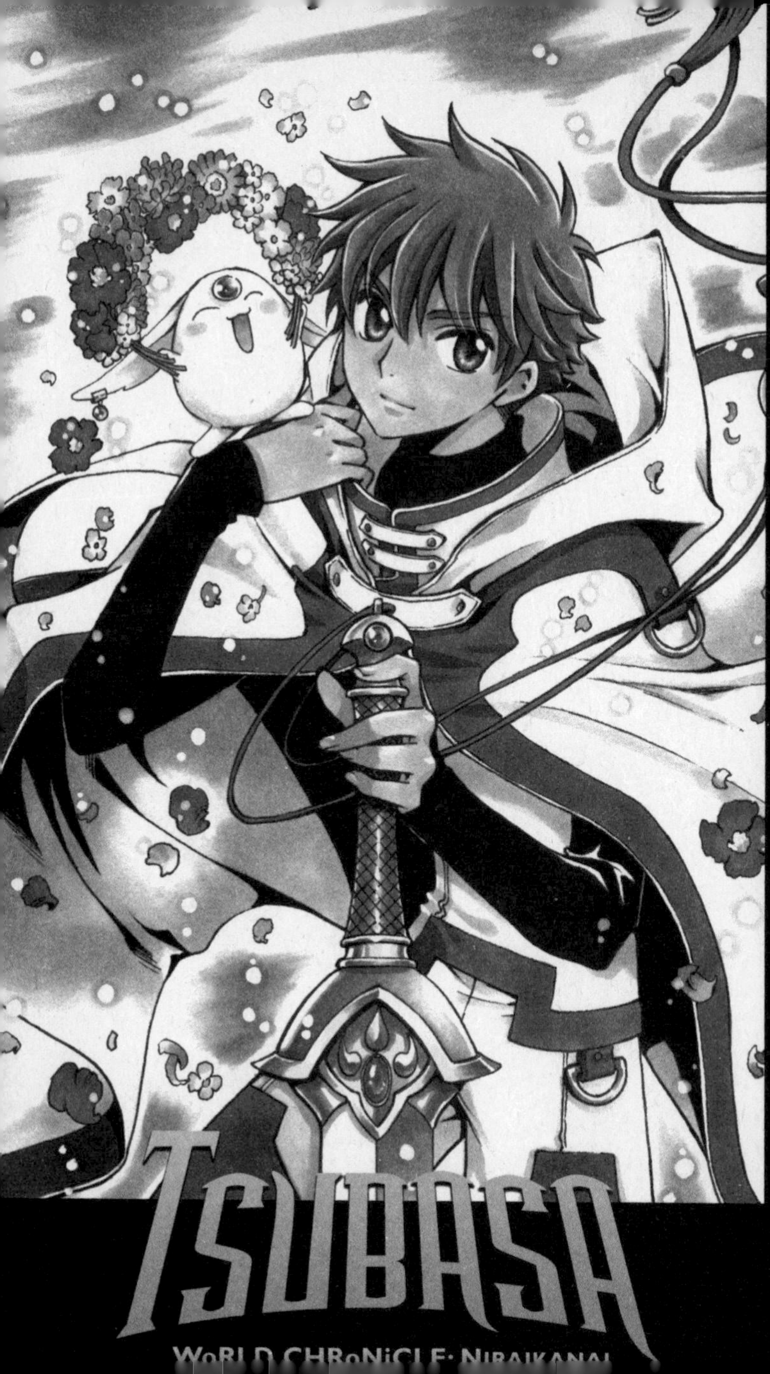
TSUBASA
WORLD CHRONICLE: NIRAIKANAI

Take a look back at Syaoran and friends' journeys from the previous series!!

Tsubasa: RESERVoir CHRoNiCLE

The Path of the Journey

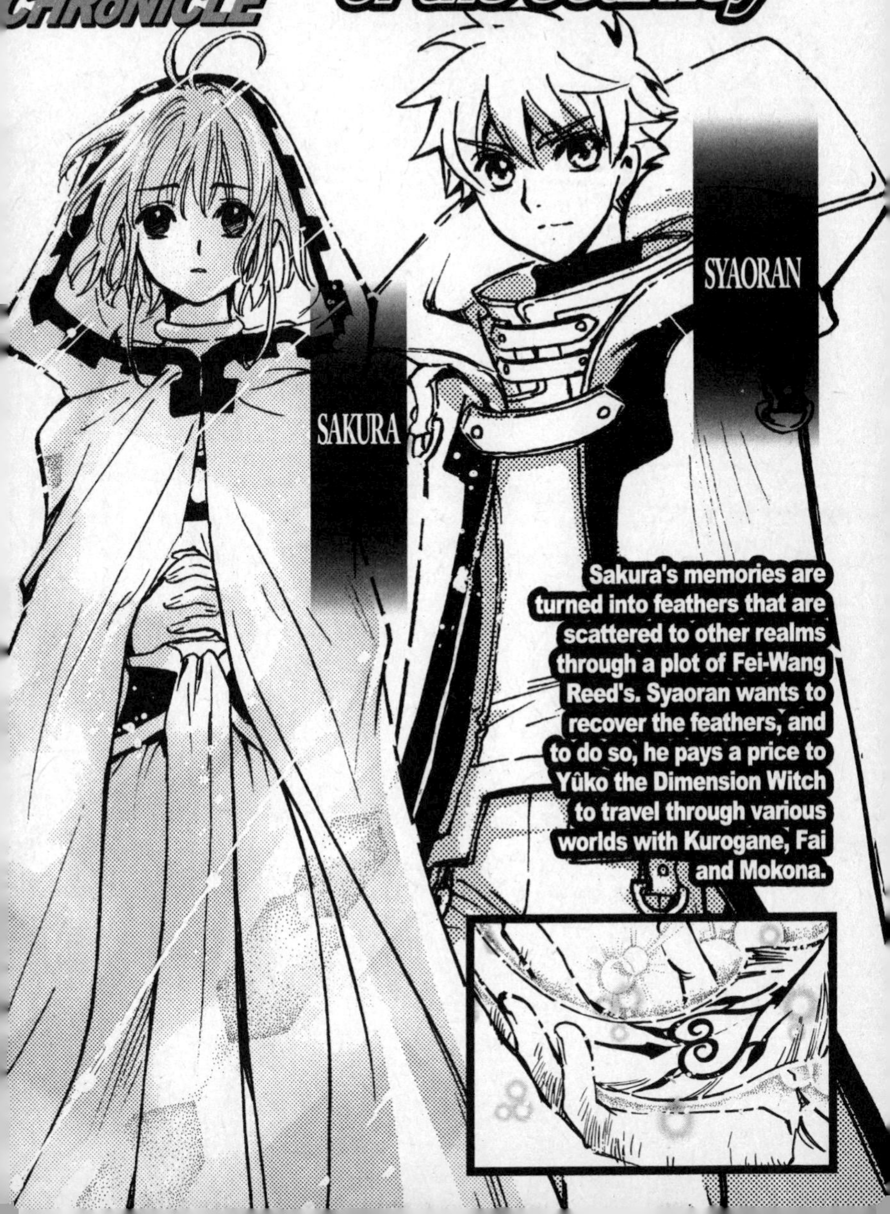
SYAORAN
SAKURA
Sakura's memories are turned into feathers that are scattered to other realms through a plot of Fei-Wang Reed's. Syaoran wants to recover the feathers, and to do so, he pays a price to Yûko the Dimension Witch to travel through various worlds with Kurogane, Fai and Mokona.

Through many trials and adventures, they succeeded in recovering Sakura's memories bit by bit, until they eventually learn that even this journey had been arranged by Fei-Wang. He destroyed the rules of time and gained Sakura's dimension-spanning power so that he could break a sacred taboo.

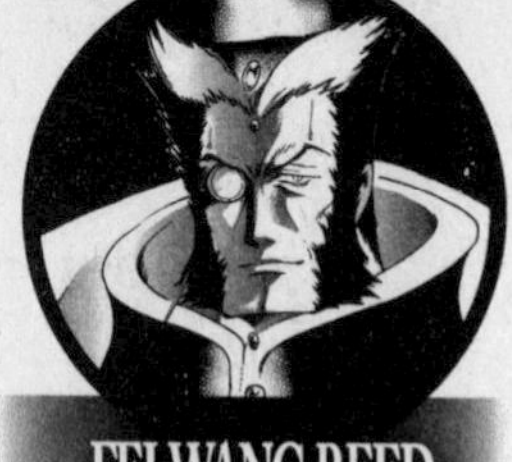

FEI-WANG REED

Despite the manipulation of their fates by Fei-Wang, Syaoran and his companions finally defeat their foe in Clow Country, returning the world to its rightful state. Fei-Wang unleashes his final curse, and in payment to undo this spell, Syaoran must leave Sakura behind and continue his journey with his friends, leaving for yet another world.

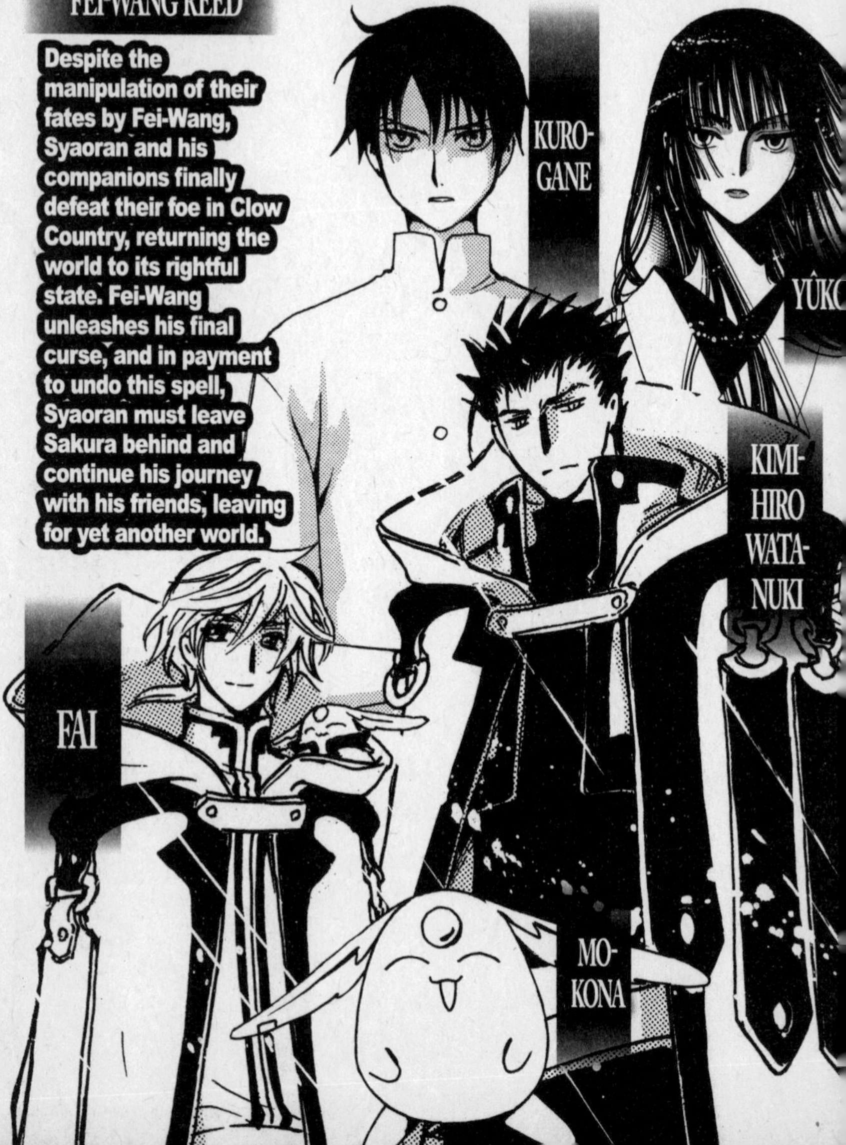
YÛKO
KURO-GANE
KIMI-HIRO WATA-NUKI
FAI
MO-KONA

TSUBASA

WoRLD CHRoNiCLE: NIRAIKANAI

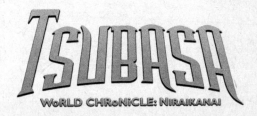

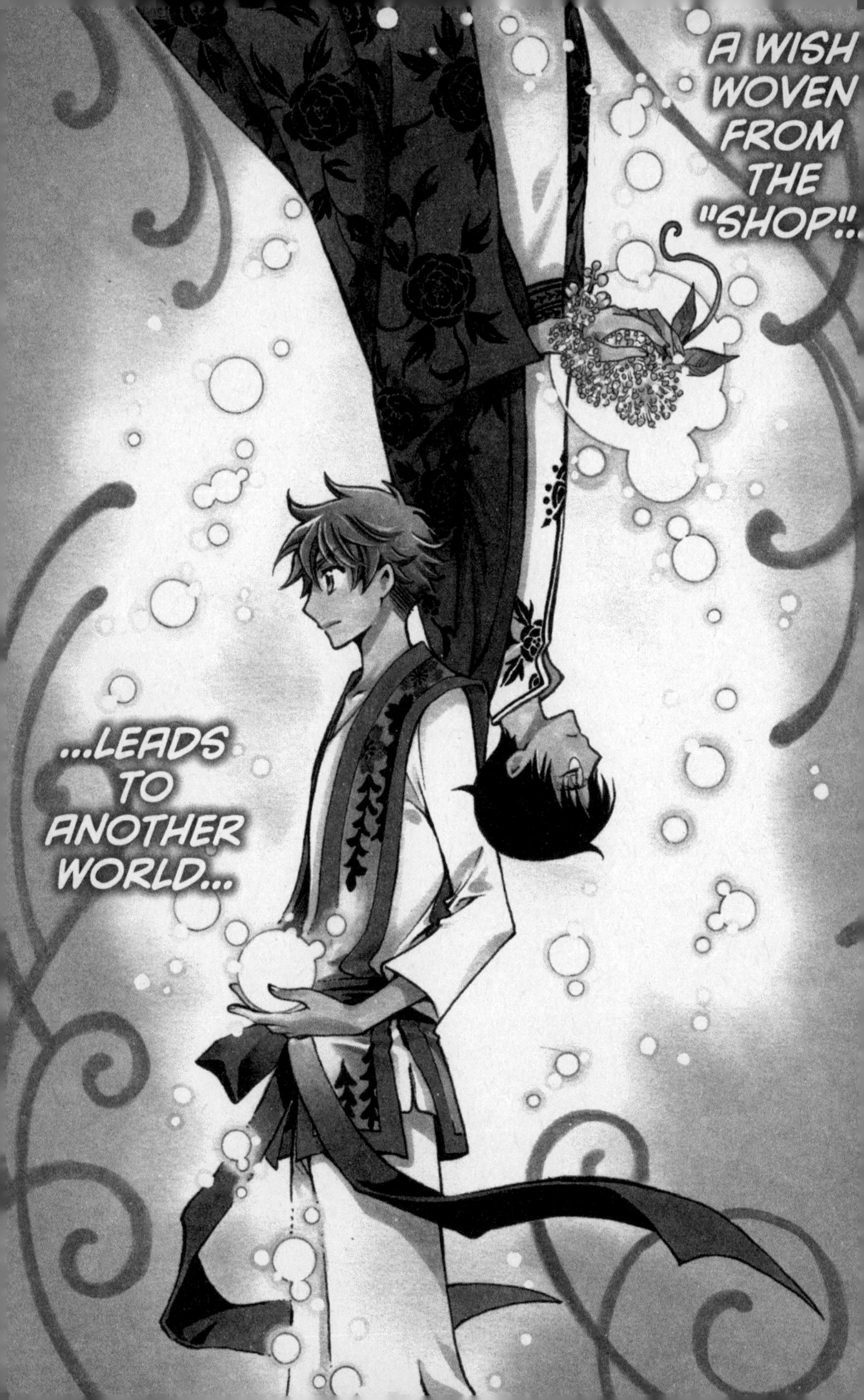
A WISH WOVEN FROM THE "SHOP"...
...LEADS TO ANOTHER WORLD...

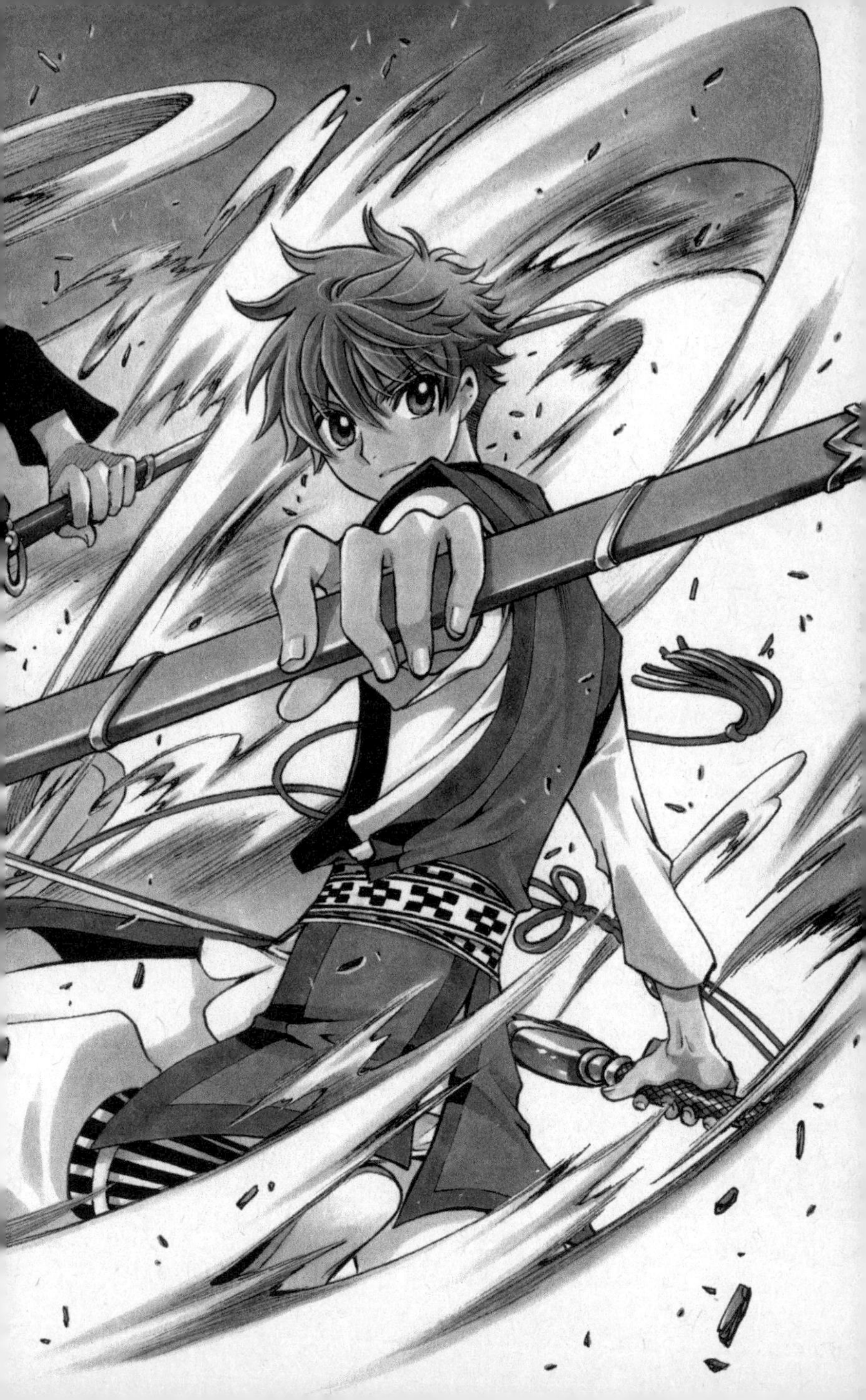

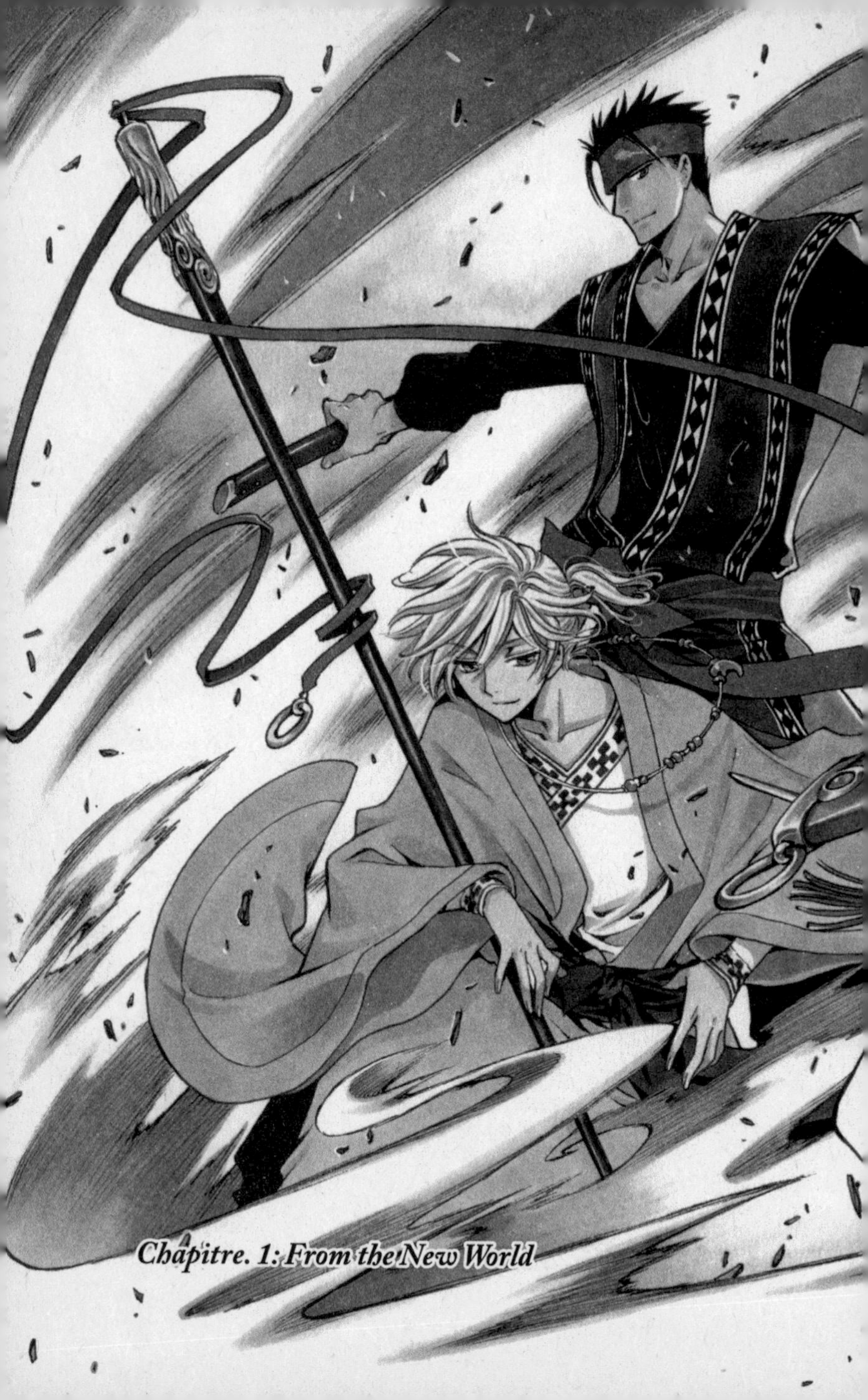
Chapitre. 1: From the New World

TSUBASA

WoRLD CHRoNiCLE: NIRAIKANAI

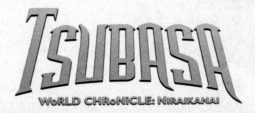

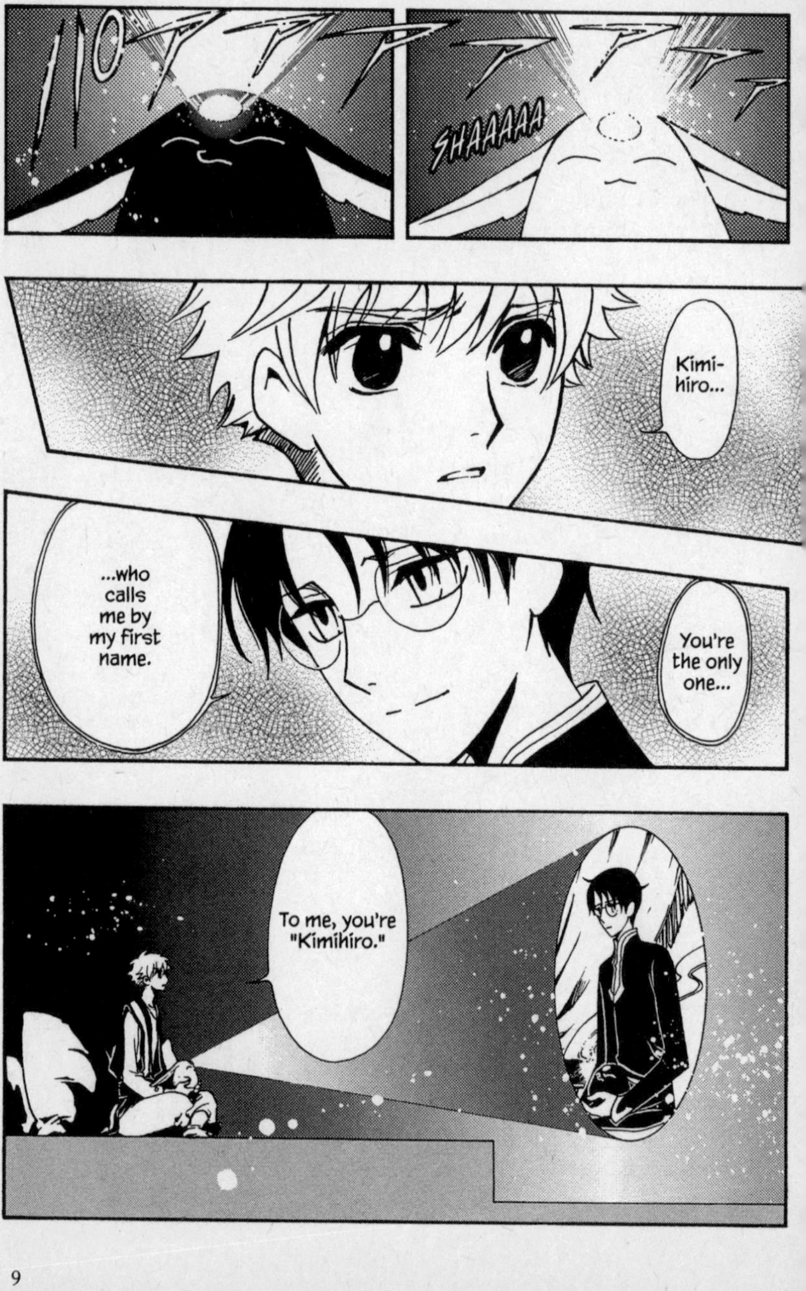
SHAAAAA
Kimi-hiro...
You're the only one...
...who calls me by my first name.
To me, you're "Kimihiro."

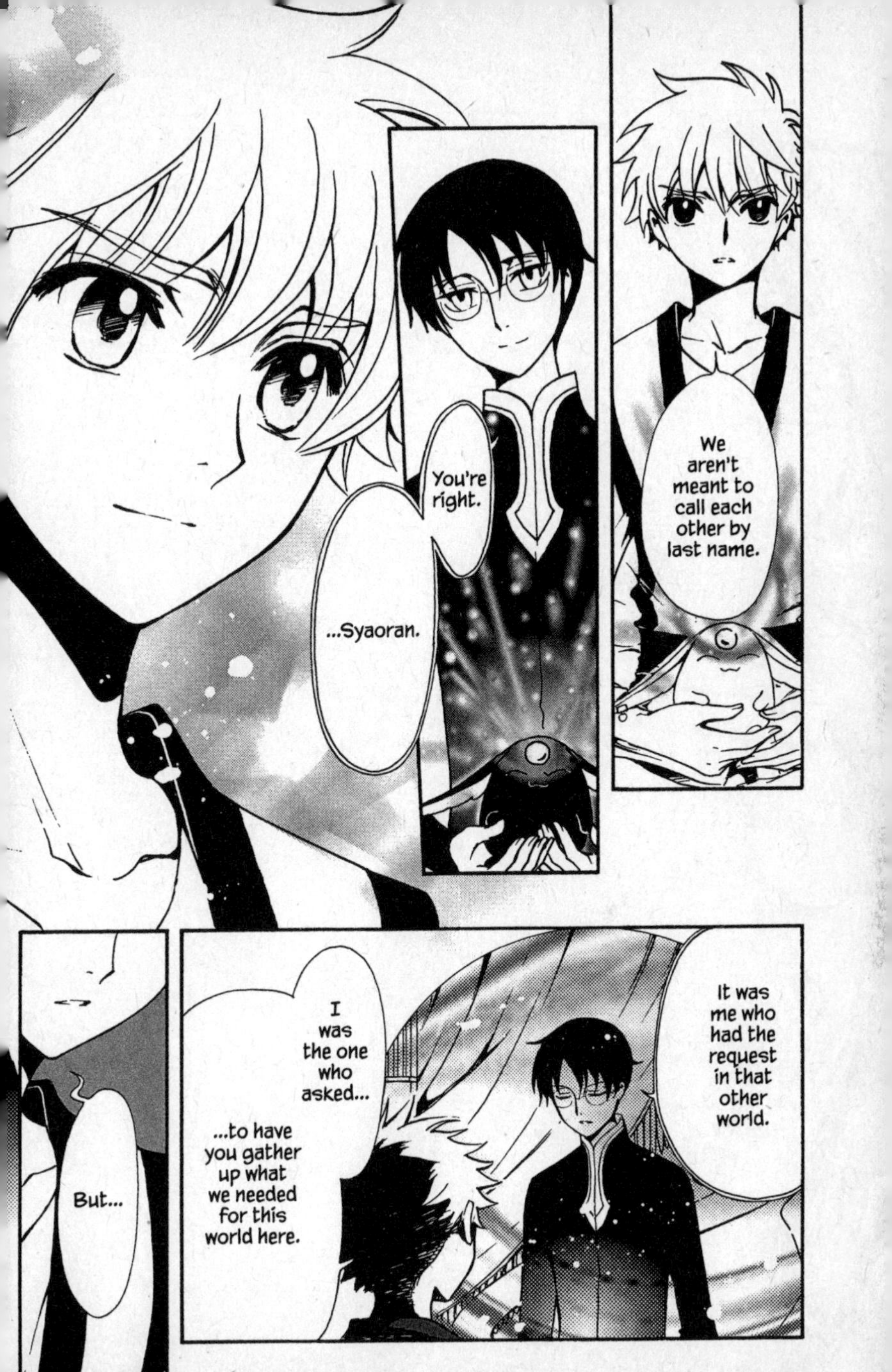

We aren't meant to call each other by last name.
You're right.
...Syaoran.
It was me who had the request in that other world.
I was the one who asked...
...to have you gather up what we needed for this world here.
But...

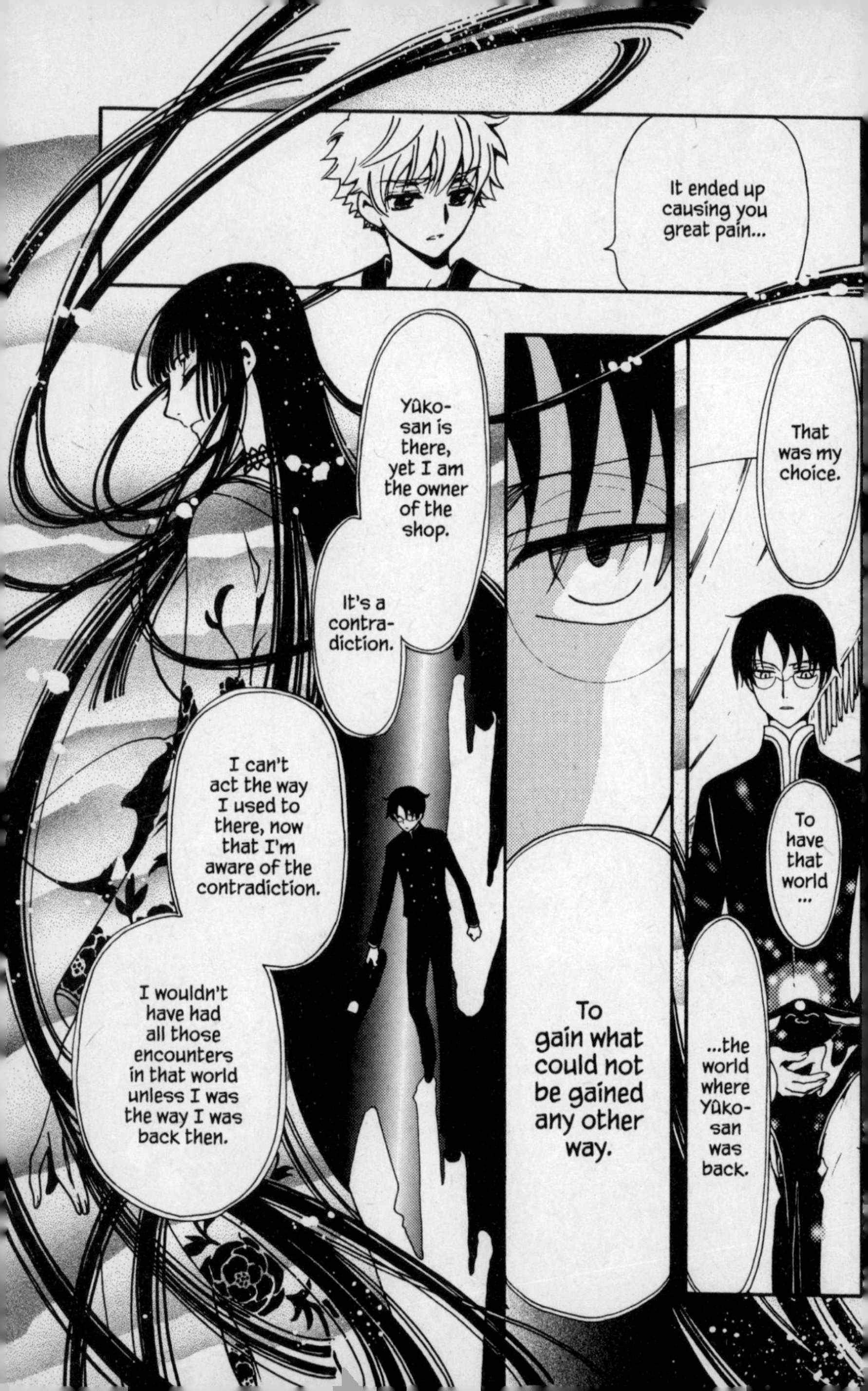
It ended up causing you great pain...
That was my choice.
To have that world...
...the world where Yūko-san was back.
To gain what could not be gained any other way.
Yūko-san is there, yet I am the owner of the shop.
It's a contradiction.
I can't act the way I used to there, now that I'm aware of the contradiction.
I wouldn't have had all those encounters in that world unless I was the way I was back then.

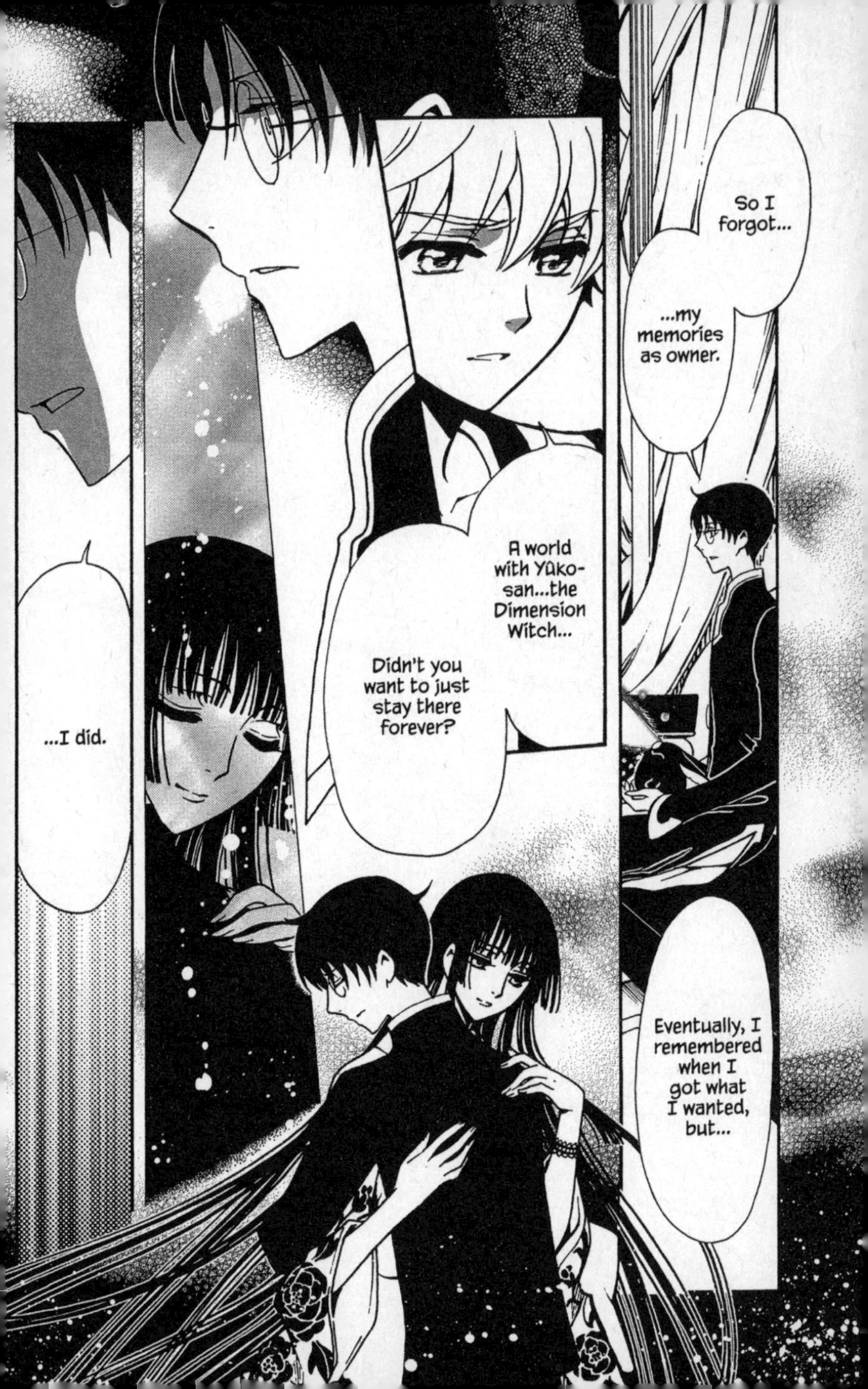
So I forgot...
...my memories as owner.
Eventually, I remembered when I got what I wanted, but...
A world with Yûko-san...the Dimension Witch...
Didn't you want to just stay there forever?
...I did.

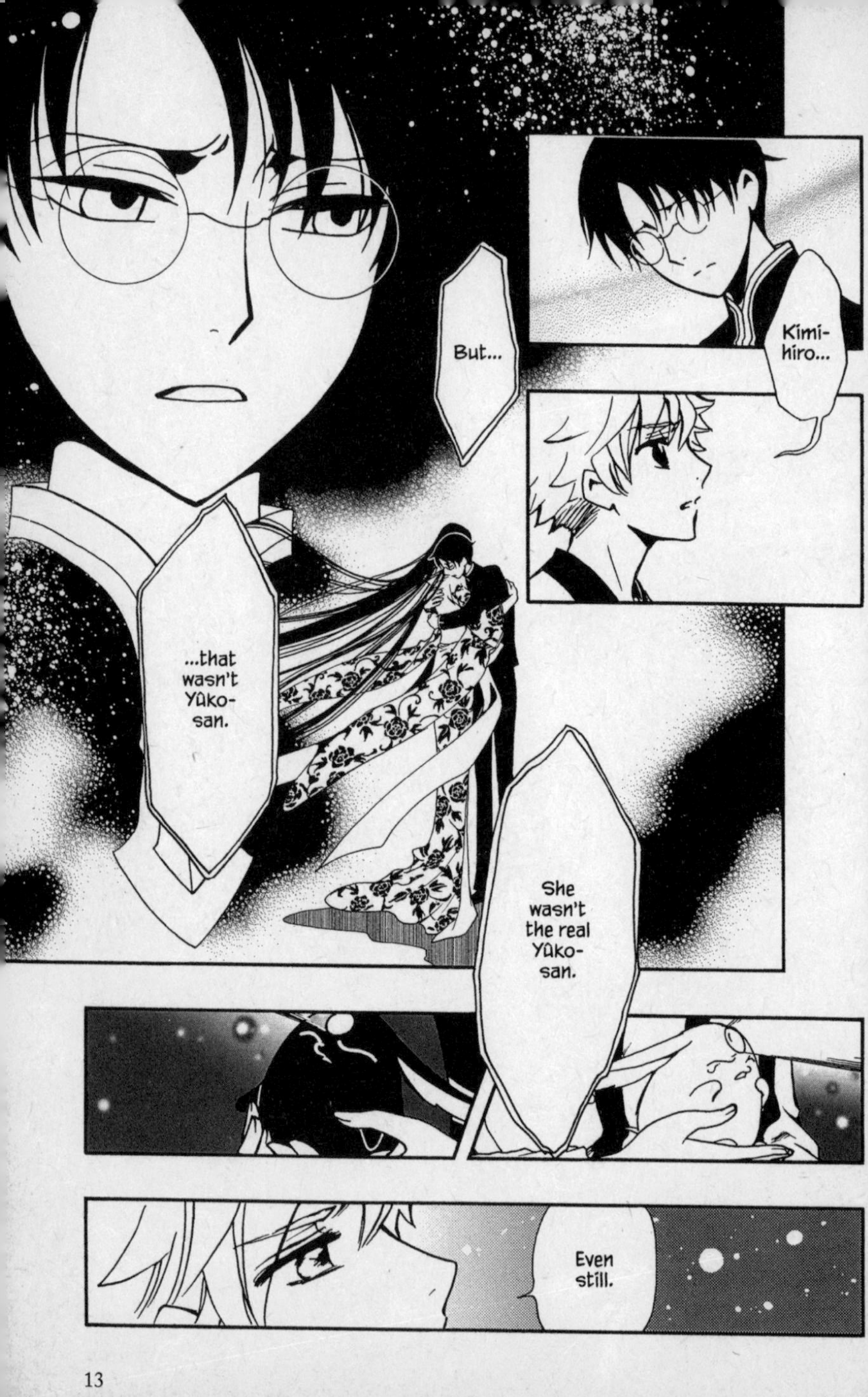
Kimi-hiro...
But...
...that wasn't Yûko-san.
She wasn't the real Yûko-san.
Even still.

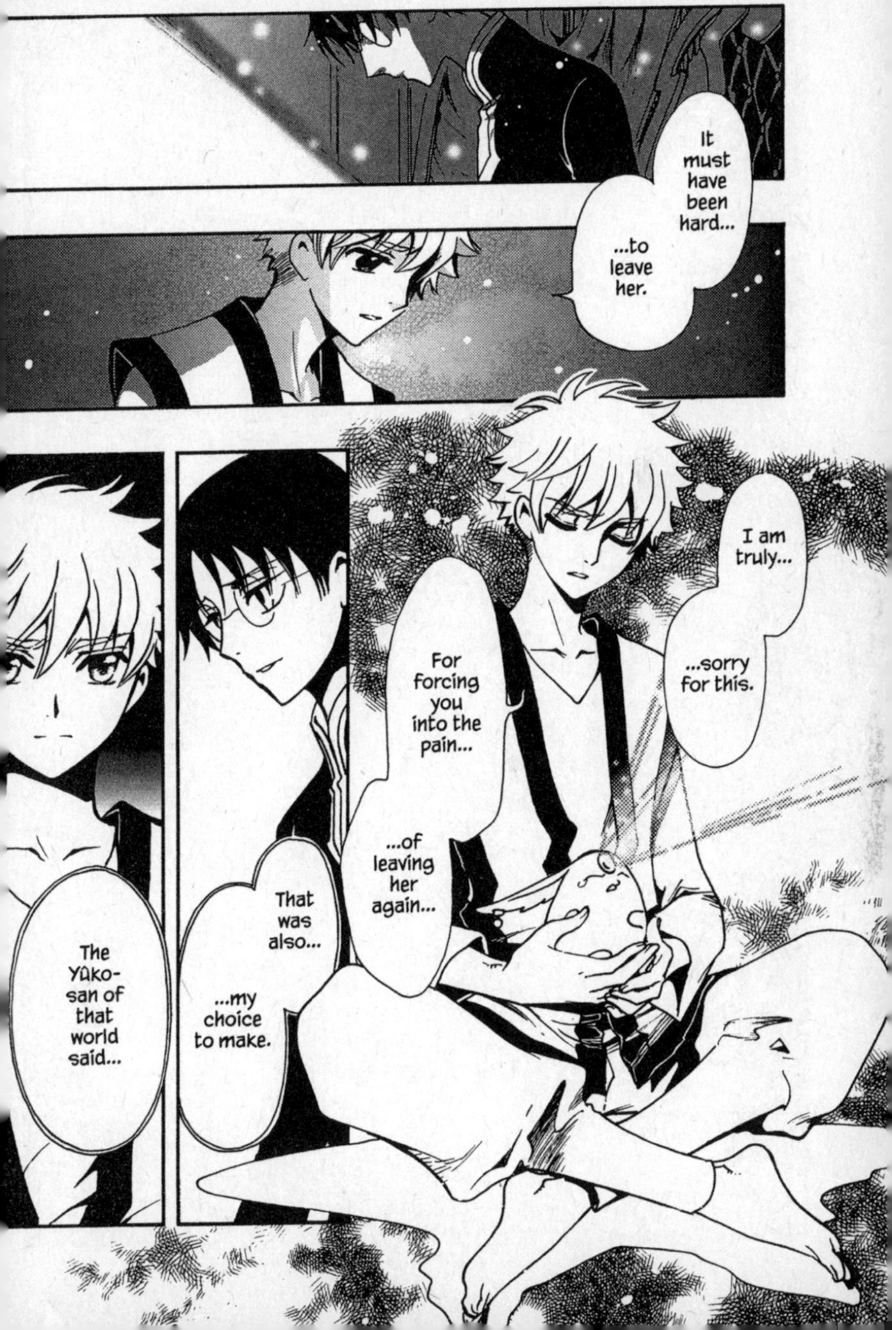
It must have been hard...
...to leave her.
I am truly...
...sorry for this.
For forcing you into the pain...
...of leaving her again...
That was also...
...my choice to make.
The Yûko-san of that world said...

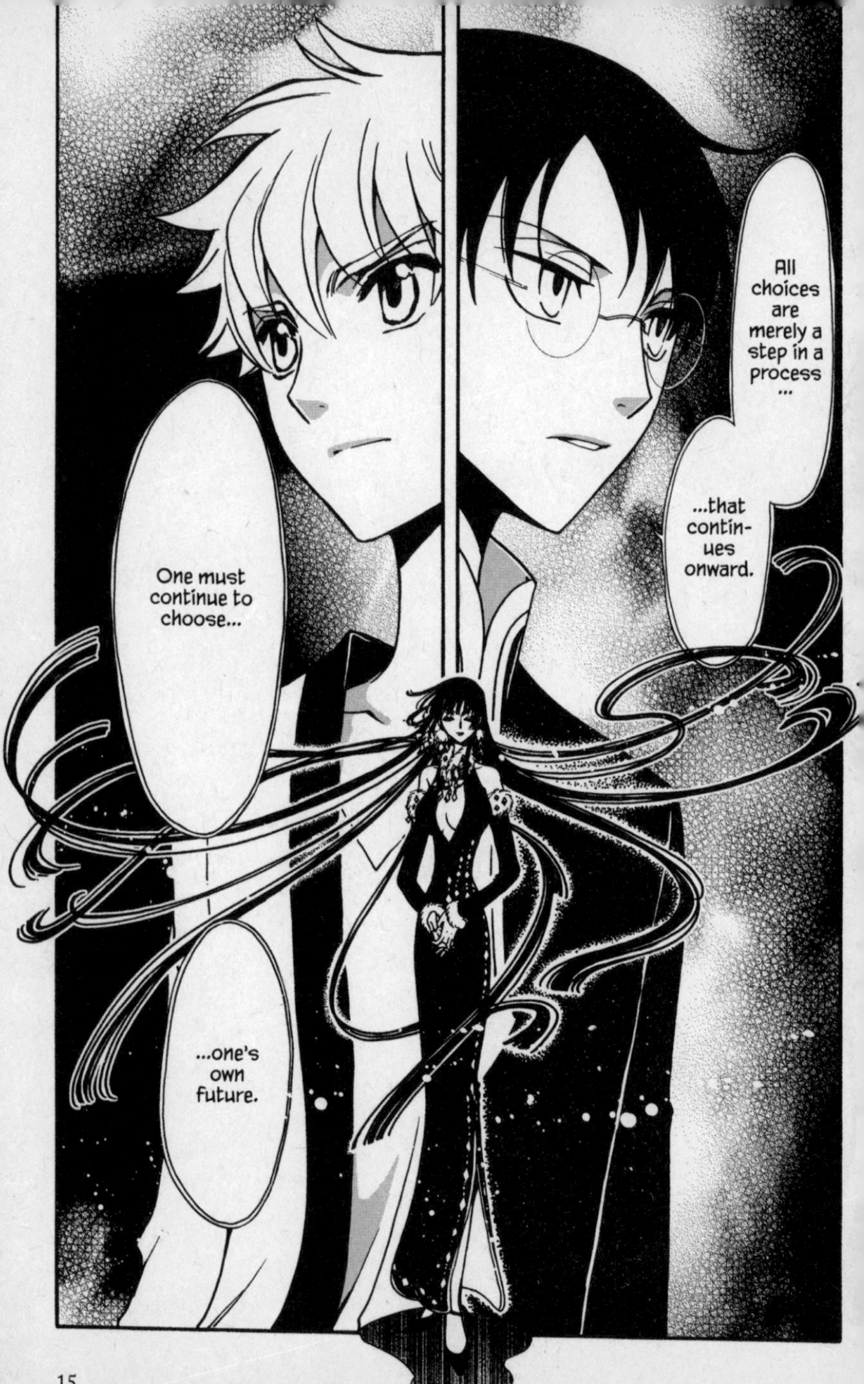
All choices are merely a step in a process ...
...that contin-ues onward.
One must continue to choose...
...one's own future.

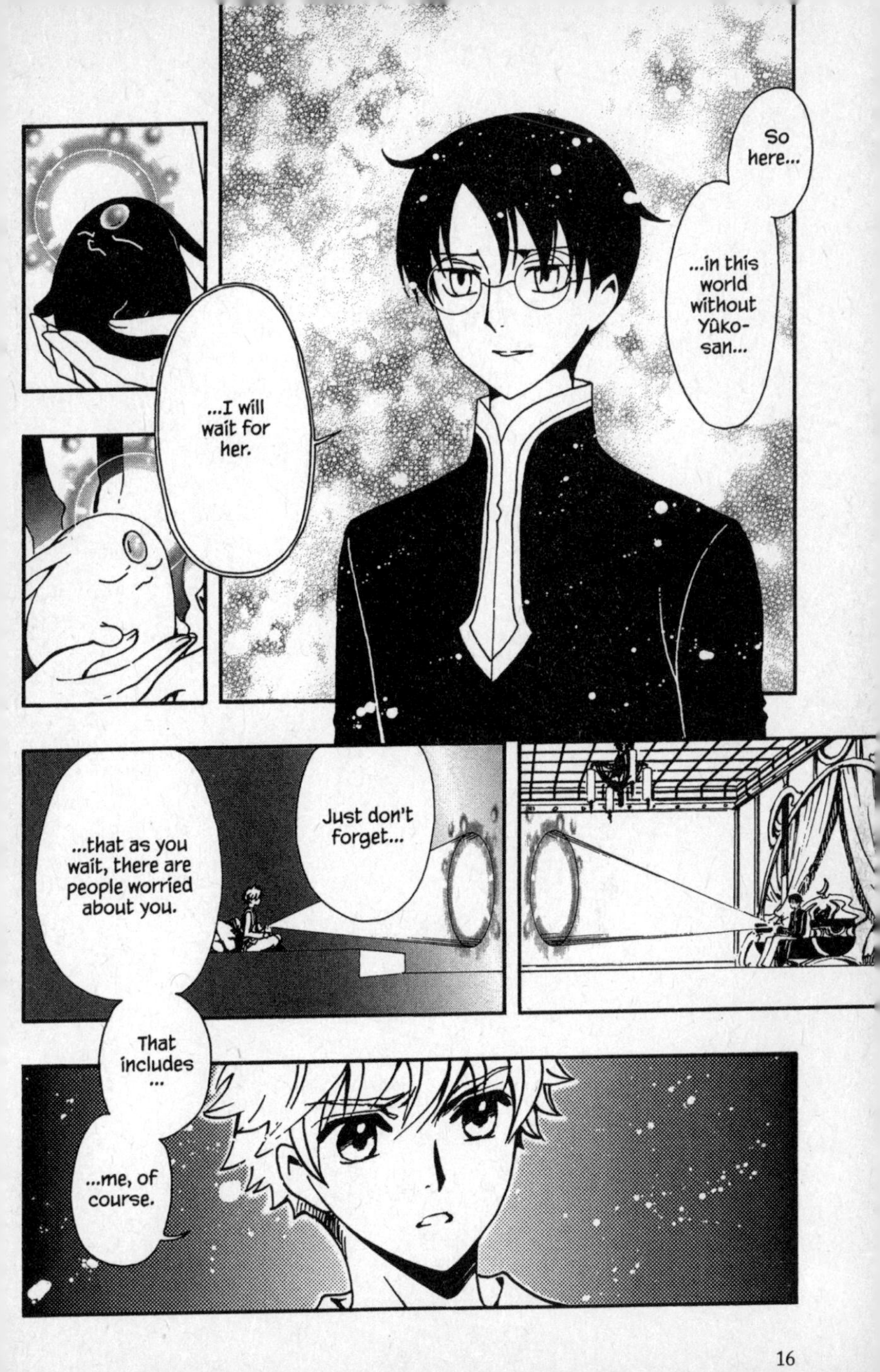
So here...
...in this world without Yûko-san...
...I will wait for her.
Just don't forget...
...that as you wait, there are people worried about you.
That includes...
...me, of course.

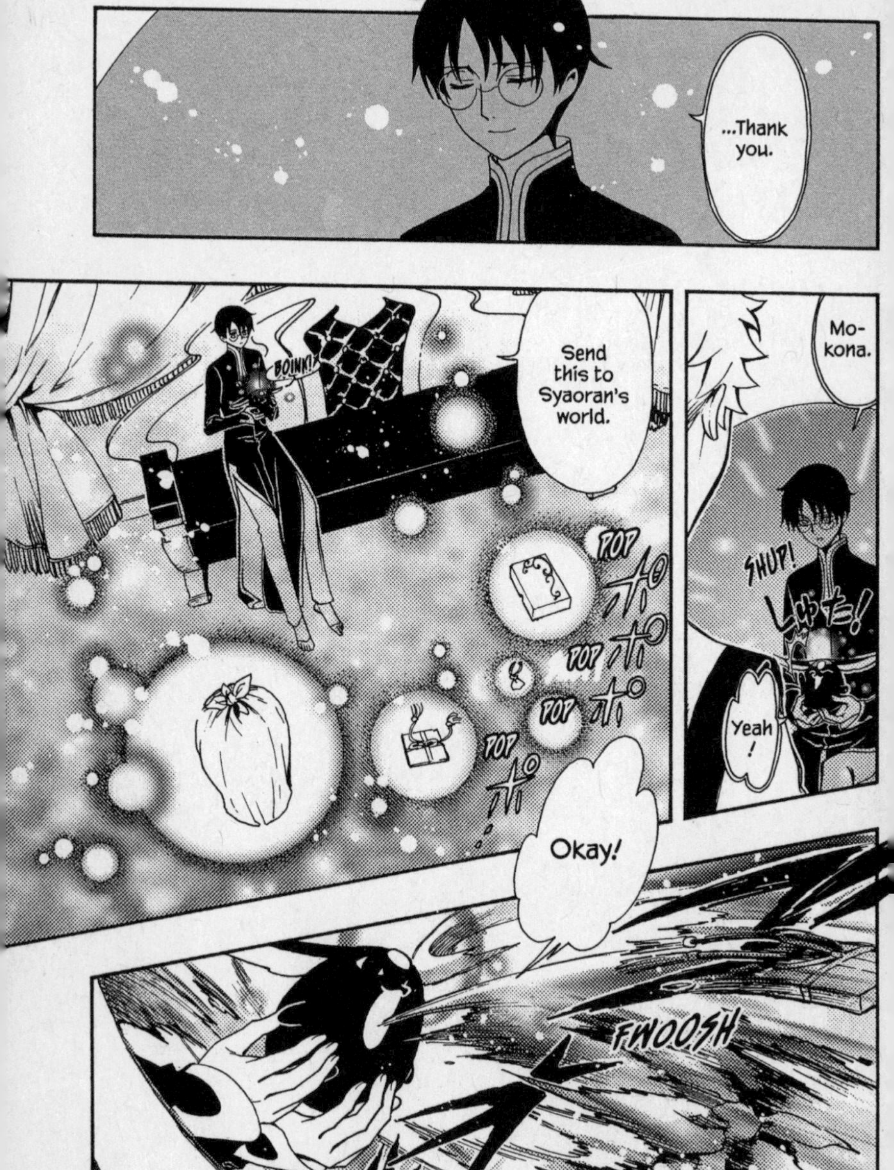
...Thank you.
Mo-kona.
SHUP!
Yeah!
Send this to Syaoran's world.
BOINK!
POP
POP
POP
POP
Okay!
FWOOSH

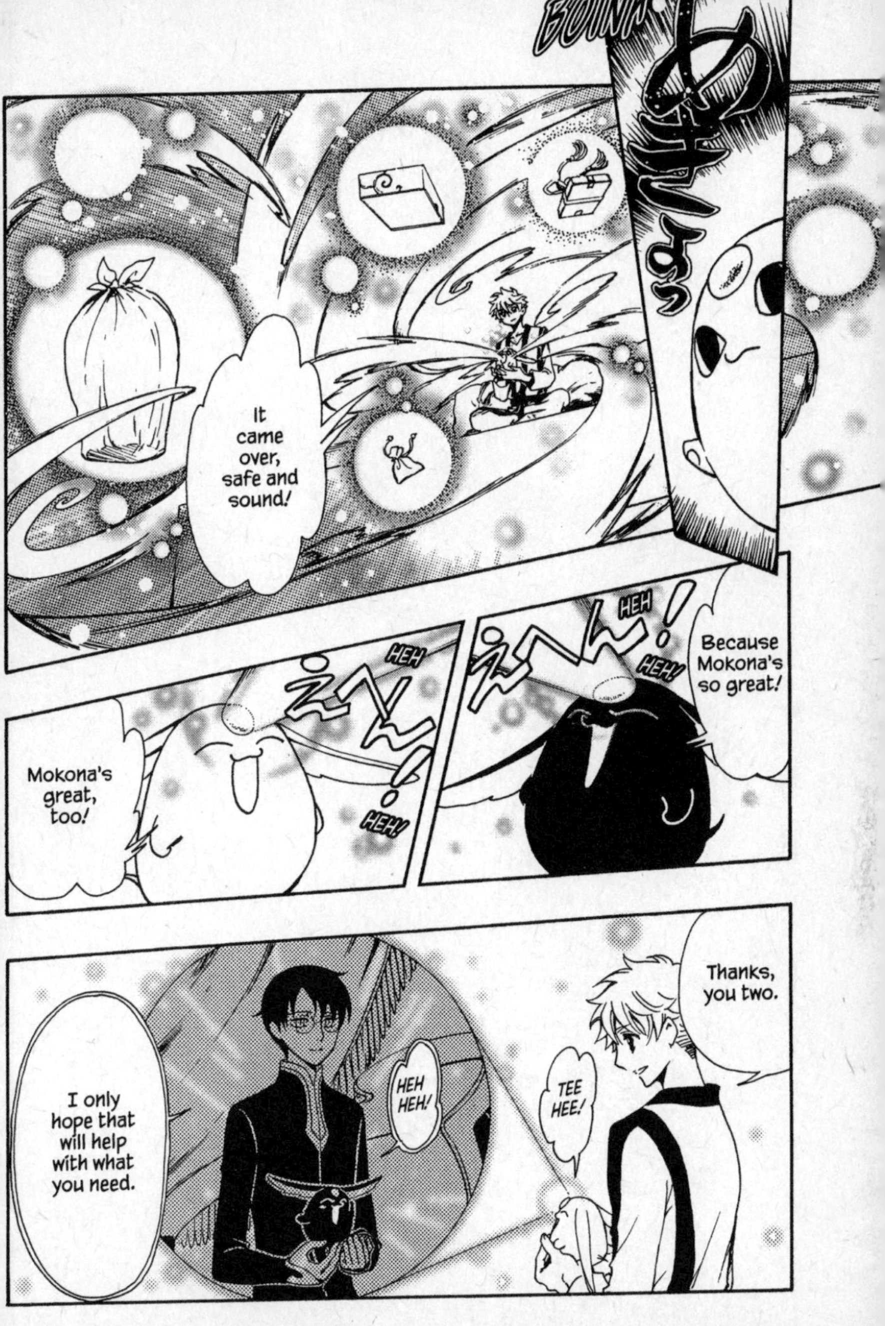
BOINK
It came over, safe and sound!
Because Mokona's so great!
HEH
HEH!
HEH
HEH!
Mokona's great, too!
Thanks, you two.
TEE HEE!
HEH HEH!
I only hope that will help with what you need.

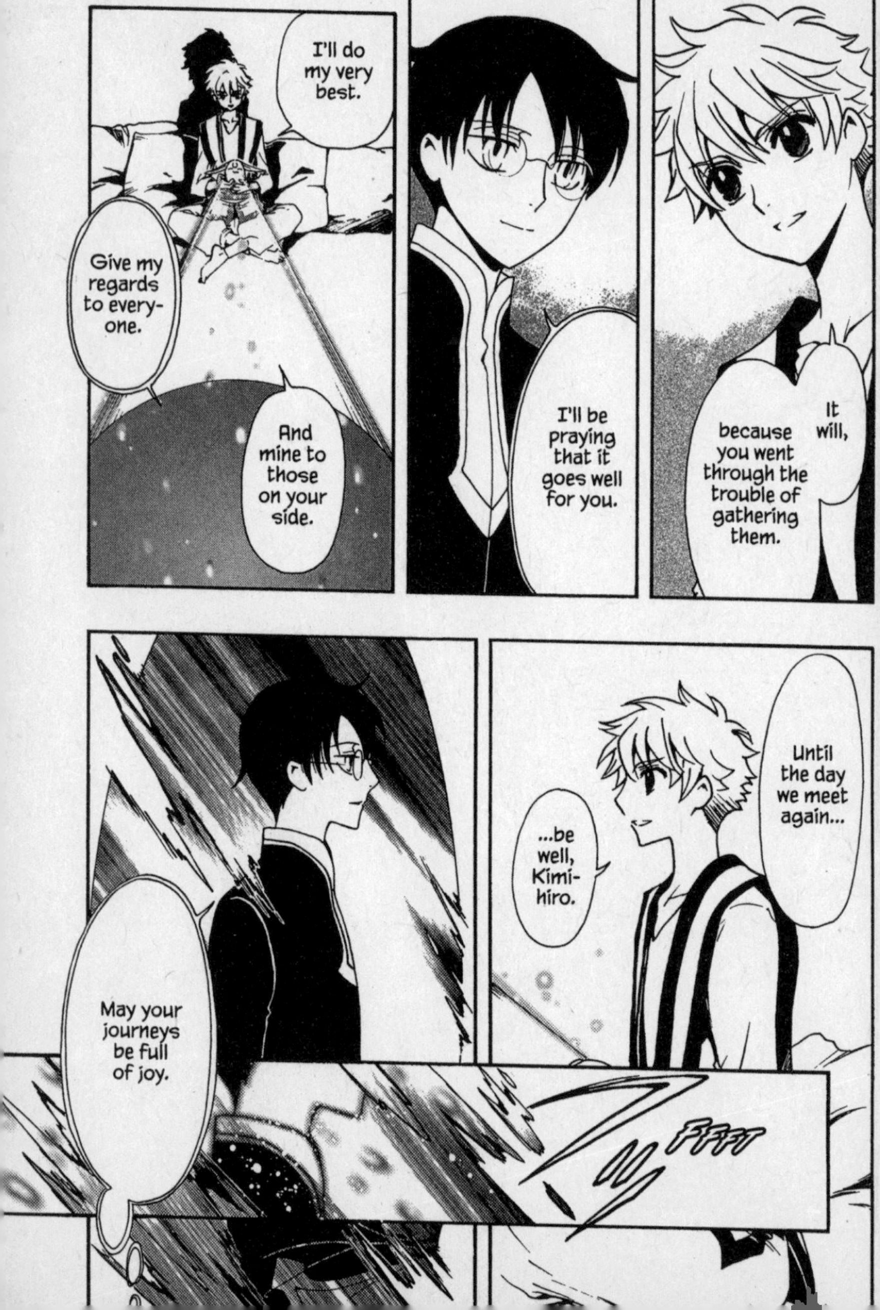
It will, because you went through the trouble of gathering them.
I'll be praying that it goes well for you.
I'll do my very best.
Give my regards to everyone.
And mine to those on your side.
Until the day we meet again...
...be well, Kimihiro.
May your journeys be full of joy.
FFFT

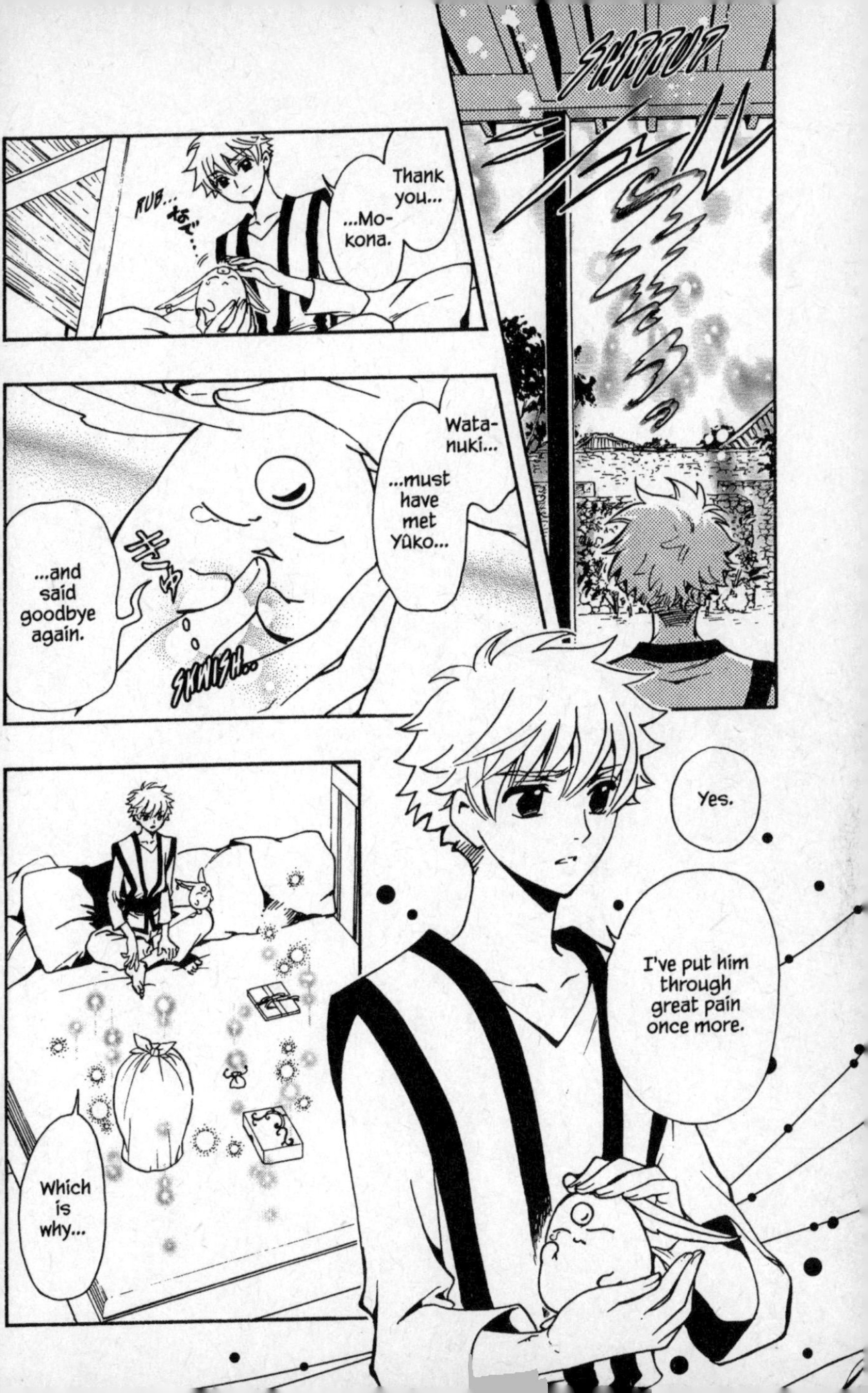
Thank you...
...Mo-kona.
RUB...
Wata-nuki...
...must have met Yûko...
...and said goodbye again.
SKWISH..
Yes.
I've put him through great pain once more.
Which is why...

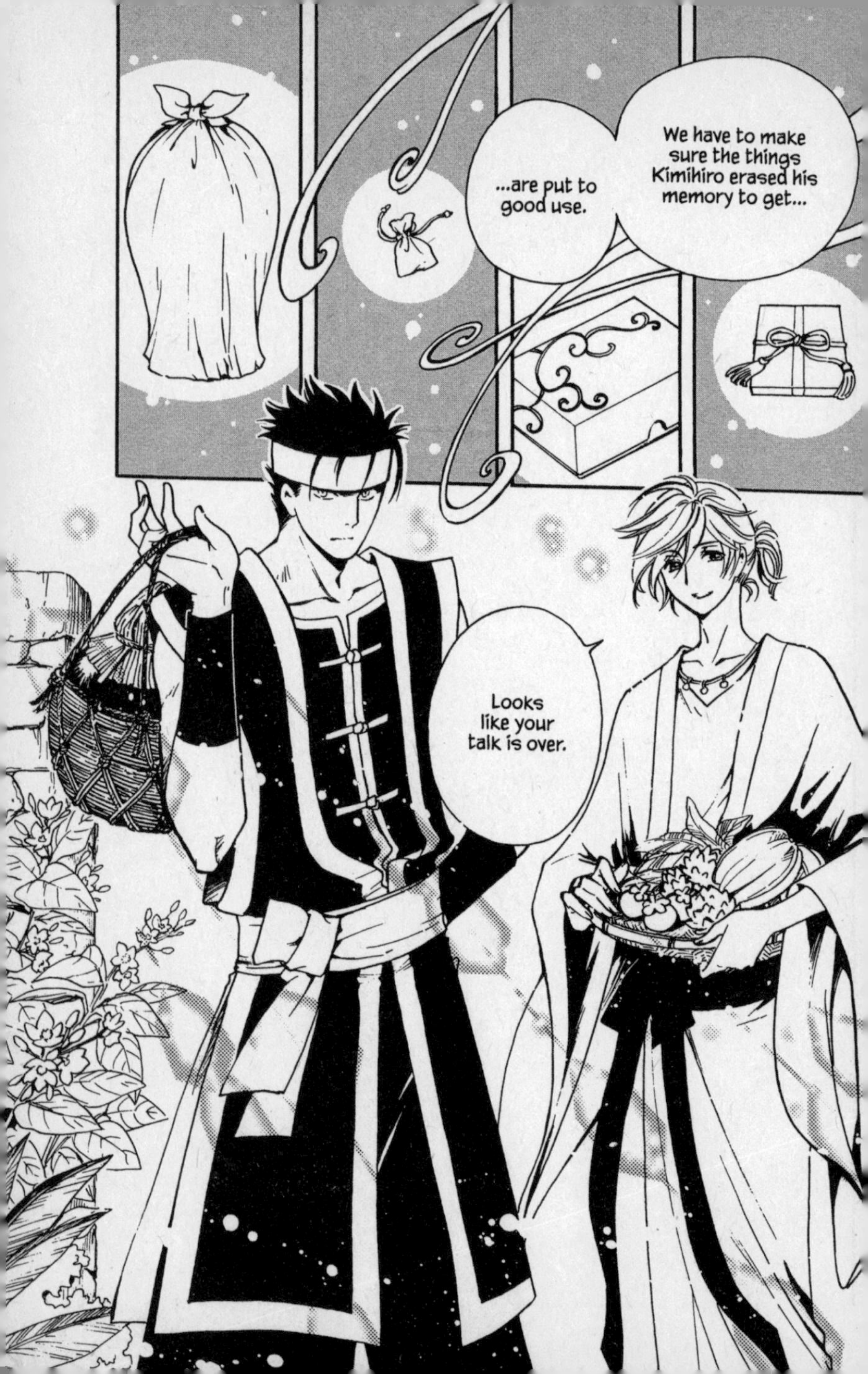
We have to make sure the things Kimihiro erased his memory to get...
...are put to good use.
Looks like your talk is over.

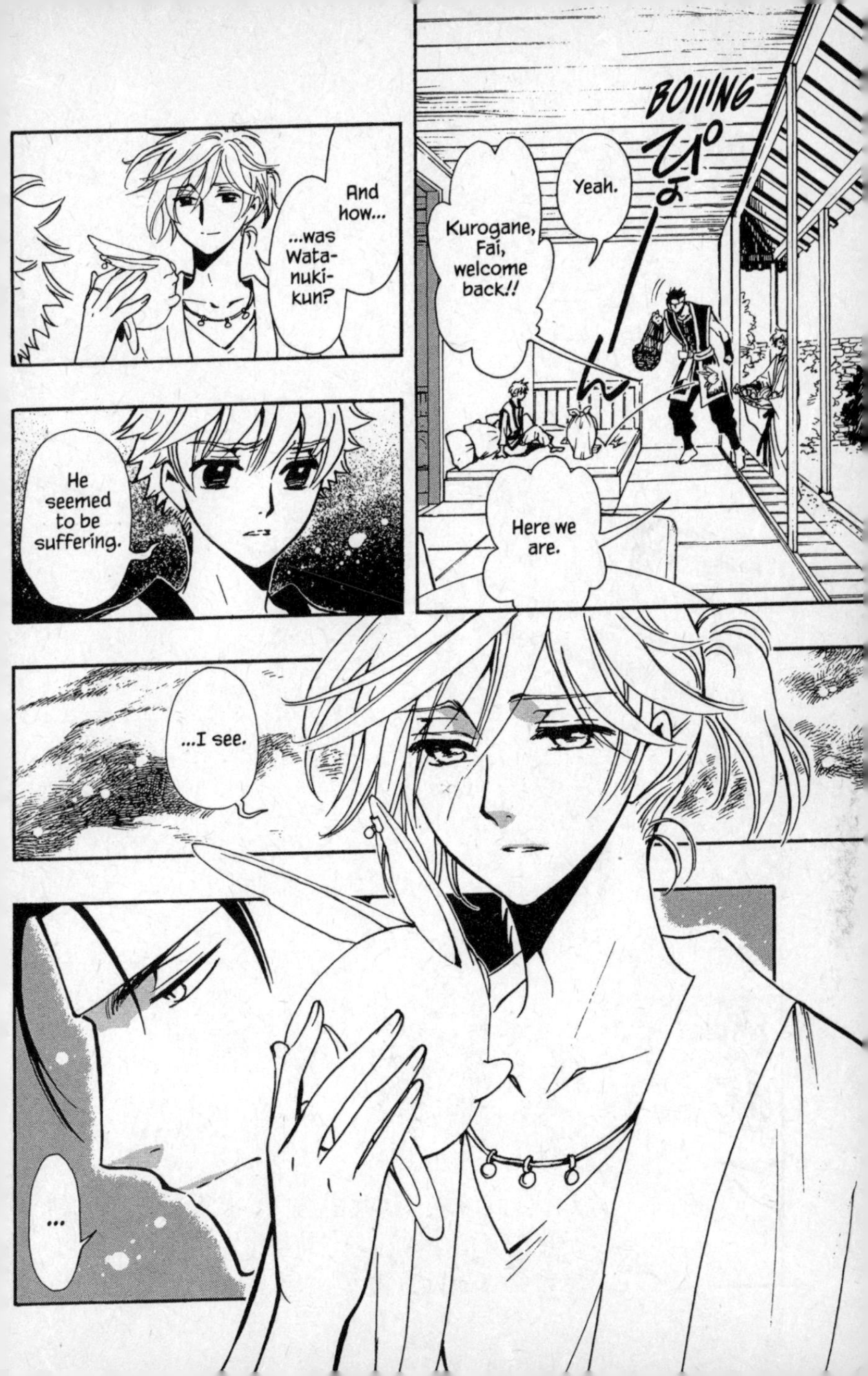
BOIIING
ぴょーん
Yeah.
Kurogane, Fai, welcome back!!
Here we are.
And how...
...was Watanuki-kun?
He seemed to be suffering.
...I see.
...

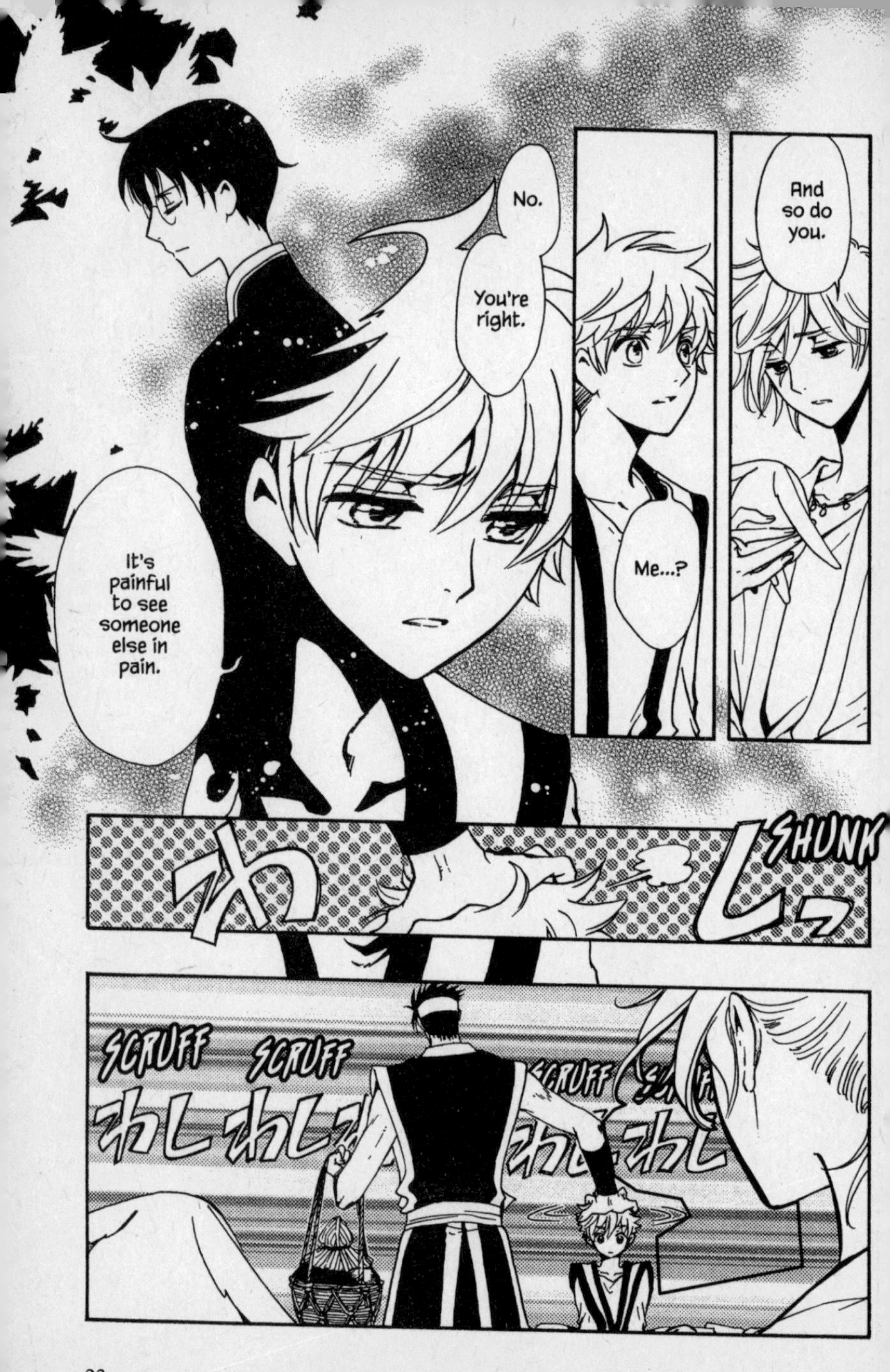
And so do you.
Me...?
No.
You're right.
It's painful to see someone else in pain.
SHUNK
SCRUFF
SCRUFF
SCRUFF

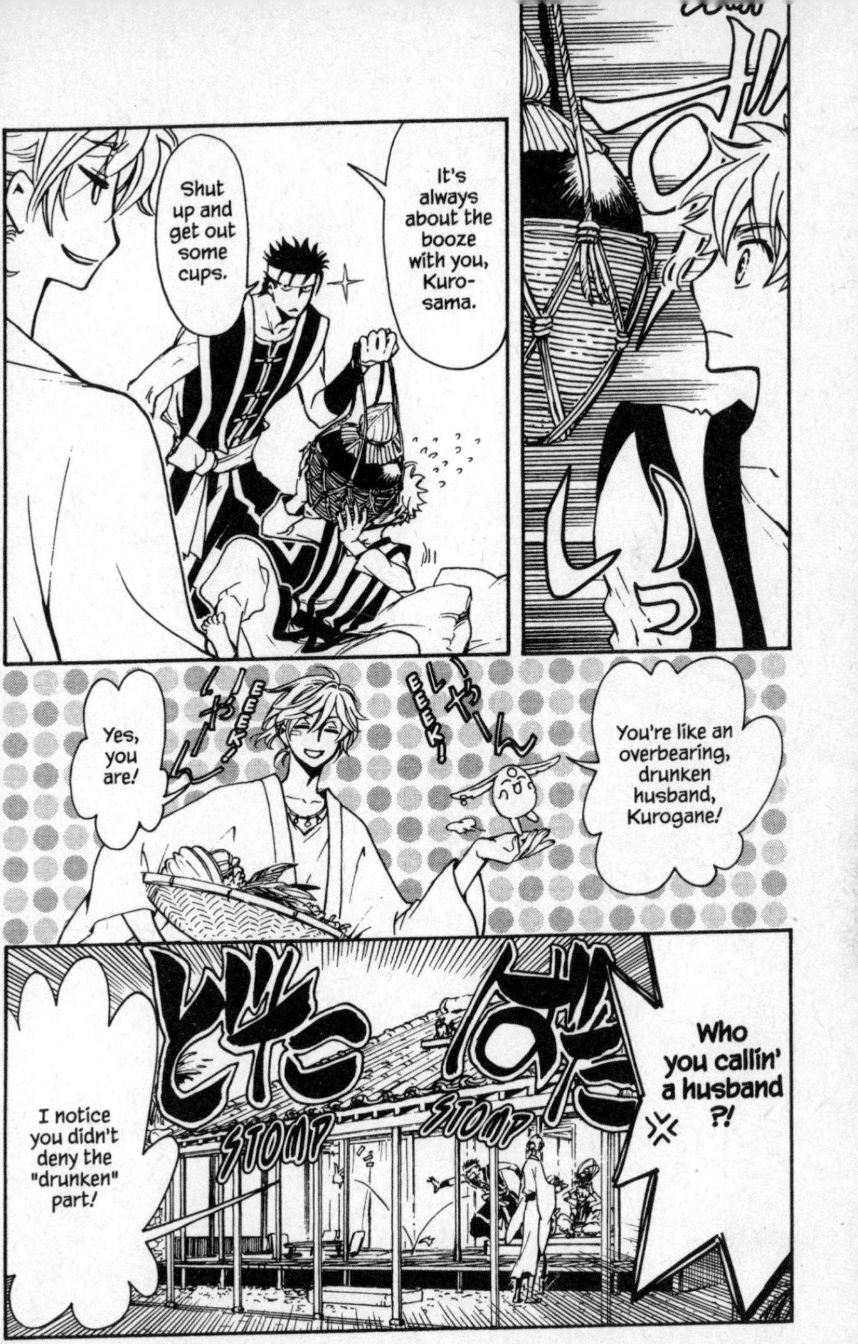
It's always about the booze with you, Kuro-sama.
Shut up and get out some cups.
You're like an overbearing, drunken husband, Kurogane!
EEEK!
EEEK-
Yes, you are!
Who you callin' a husband ?!
STOMP
STOMP
I notice you didn't deny the "drunken" part!

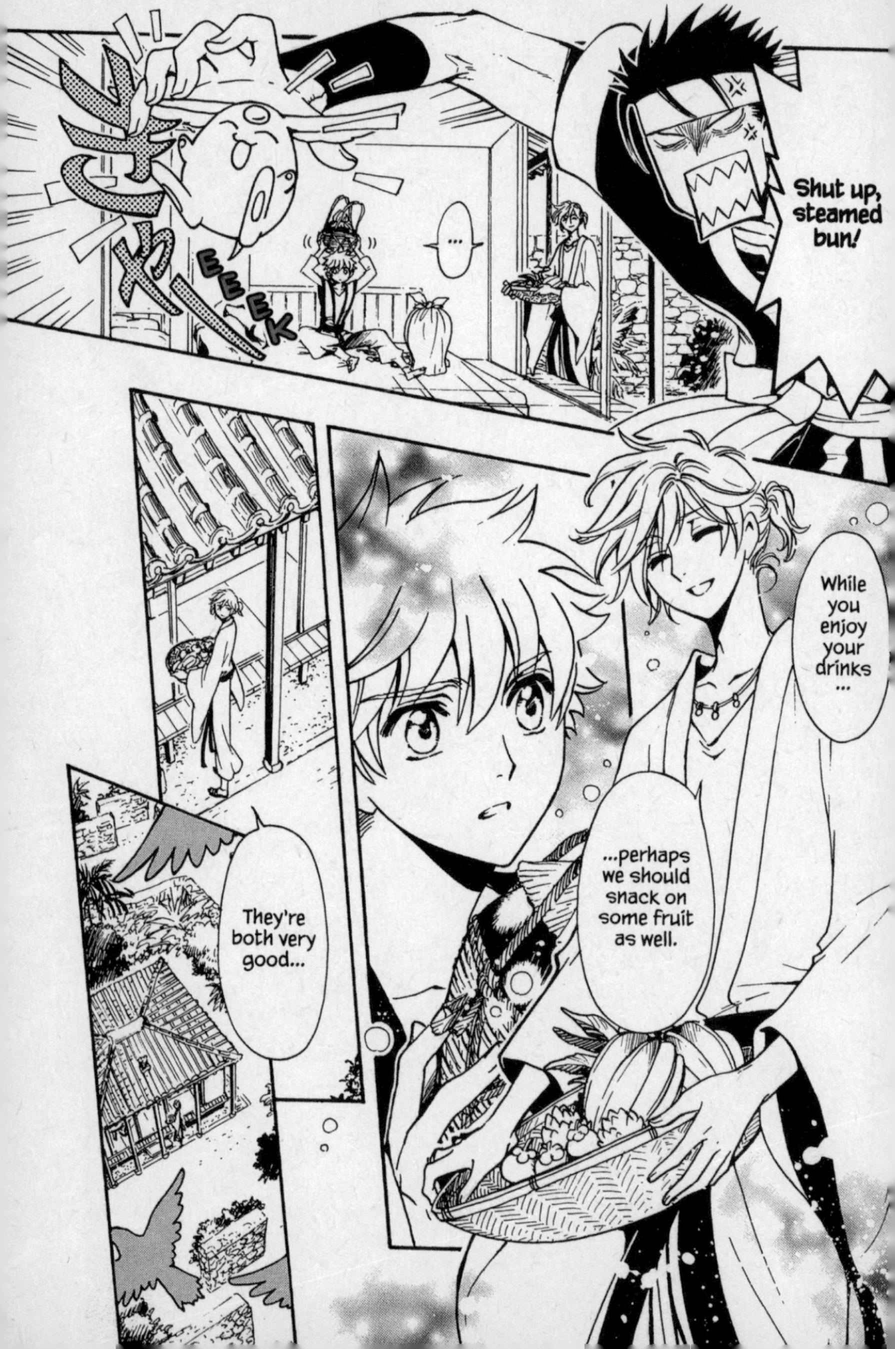
Shut up, steamed bun!
...
EEEEK
While you enjoy your drinks...
...perhaps we should snack on some fruit as well.
They're both very good...

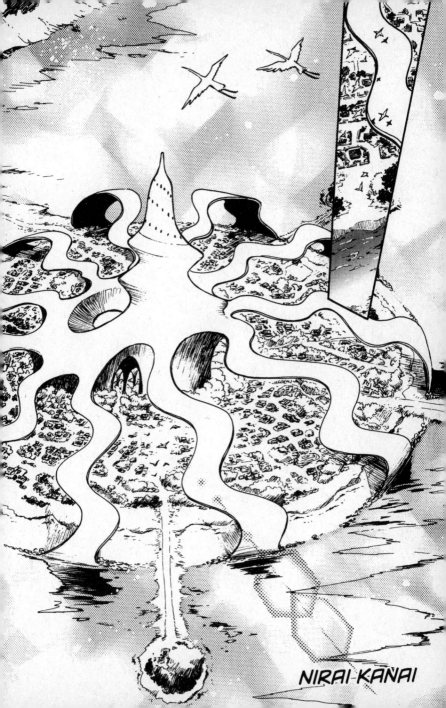

NIRAI KANAI

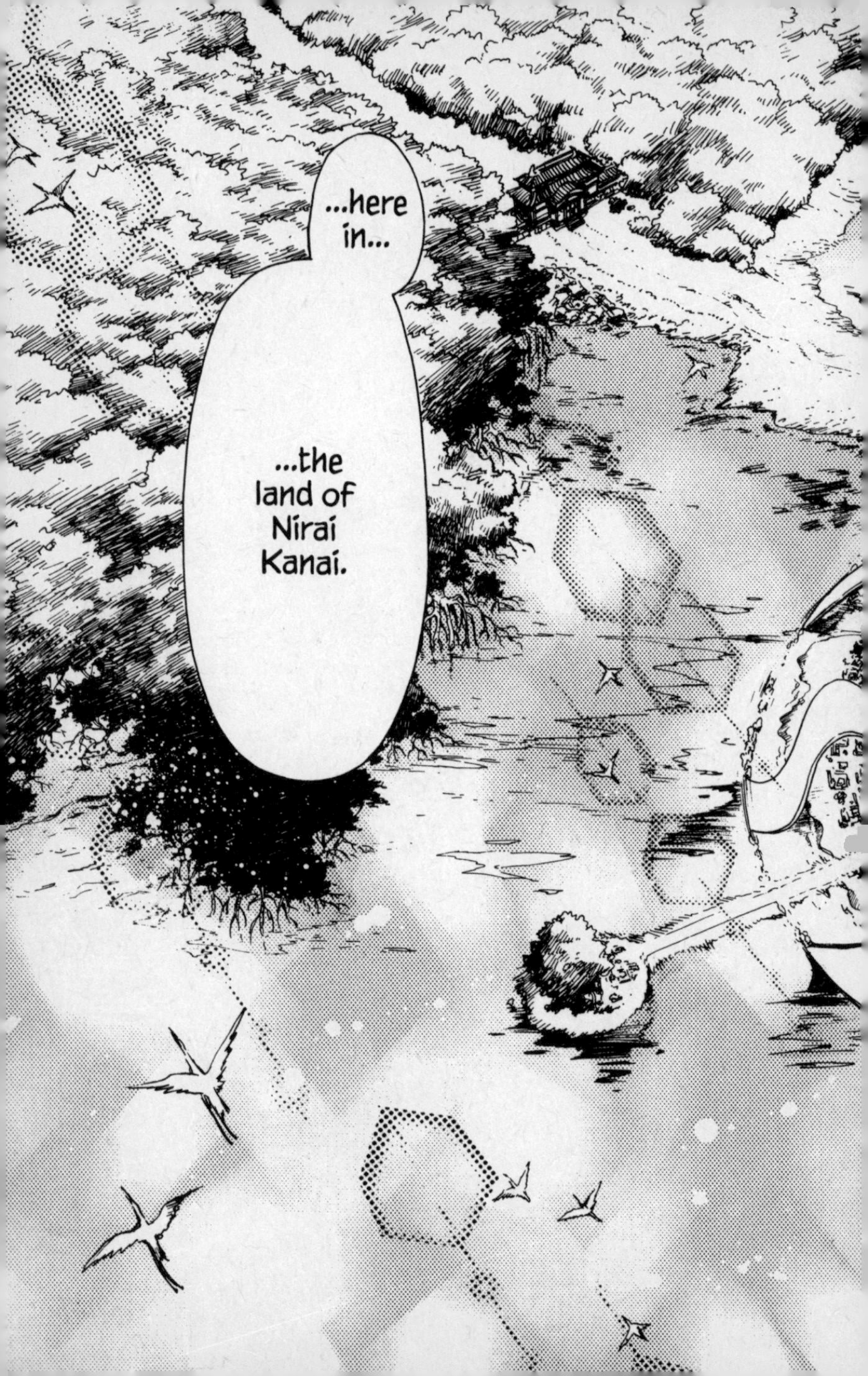
...here in...
...the land of Nirai Kanai.

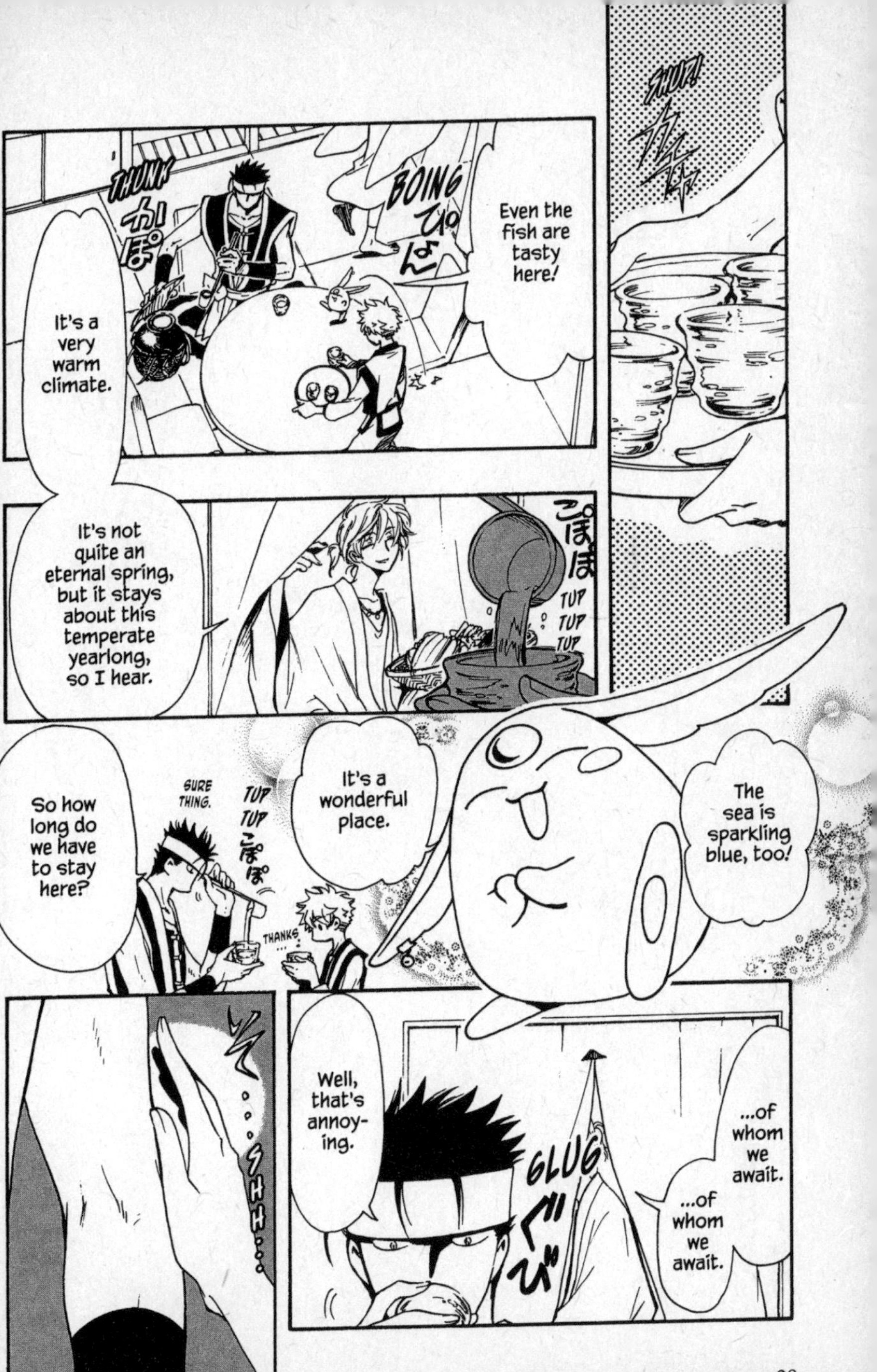
SHUTA!
Even the fish are tasty here!
BOING
ぴょん
THUNK
かぽ
It's a very warm climate.
こぽぽ
TUP TUP TUP
It's not quite an eternal spring, but it stays about this temperate yearlong, so I hear.
The sea is sparkling blue, too!
It's a wonderful place.
TUP TUP
こぽぽ
SURE THING.
THANKS...
So how long do we have to stay here?
...of whom we await.
...of whom we await.
GLUG
ぐび
Well, that's annoying.
SHHH...

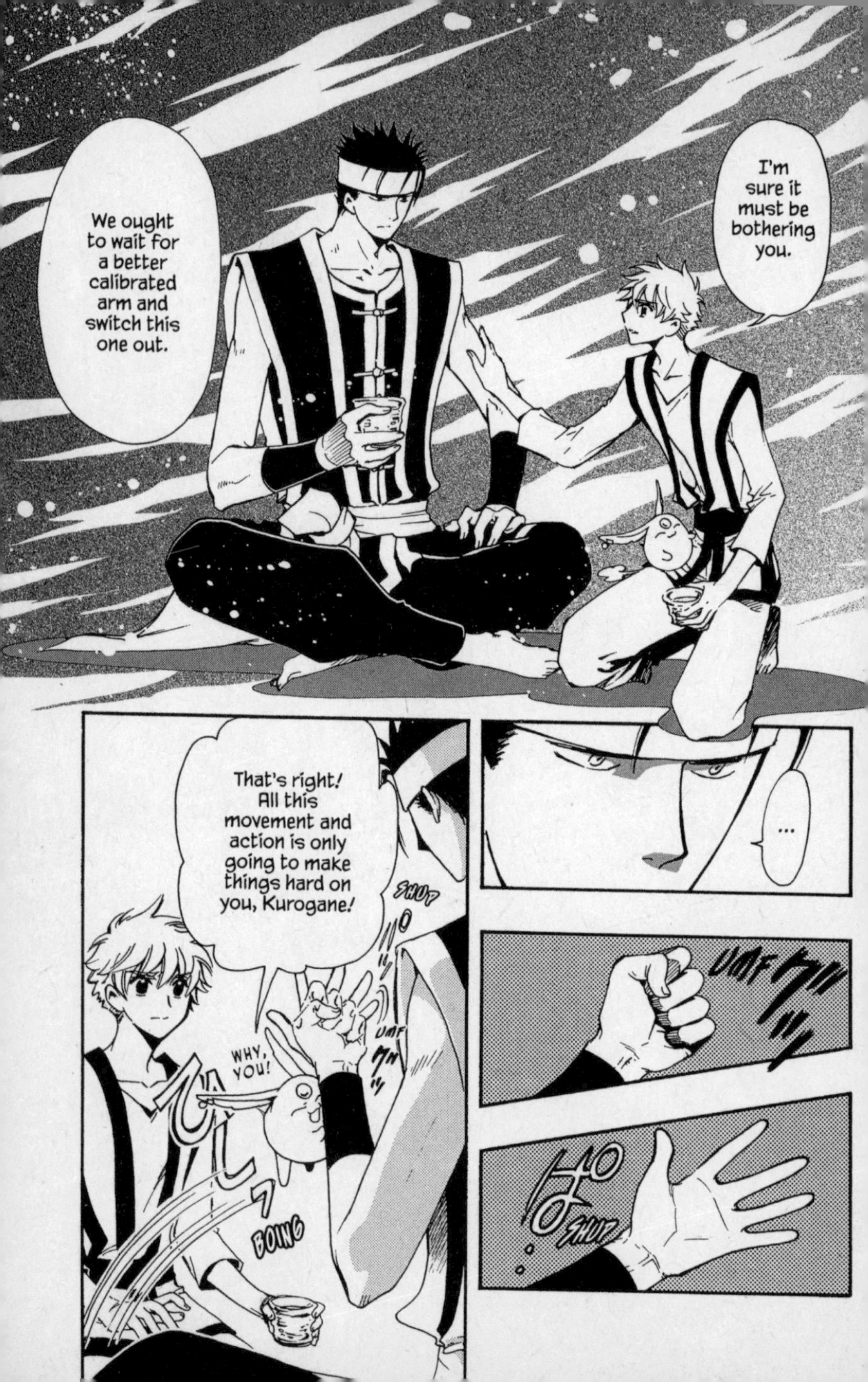
I'm sure it must be bothering you.
We ought to wait for a better calibrated arm and switch this one out.
...
UMF
SHUP
That's right! All this movement and action is only going to make things hard on you, Kurogane!
SHUP
UMF
WHY, YOU!
BOING

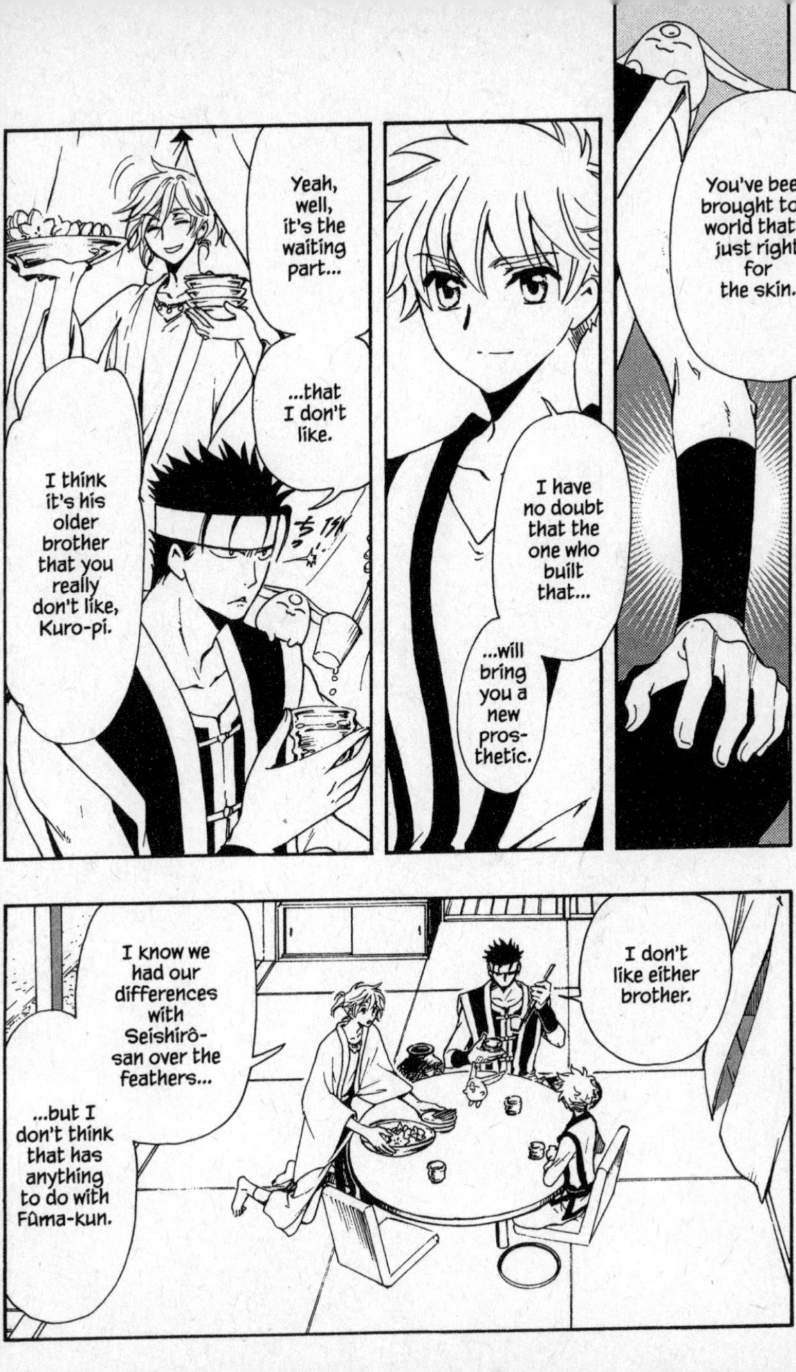
You've been brought to a world that's just right for the skin.
I have no doubt that the one who built that...
...will bring you a new prosthetic.
Yeah, well, it's the waiting part...
...that I don't like.
TSK
I think it's his older brother that you really don't like, Kuro-pi.
I don't like either brother.
I know we had our differences with Seishirô-san over the feathers...
...but I don't think that has anything to do with Fûma-kun.

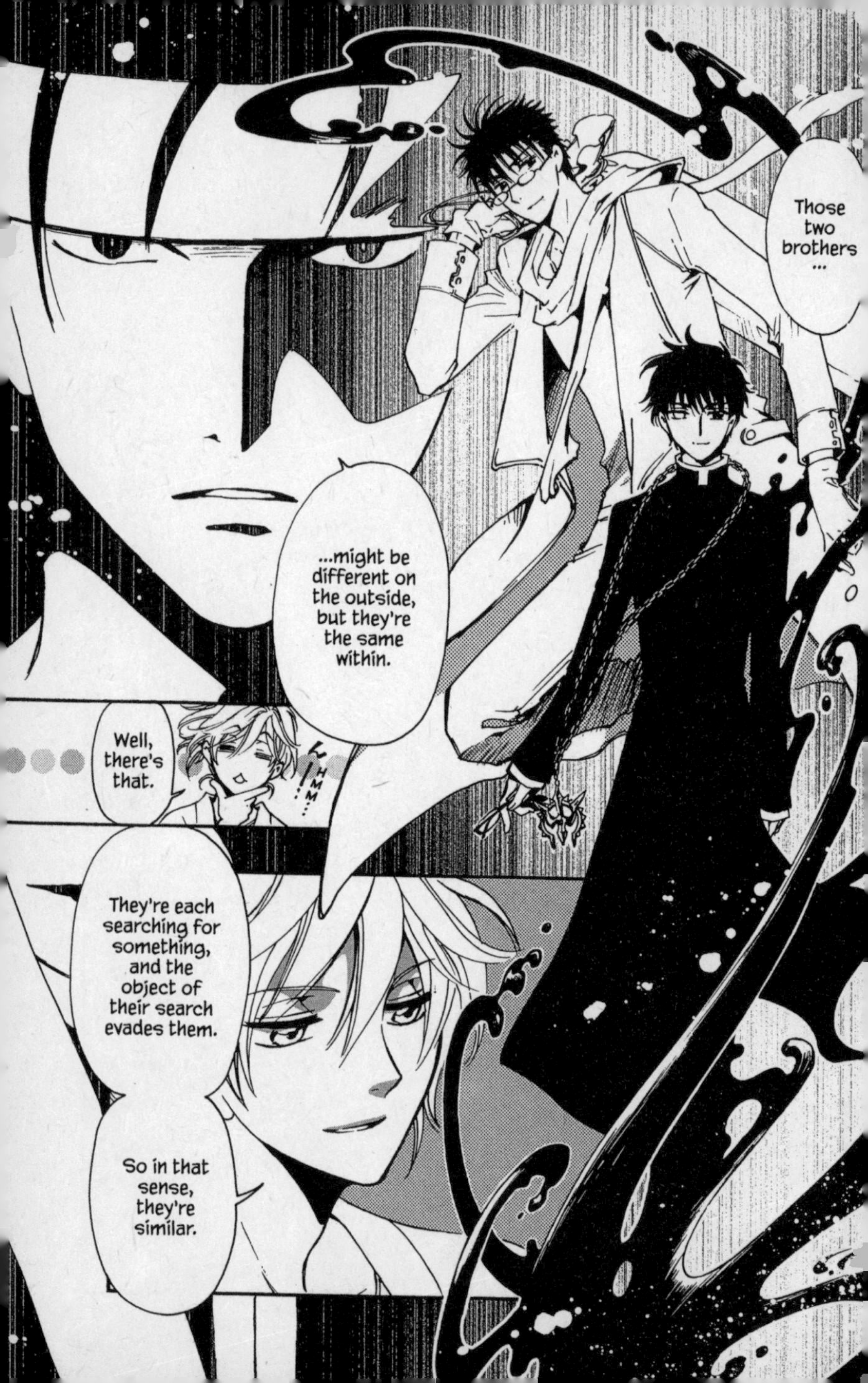
Those two brothers ...
...might be different on the outside, but they're the same within.
Well, there's that.
HMM...
They're each searching for something, and the object of their search evades them.
So in that sense, they're similar.

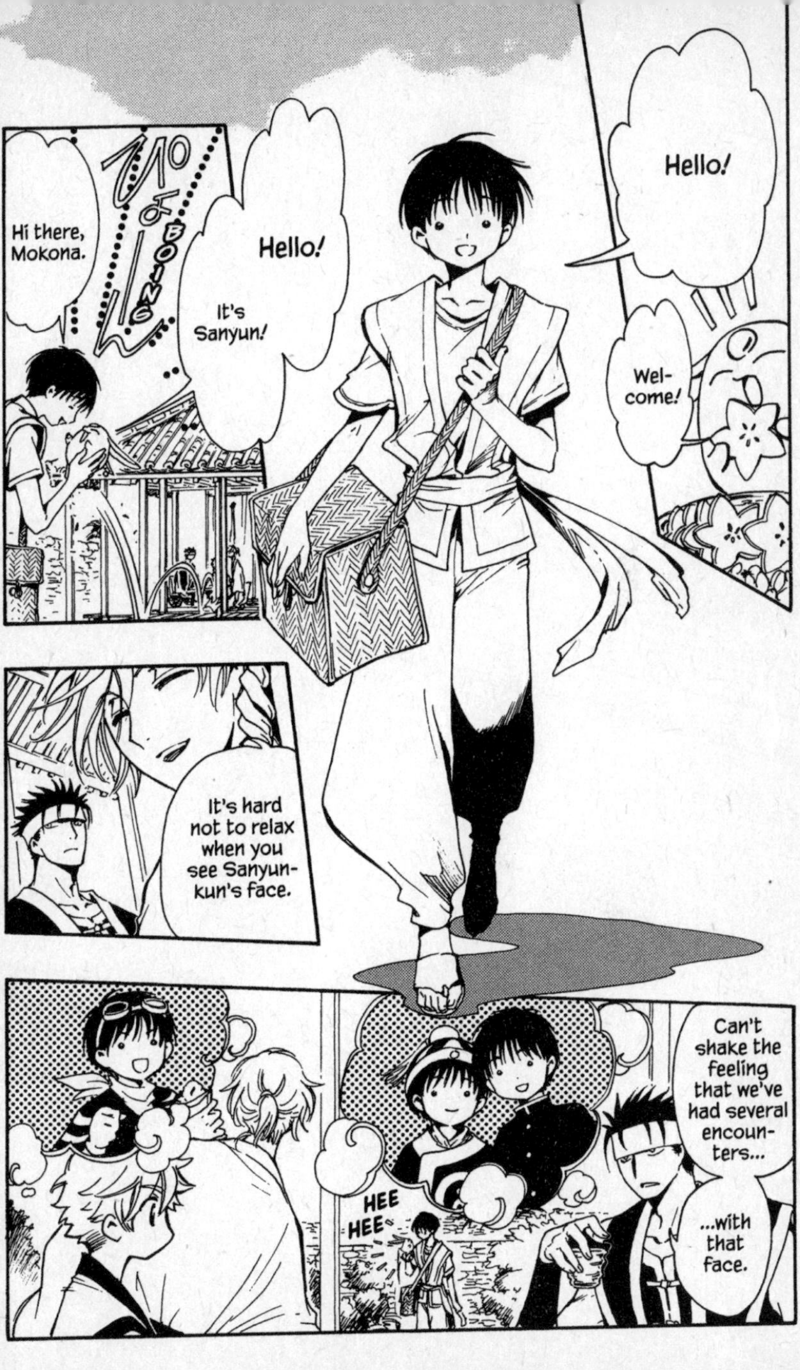
Hello!
Wel-come!
Hello!
It's Sanyun!
Hi there, Mokona.
BOING
It's hard not to relax when you see Sanyun-kun's face.
Can't shake the feeling that we've had several encoun-ters...
...with that face.
HEE HEE

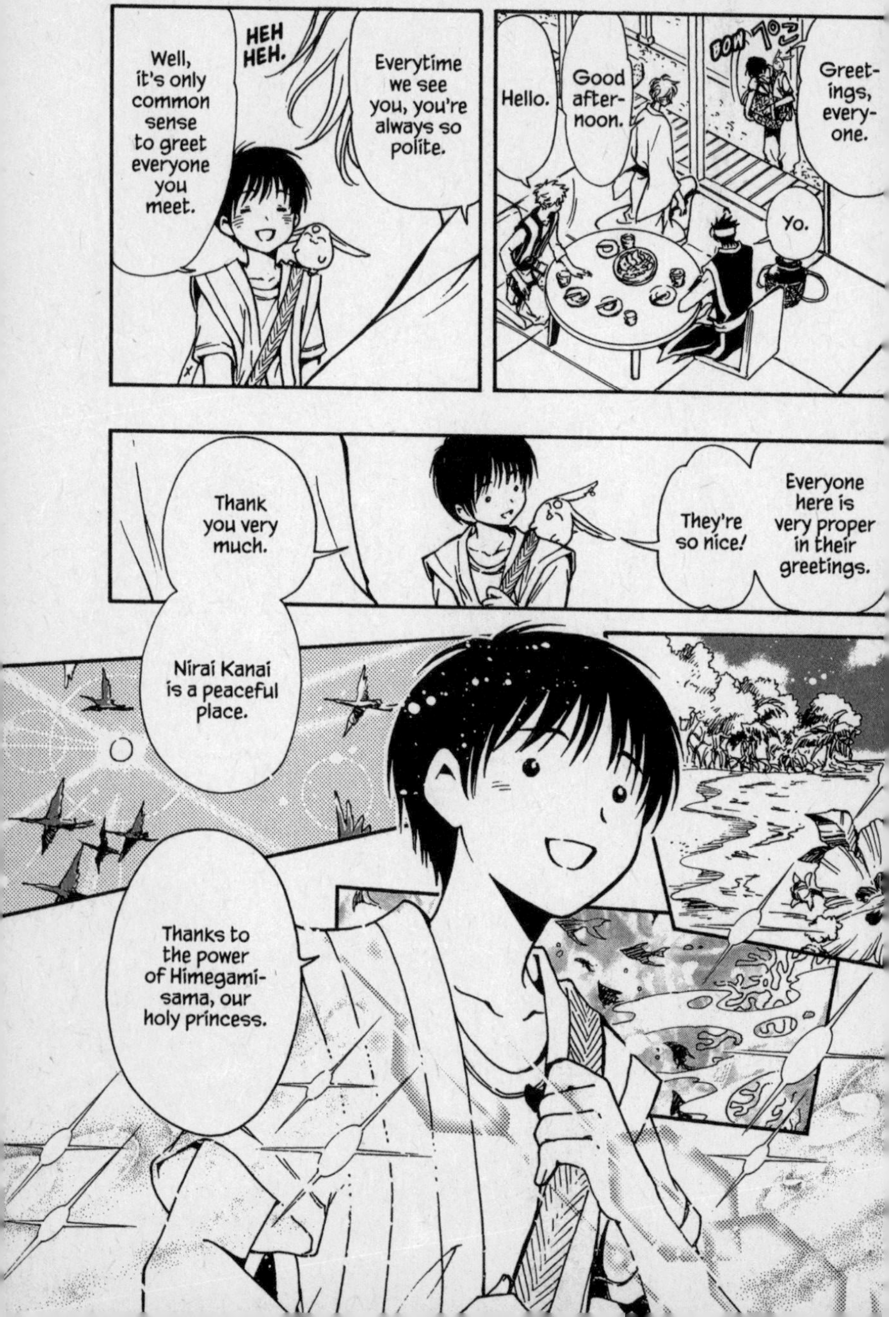
BOW
Greetings, everyone.
Good afternoon.
Hello.
Yo.
Everytime we see you, you're always so polite.
HEH HEH.
Well, it's only common sense to greet everyone you meet.
Everyone here is very proper in their greetings.
They're so nice!
Thank you very much.
Nirai Kanai is a peaceful place.
Thanks to the power of Himegami-sama, our holy princess.

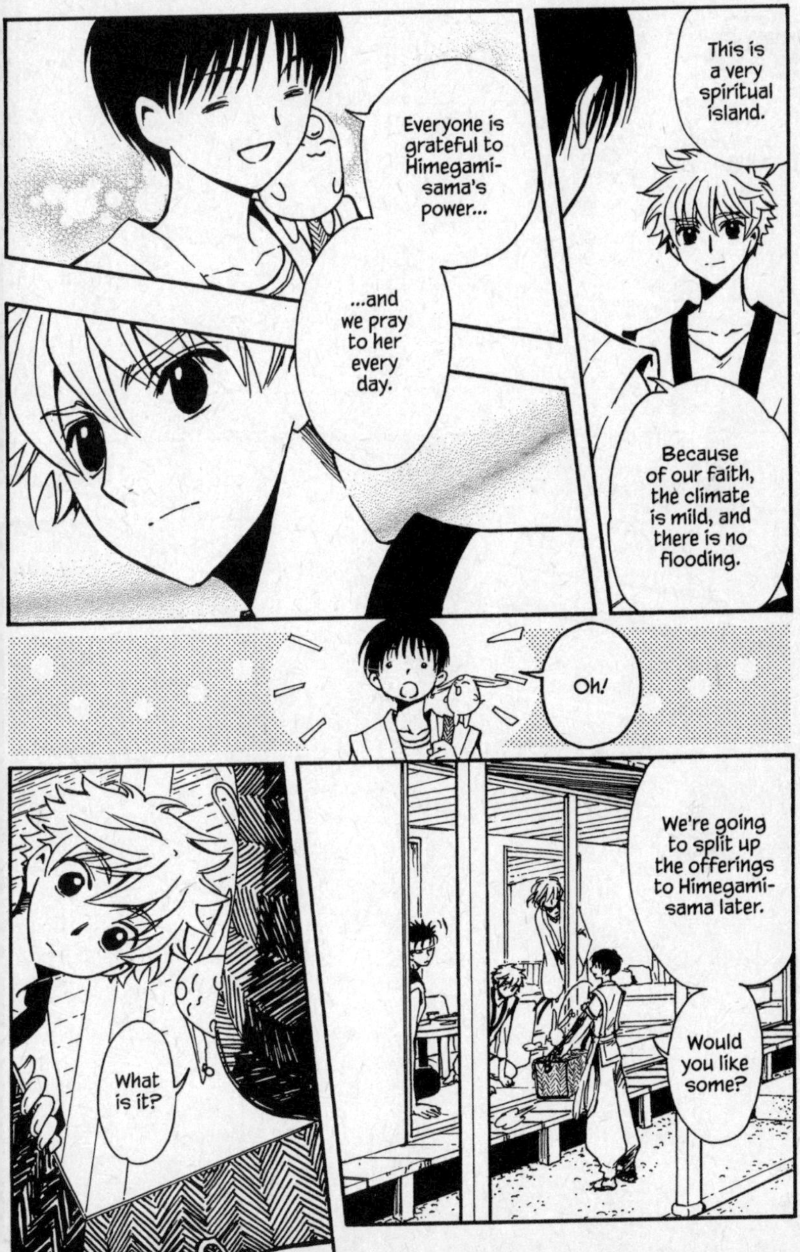
This is a very spiritual island.
Because of our faith, the climate is mild, and there is no flooding.
Everyone is grateful to Himegami-sama's power...
...and we pray to her every day.
Oh!
We're going to split up the offerings to Himegami-sama later.
Would you like some?
What is it?

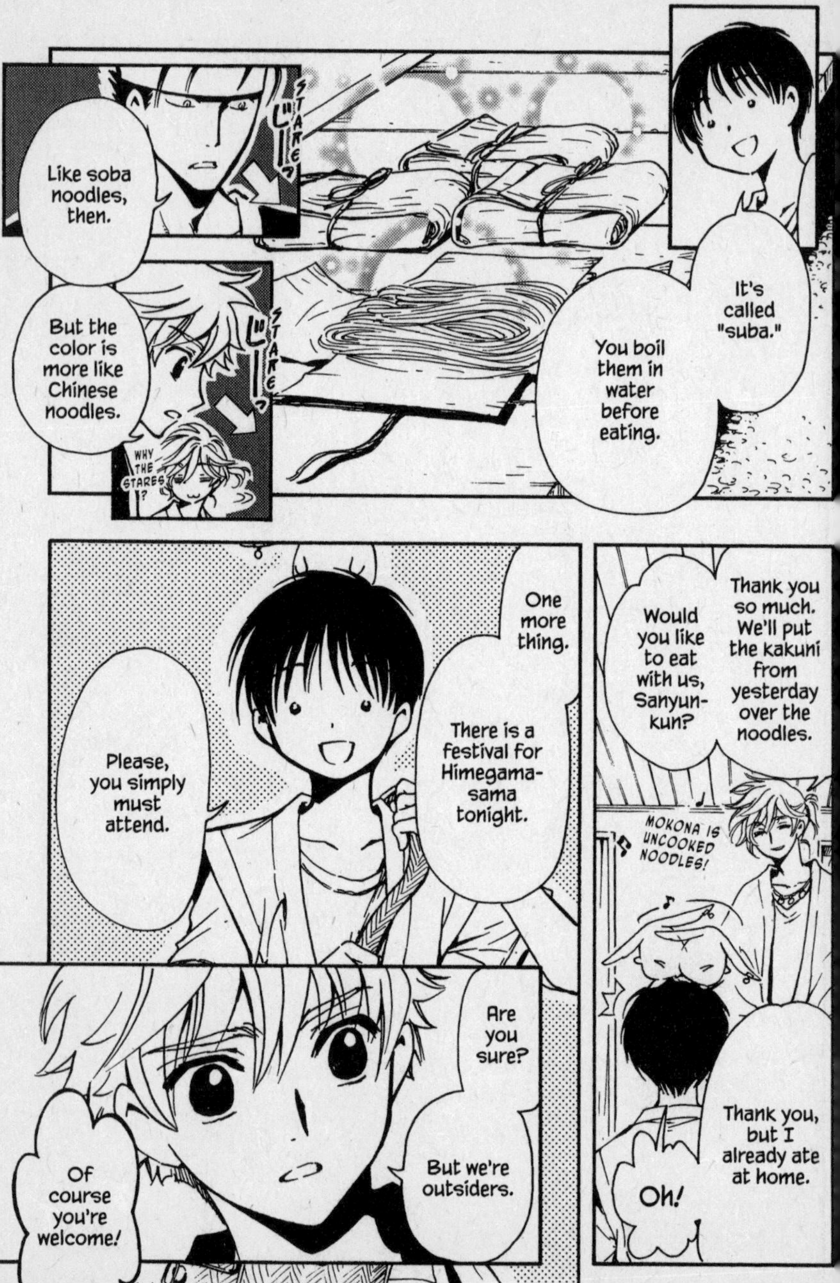
It's called "suba."
You boil them in water before eating.
Like soba noodles, then.
STARE
But the color is more like Chinese noodles.
STARE
WHY THE STARES?
Thank you so much. We'll put the kakuni from yesterday over the noodles.
Would you like to eat with us, Sanyun-kun?
MOKONA IS UNCOOKED NOODLES!
Thank you, but I already ate at home.
Oh!
One more thing.
There is a festival for Himegama-sama tonight.
Please, you simply must attend.
Are you sure?
But we're outsiders.
Of course you're welcome!

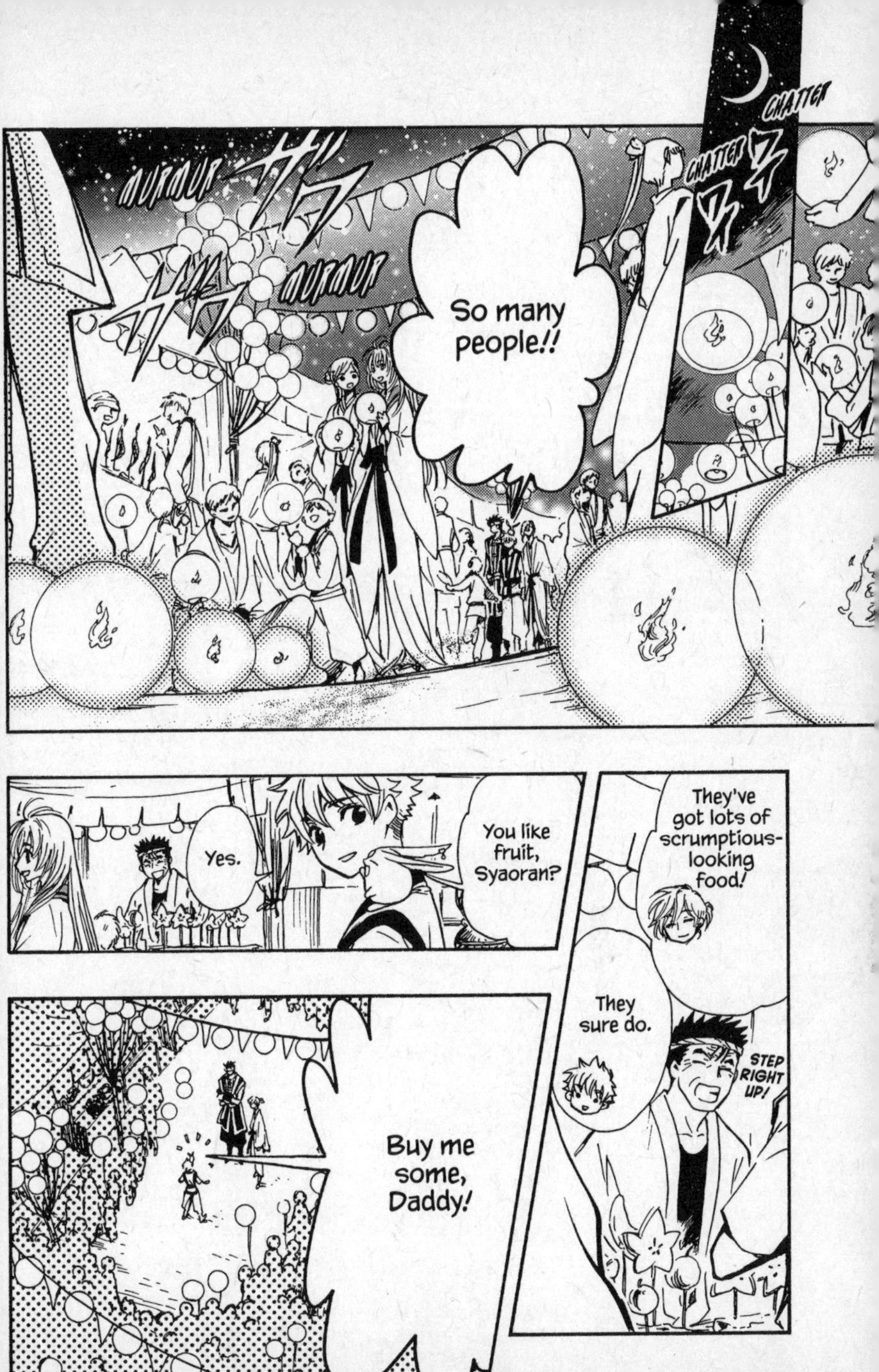
CHATTER CHATTER
So many people!!
MURMUR MURMUR
They've got lots of scrumptious-looking food!
They sure do.
STEP RIGHT UP!
You like fruit, Syaoran?
Yes.
Buy me some, Daddy!

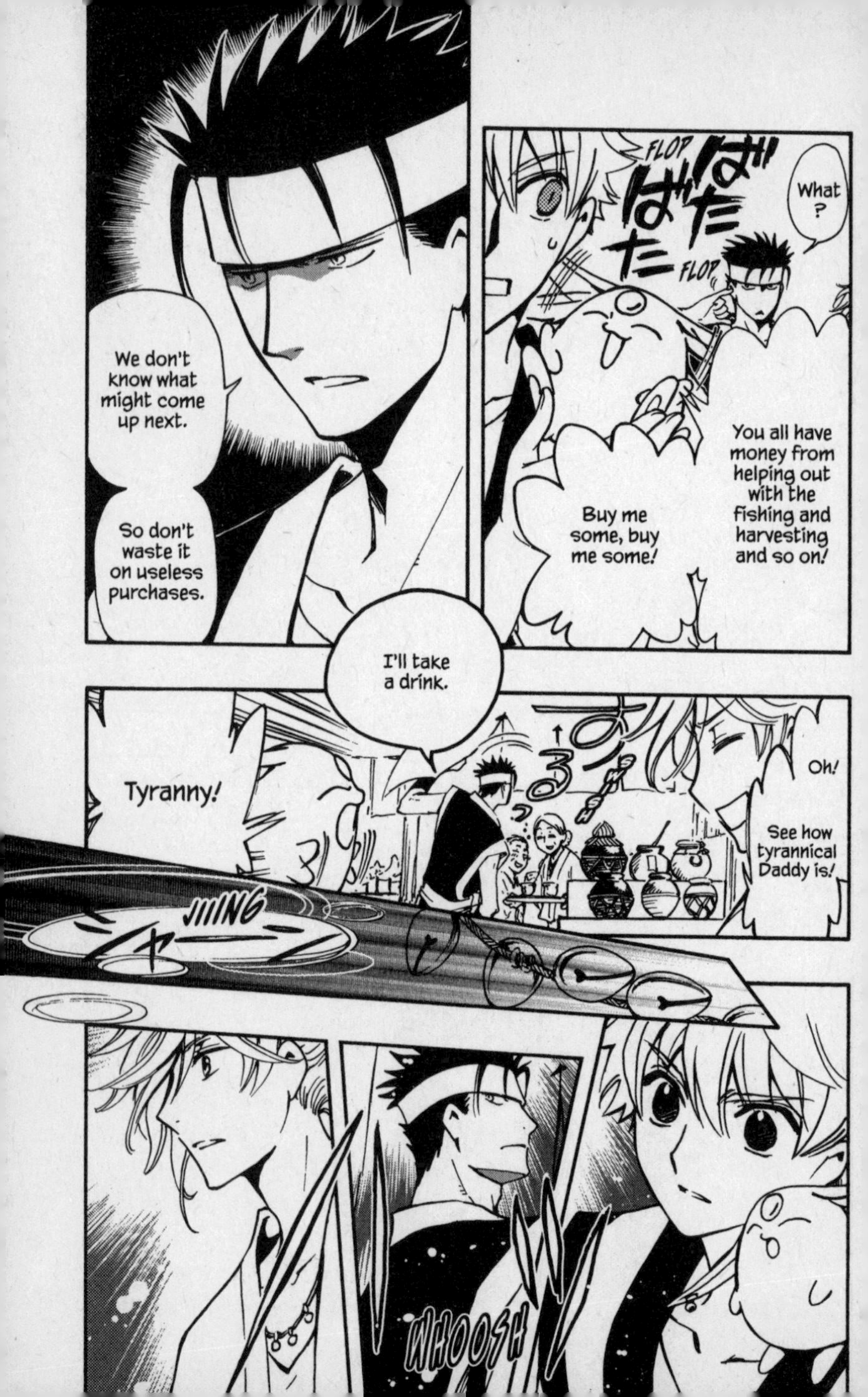
FLOP
ばた
ばた
FLOP
What?
You all have money from helping out with the fishing and harvesting and so on!
Buy me some, buy me some!
We don't know what might come up next.
So don't waste it on useless purchases.
Oh!
See how tyrannical Daddy is!
I'll take a drink.
Tyranny!
JIIING
WHOOSH

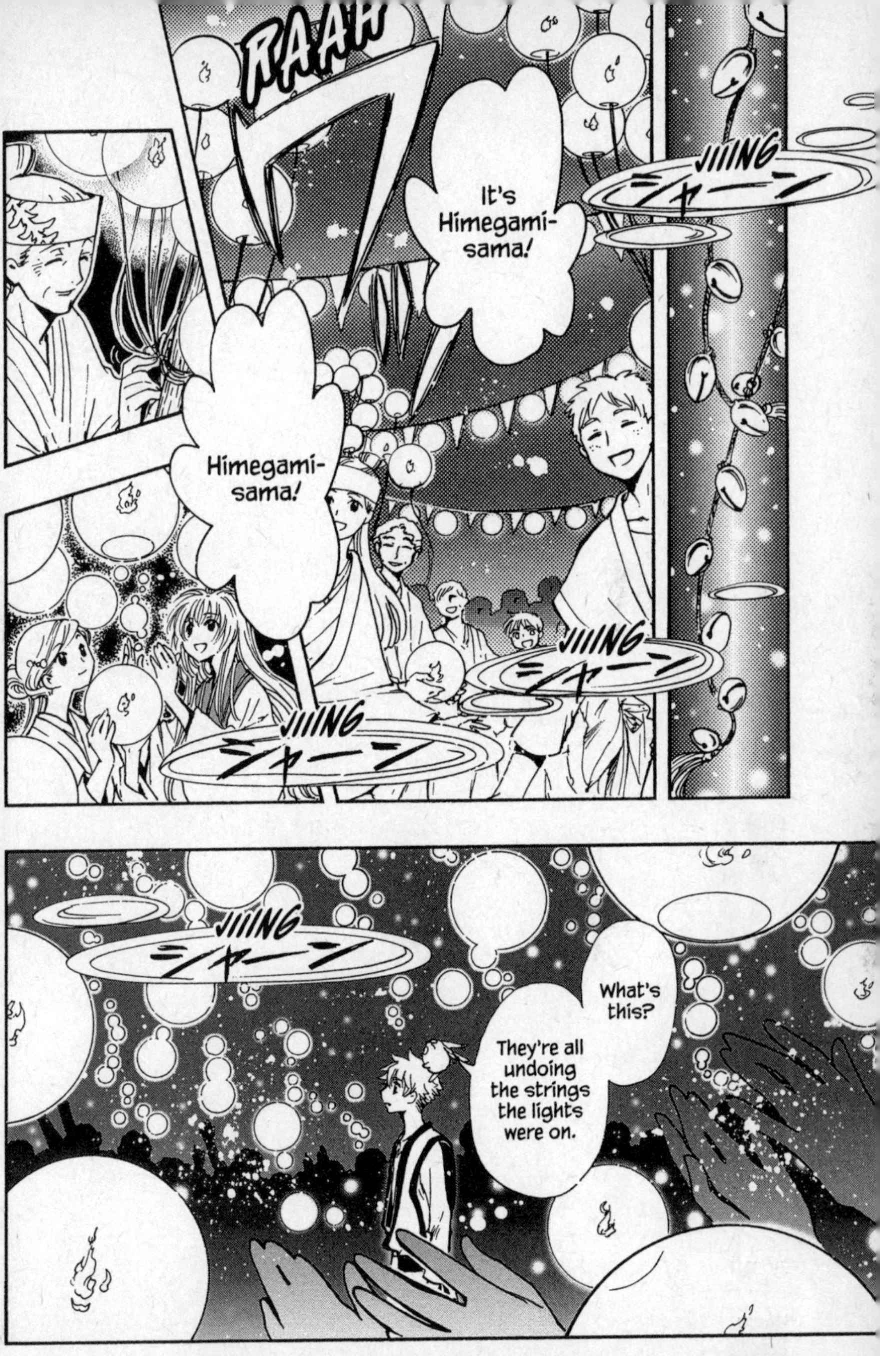
RAAH
It's Himegami-sama!
JIIING
シャーン
Himegami-sama!
JIIING
シャーン
JIIING
シャーン
JIIING
シャーン
What's this?
They're all undoing the strings the lights were on.

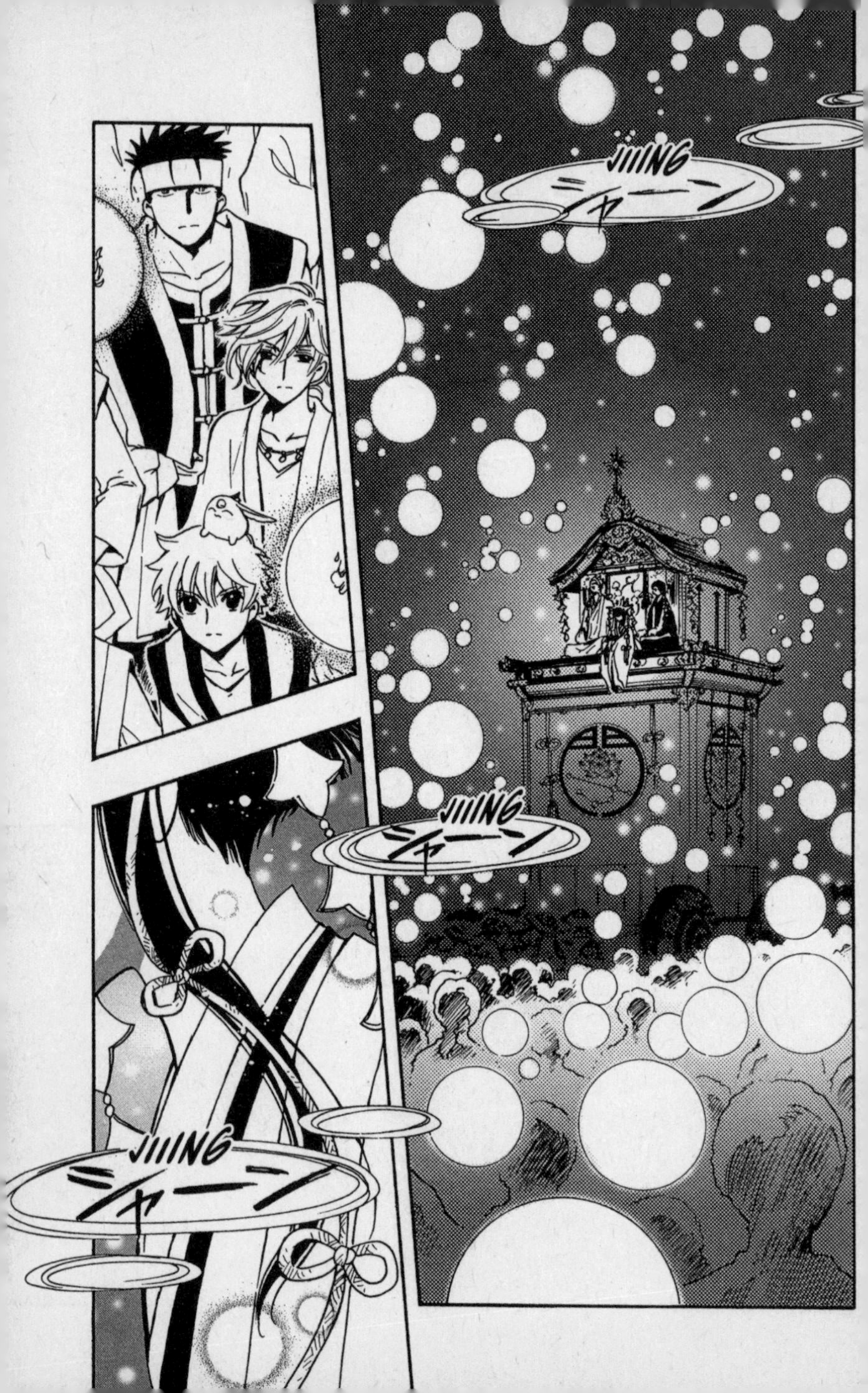
JIIING
JIIING
JIIING

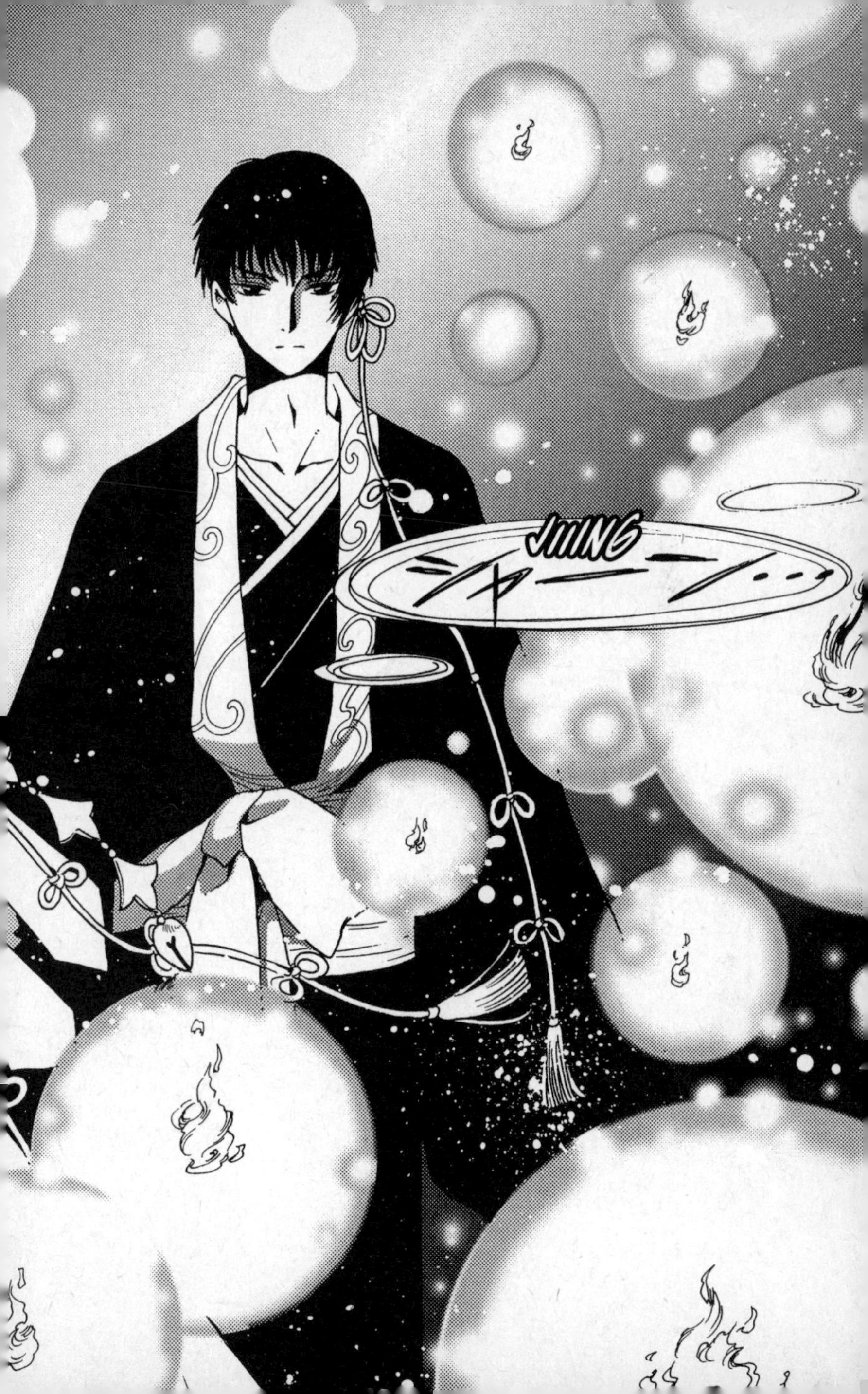
JIIING
シャーーン…

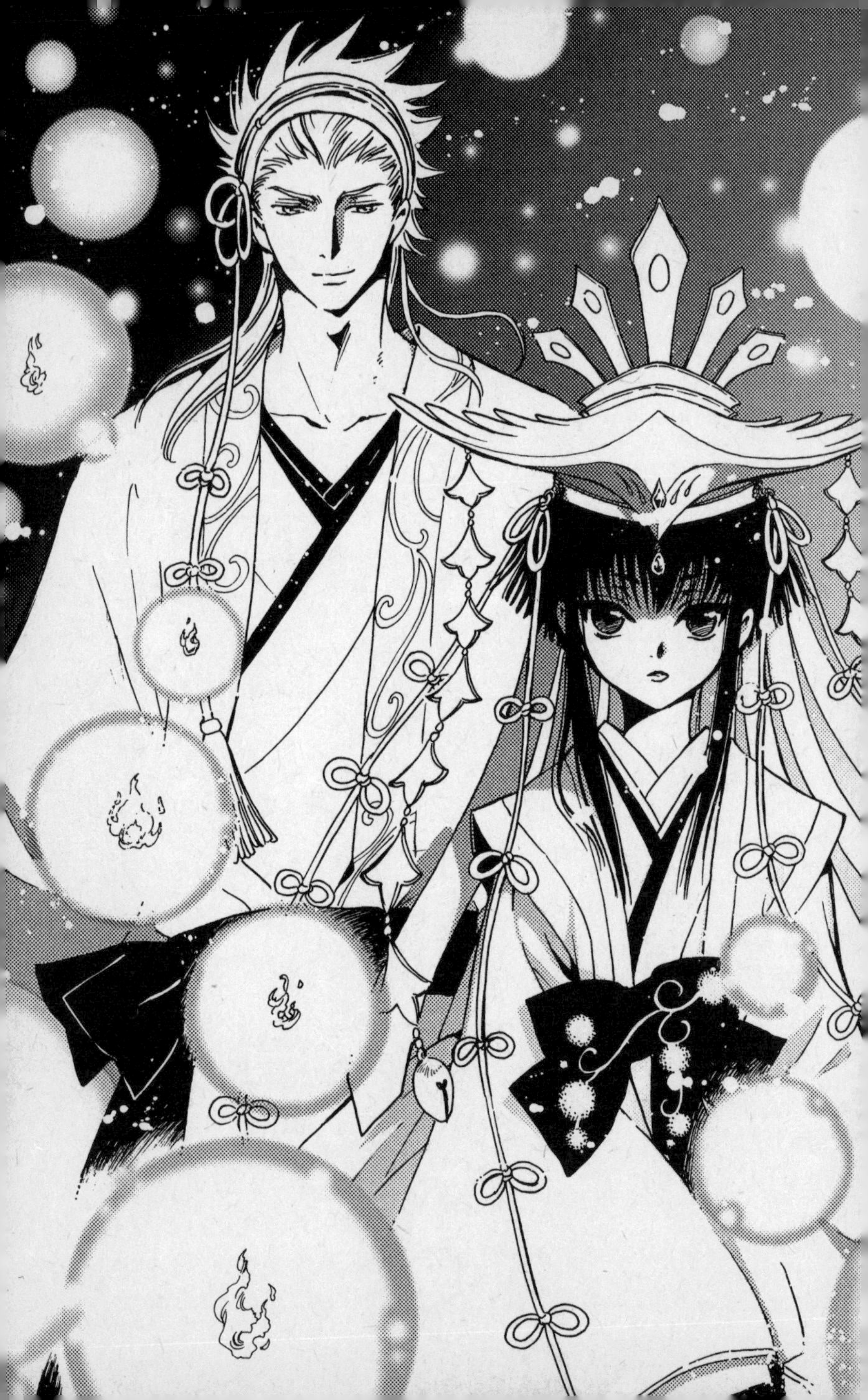

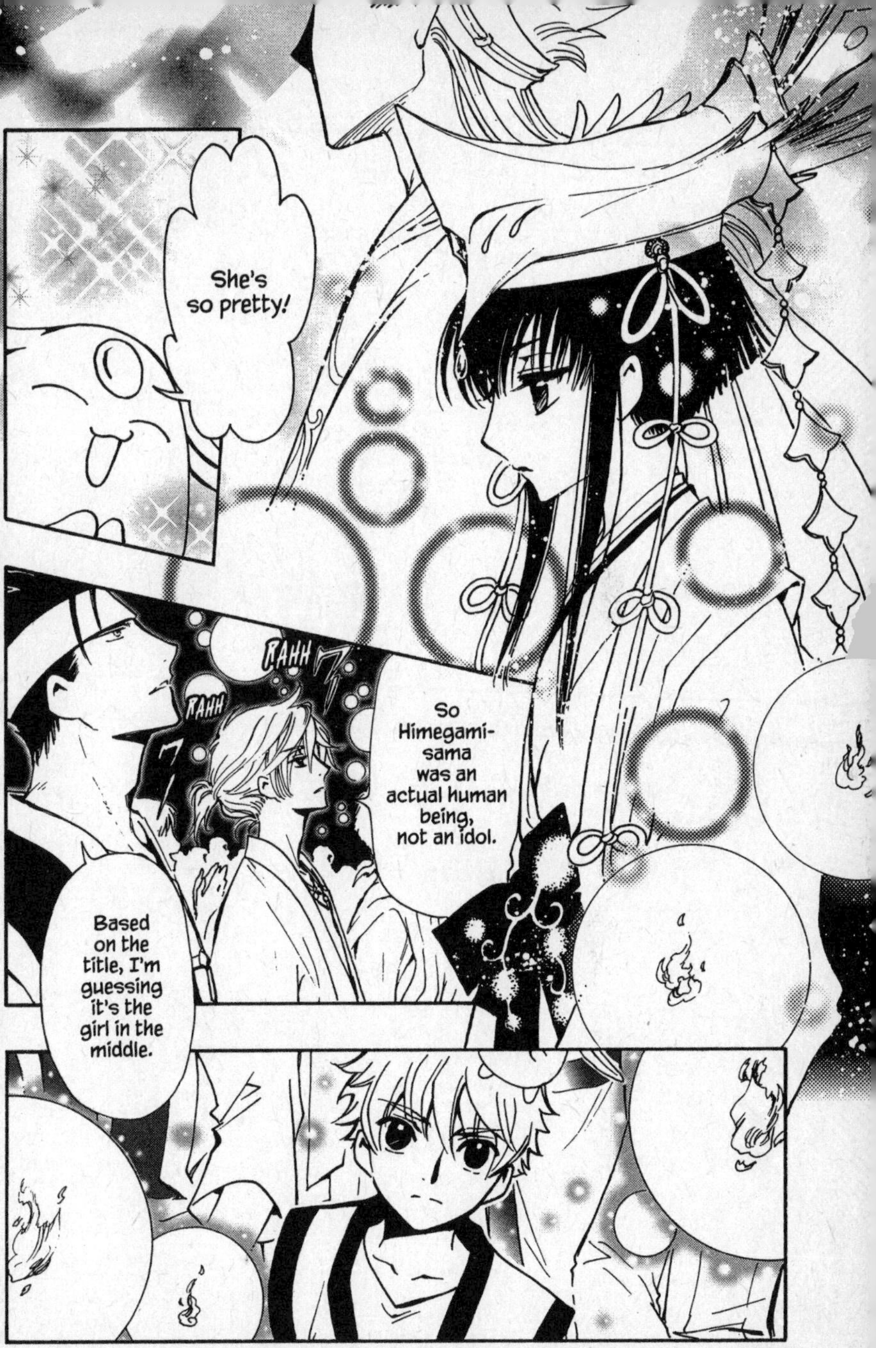
She's so pretty!
RAHH
RAHH
So Himegami-sama was an actual human being, not an idol.
Based on the title, I'm guessing it's the girl in the middle.

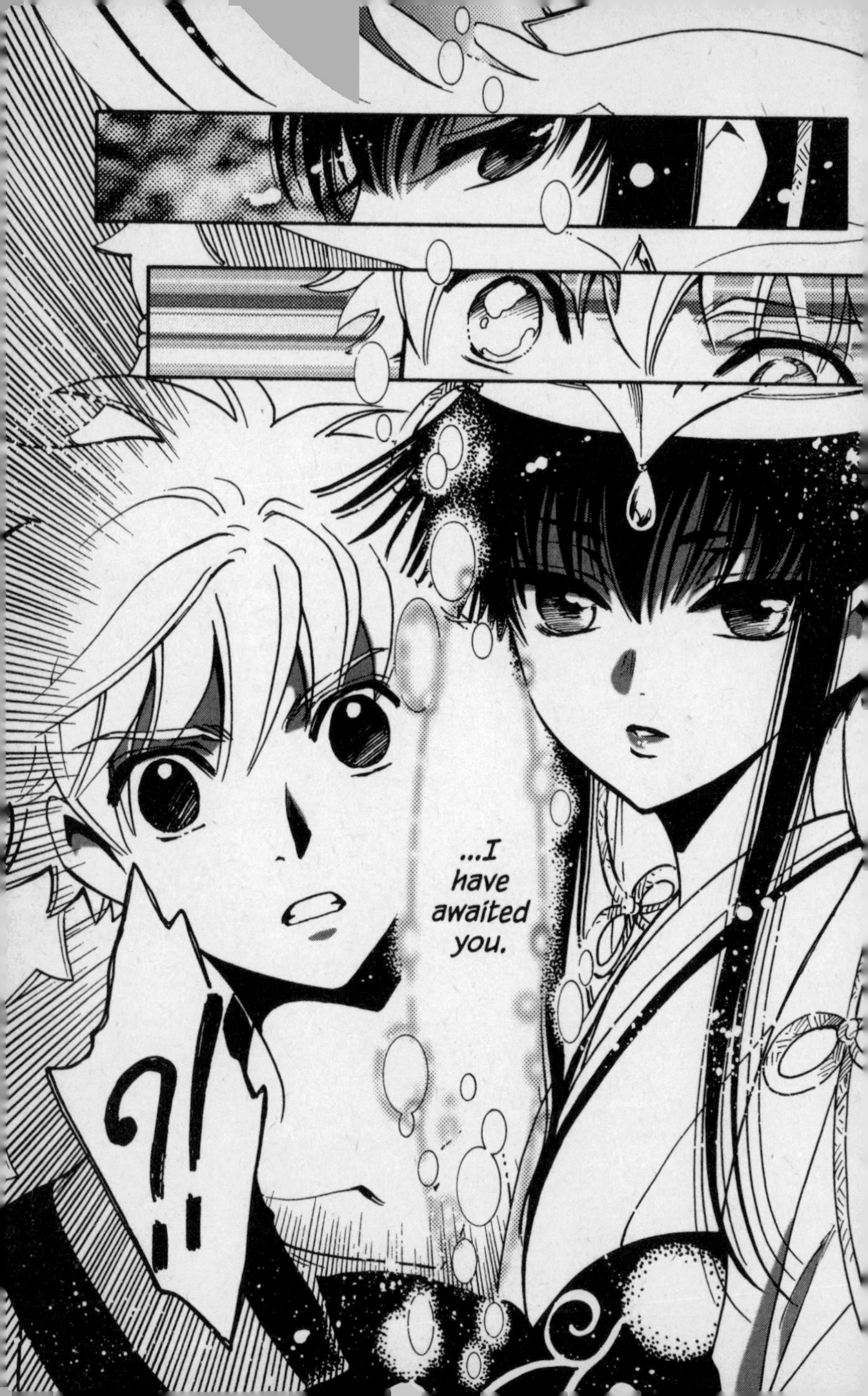
...I have awaited you.
?!

TSUBASA

WoRLD CHRoNiCLE: NIRAIKANAI

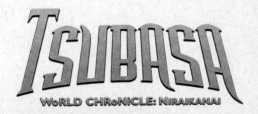

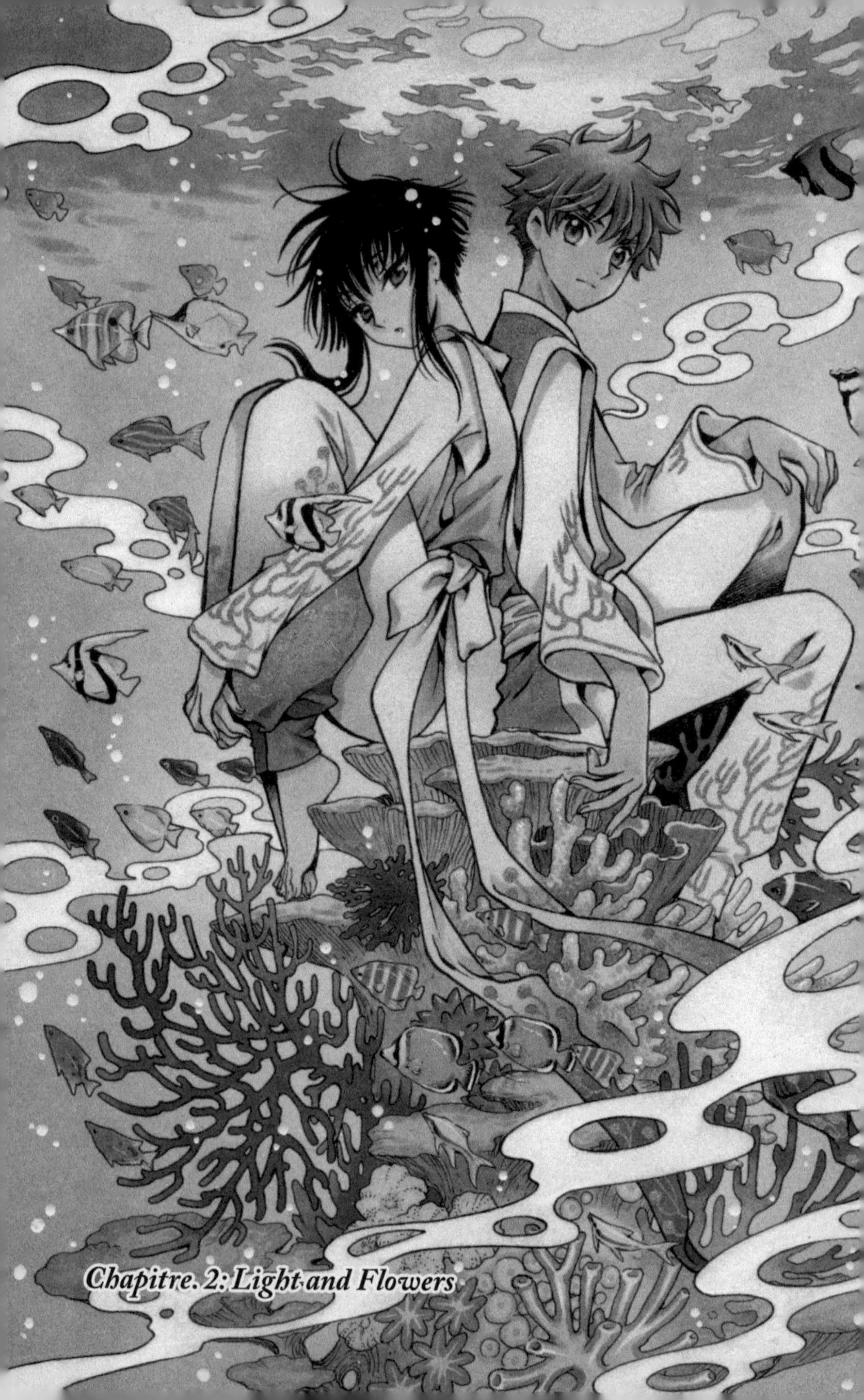

Chapitre. 2: Light and Flowers

TSUBASA
WoRLD CHRoNiCLE: NIRAIKANAI

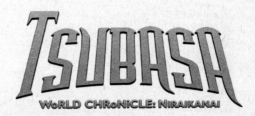

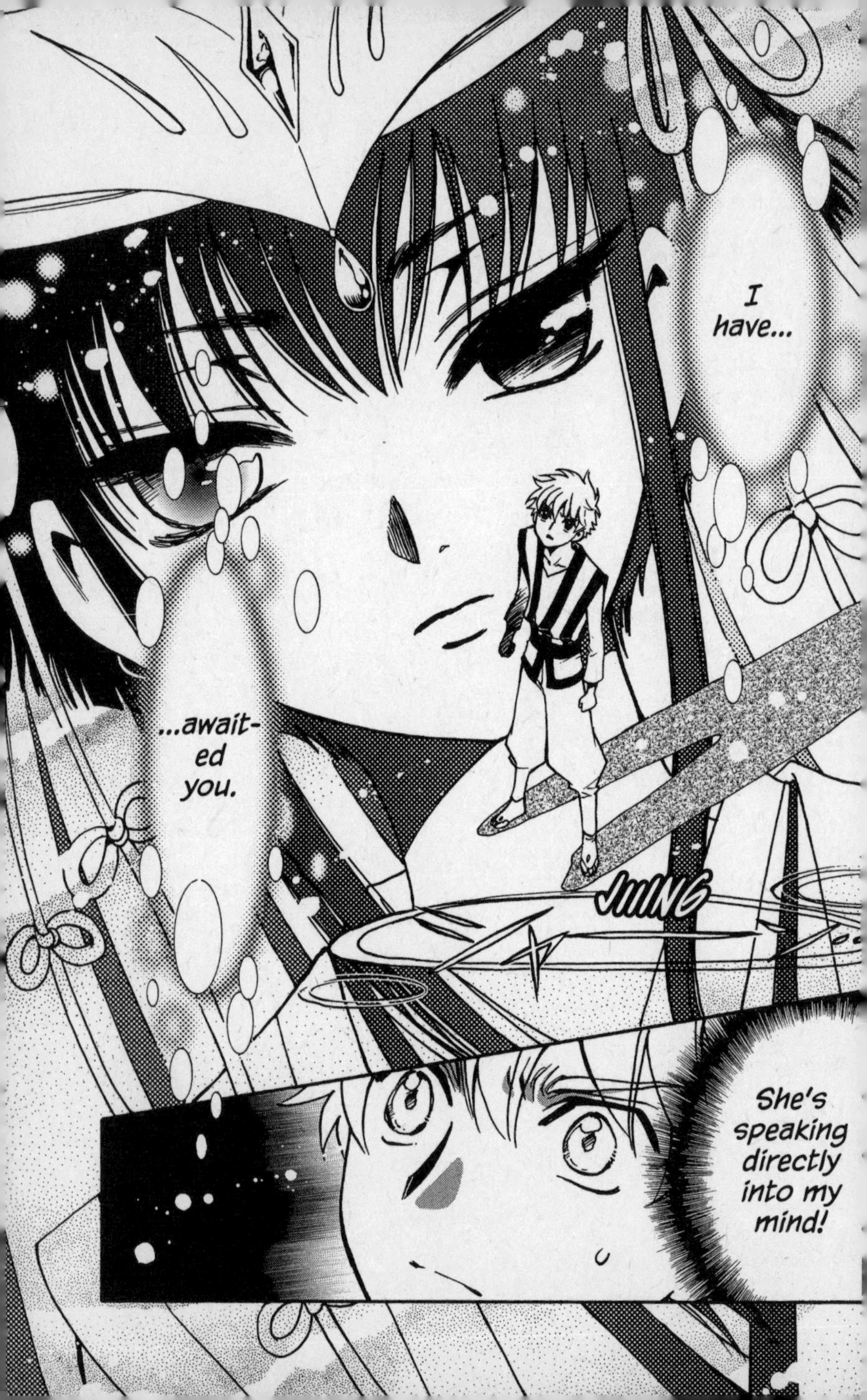
I have...
...await-ed you.
JIIING
She's speaking directly into my mind!

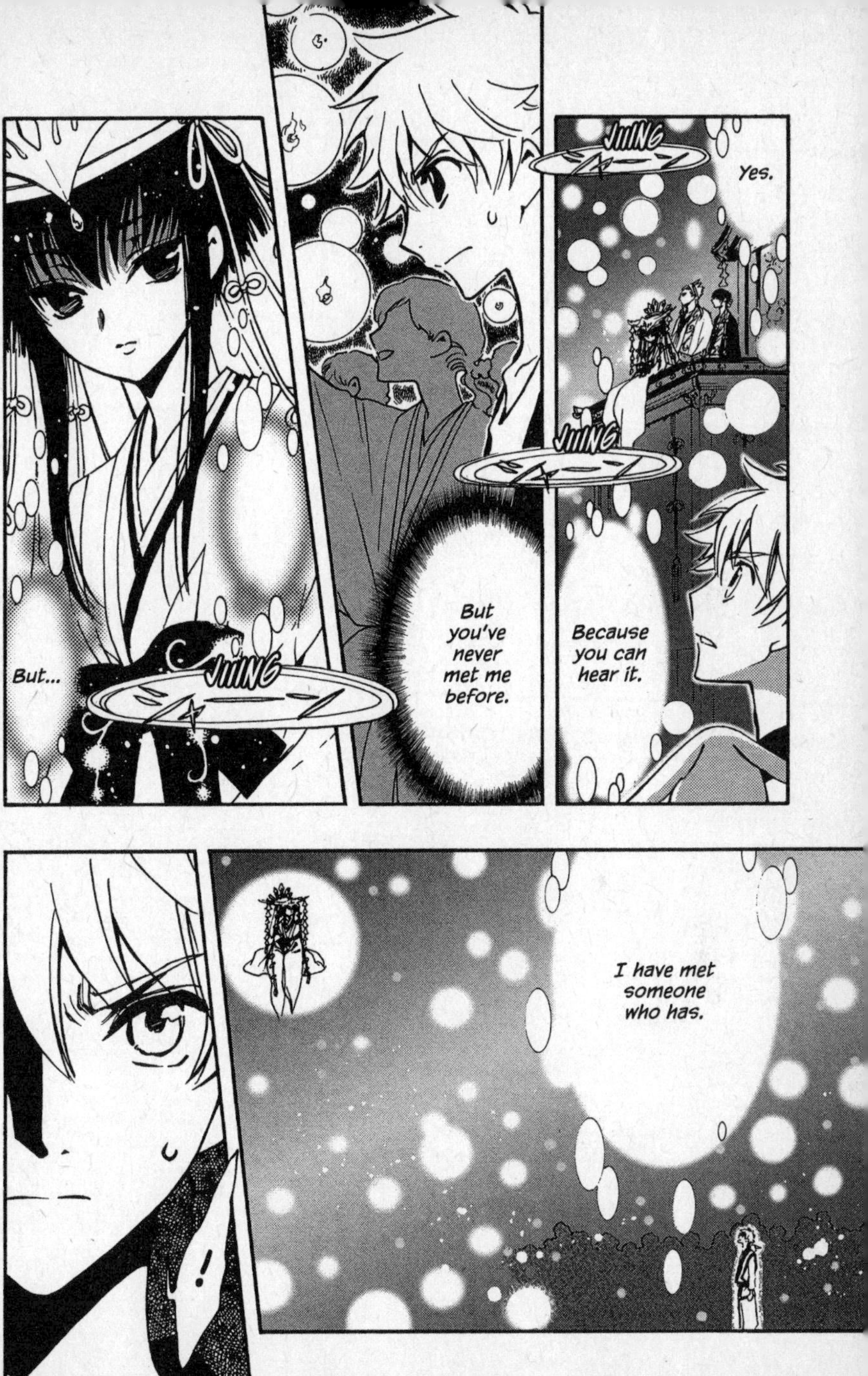
JIIING
Yes.
JIIING
Because you can hear it.
But you've never met me before.
But...
JIIING
I have met someone who has.
!

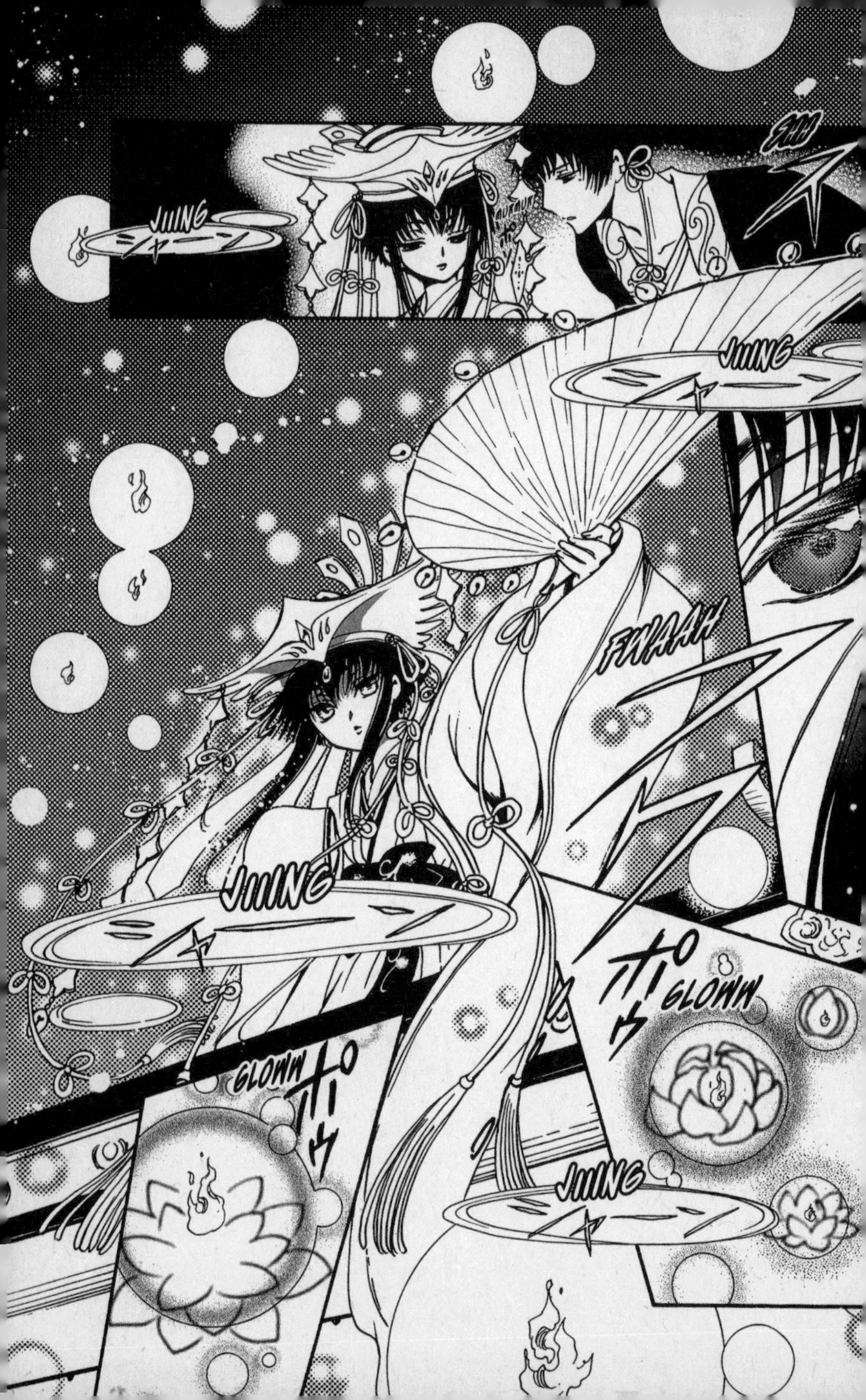
SHH
JIIING
JIIING
FWAAH
GLOWW
JIIING
GLOWW
JIIING

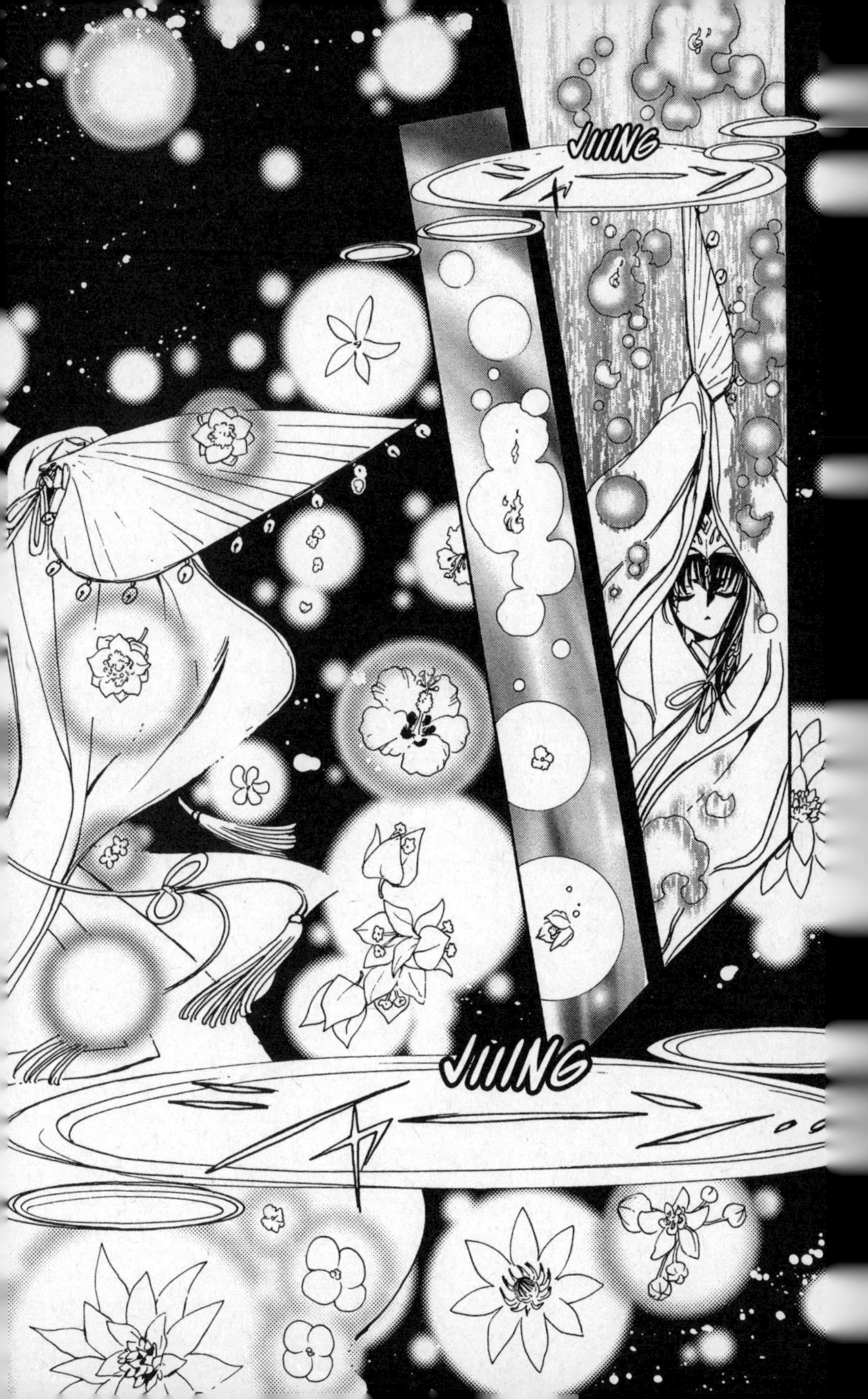
JIIING
JIIING

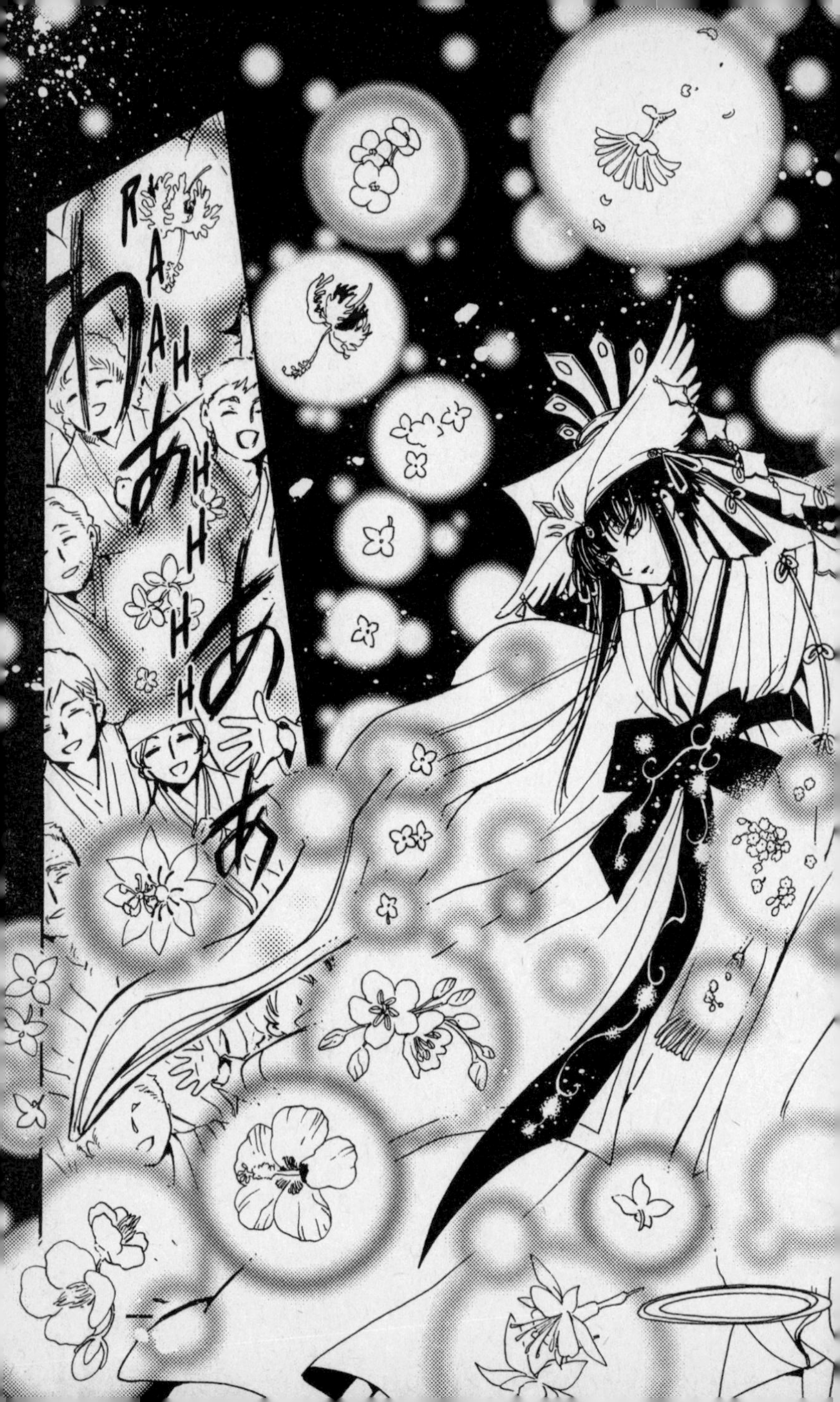
わあぁぁ
RAAHHHHHH

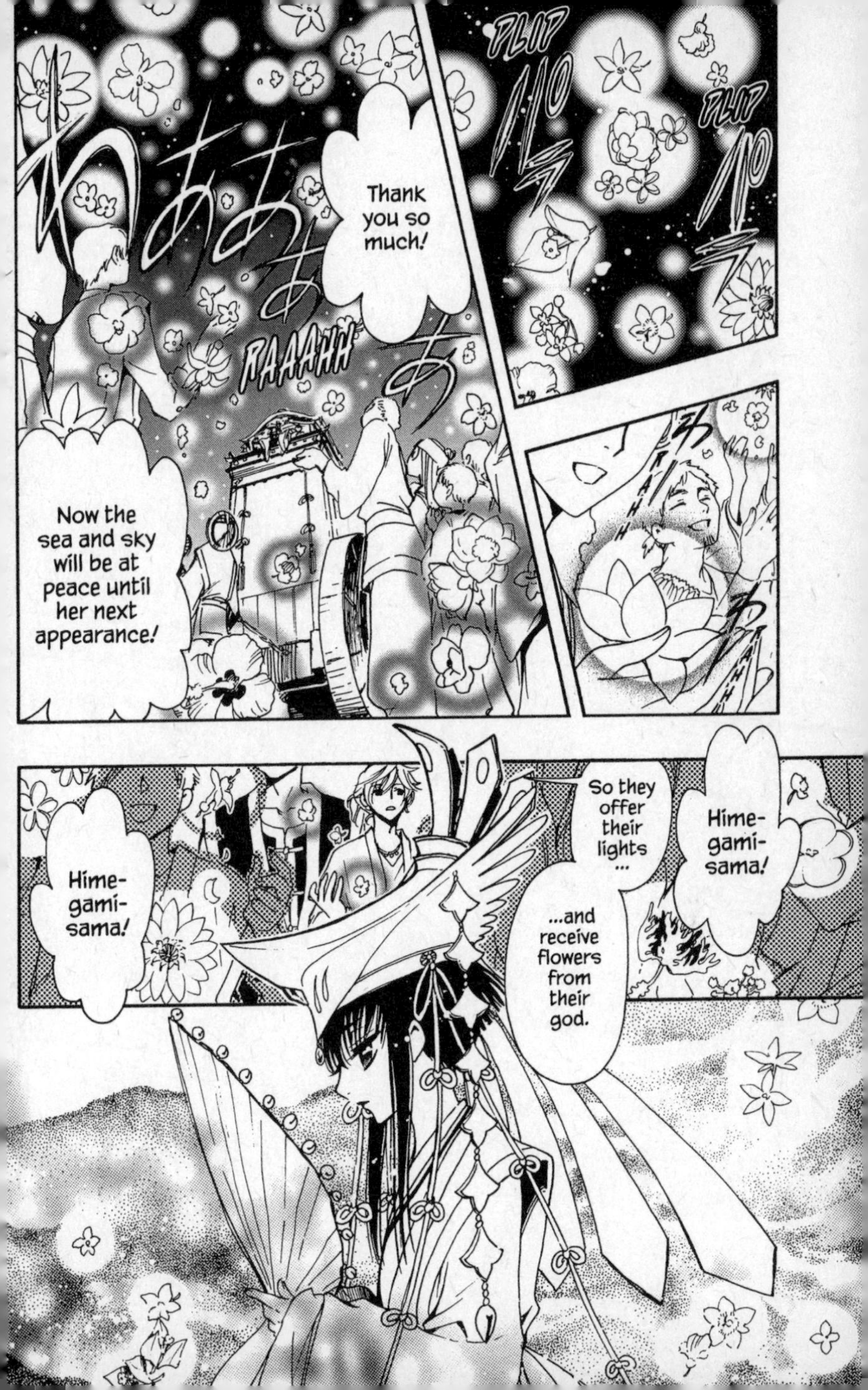
PLIP
PLIP
RAAHH
Thank you so much!
RAAAHH
Now the sea and sky will be at peace until her next appearance!
Hime-gami-sama!
So they offer their lights...
...and receive flowers from their god.
Hime-gami-sama!

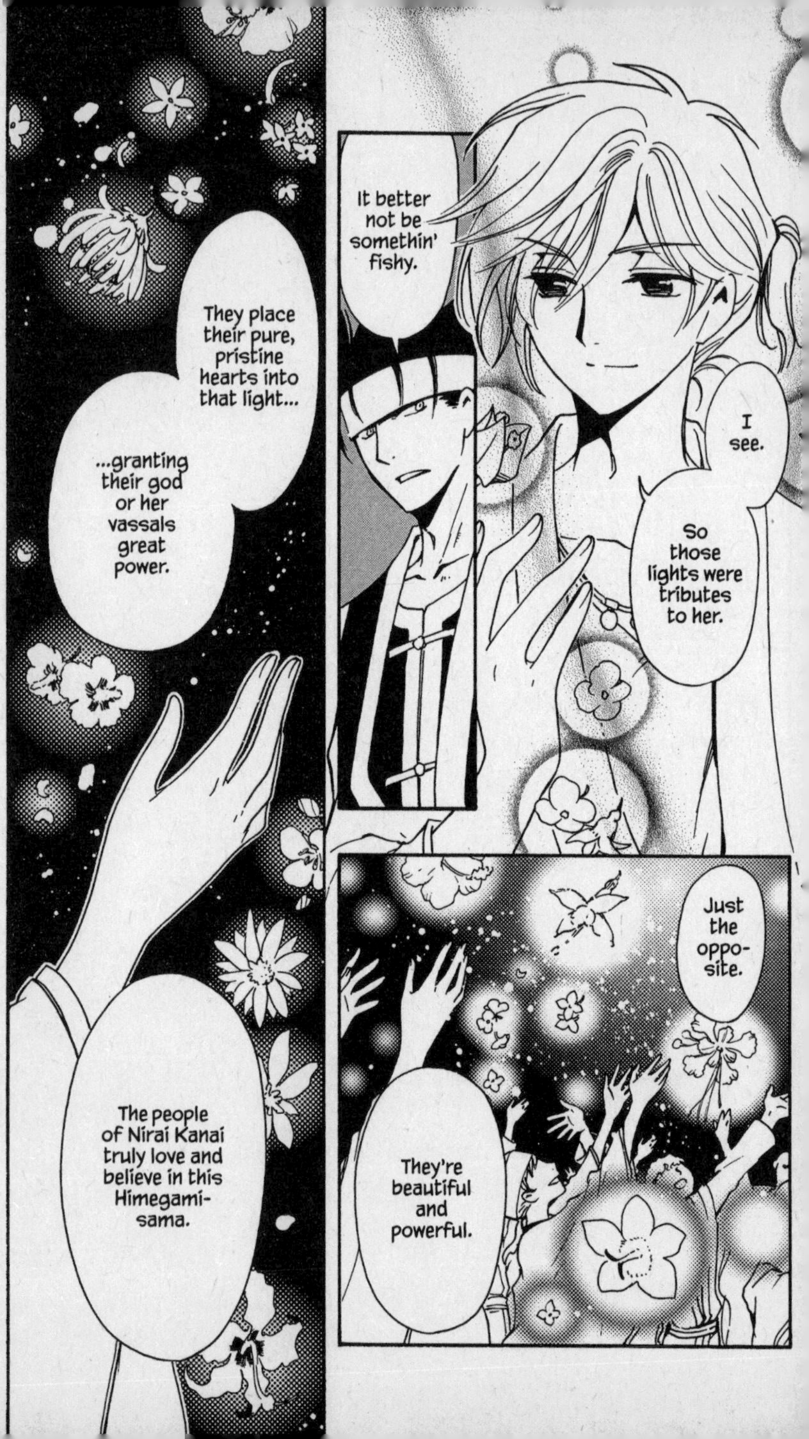
It better not be somethin' fishy.
I see.
So those lights were tributes to her.
Just the oppo-site.
They're beautiful and powerful.
They place their pure, pristine hearts into that light...
...granting their god or her vassals great power.
The people of Nirai Kanai truly love and believe in this Himegami-sama.

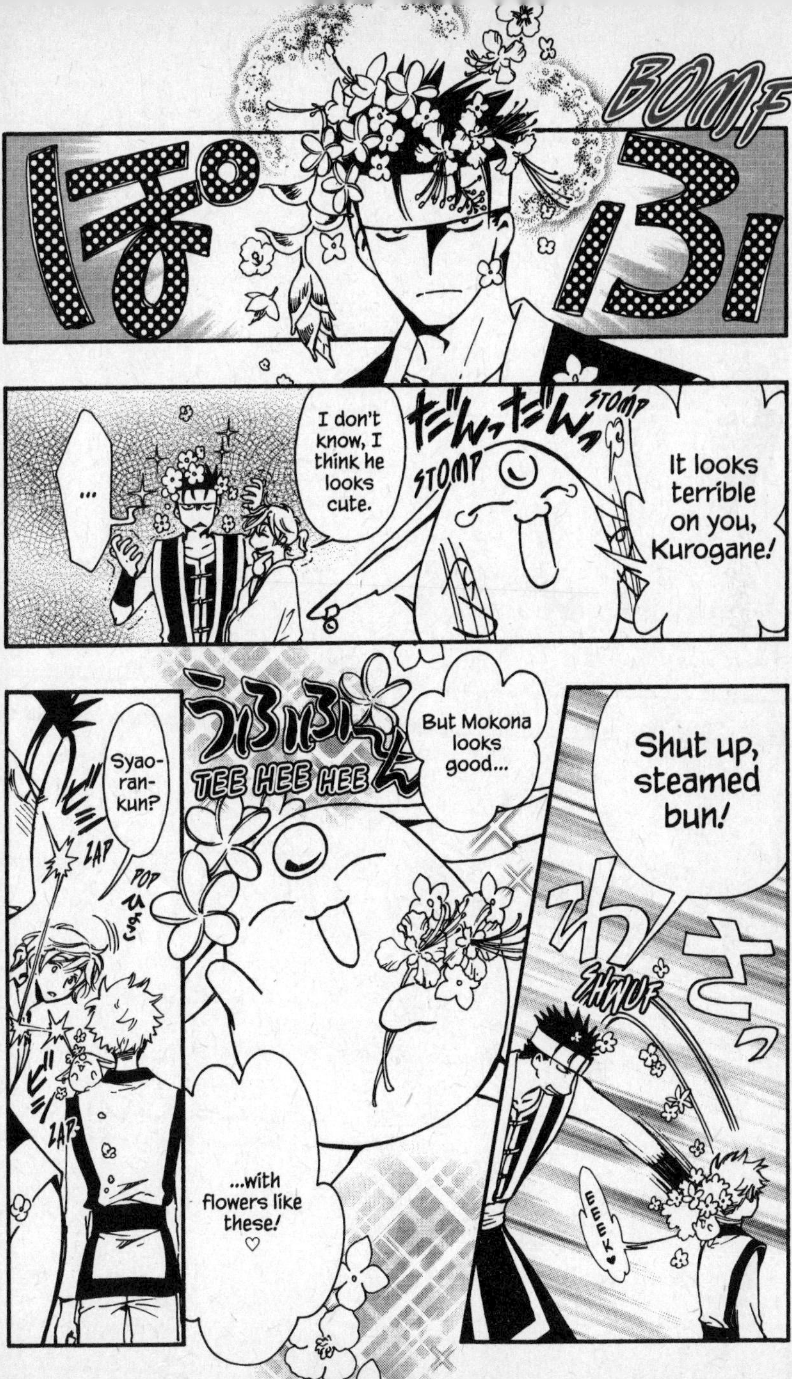
BONF
It looks terrible on you, Kurogane!
STOMP
STOMP
I don't know, I think he looks cute.
...
Shut up, steamed bun!
SHWUF
EEEK♥
But Mokona looks good...
TEE HEE HEE
...with flowers like these! ♡
Syao-ran-kun?
ZAP
POP
ZAP

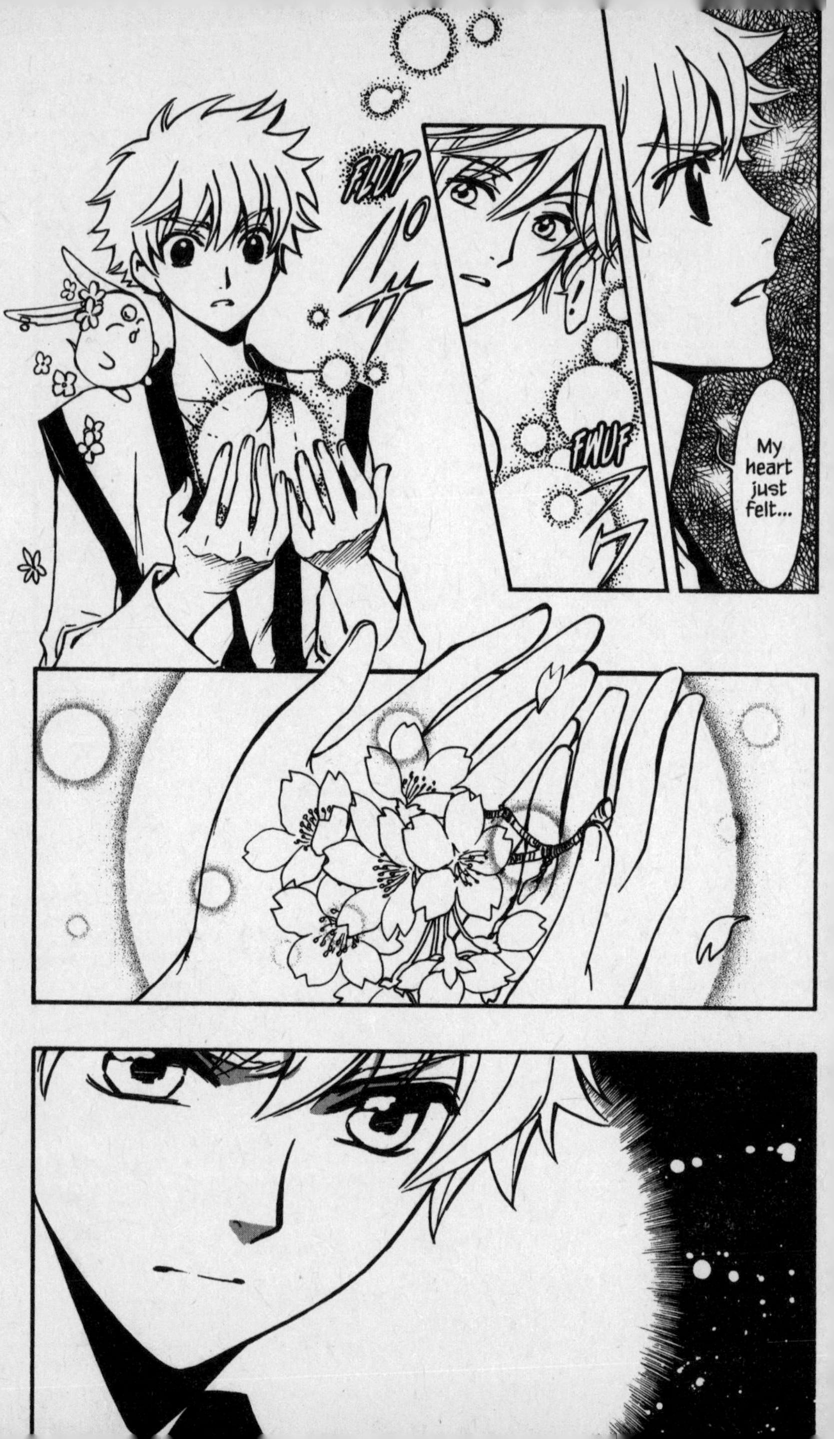
My heart just felt...
FWUF
FLUP

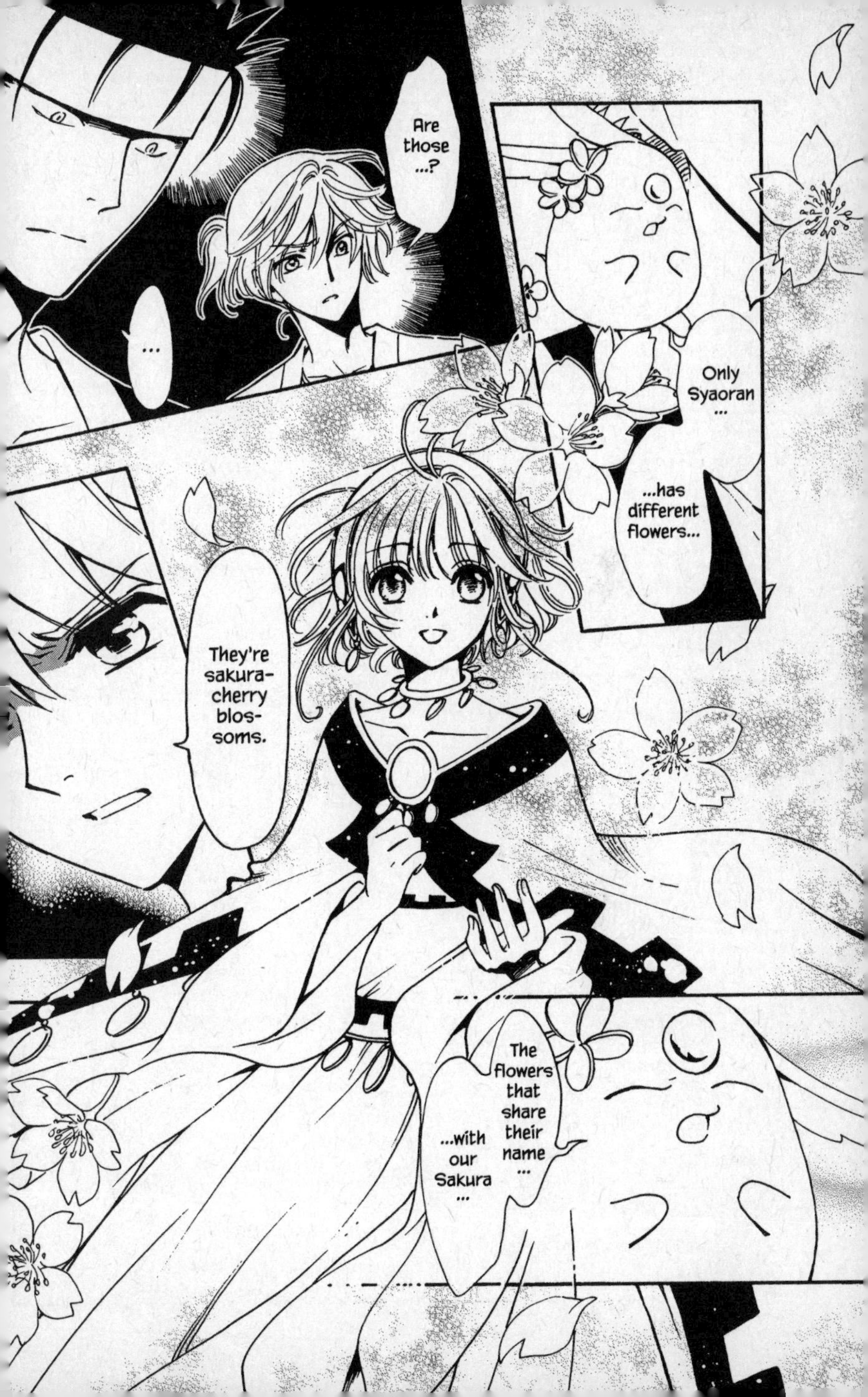

Only Syaoran ...
...has different flowers...
Are those ...?
...
They're sakura-cherry blossoms.
The flowers that share their name ...
...with our Sakura ...

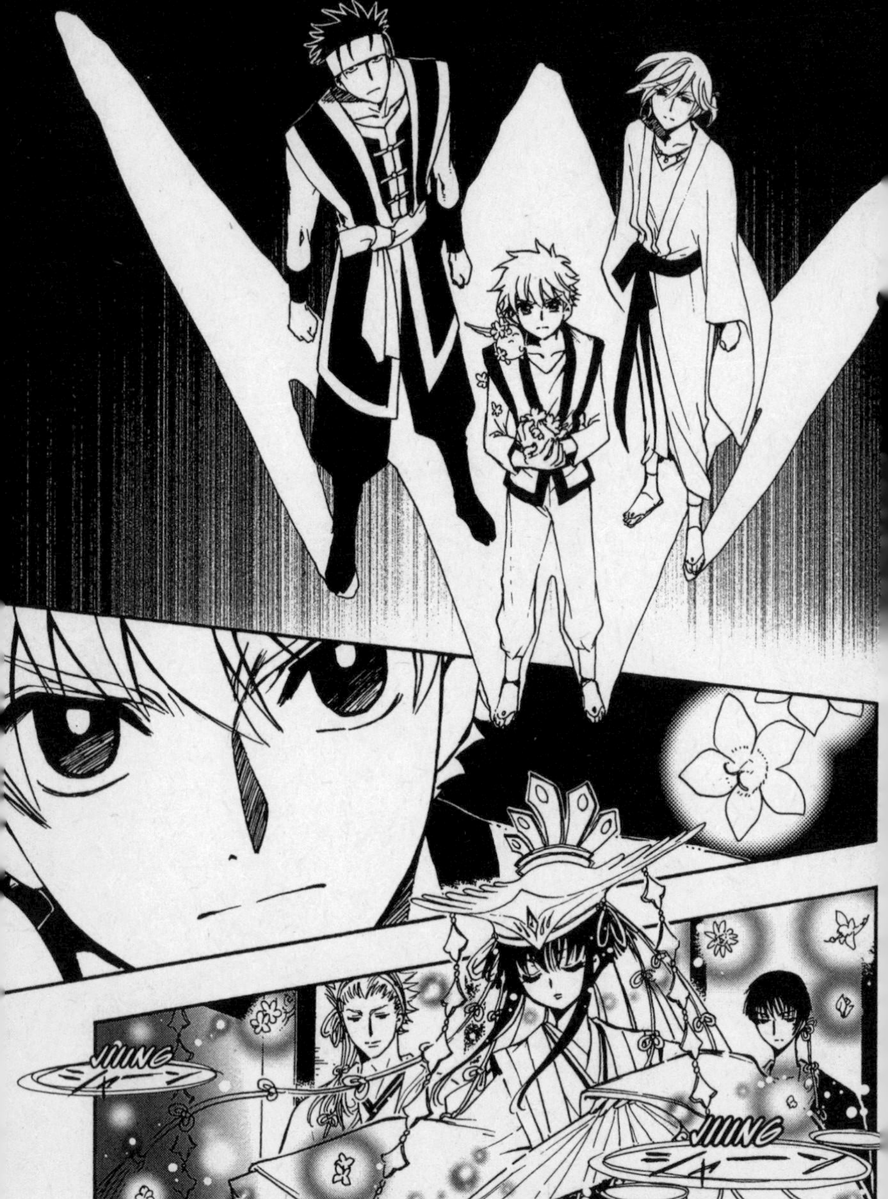
JIIING
JIIING

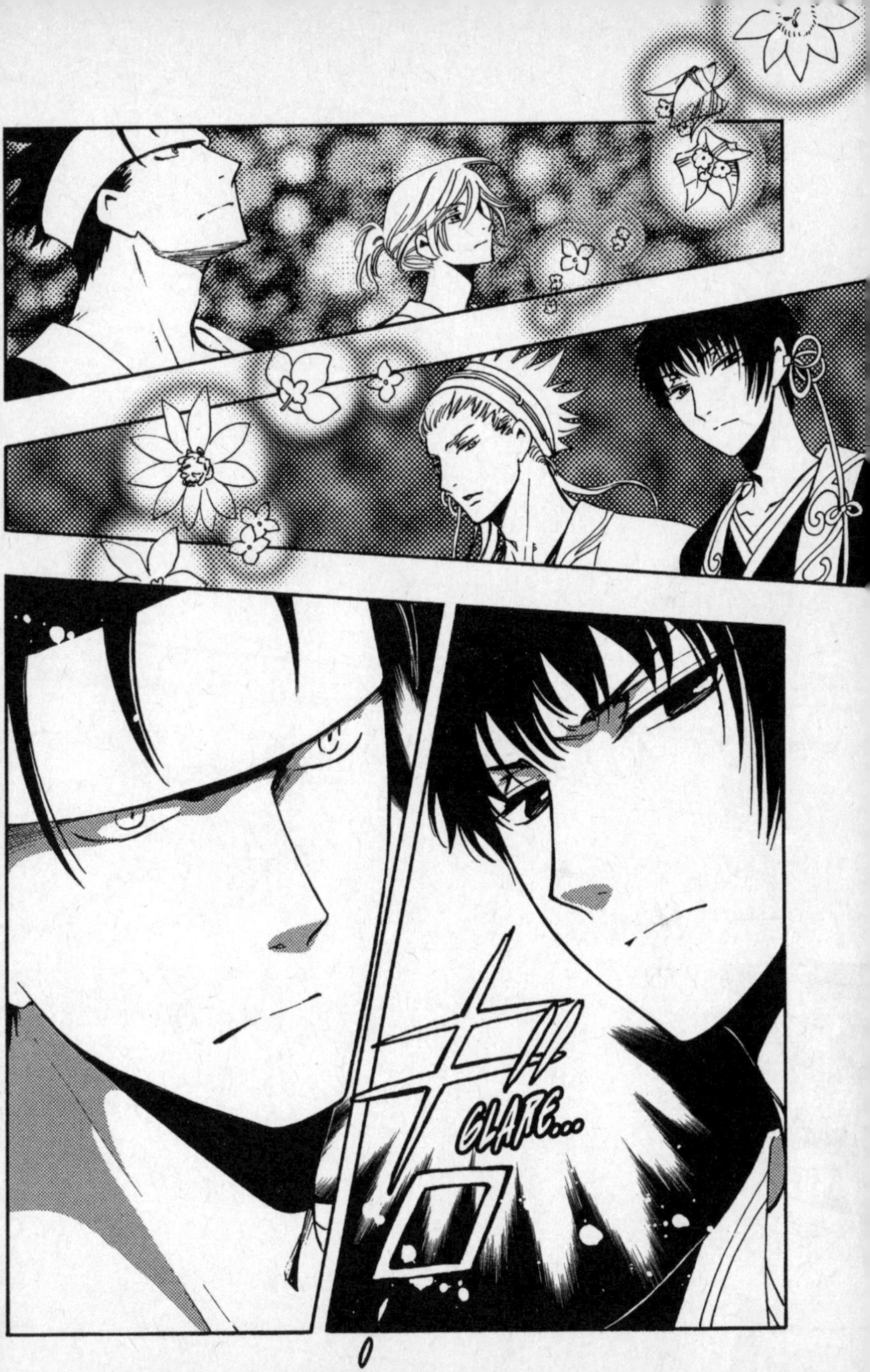
GLARE...

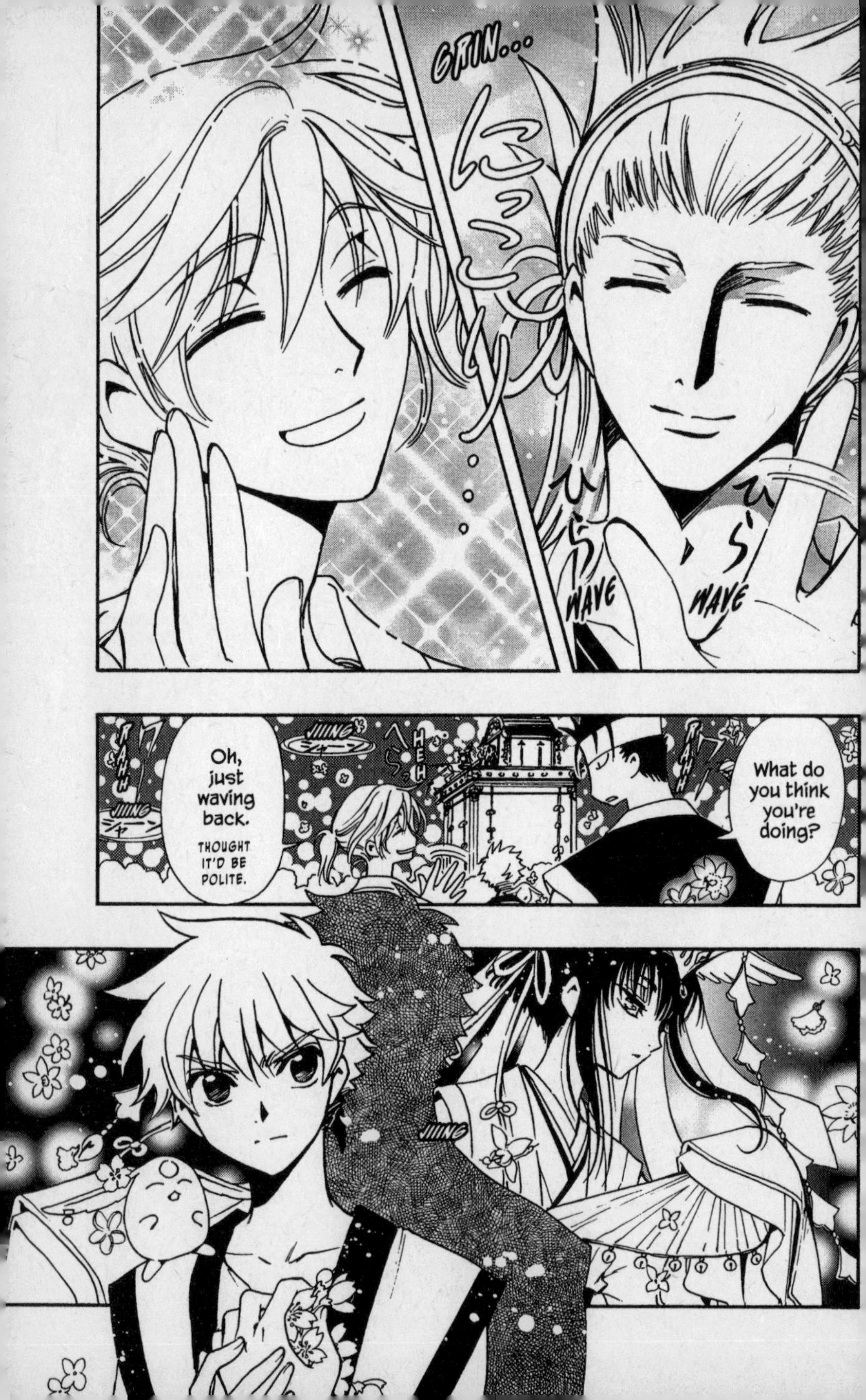
GRIN...
WAVE
WAVE
What do you think you're doing?
RAHH
JIIING
HEH
Oh, just waving back.
THOUGHT IT'D BE POLITE.
JIIING
RAHH
JIIING

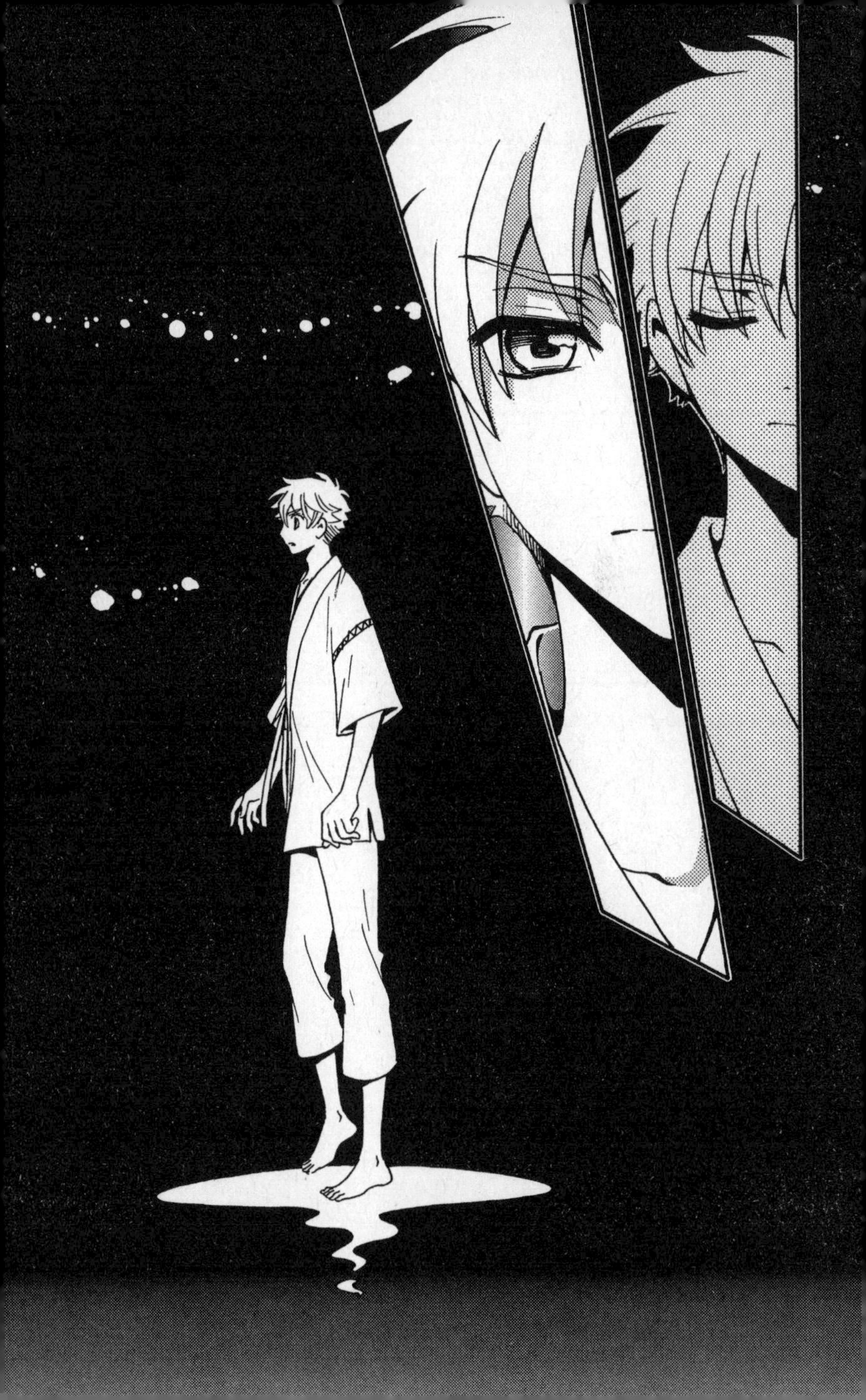

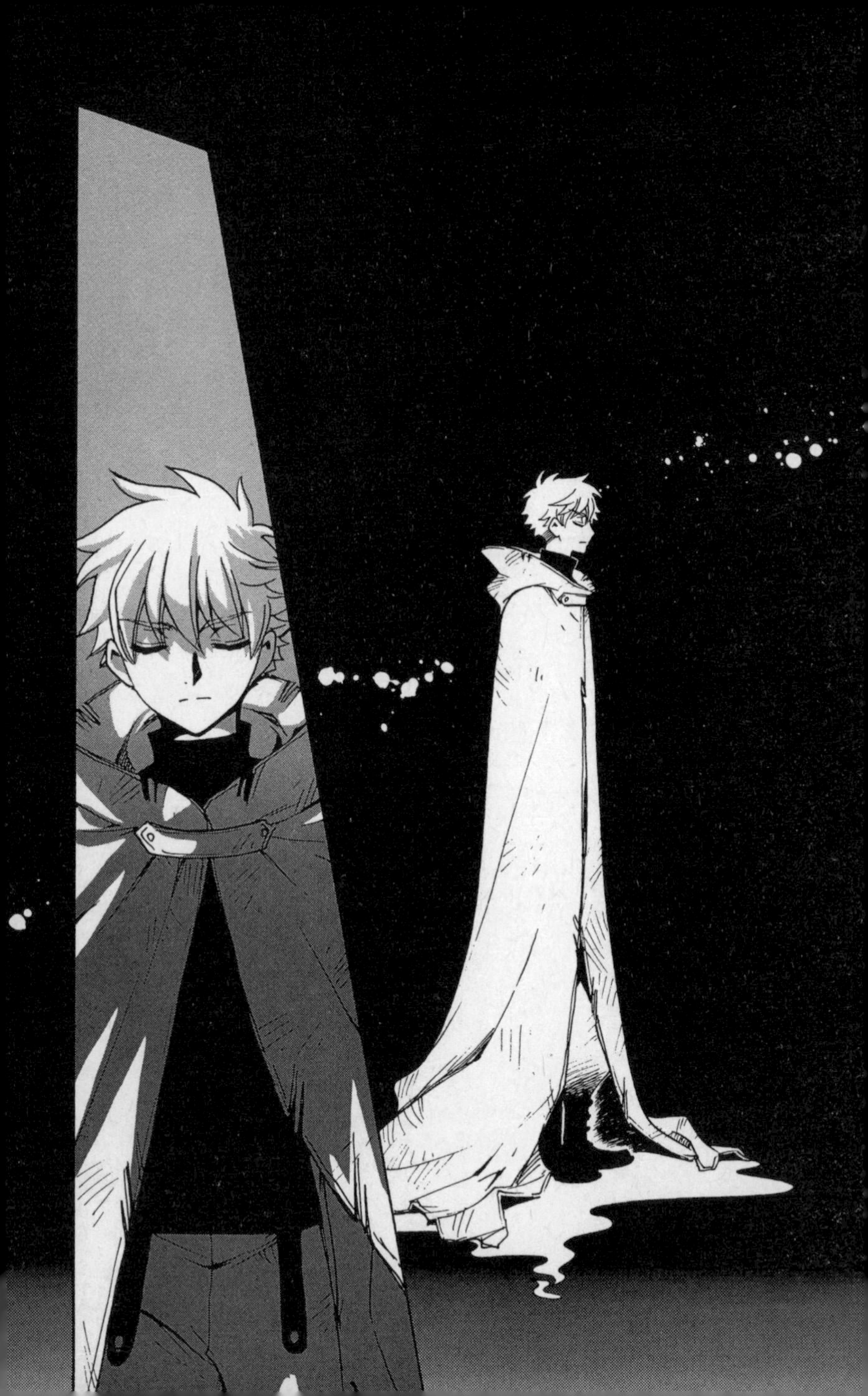

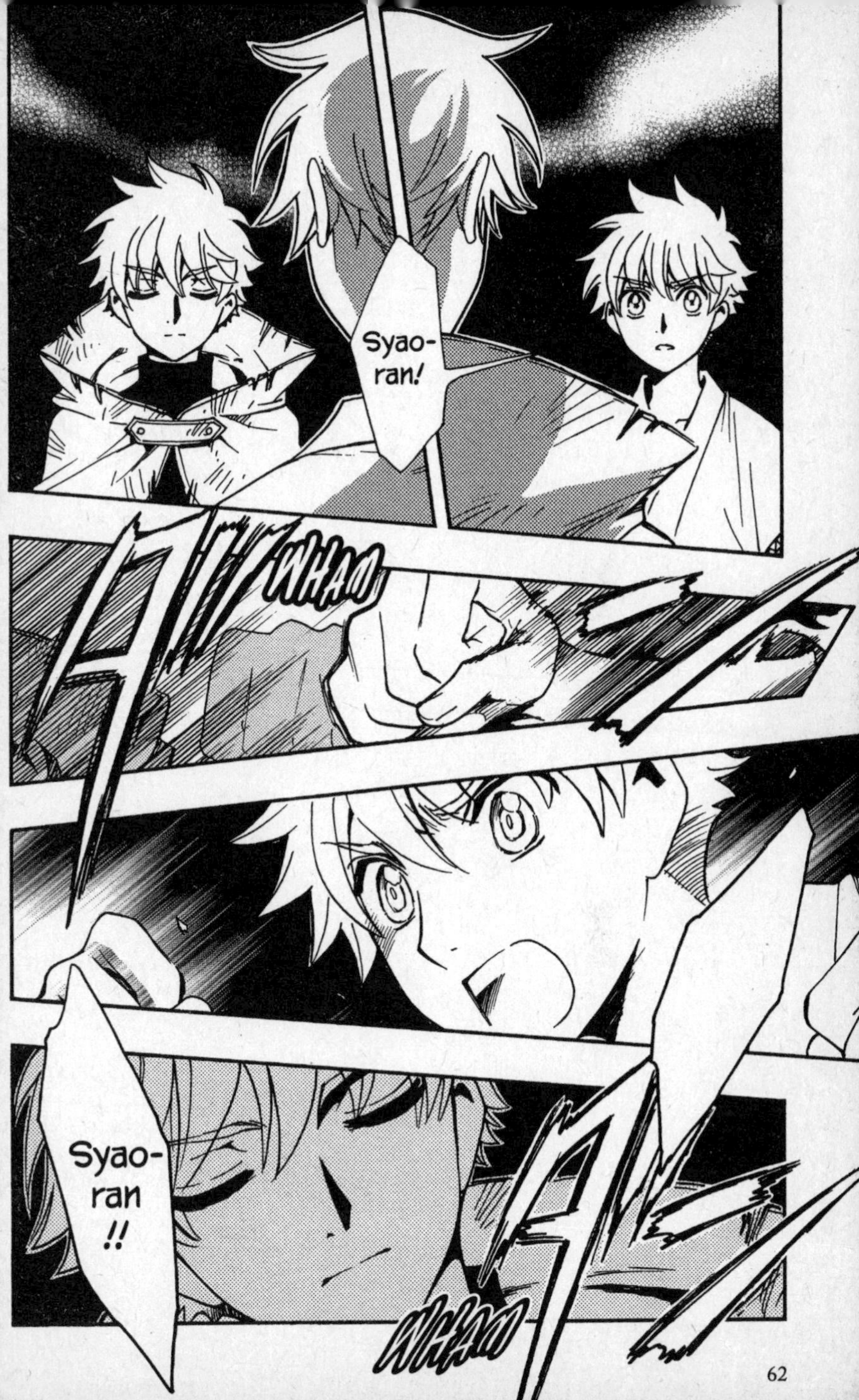
Syao-
ran!
WHAM
Syao-
ran
!!
WHAM

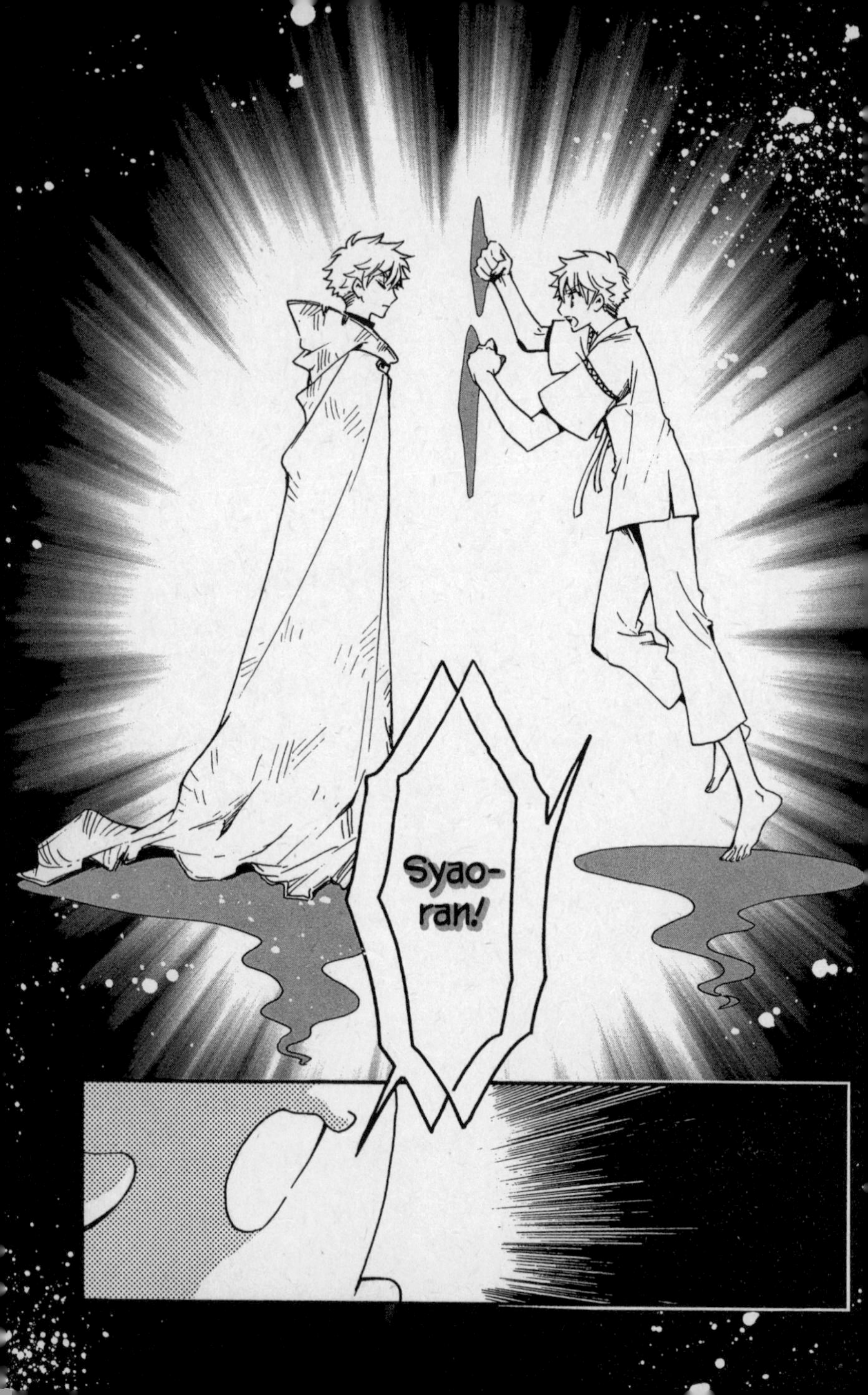
Syao-
ran!

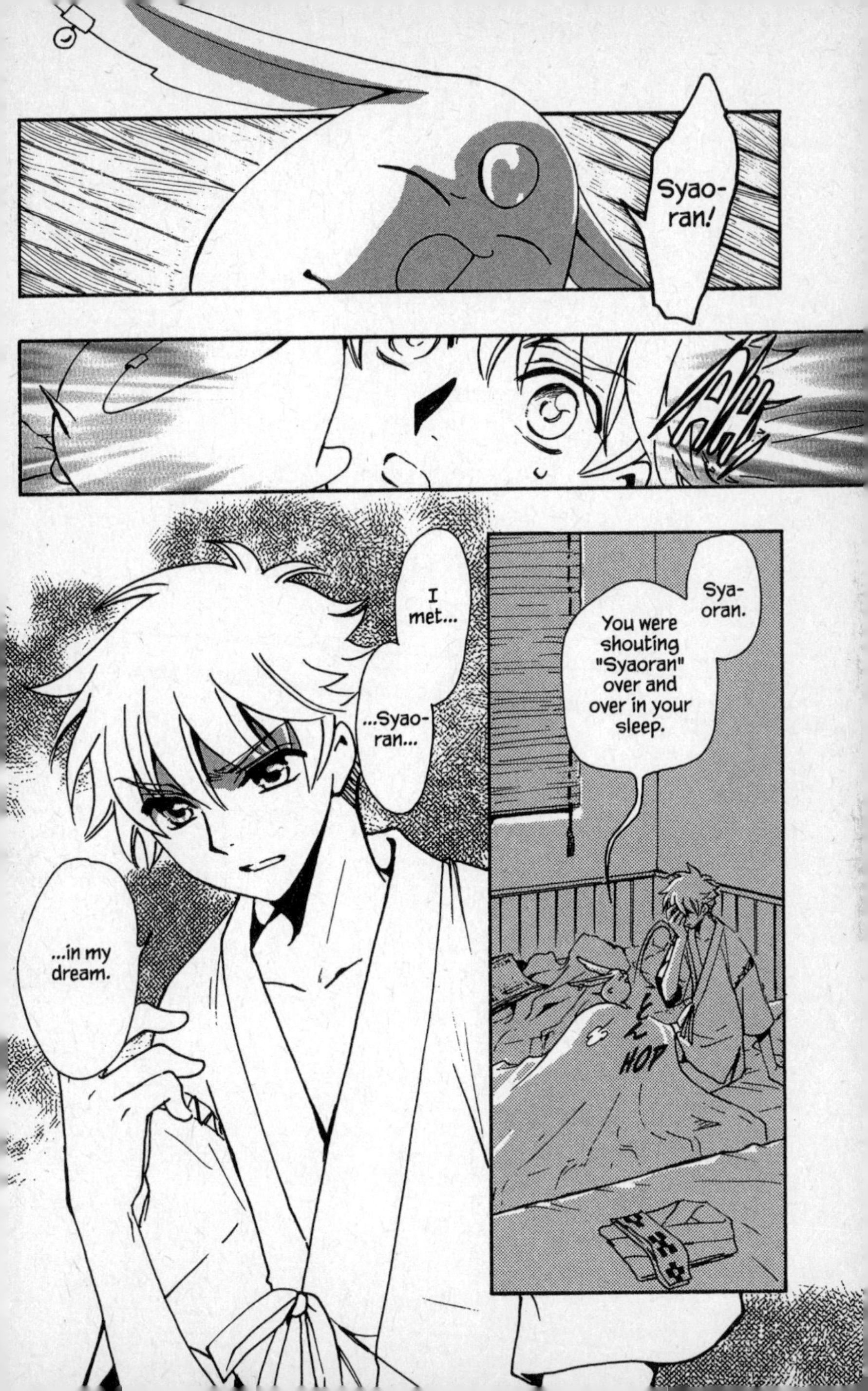
Syaoran!
Sya-oran.
You were shouting "Syaoran" over and over in your sleep.
HOP
I met...
...Syaoran...
...in my dream.

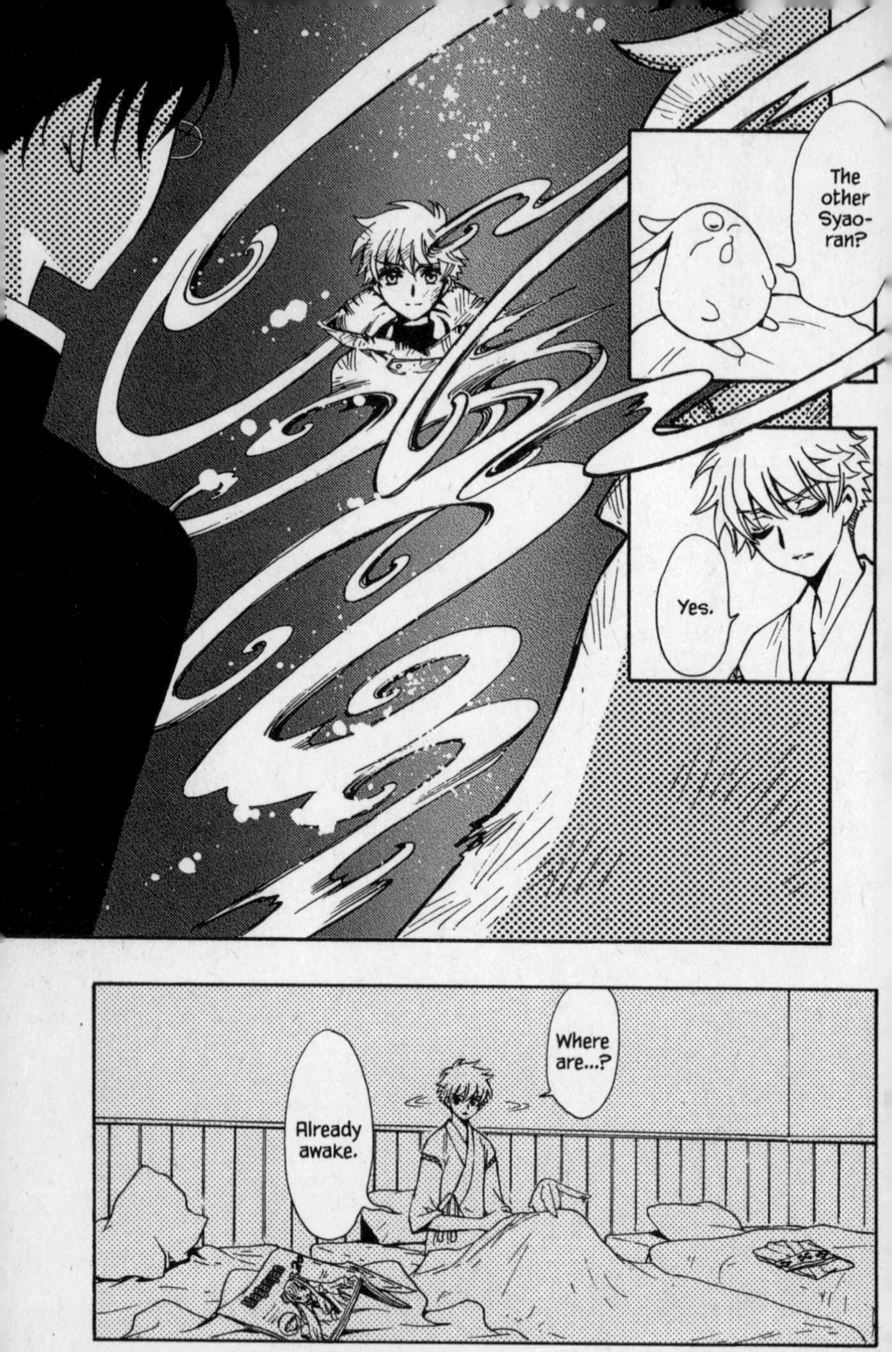
The other Syao-ran?
Yes.
Where are...?
Already awake.

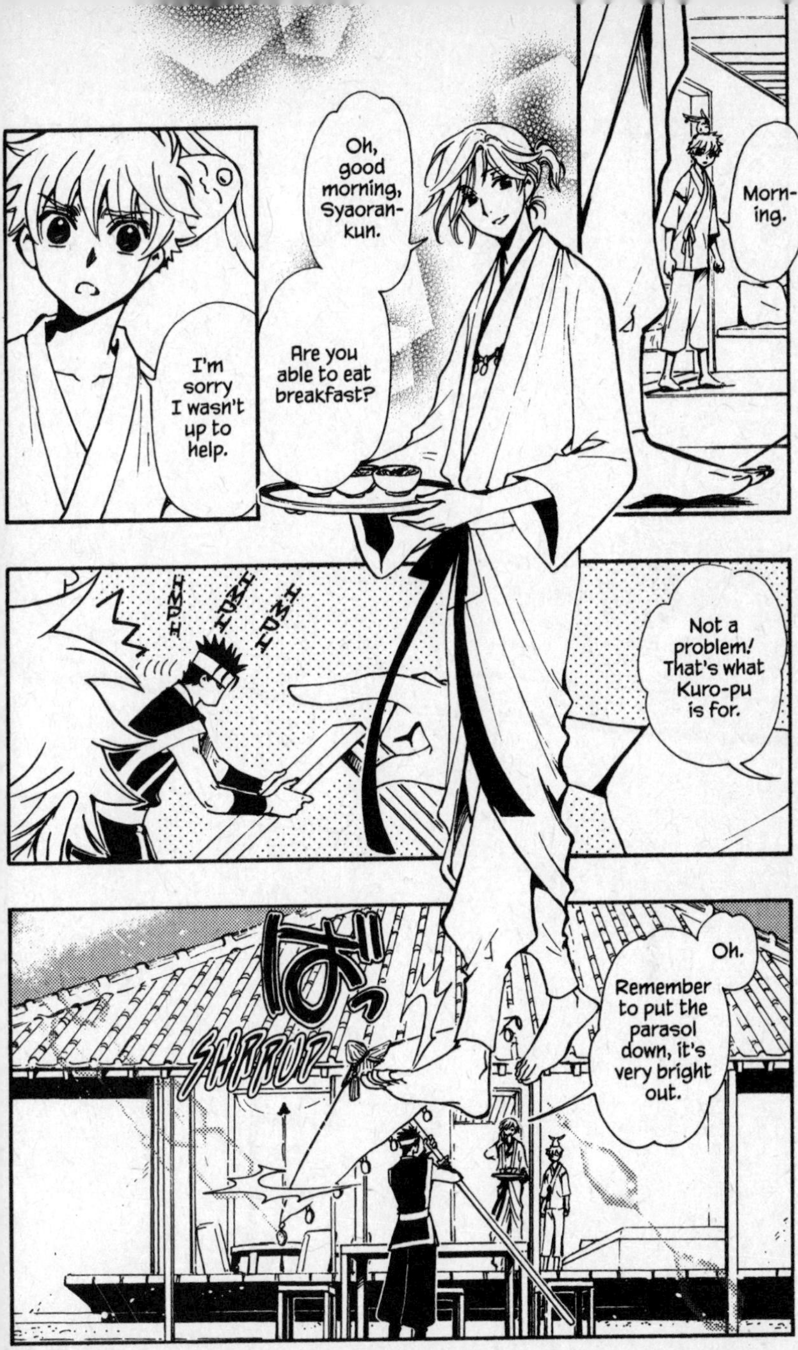
Morning.
Oh, good morning, Syaoran-kun.
Are you able to eat breakfast?
I'm sorry I wasn't up to help.
Not a problem! That's what Kuro-pu is for.
HMPH
HMPH
HMPH
Oh.
Remember to put the parasol down, it's very bright out.
ばっ

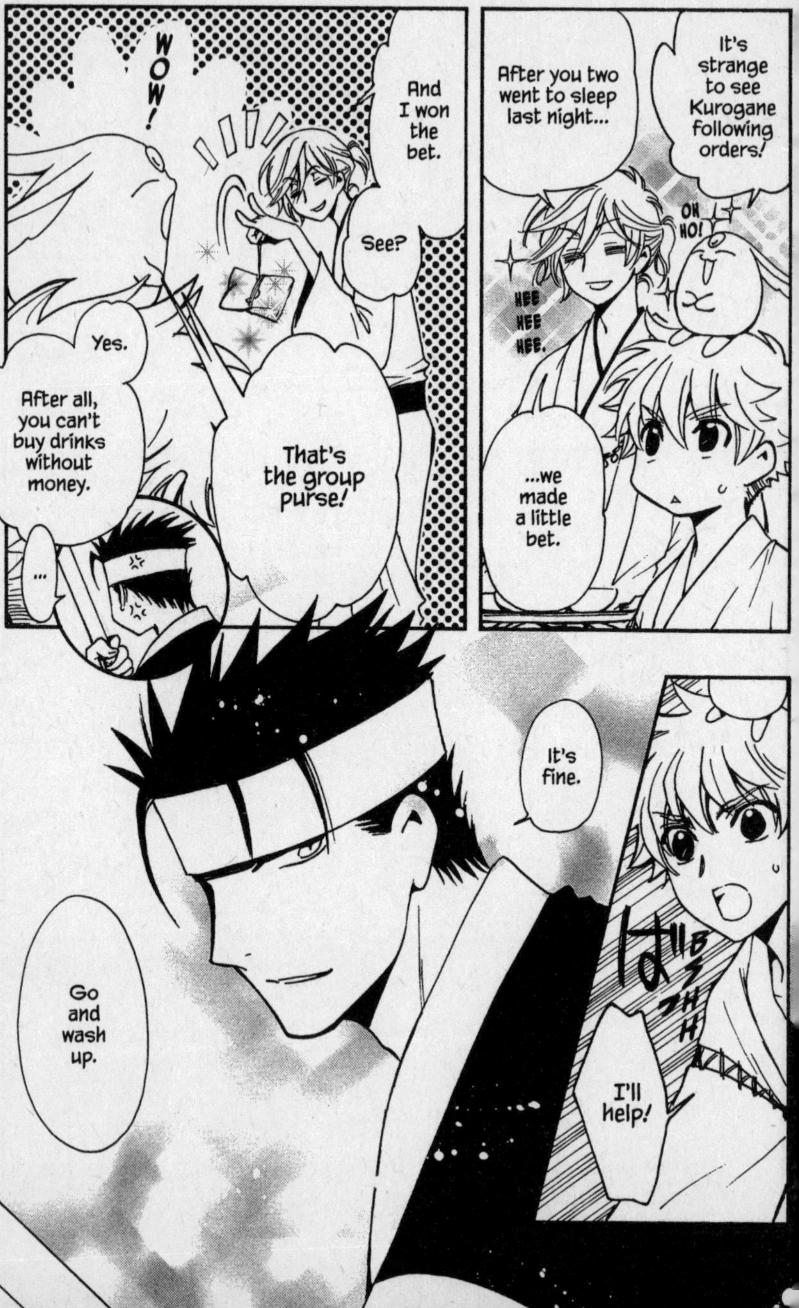
It's strange to see Kurogane following orders!
After you two went to sleep last night...
OH HO!
HEE HEE HEE.
...we made a little bet.
And I won the bet.
WOW!
See?
Yes.
That's the group purse!
After all, you can't buy drinks without money.
...
は BSHH
I'll help!
It's fine.
Go and wash up.

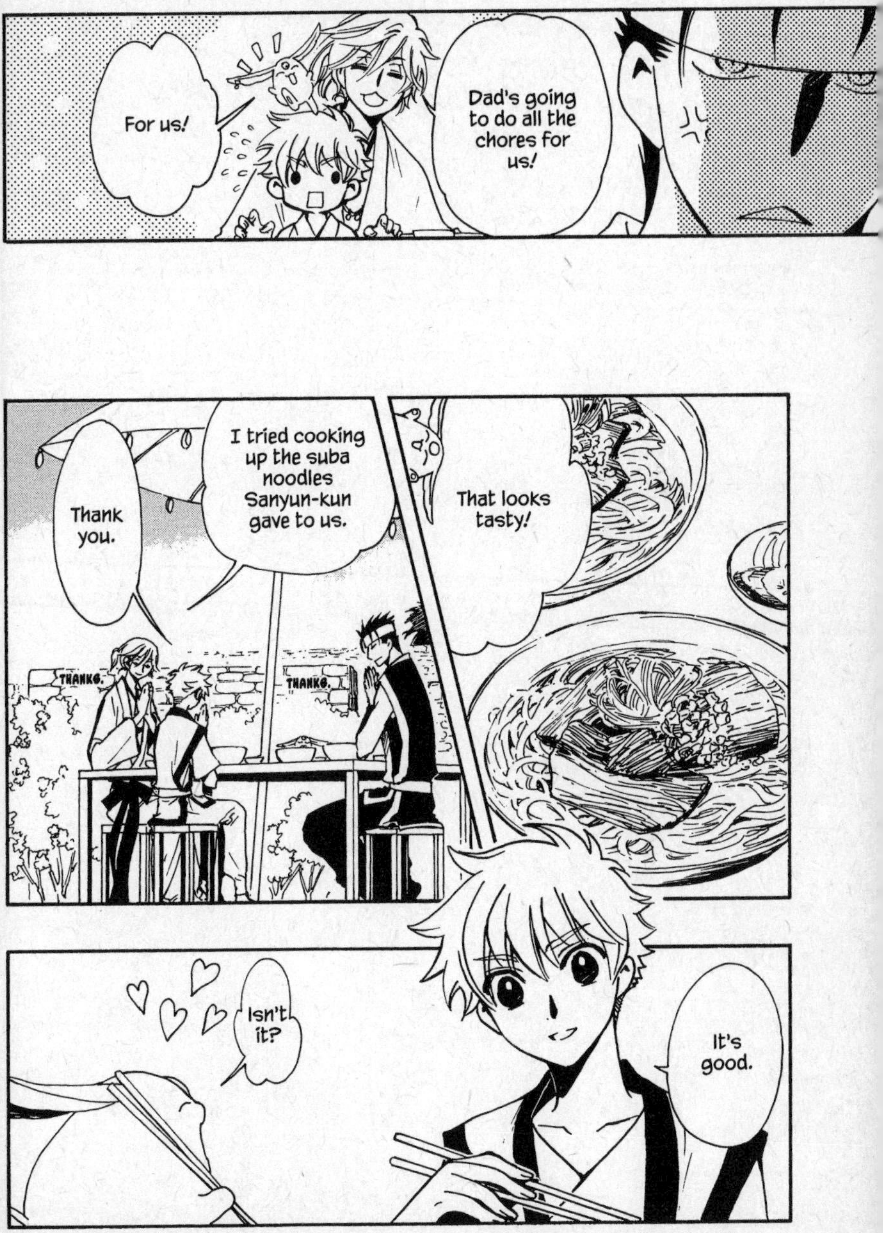
Dad's going to do all the chores for us!
For us!
That looks tasty!
I tried cooking up the suba noodles Sanyun-kun gave to us.
Thank you.
THANKS.
THANKS.
It's good.
Isn't it?

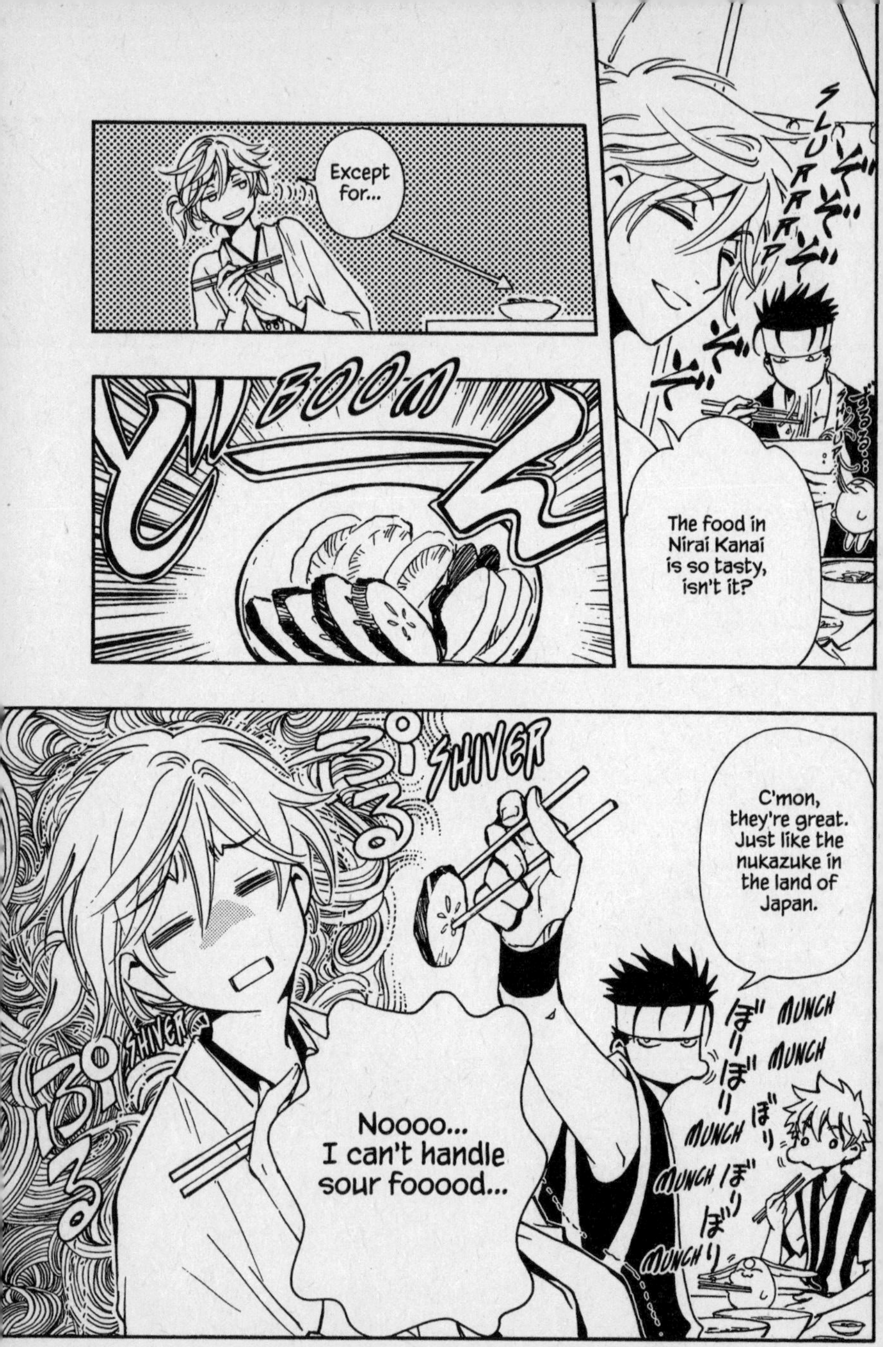
SLURRRRP
The food in Nirai Kanai is so tasty, isn't it?
Except for...
BOOM
C'mon, they're great. Just like the nukazuke in the land of Japan.
SHIVER
MUNCH
MUNCH
MUNCH
MUNCH
MUNCH
SHIVER
Noooo... I can't handle sour fooood...

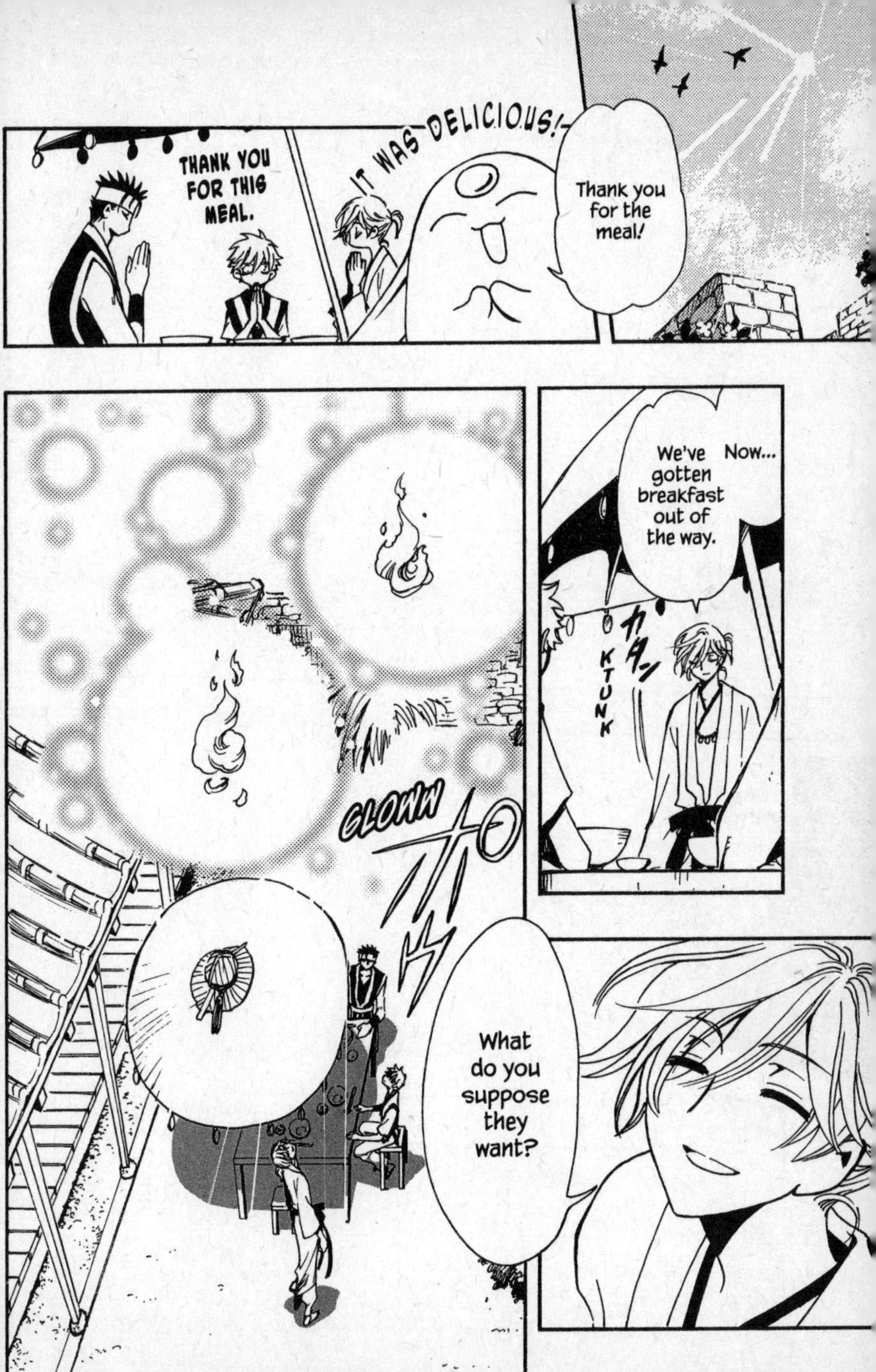
Thank you for the meal!
IT WAS DELICIOUS!
THANK YOU FOR THIS MEAL.
Now... We've gotten breakfast out of the way.
KTUNK
What do you suppose they want?
GLOWW

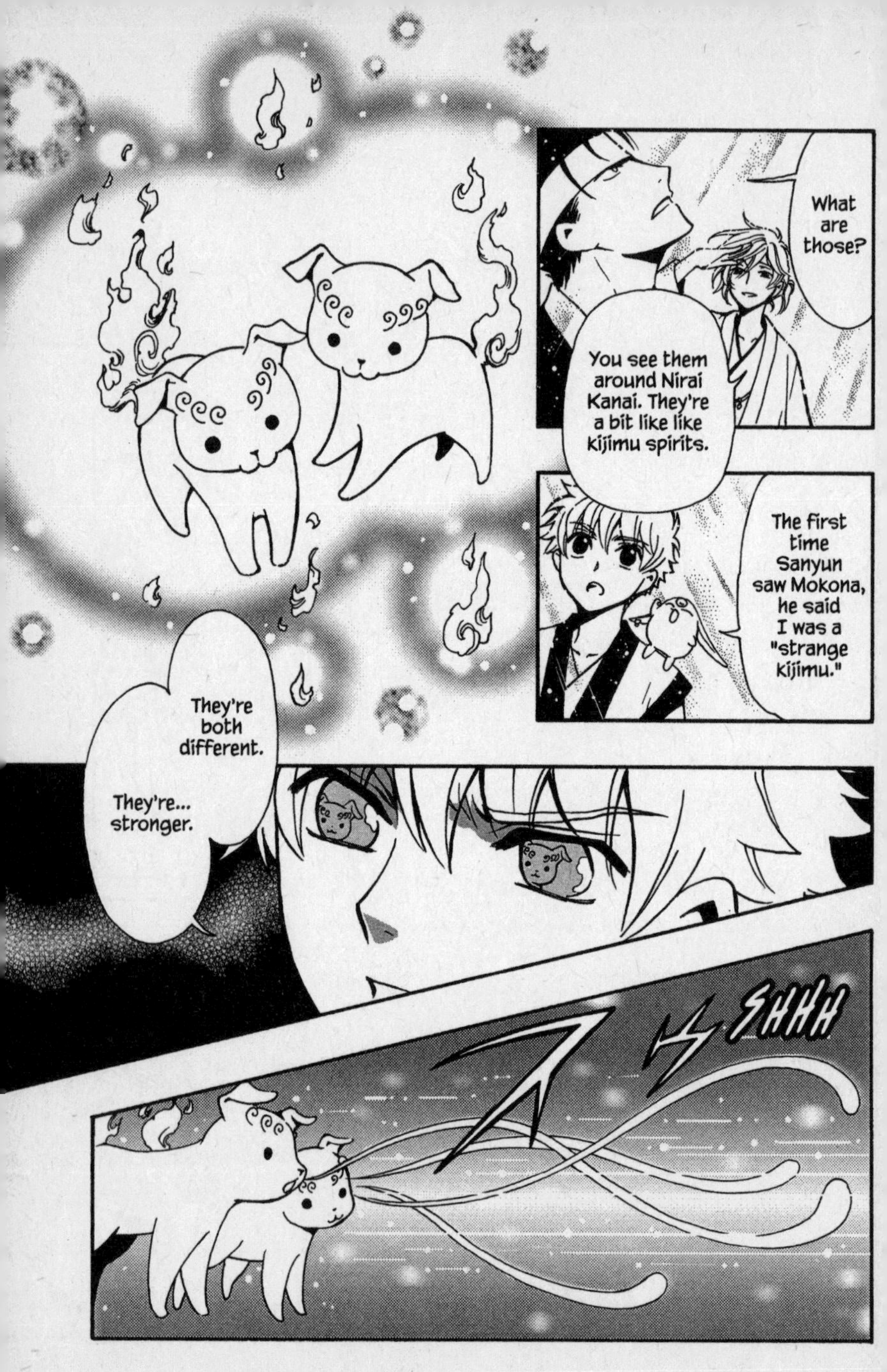
What are those?
You see them around Nirai Kanai. They're a bit like like kijimu spirits.
The first time Sanyun saw Mokona, he said I was a "strange kijimu."
They're both different.
They're... stronger.
SHHH

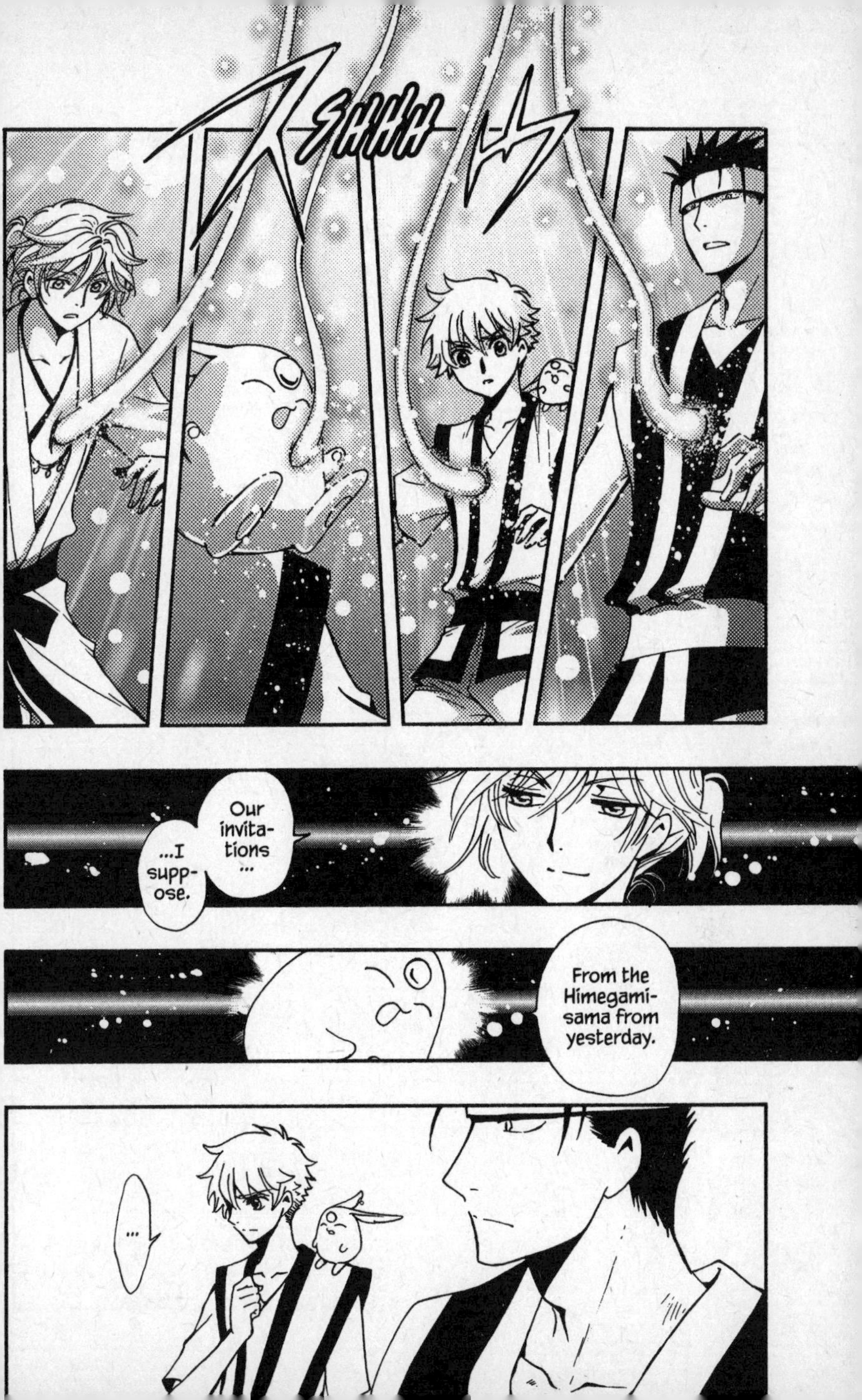
SHHHH
Our invitations...
...I suppose.
From the Himegami-sama from yesterday.
...

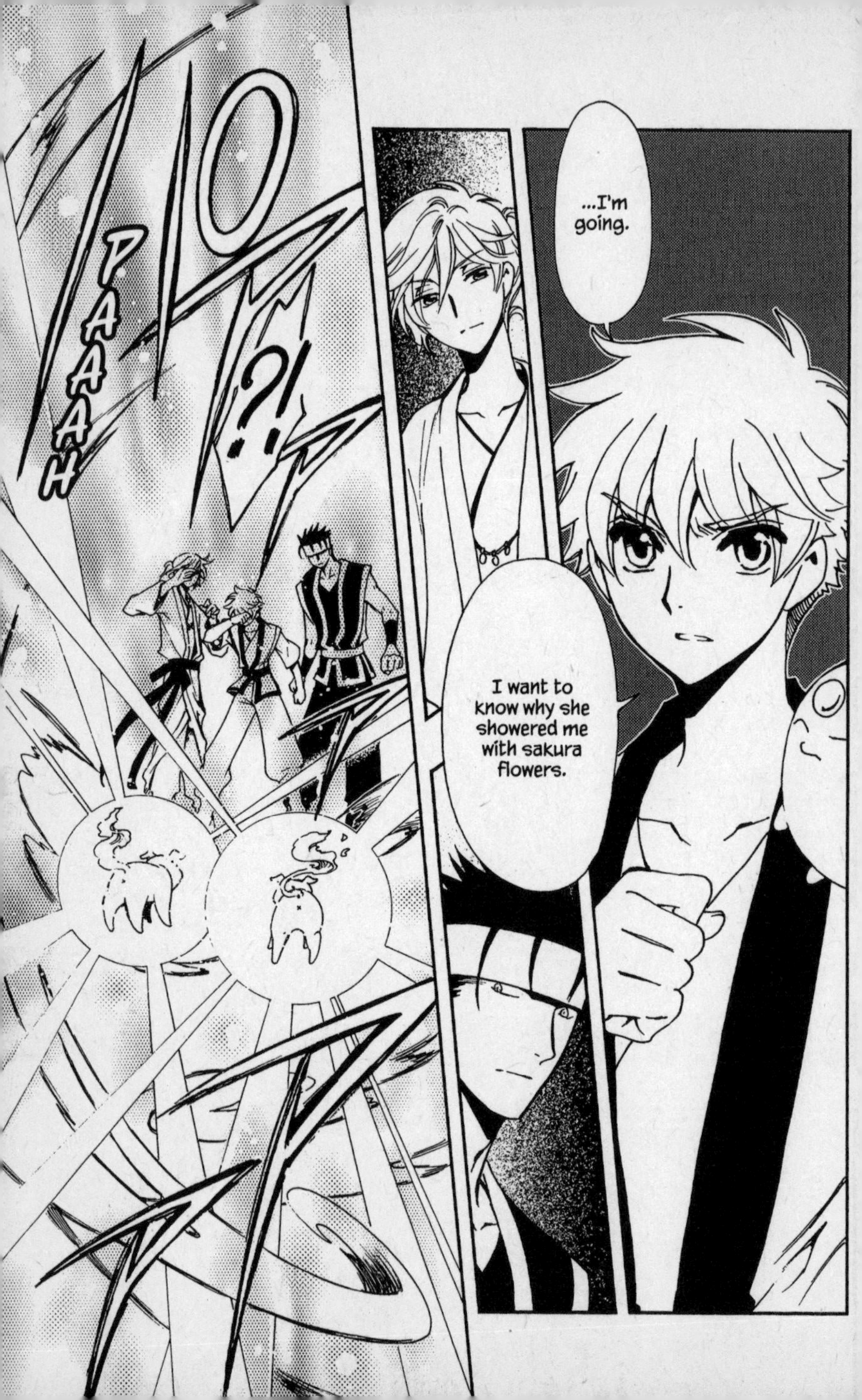
...I'm going.
I want to know why she showered me with sakura flowers.
PAAAAH
?!

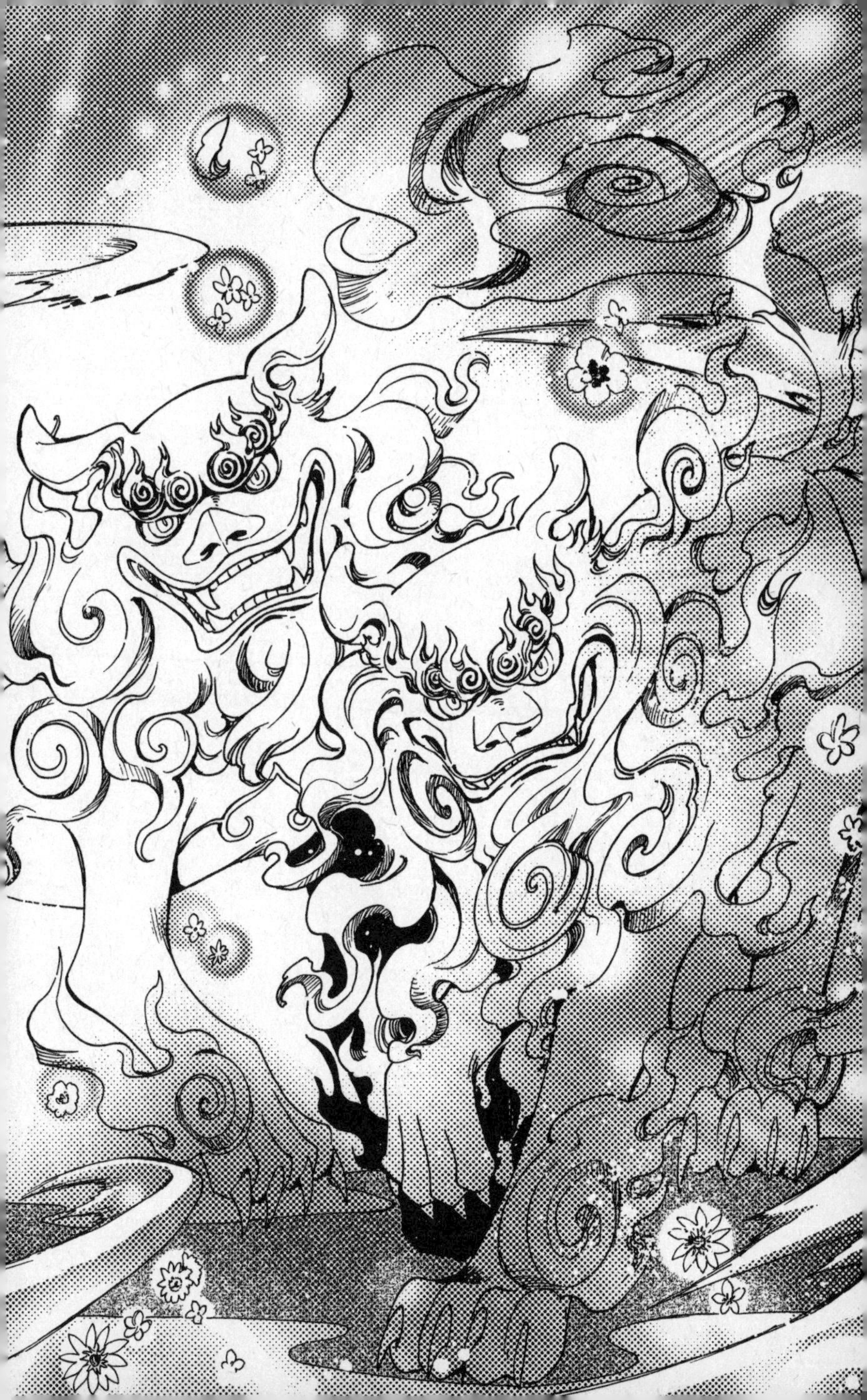

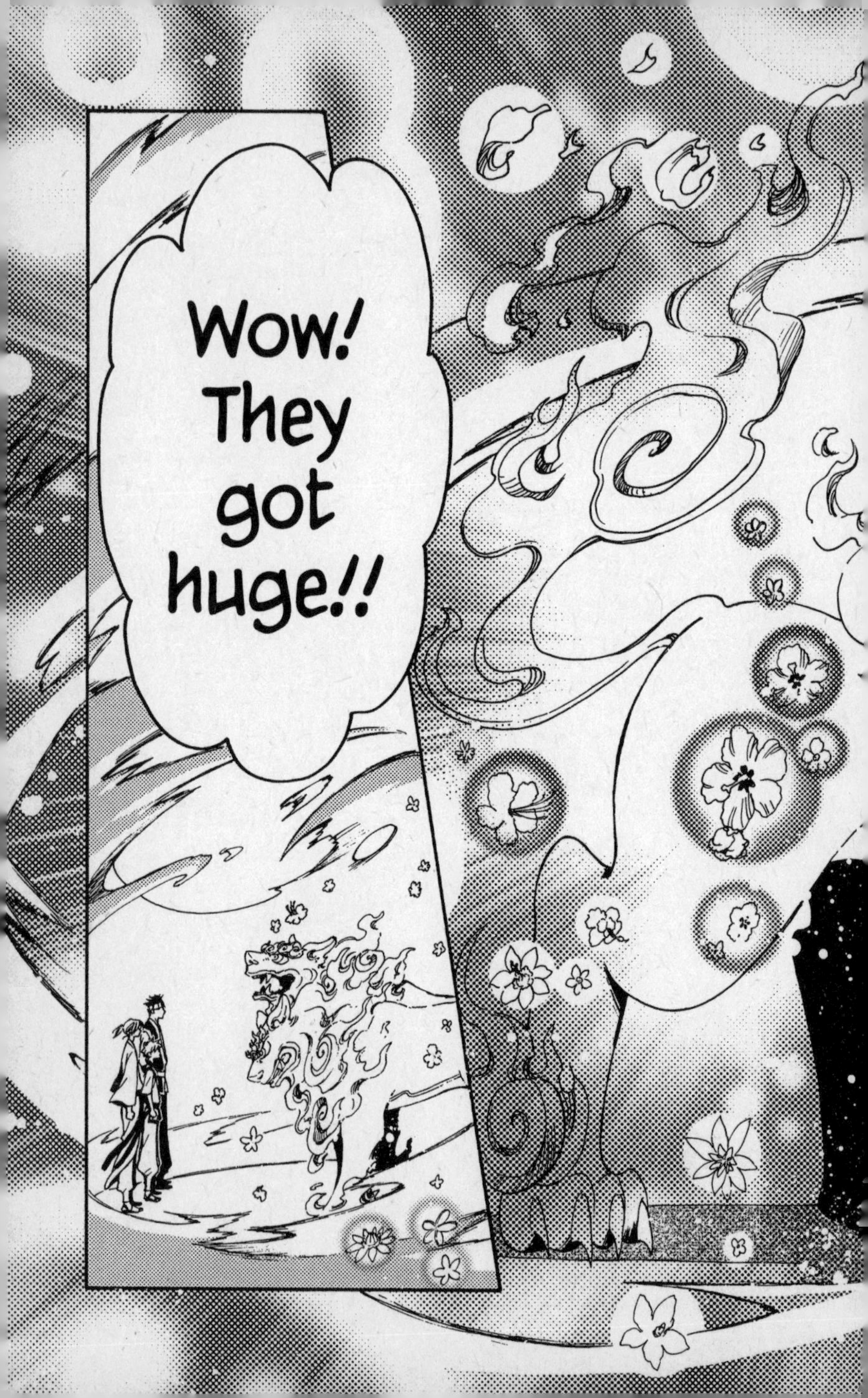
Wow! They got huge!!

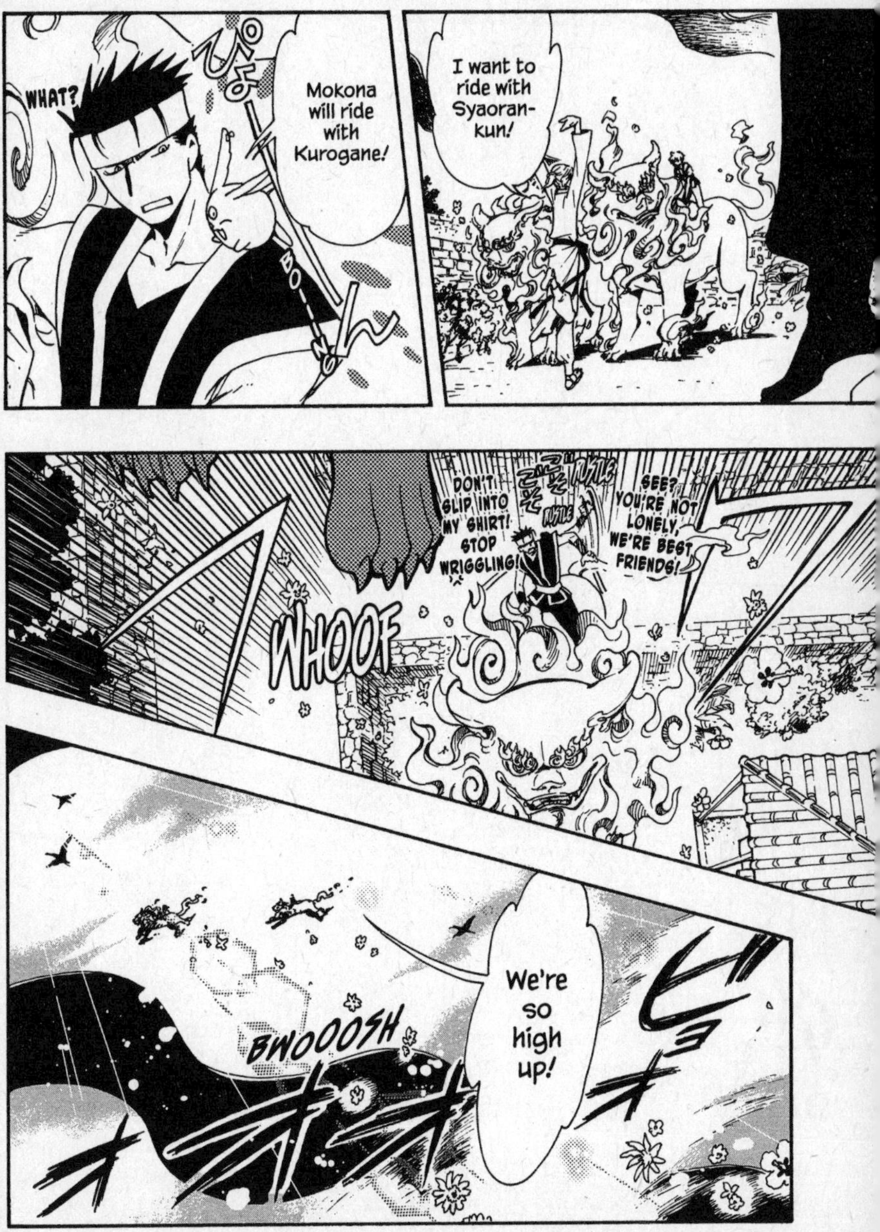
I want to ride with Syaoran-kun!
Mokona will ride with Kurogane!
WHAT?
BO-I-N
SEE? YOU'RE NOT LONELY, WE'RE BEST FRIENDS!
RUSTLE
RUSTLE
DON'T SLIP INTO MY SHIRT! STOP WRIGGLING!
WHOOF
We're so high up!
BWOOOSH

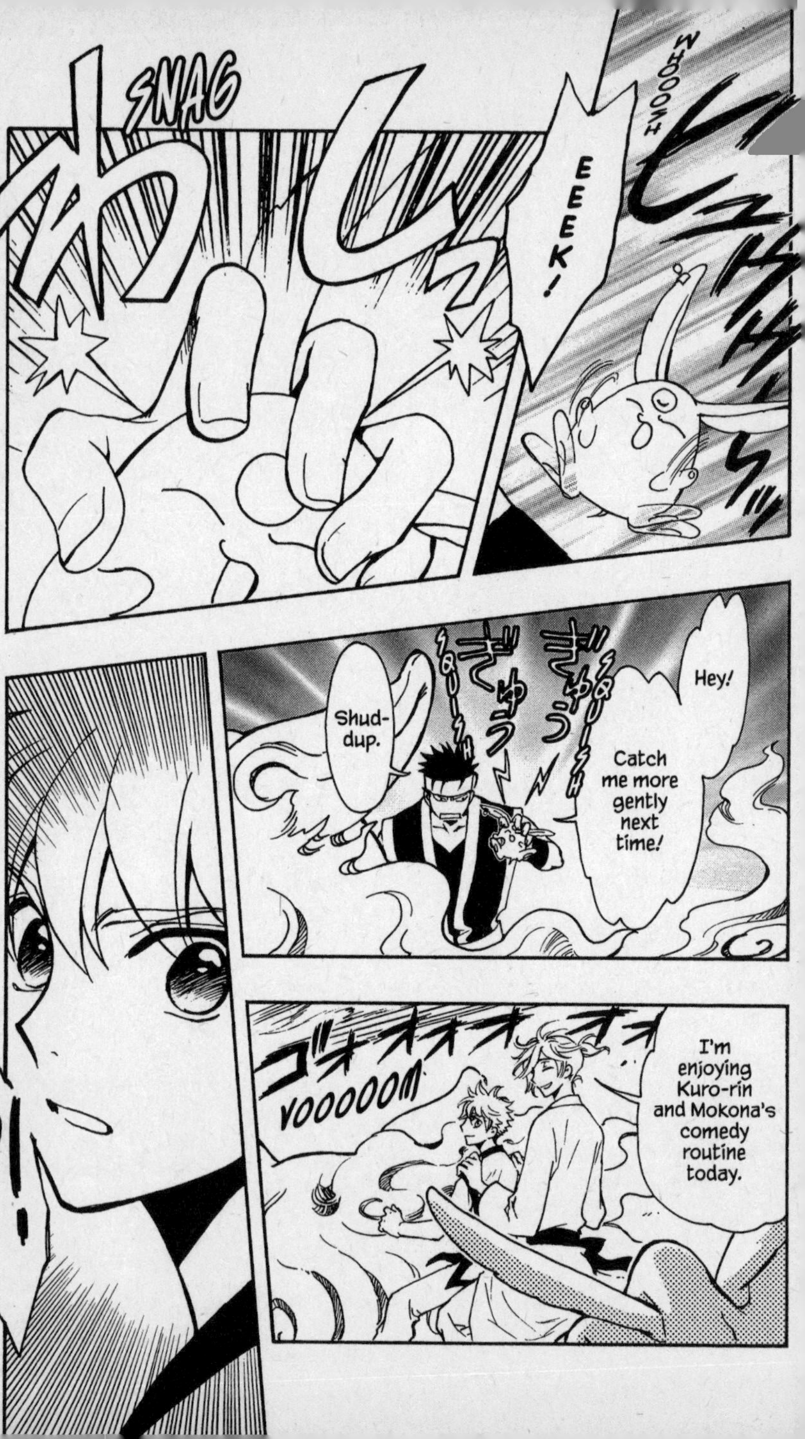
WHOOOOSH
EEEEK!
SNAG
Hey!
Catch me more gently next time!
Shud-dup.
I'm enjoying Kuro-rin and Mokona's comedy routine today.
VOOOOOM
?!

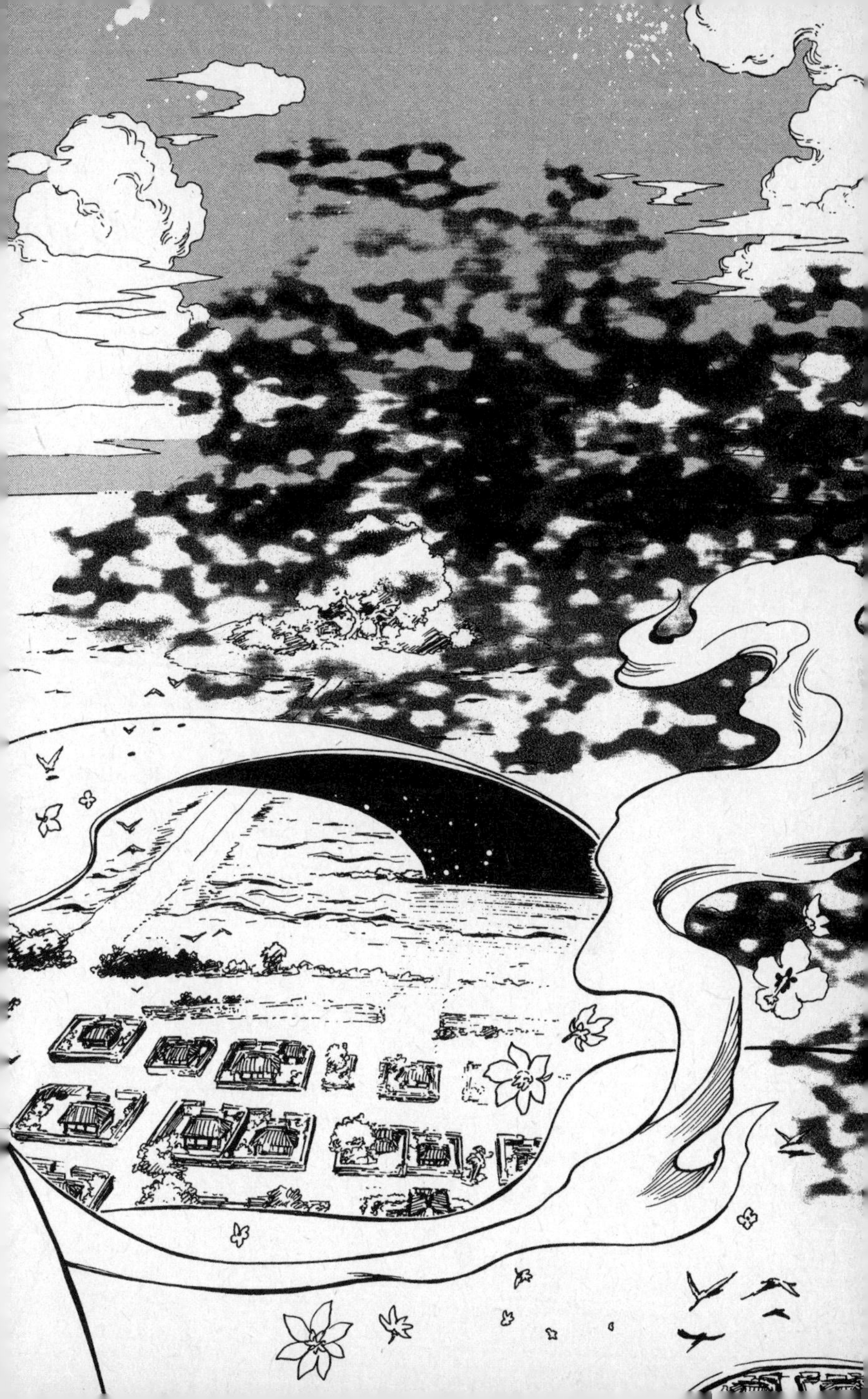

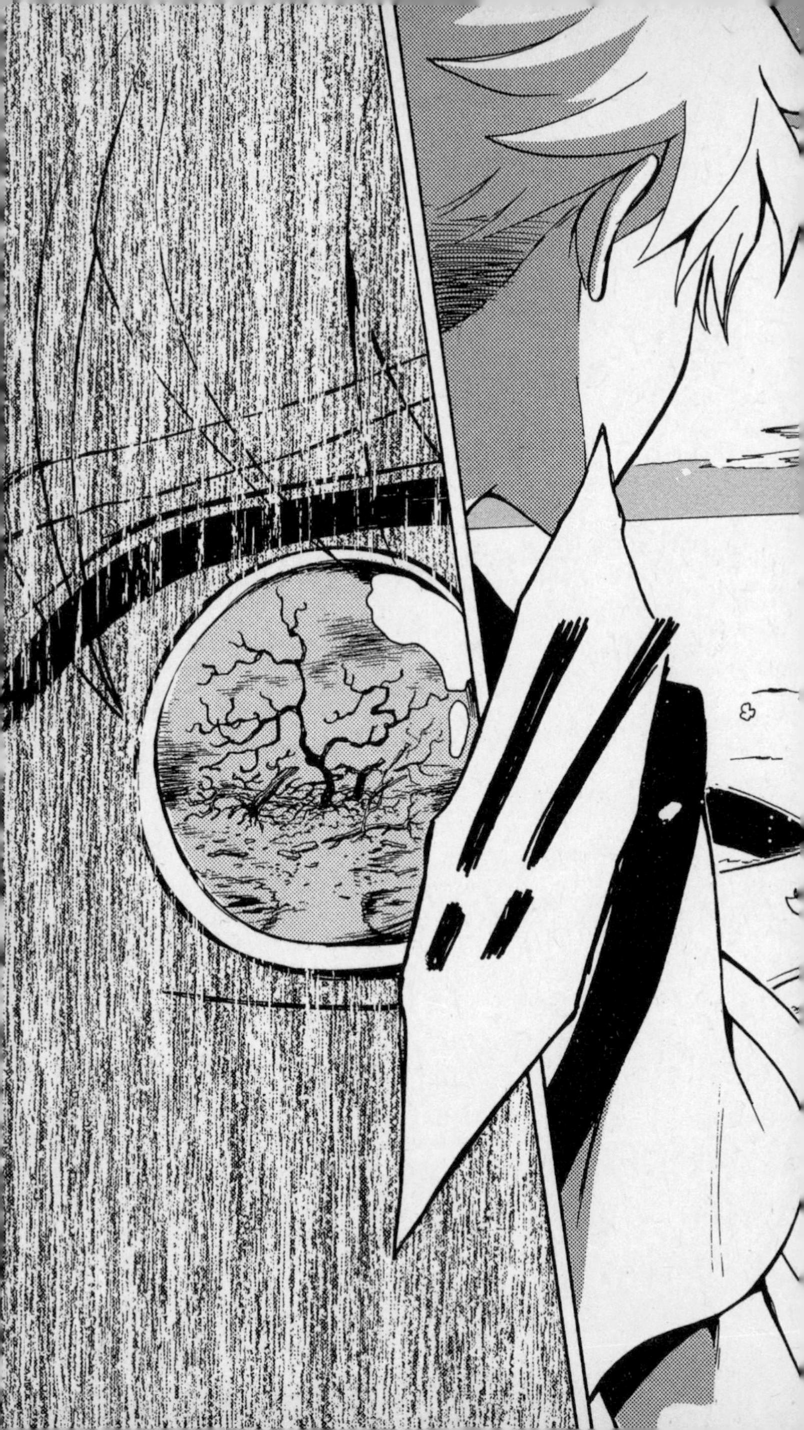

TSUBASA

WoRLD CHRoNiCLE: NIRAIKANAI

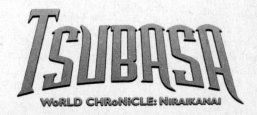

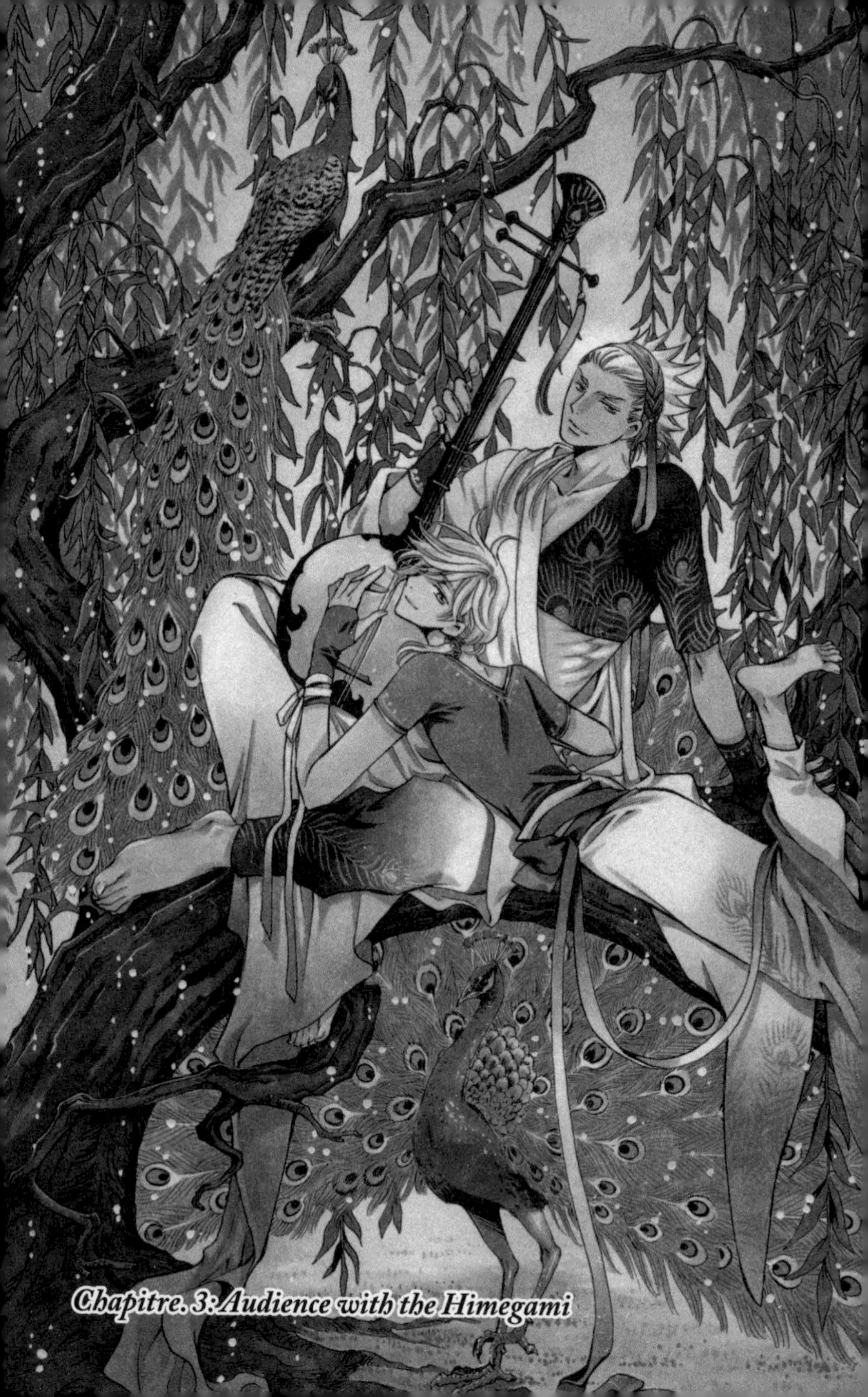
Chapitre. 3: Audience with the Himegami

TSUBASA
WoRLD CHRoNiCLE: NiRAiKANAi

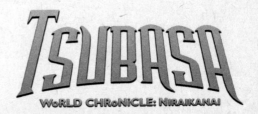

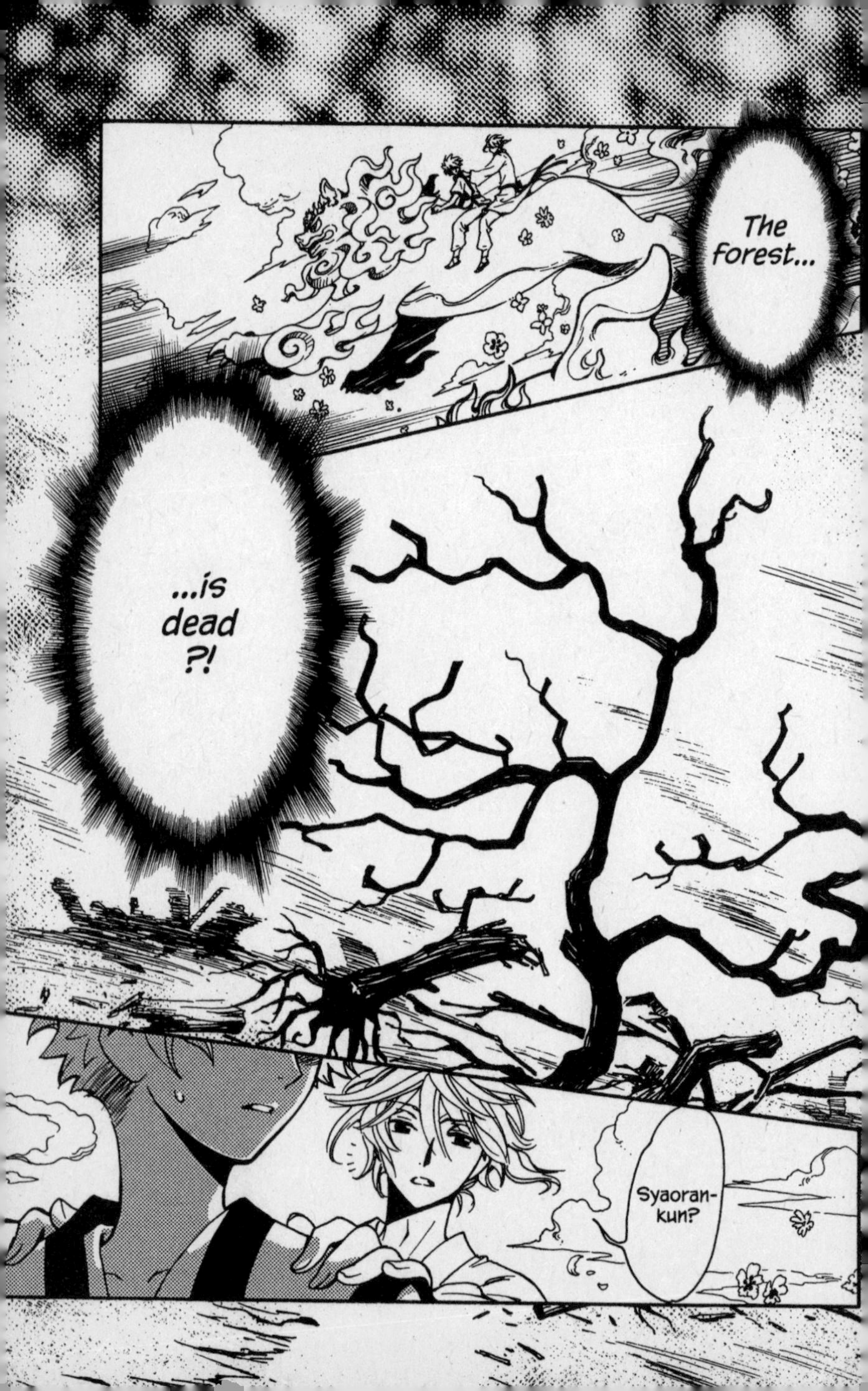
The forest...
...is dead ?!
Syaoran-kun?

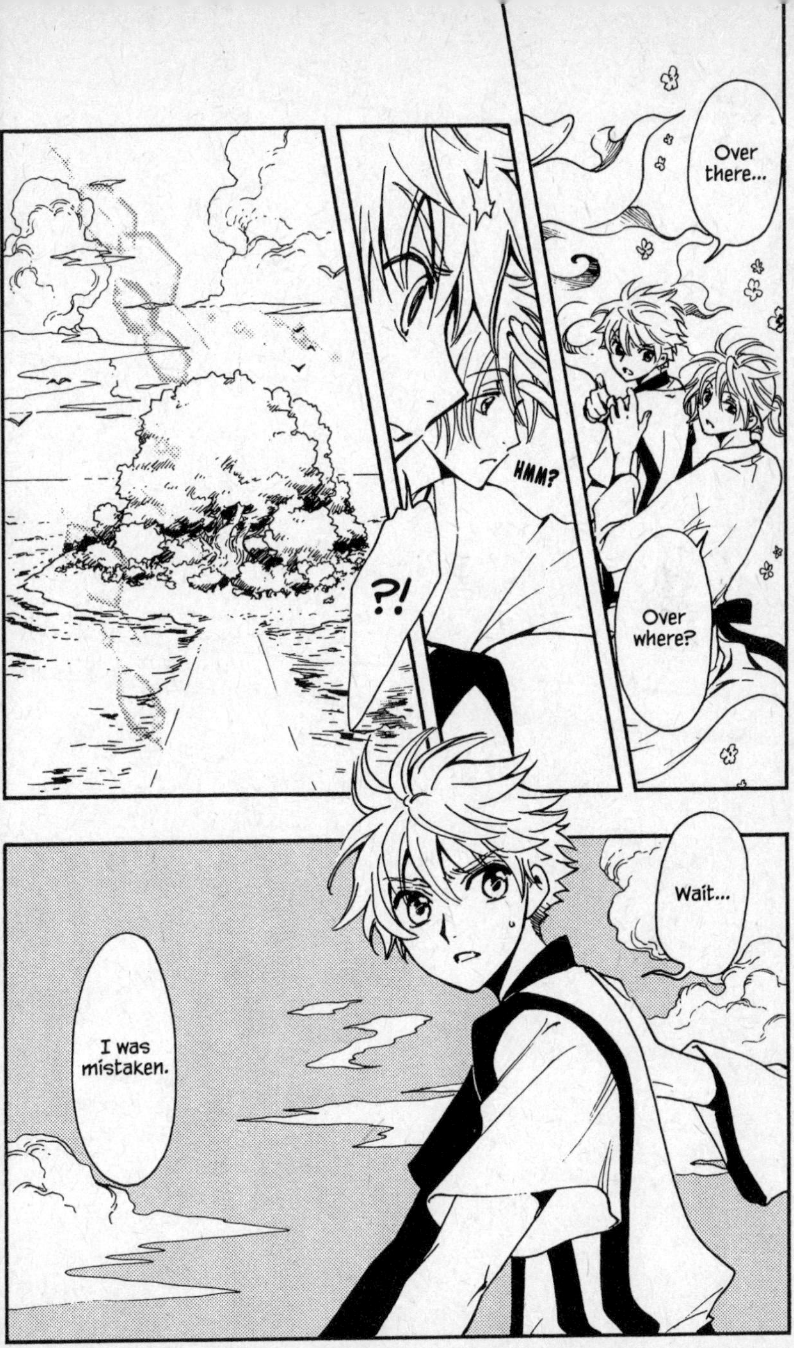
Over there...
Over where?
HMM?
?!
Wait...
I was mistaken.

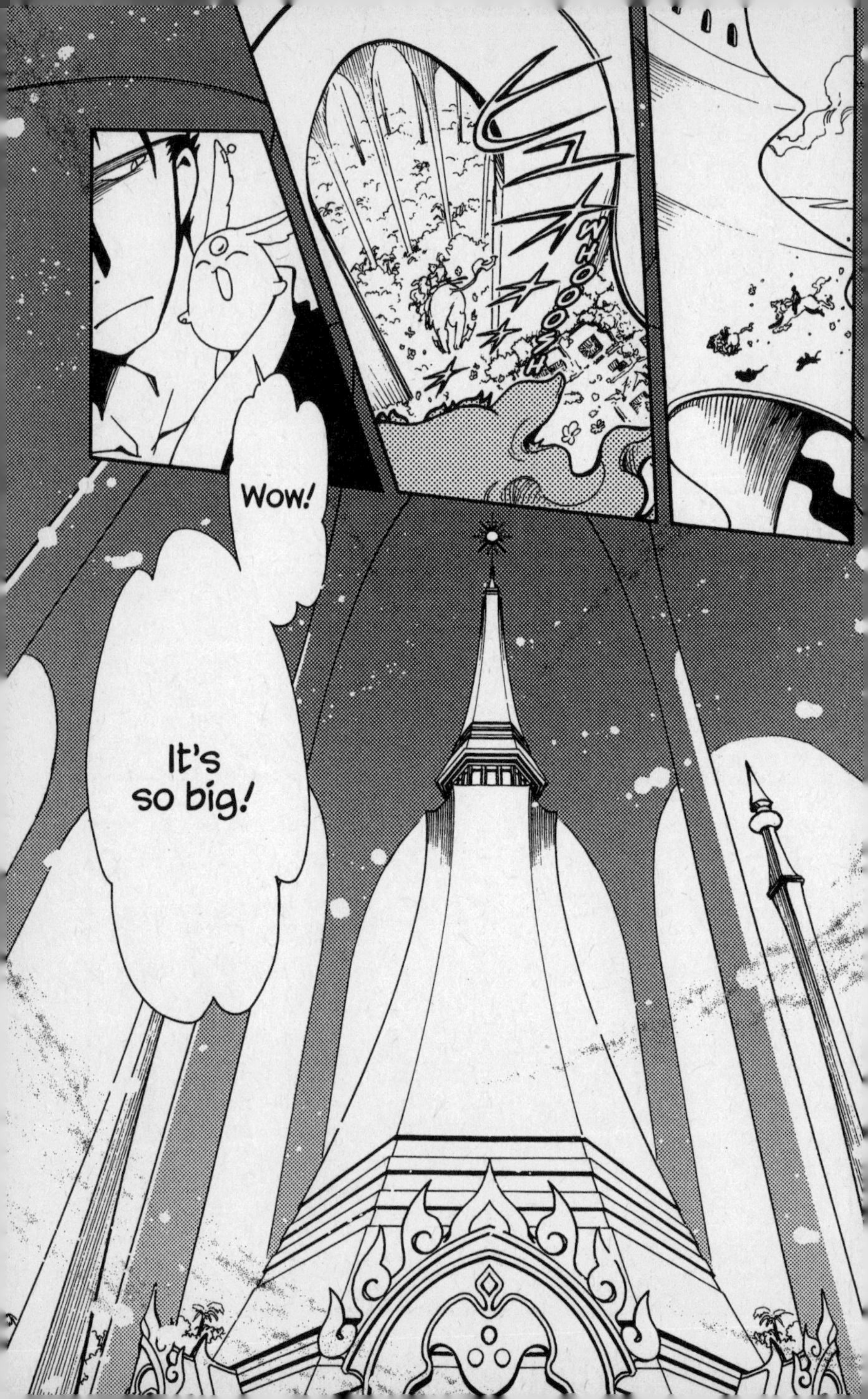
WHOOOOOSH
Wow!
It's so big!

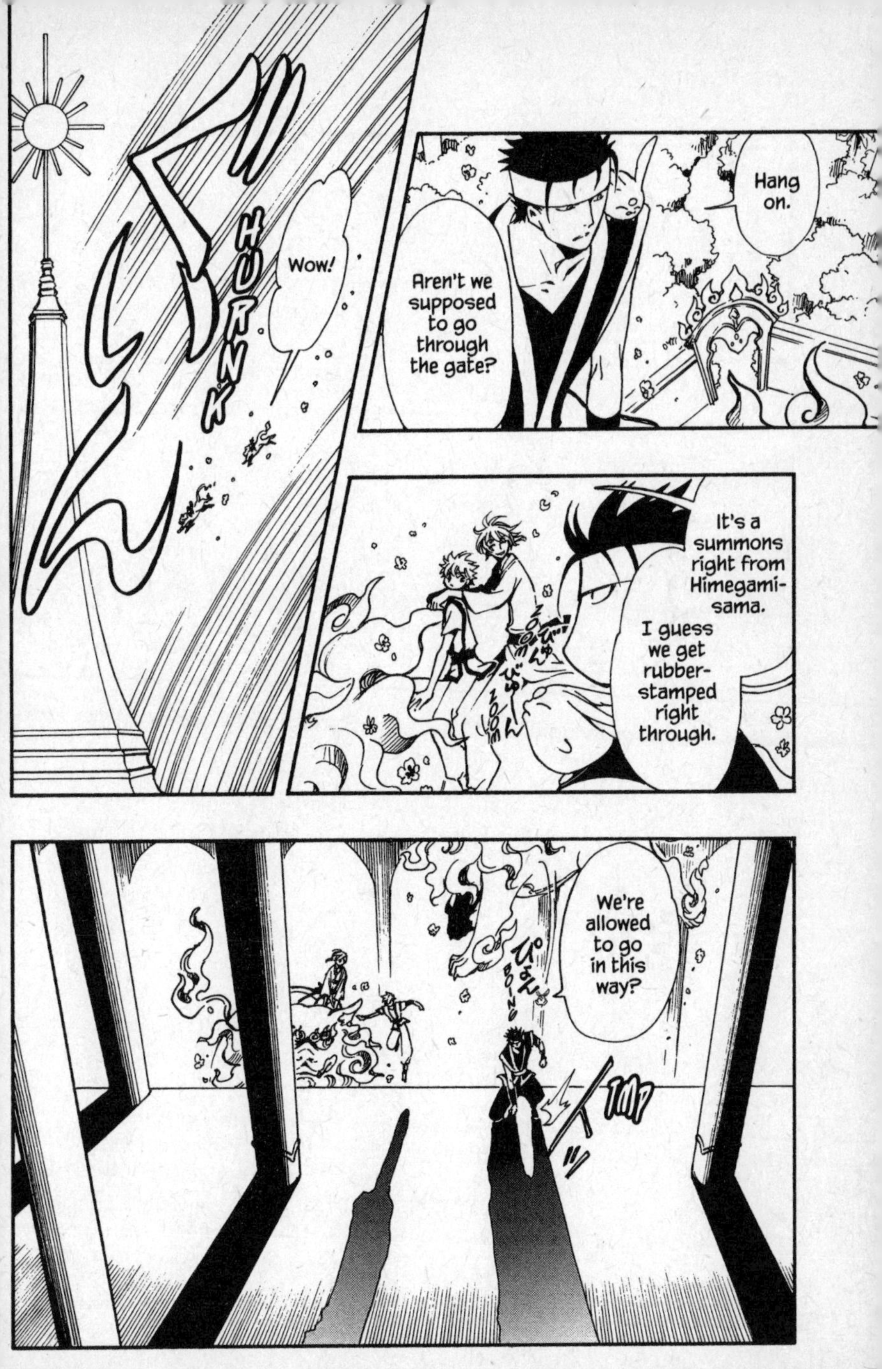
Hang on.
Aren't we supposed to go through the gate?
It's a summons right from Himegami-sama.
I guess we get rubber-stamped right through.
Wow!
HURNK
We're allowed to go in this way?
BOING
TMP

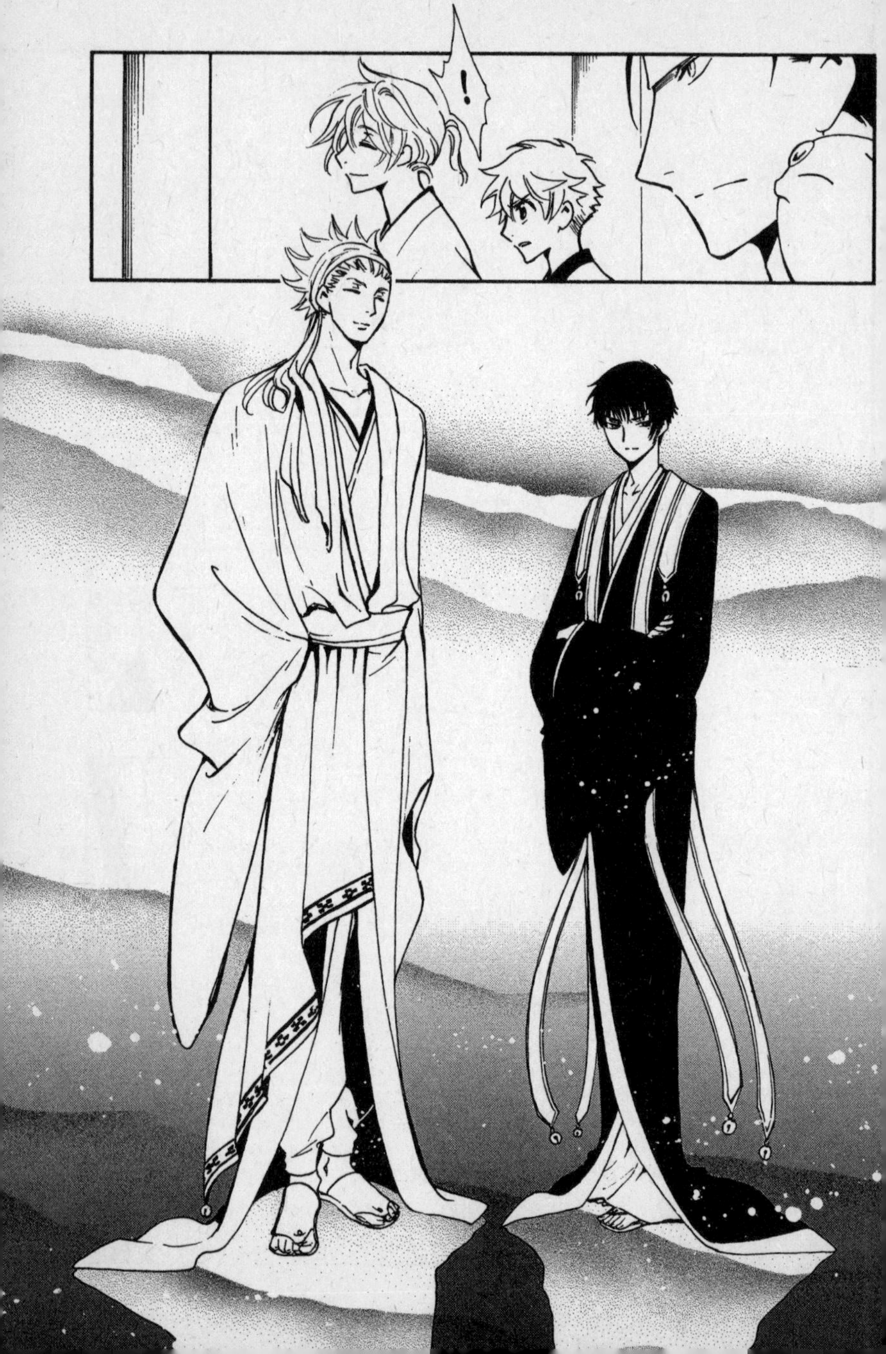
!

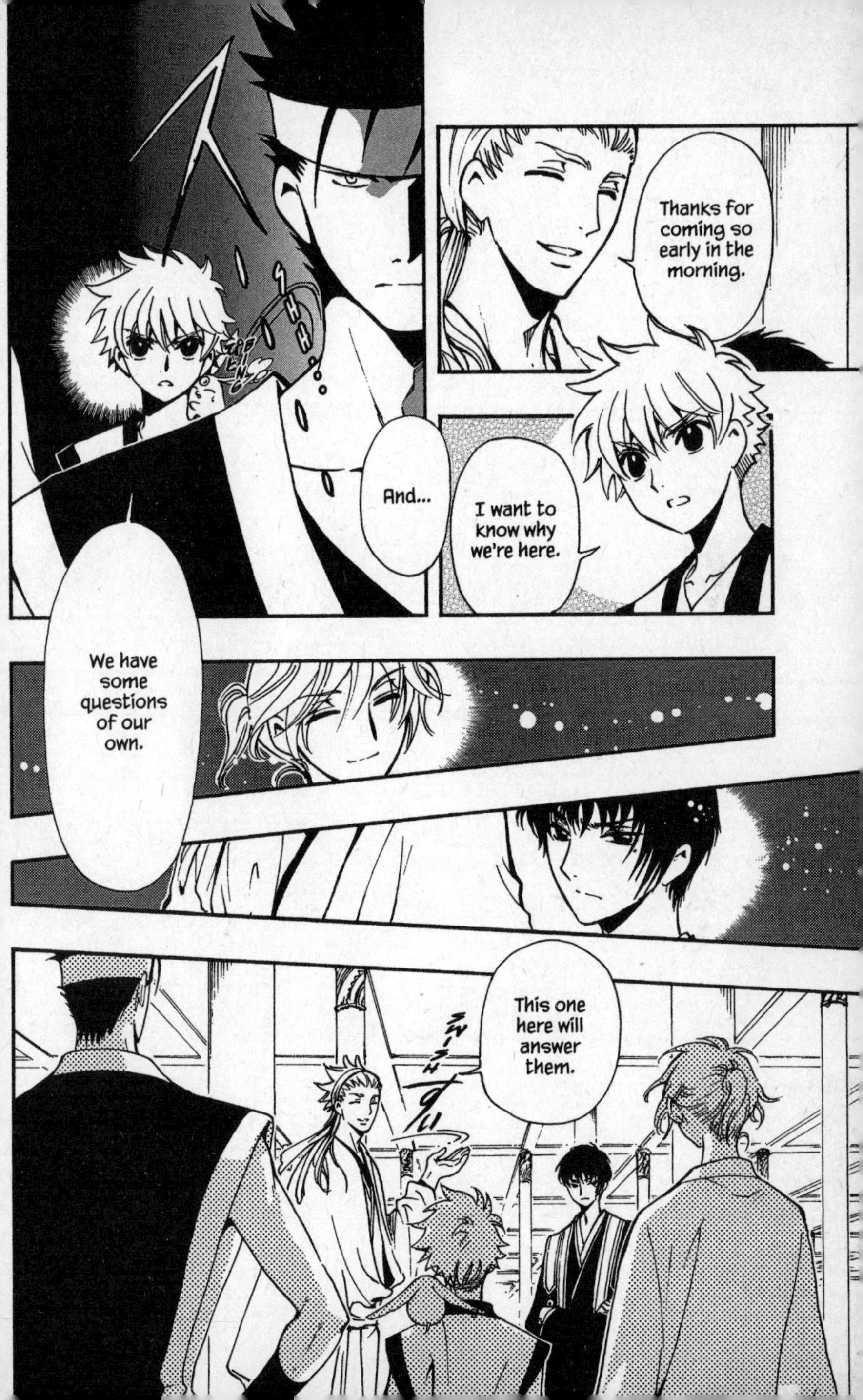
Thanks for coming so early in the morning.
I want to know why we're here.
And...
SHHH
We have some questions of our own.
This one here will answer them.
SWISH

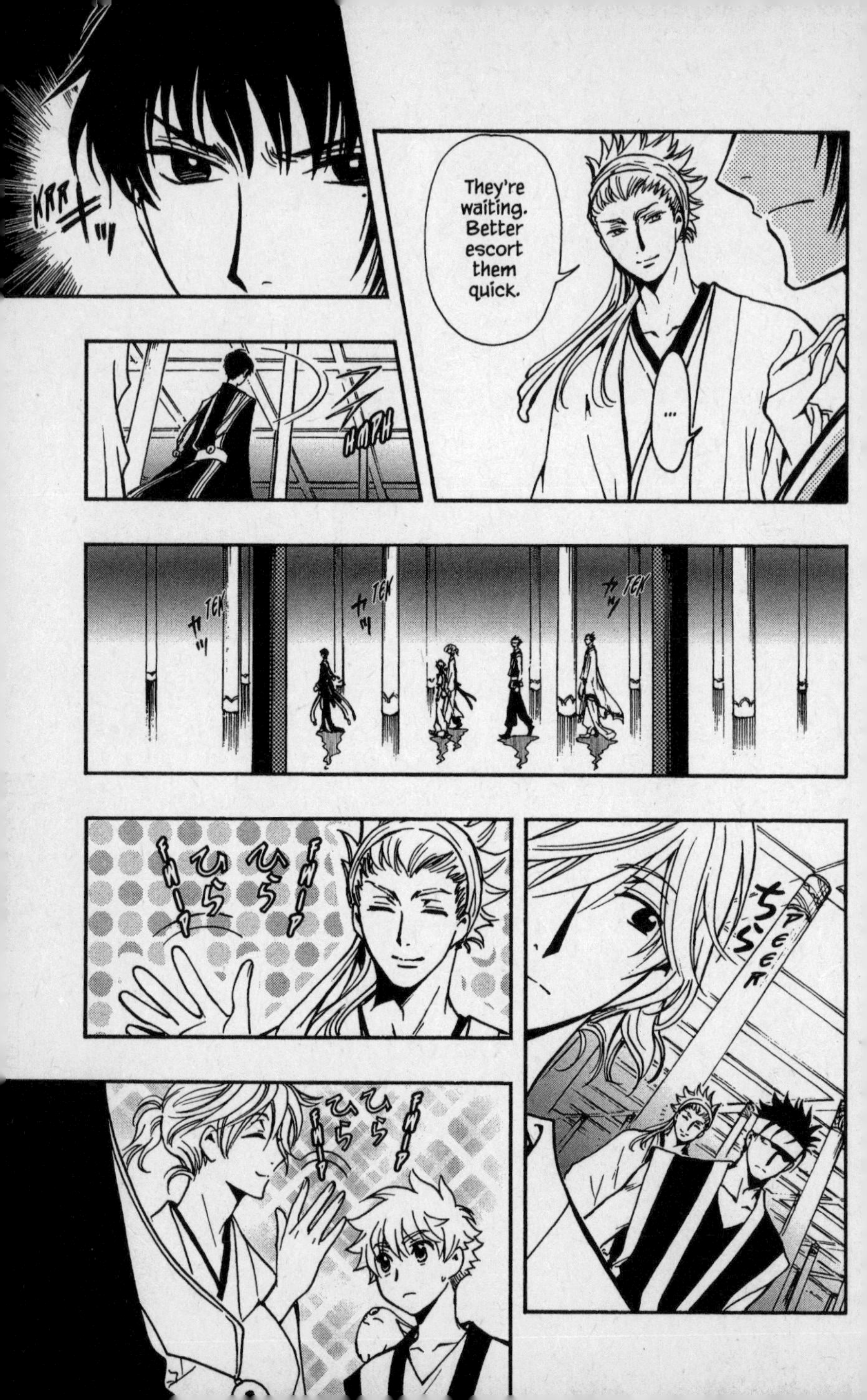

They're waiting. Better escort them quick.
...
KRR
HMPH
TEN
TEN
TEN
SPEER
FWIP FWIP
FWIP FWIP

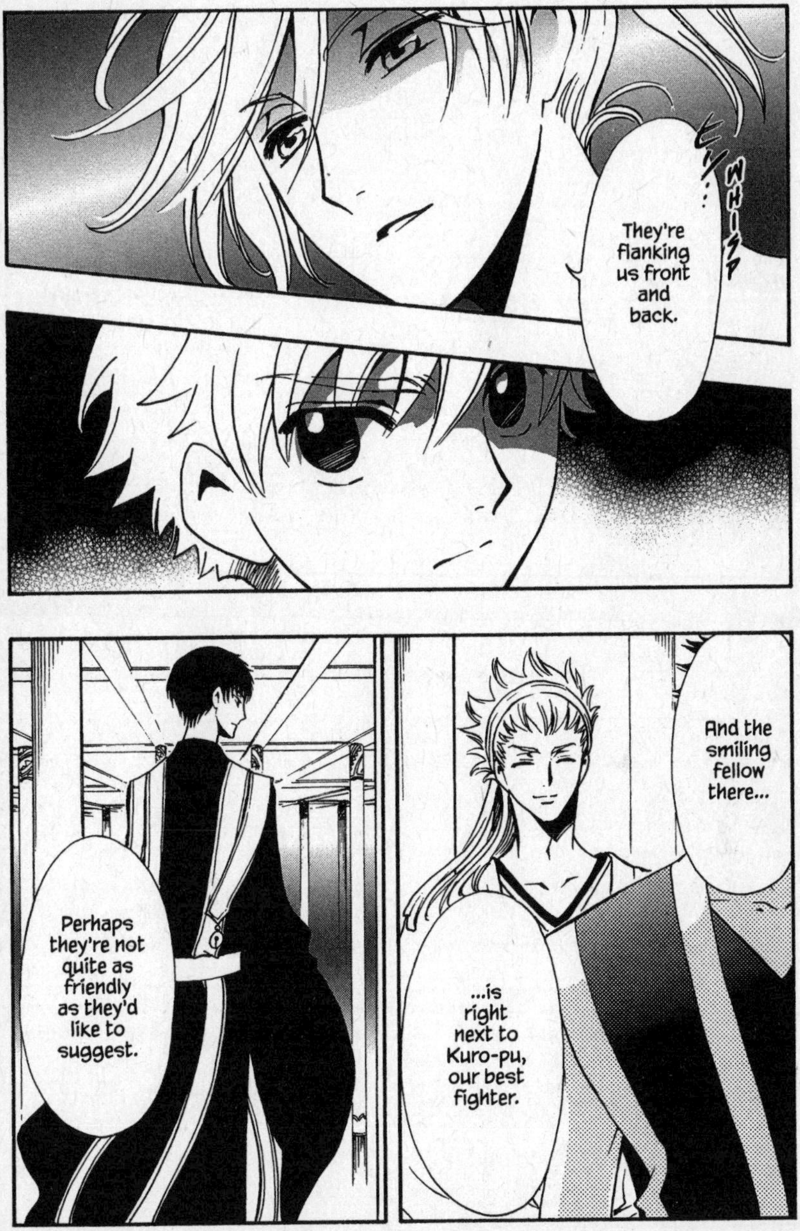
WHISP
They're flanking us front and back.
And the smiling fellow there...
...is right next to Kuro-pu, our best fighter.
Perhaps they're not quite as friendly as they'd like to suggest.

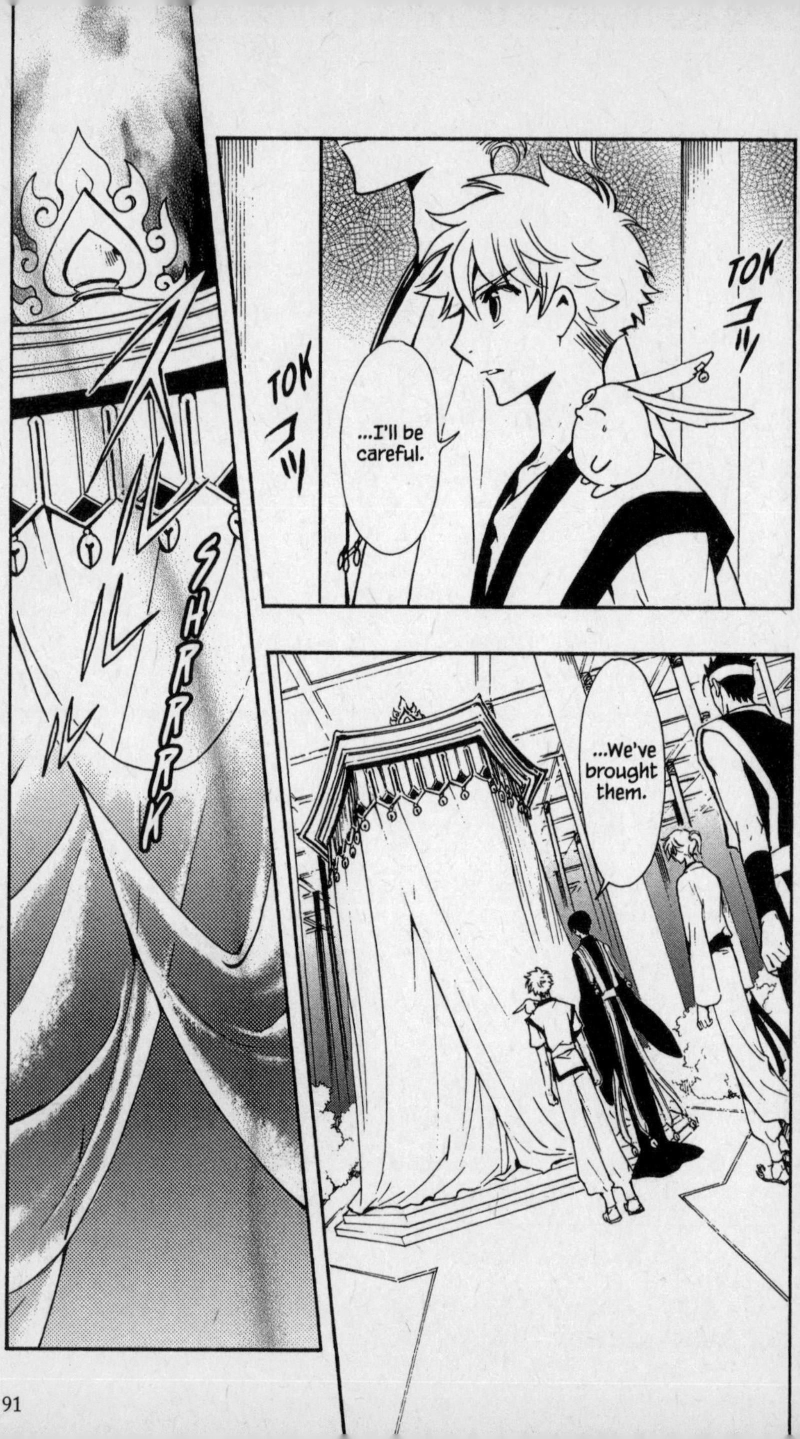
TOK
コッ
...I'll be careful.
TOK
コッ
...We've brought them.
SHRRRRK

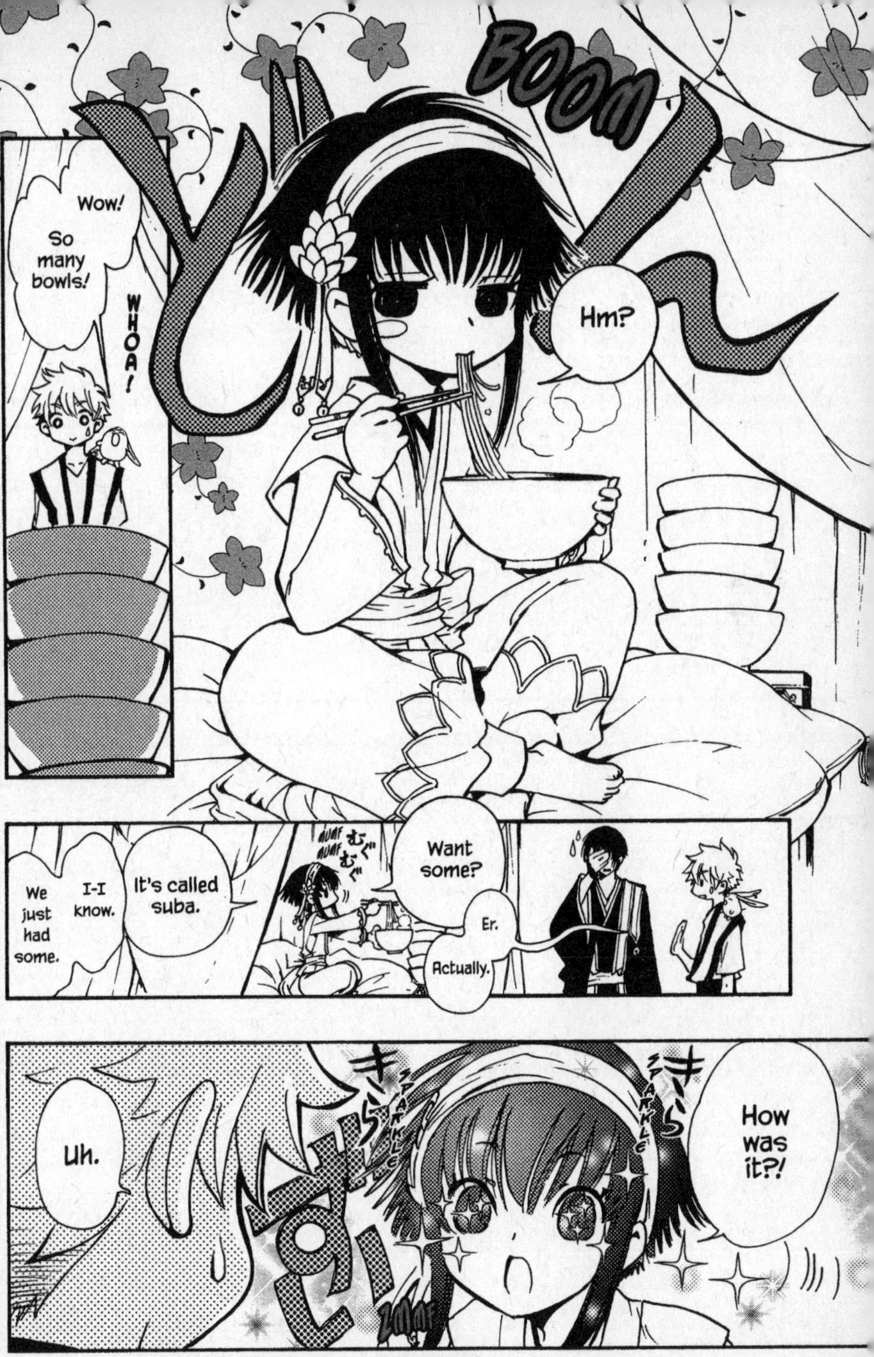
BOOM
Hm?
Wow! So many bowls!
WHOA!
Er. Actually.
むぐむぐ
Want some?
It's called suba.
I-I know.
We just had some.
How was it?!
SPARKLE
SPARKLE
Uh.

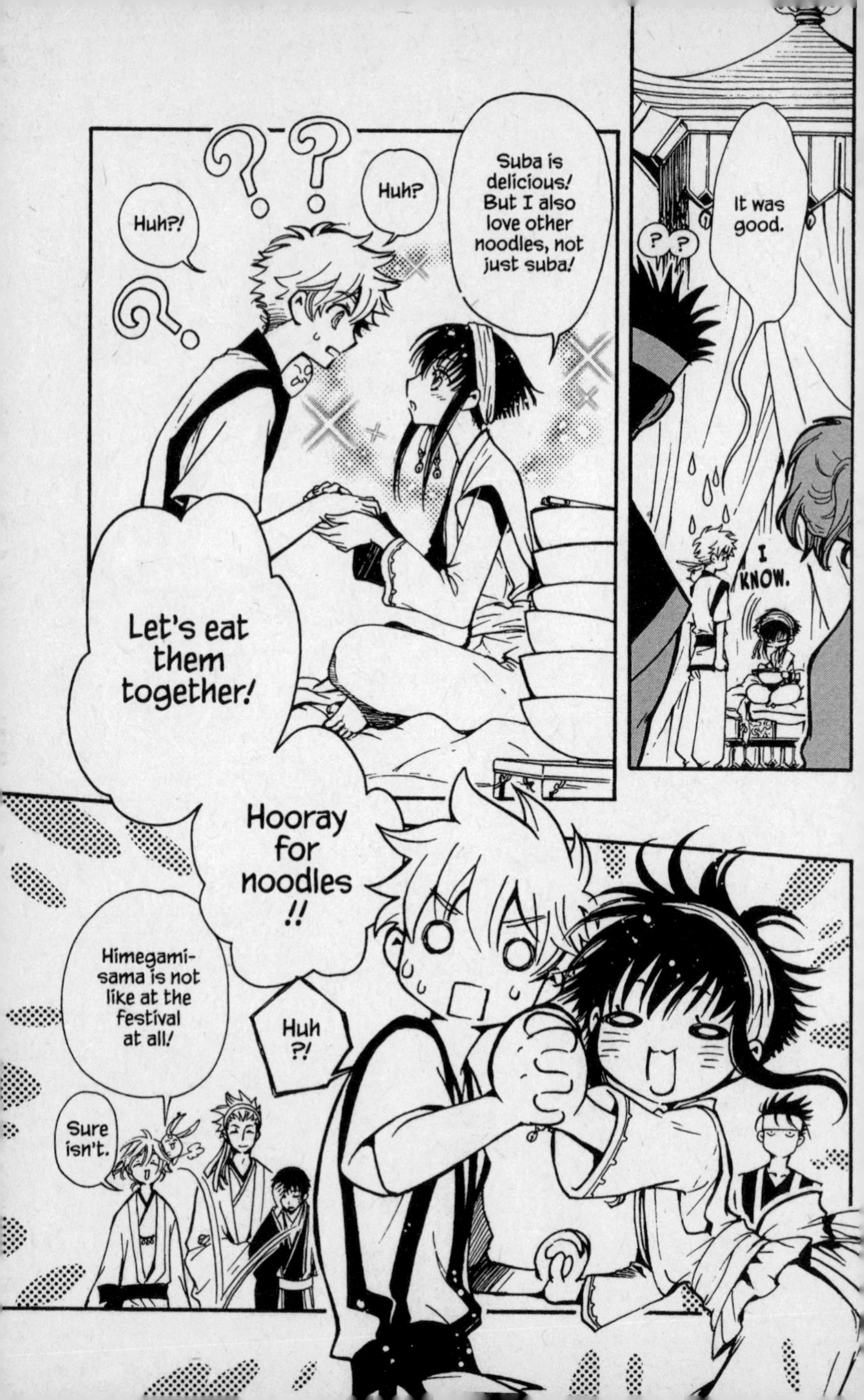
It was good.
I KNOW.
Suba is delicious! But I also love other noodles, not just suba!
Huh?
Huh?!
Let's eat them together!
Hooray for noodles !!
Huh ?!
Himegami-sama is not like at the festival at all!
Sure isn't.

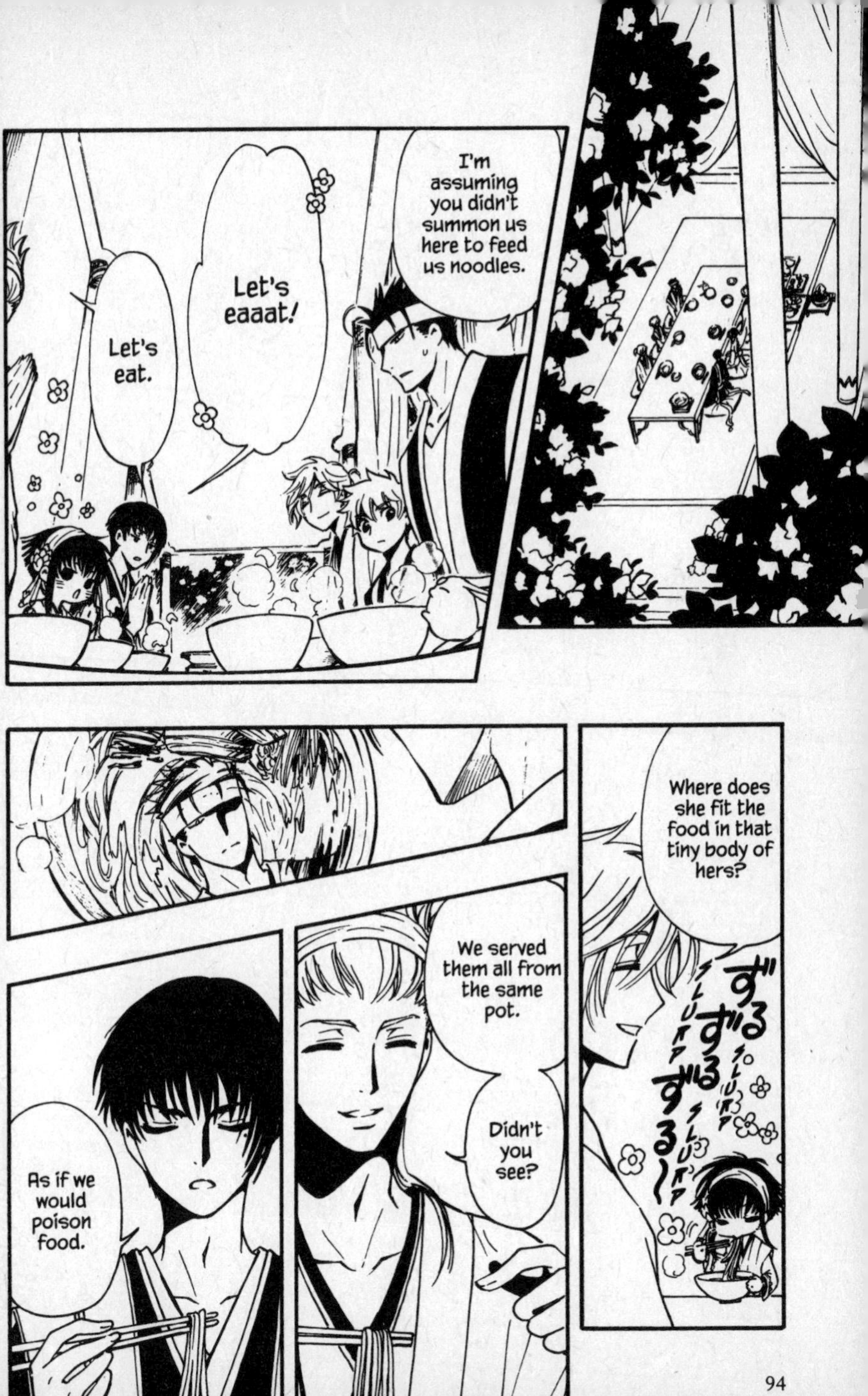
I'm assuming you didn't summon us here to feed us noodles.
Let's eaaat!
Let's eat.
Where does she fit the food in that tiny body of hers?
ずるずるずるずる〜
We served them all from the same pot.
Didn't you see?
As if we would poison food.

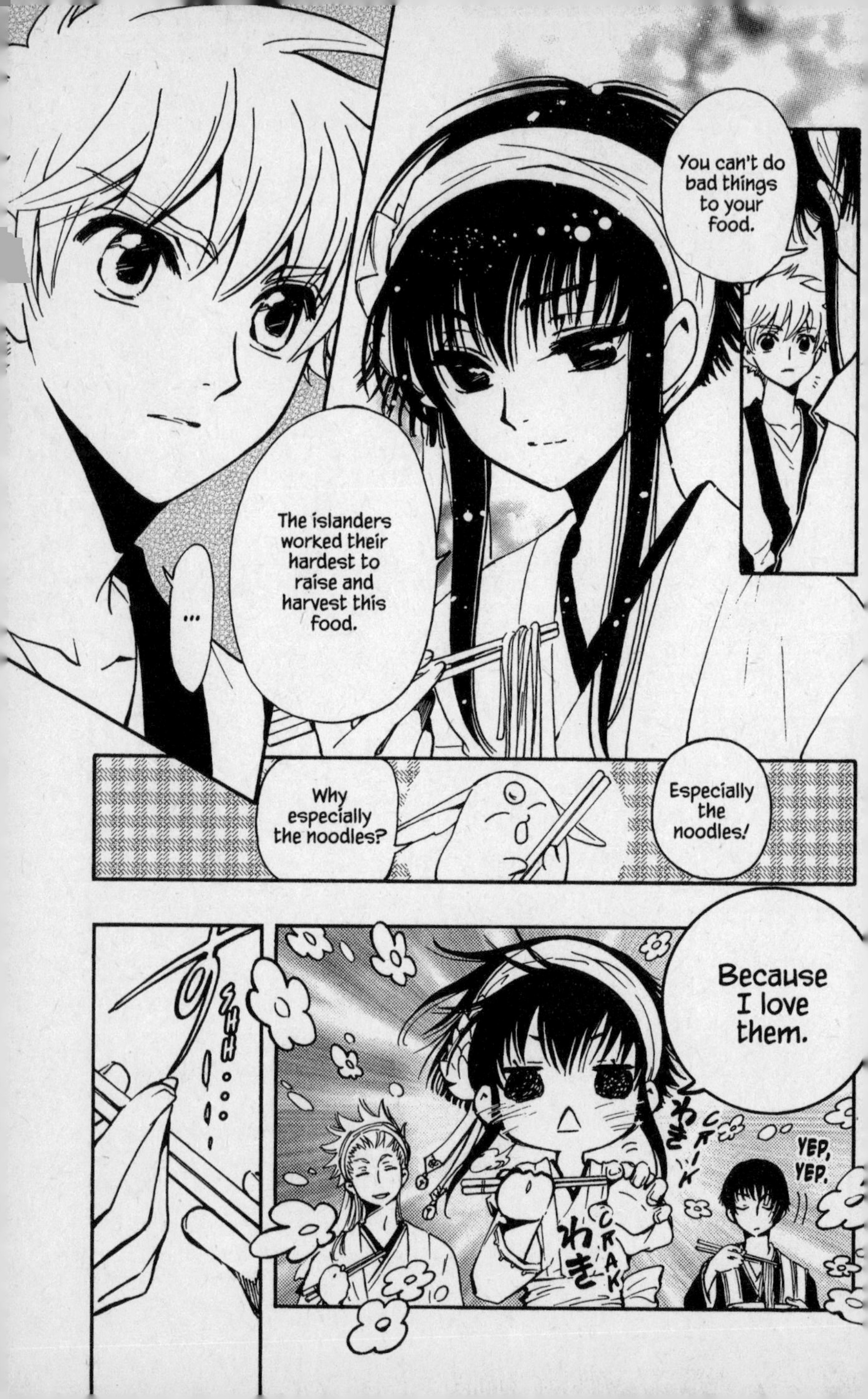
You can't do bad things to your food.
The islanders worked their hardest to raise and harvest this food.
...
Especially the noodles!
Why especially the noodles?
Because I love them.
わき
CRAK
YEP, YEP.
わき
CRAK
SHHH...

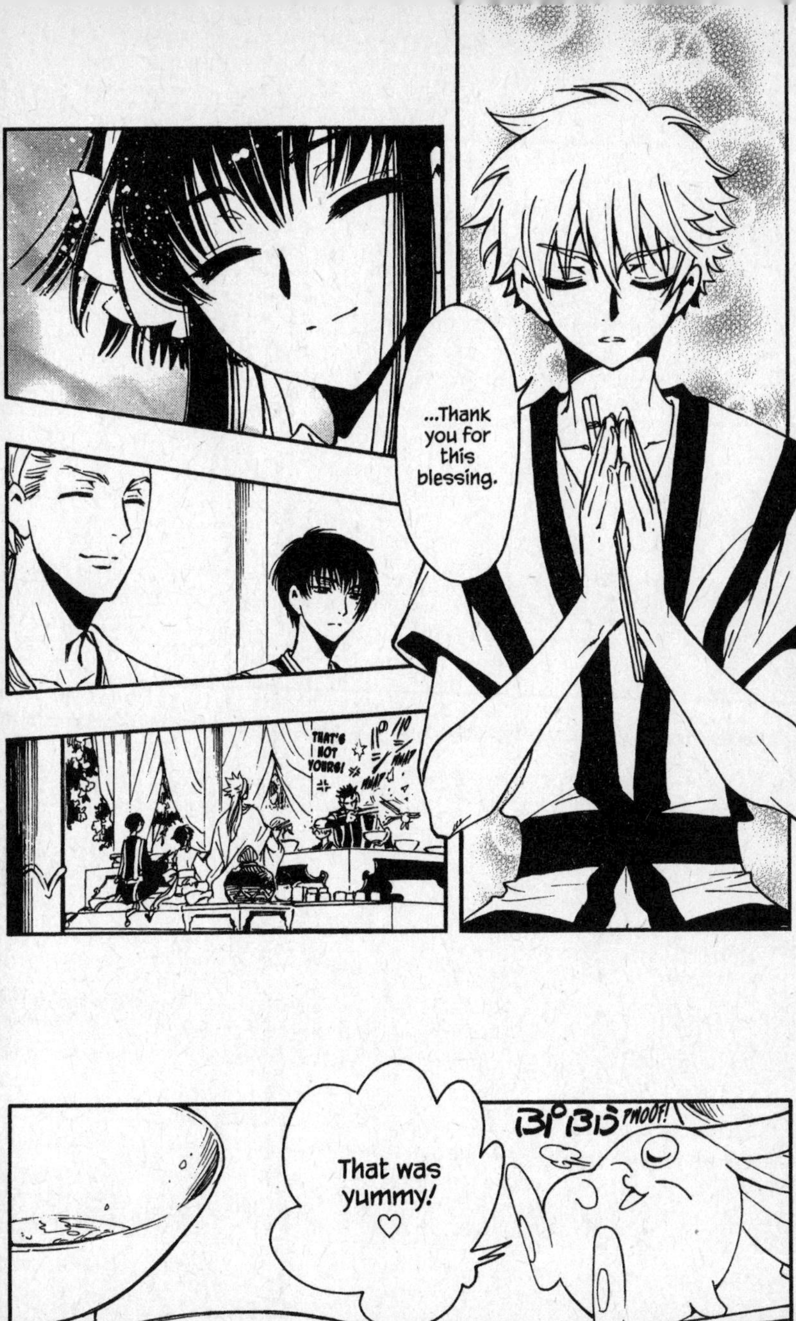
...Thank you for this blessing.
THAT'S NOT YOURS!
That was yummy! ♡
PWOOF!

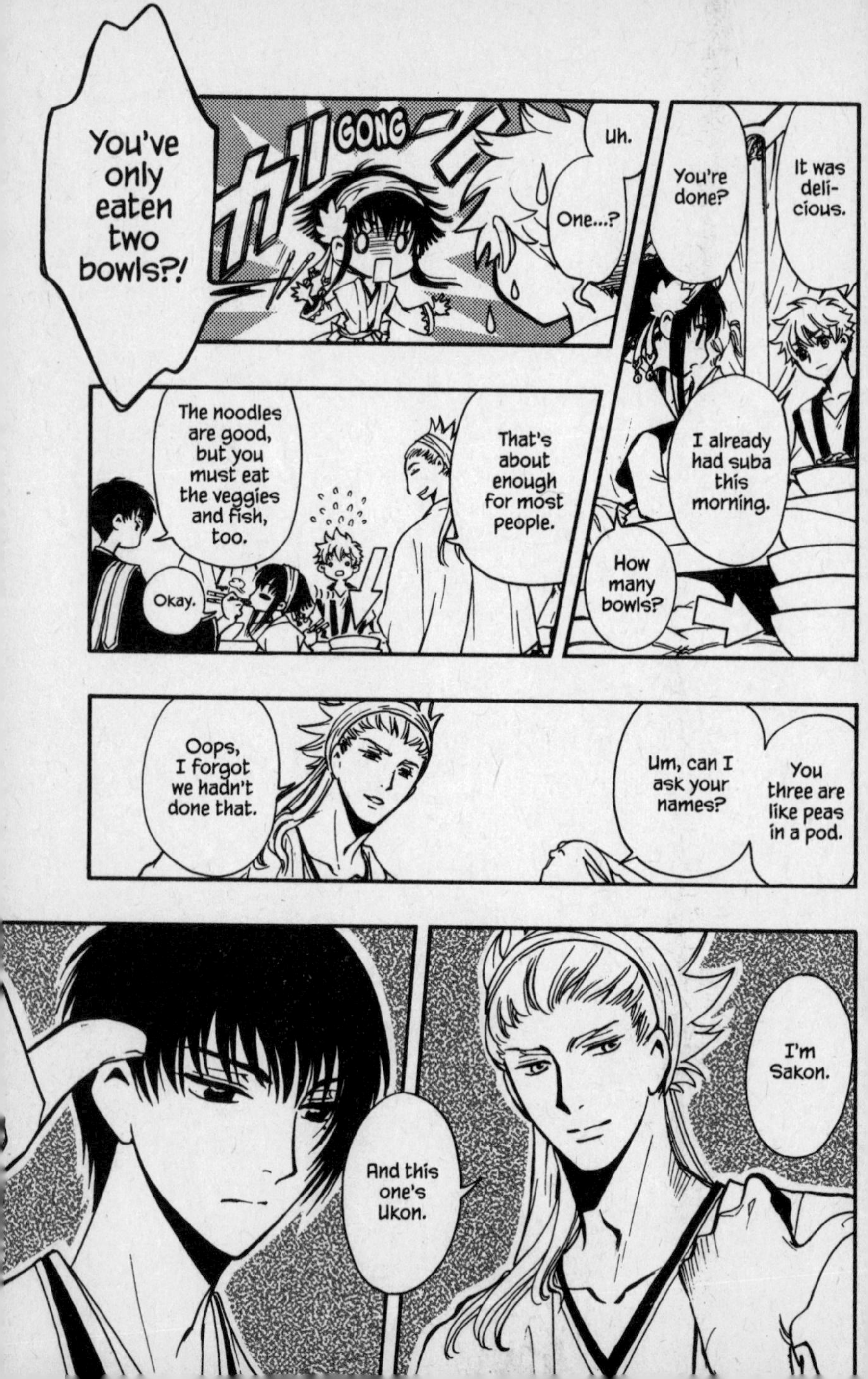
It was delicious.
You're done?
I already had suba this morning.
How many bowls?
Uh.
One...?
GONG
You've only eaten two bowls?!
That's about enough for most people.
The noodles are good, but you must eat the veggies and fish, too.
Okay.
You three are like peas in a pod.
Um, can I ask your names?
Oops, I forgot we hadn't done that.
I'm Sakon.
And this one's Ukon.

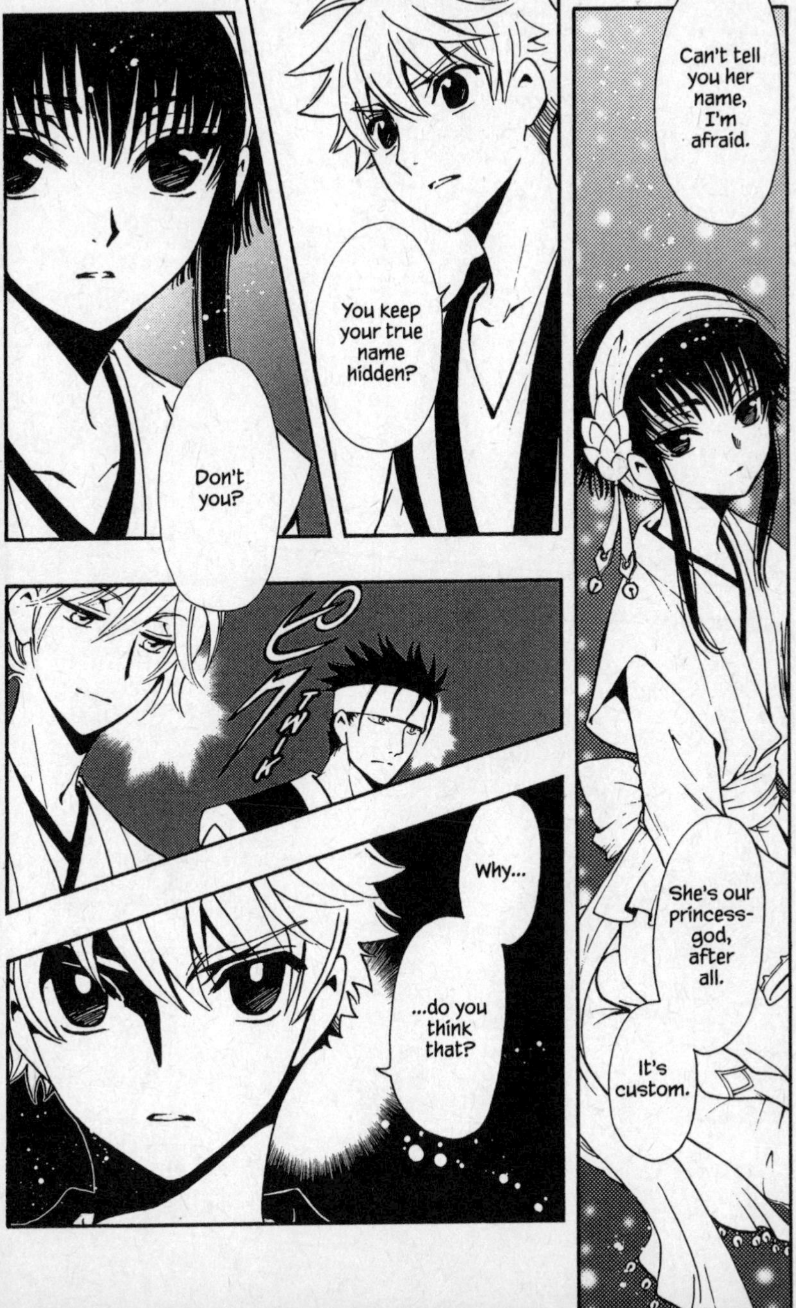
Can't tell you her name, I'm afraid.
She's our princess-god, after all.
It's custom.
You keep your true name hidden?
Don't you?
TWIK
Why...
...do you think that?

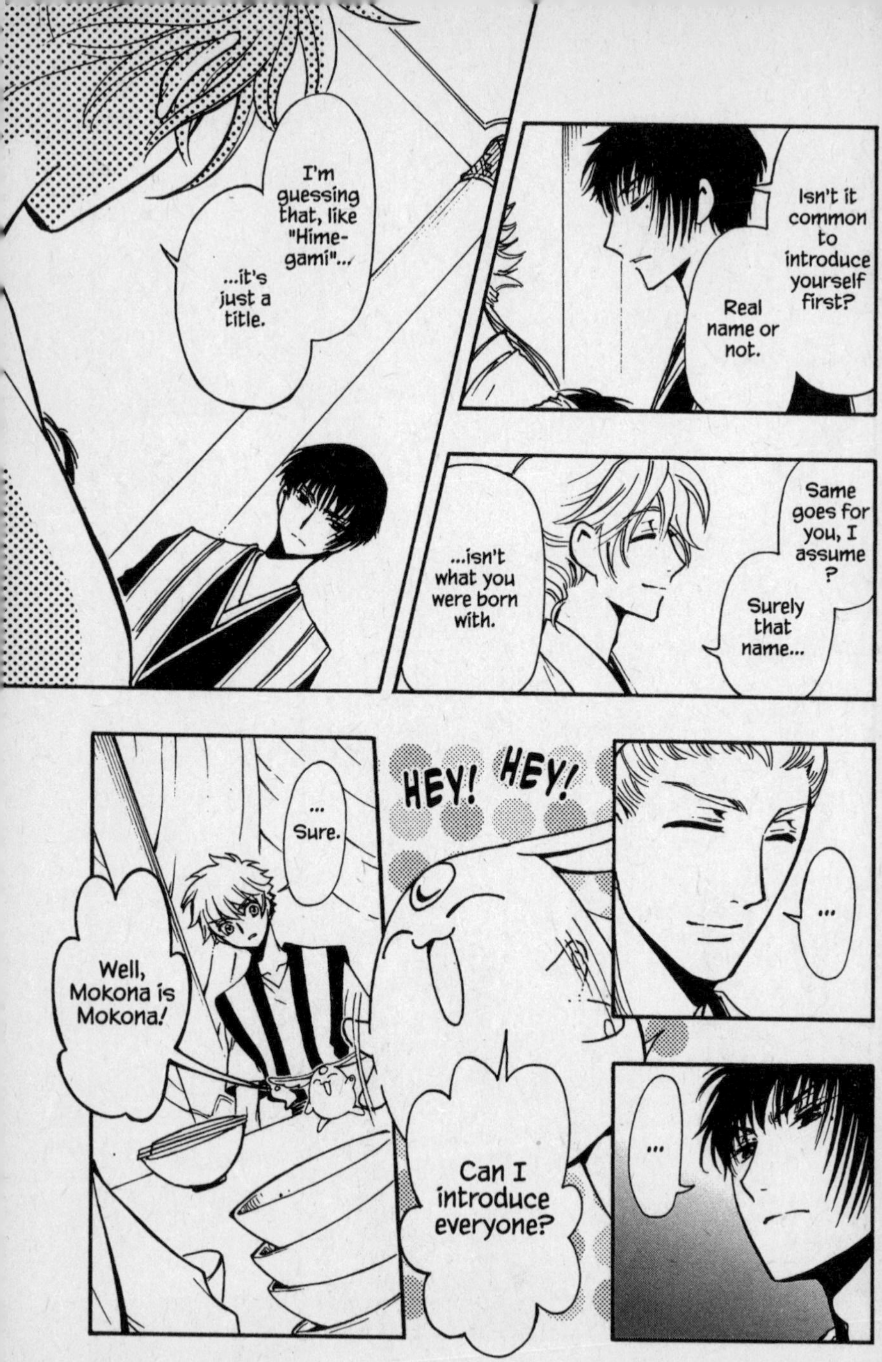
Isn't it common to introduce yourself first?
Real name or not.
Same goes for you, I assume?
Surely that name...
...isn't what you were born with.
I'm guessing that, like "Hime-gami"...
...it's just a title.
...
...
HEY! HEY!
Can I introduce everyone?
... Sure.
Well, Mokona is Mokona!

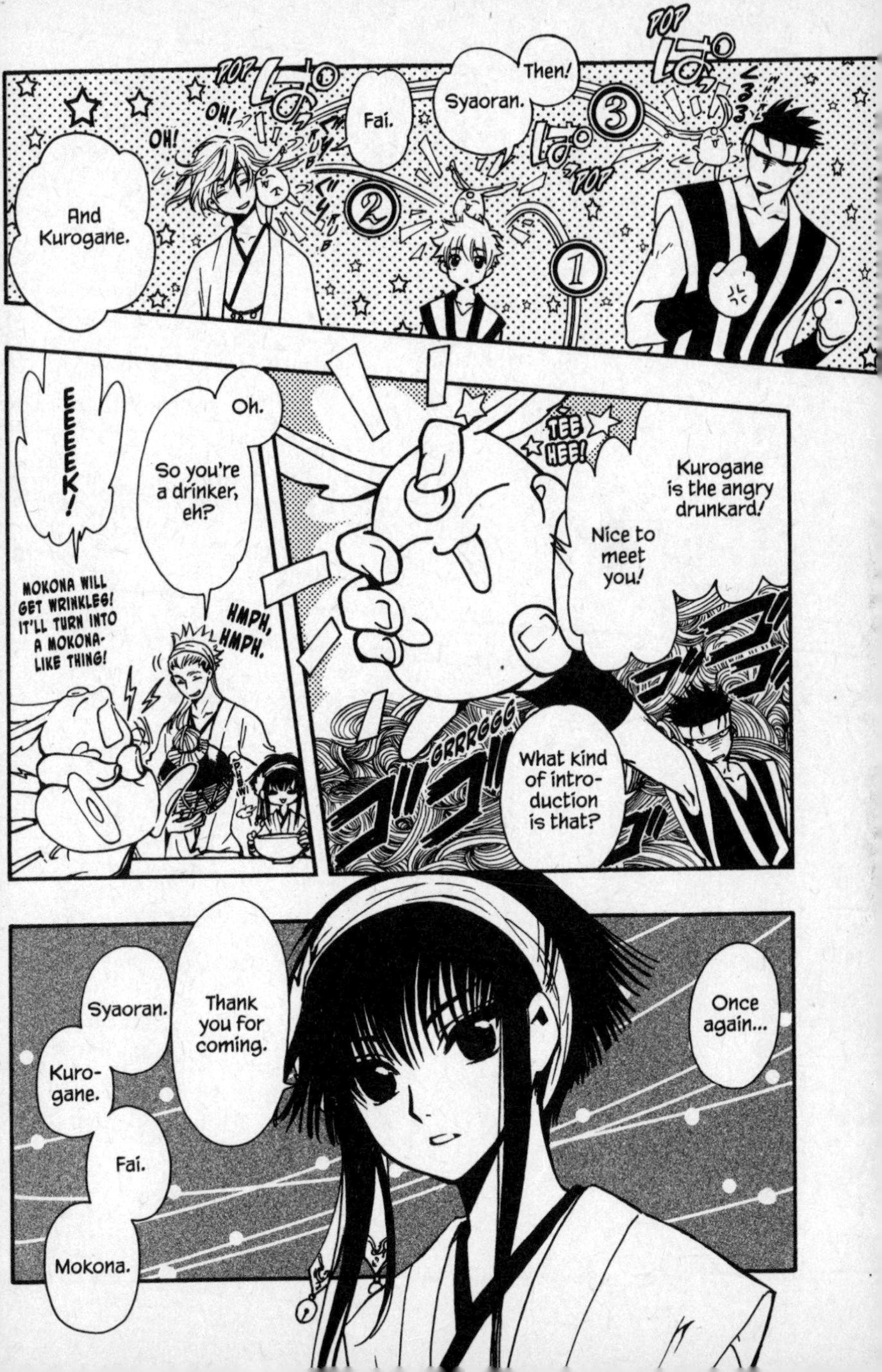
POP
Then!
Syaoran.
POP
Fai.
POP
OH!
OH!
And Kurogane.
TEE HEE!
Kurogane is the angry drunkard!
Nice to meet you!
GRRRGGG
What kind of intro-duction is that?
Oh.
So you're a drinker, eh?
EEEEEK!
HMPH, HMPH.
MOKONA WILL GET WRINKLES! IT'LL TURN INTO A MOKONA-LIKE THING!
Once again...
Thank you for coming.
Syaoran.
Kuro-gane.
Fai.
Mokona.

May I ask a question first?

Yes.

You made...

...this flower fall on me, and only me.

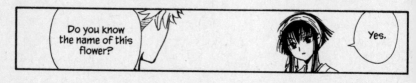

Do you know the name of this flower?

Yes.

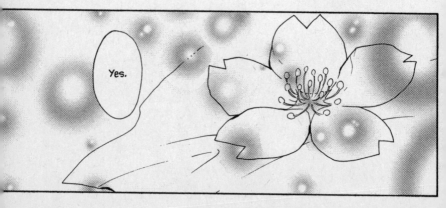

Yes.

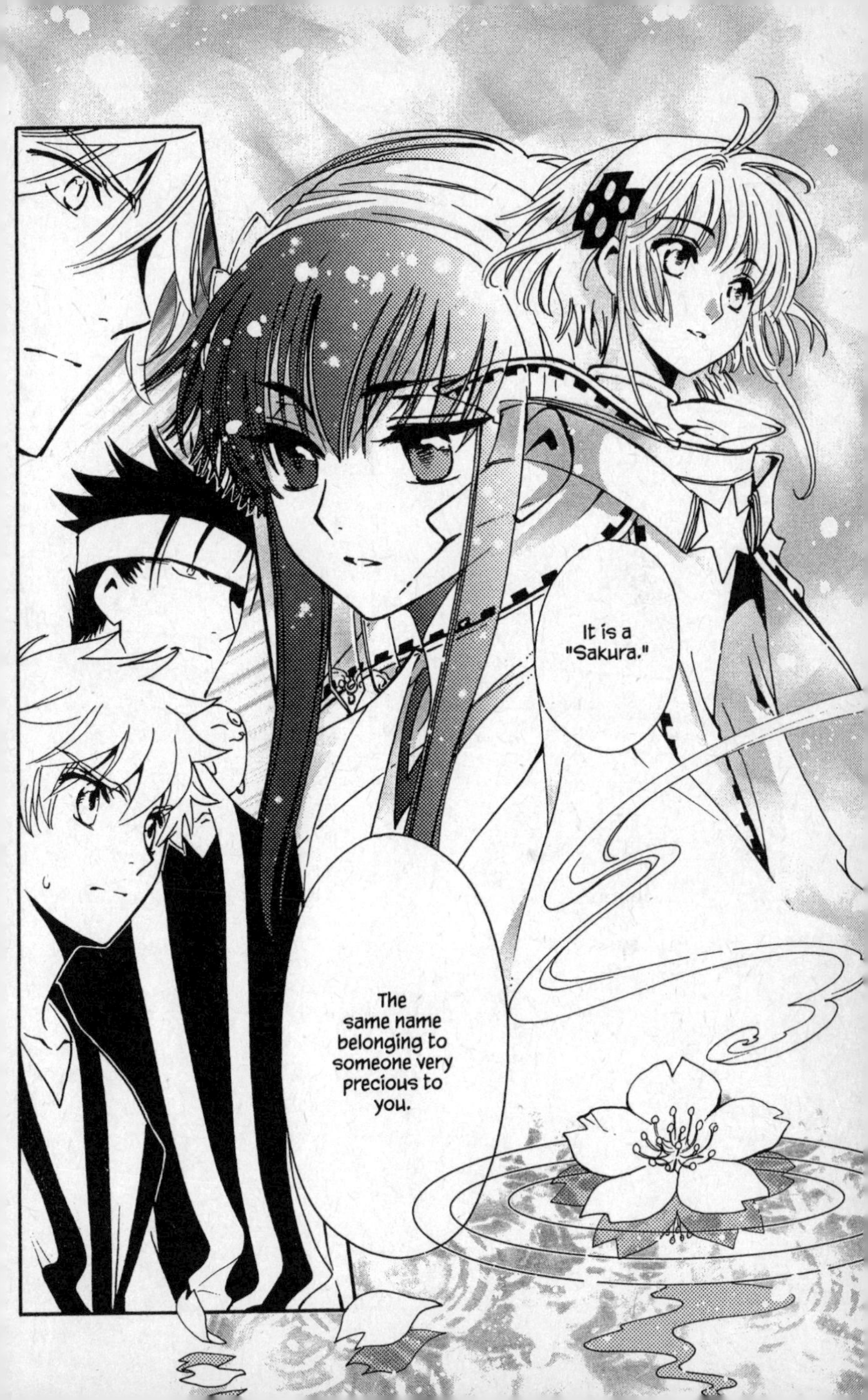
It is a "Sakura."
The same name belonging to someone very precious to you.

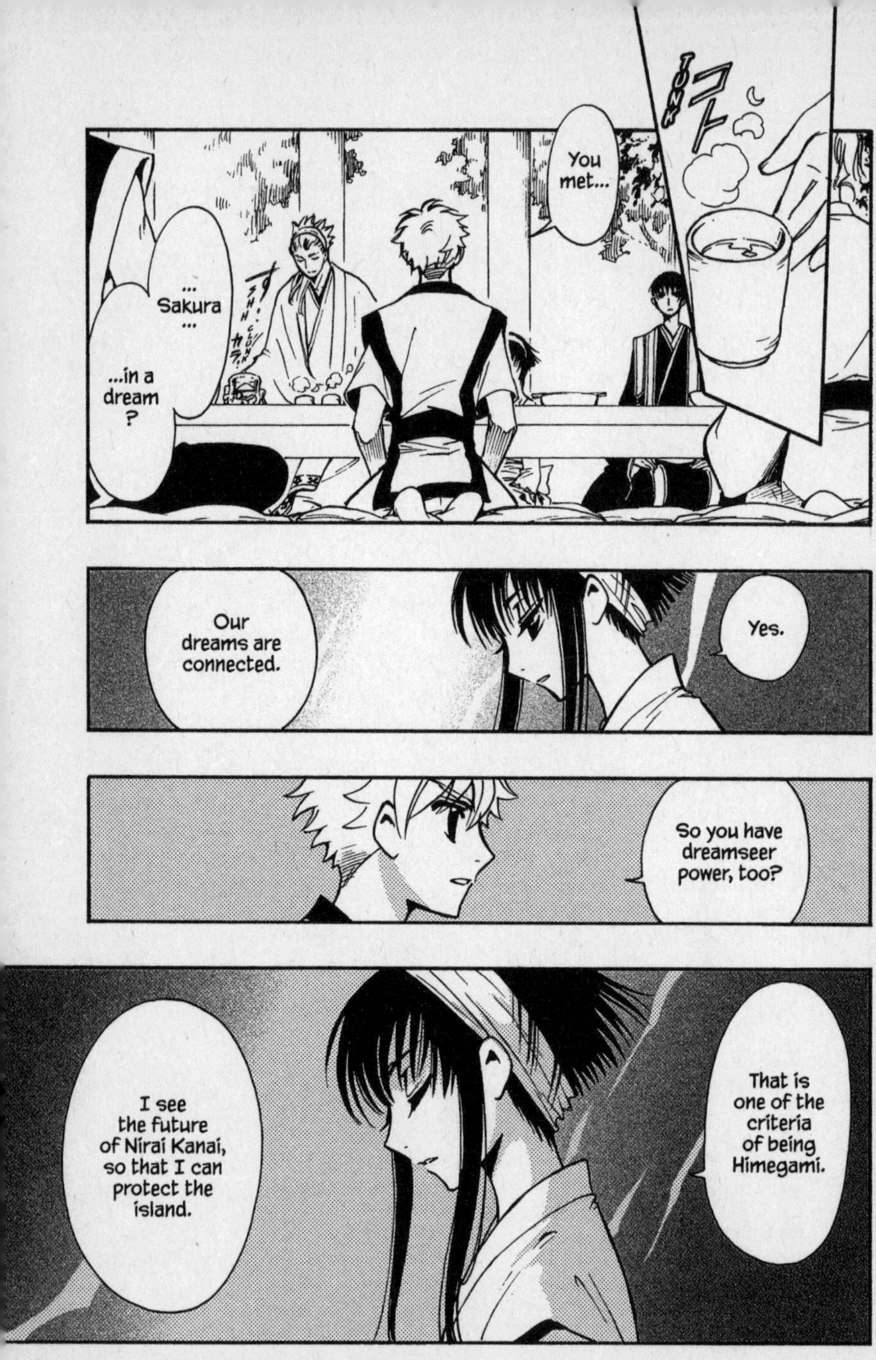
TONK
You met...
...Sakura...
...in a dream?
Yes.
Our dreams are connected.
So you have dreamseer power, too?
That is one of the criteria of being Himegami.
I see the future of Nirai Kanai, so that I can protect the island.

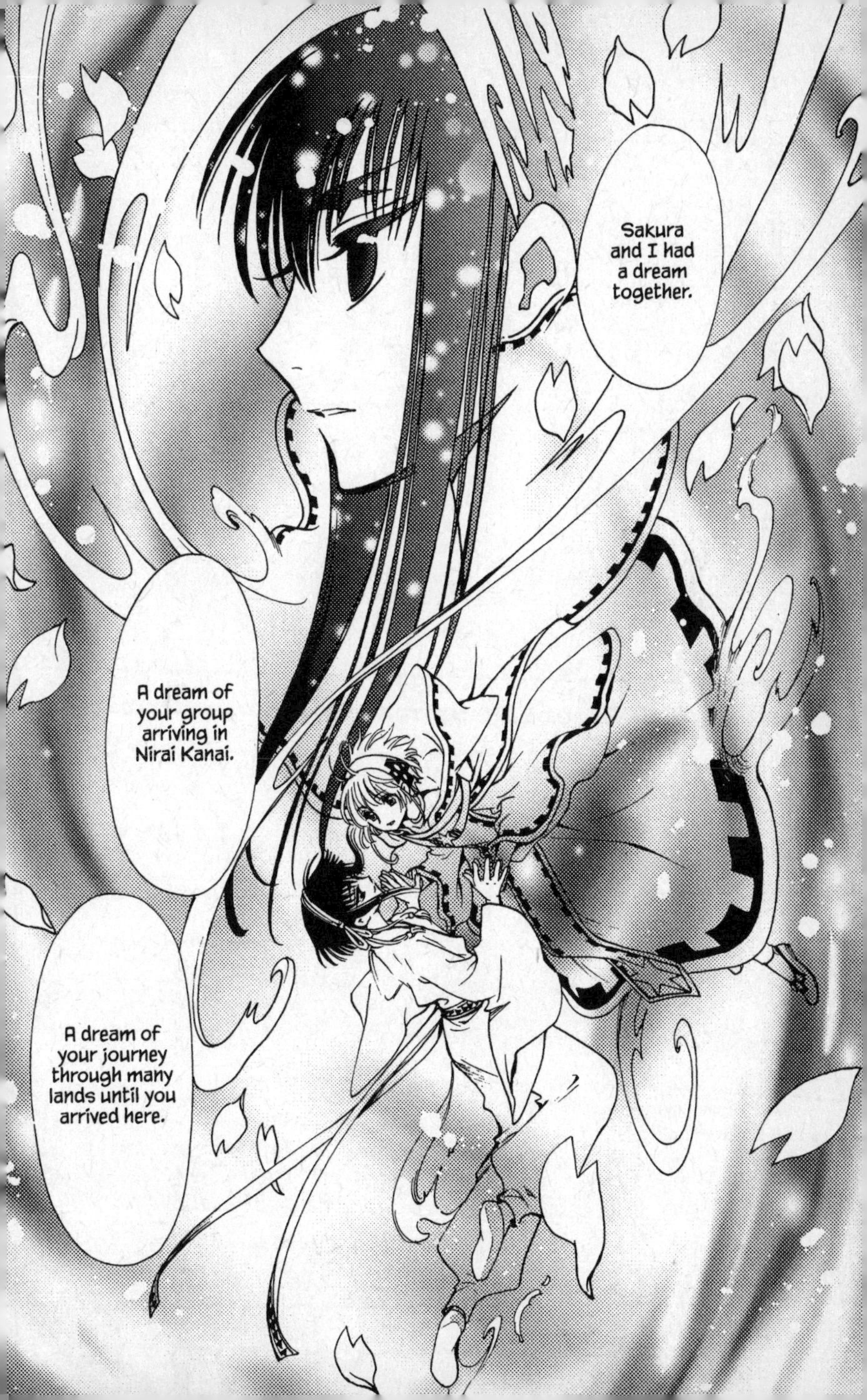
Sakura and I had a dream together.
A dream of your group arriving in Nirai Kanai.
A dream of your journey through many lands until you arrived here.

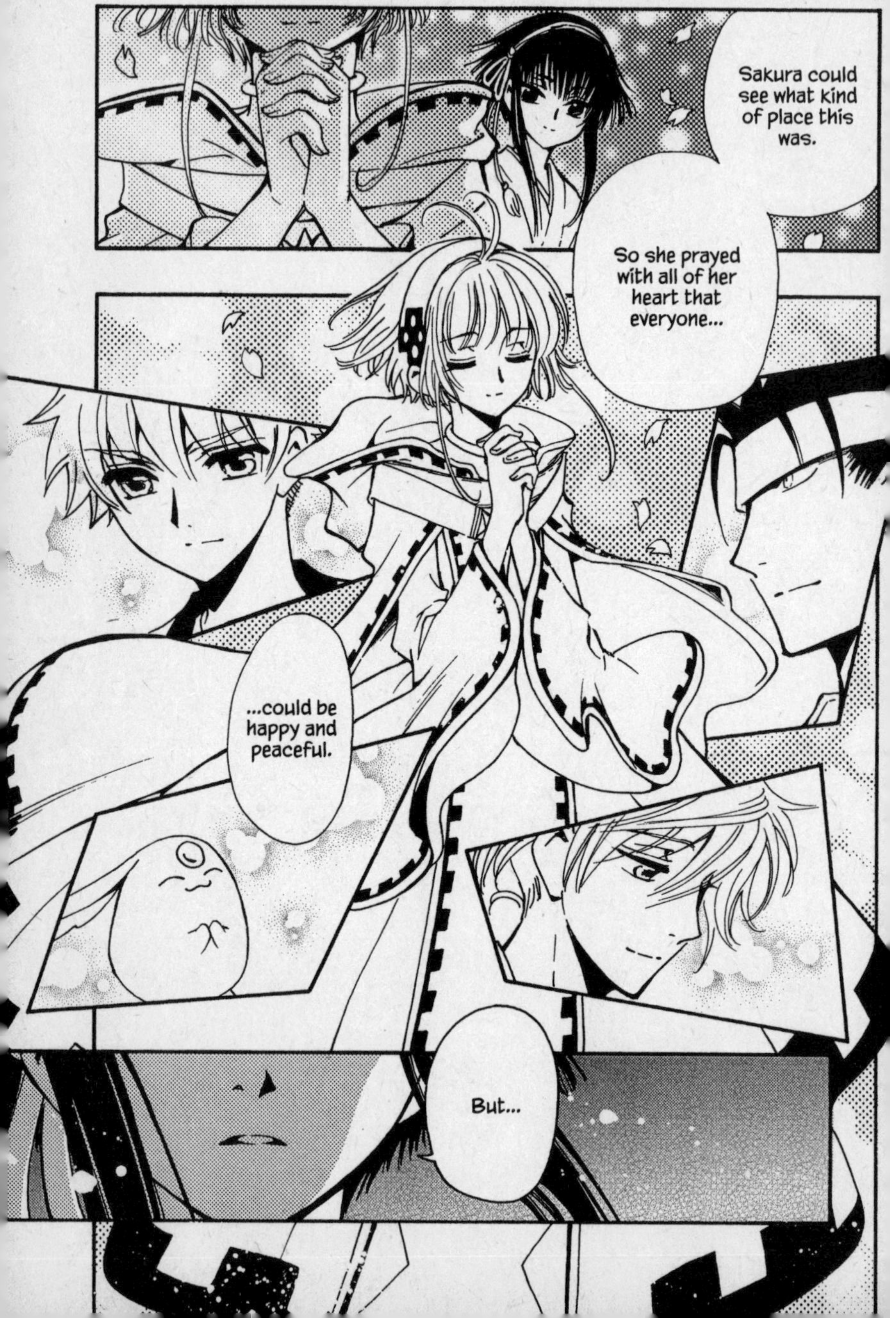
Sakura could see what kind of place this was.
So she prayed with all of her heart that everyone...
...could be happy and peaceful.
But...

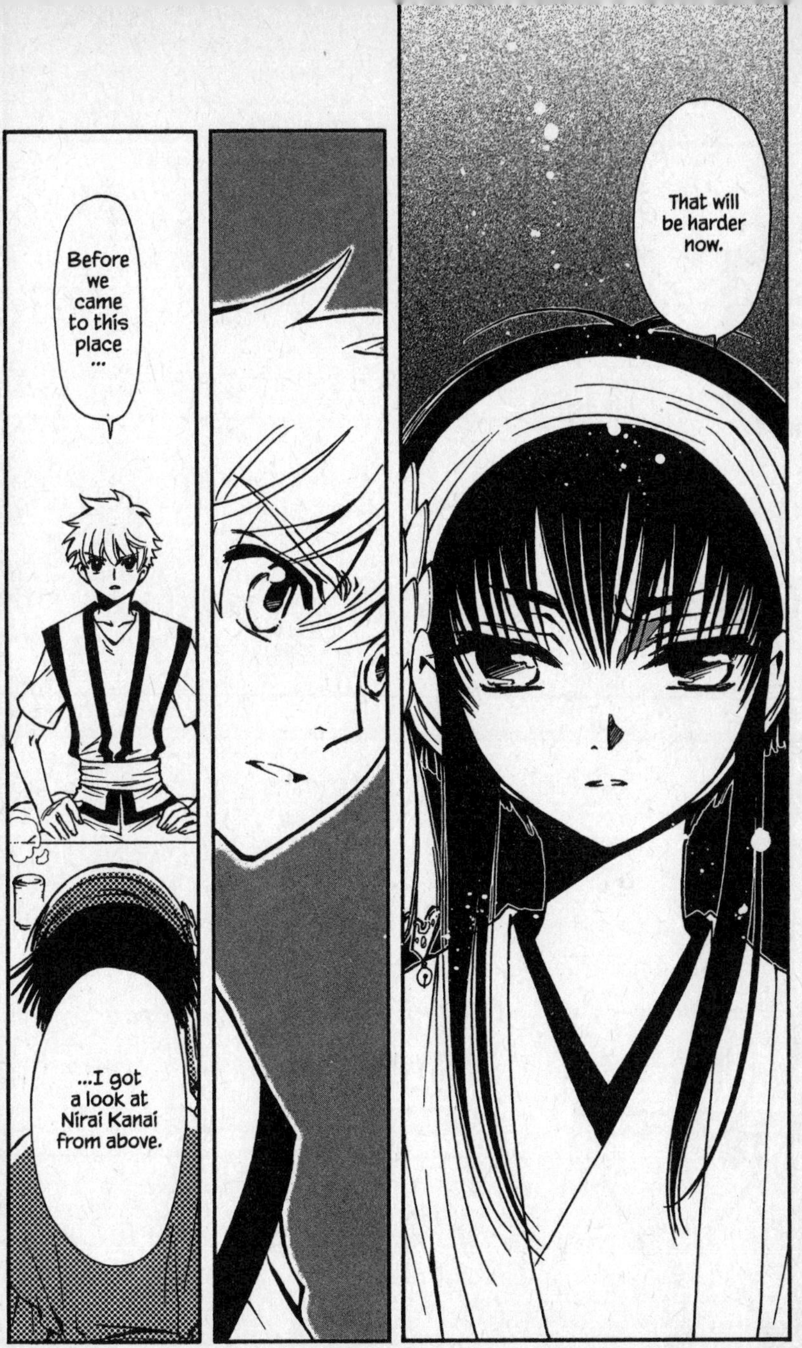
That will be harder now.
Before we came to this place ...
...I got a look at Nirai Kanai from above.

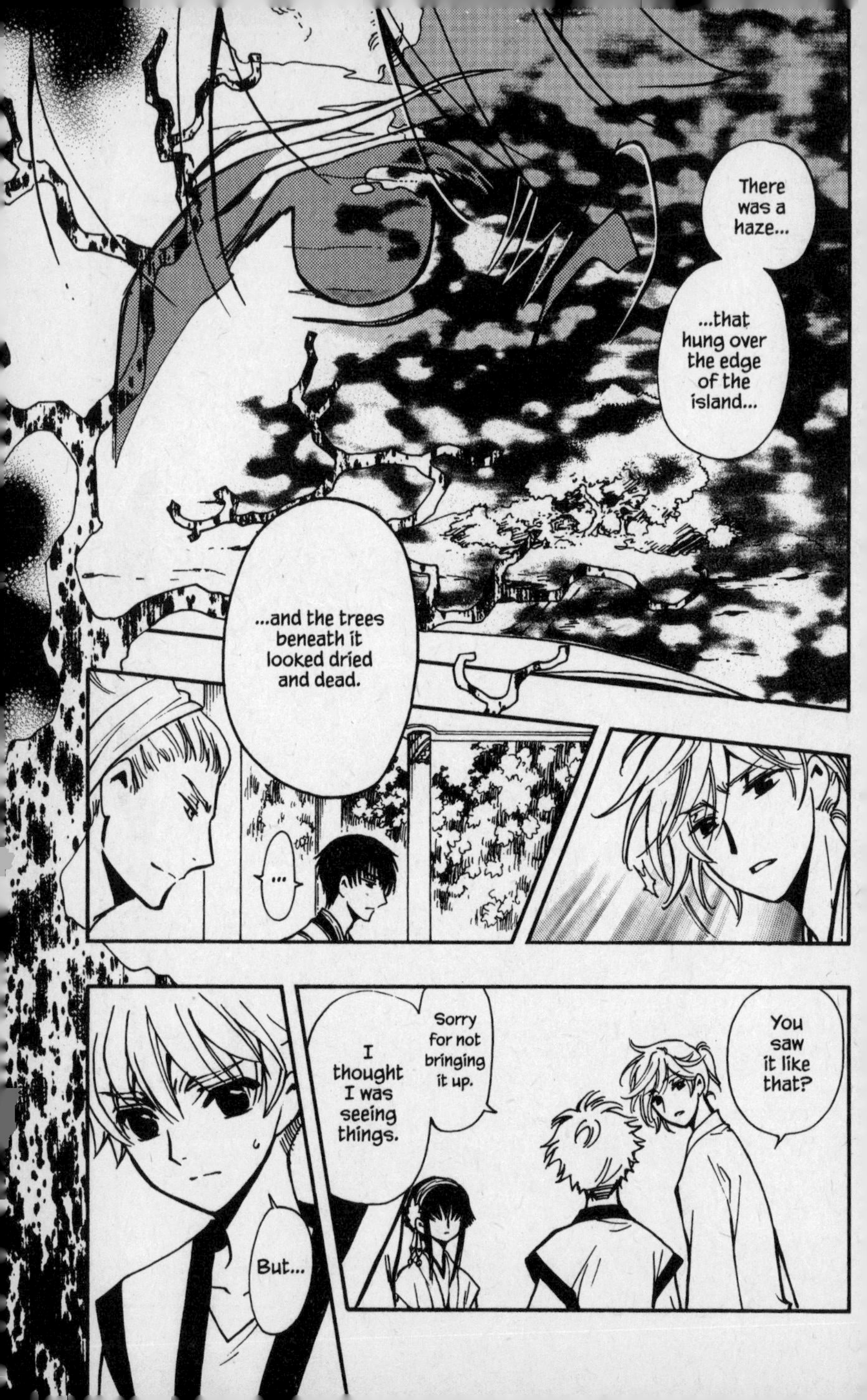
There was a haze...
...that hung over the edge of the island...
...and the trees beneath it looked dried and dead.
...
You saw it like that?
Sorry for not bringing it up.
I thought I was seeing things.
But...

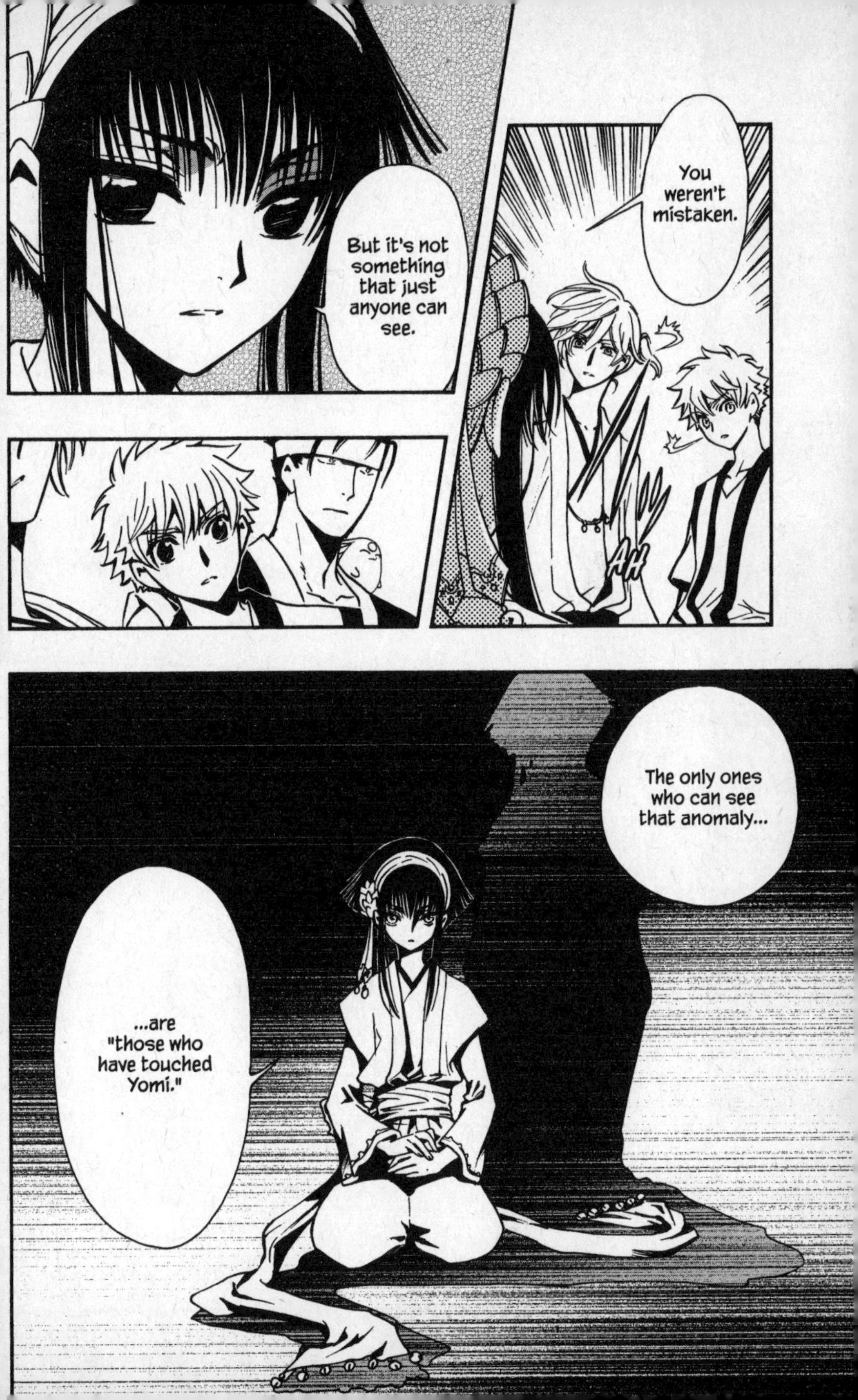
You weren't mistaken.
AH
But it's not something that just anyone can see.
The only ones who can see that anomaly...
...are "those who have touched Yomi."

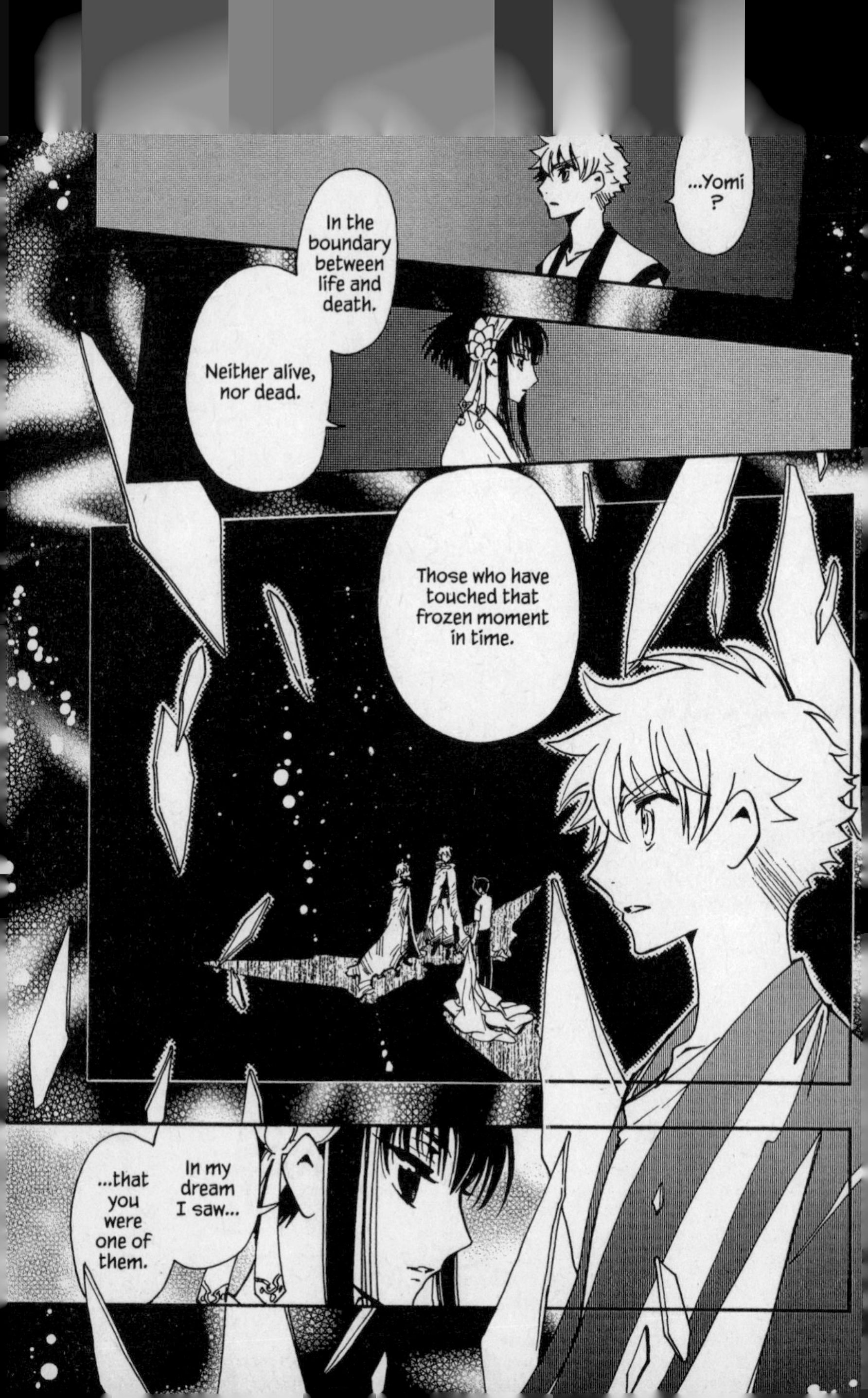
...Yomi?
In the boundary between life and death.
Neither alive, nor dead.
Those who have touched that frozen moment in time.
In my dream I saw...
...that you were one of them.

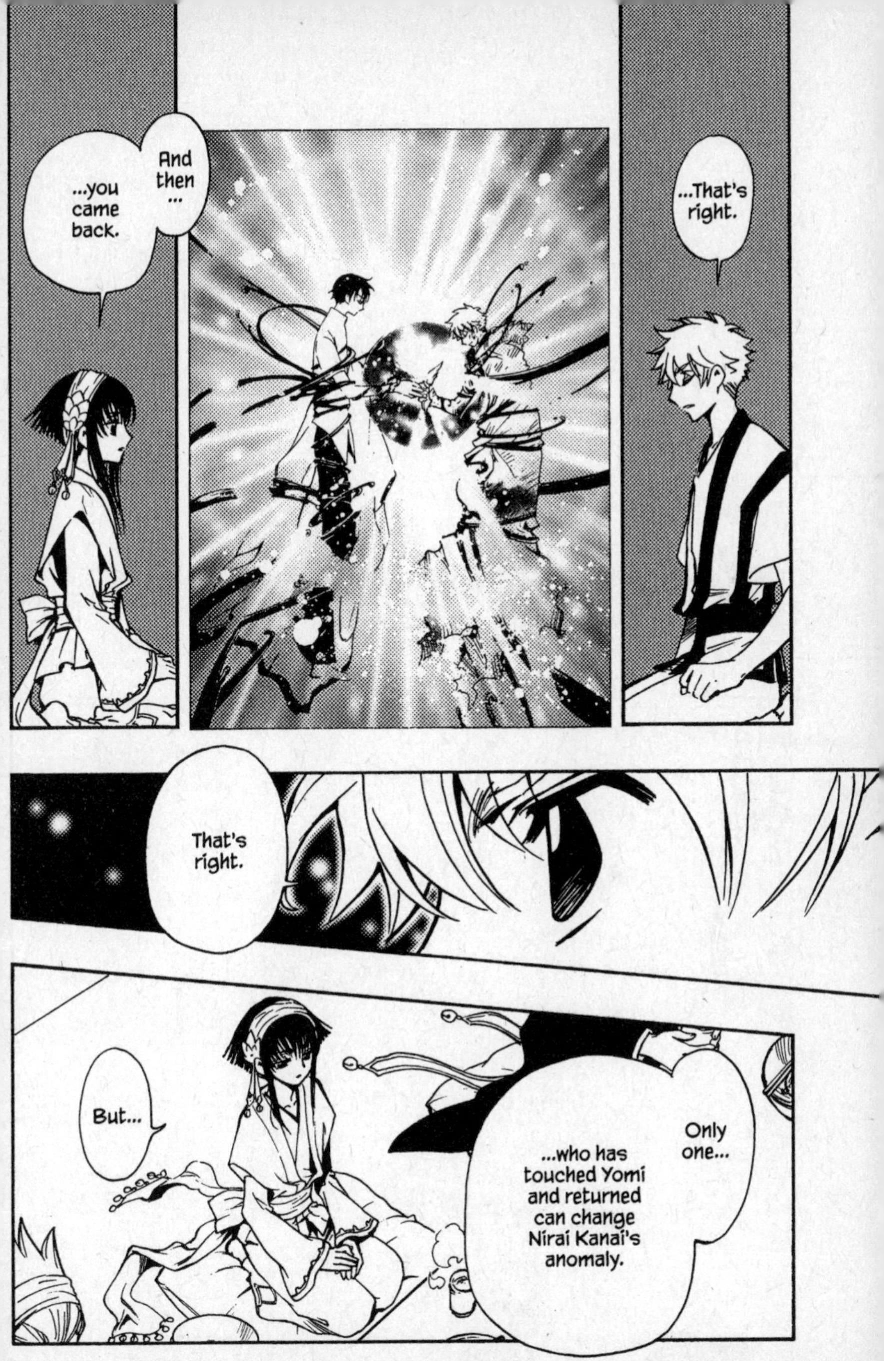
...That's right.
And then ...
...you came back.
That's right.
Only one...
...who has touched Yomi and returned can change Nirai Kanai's anomaly.
But...

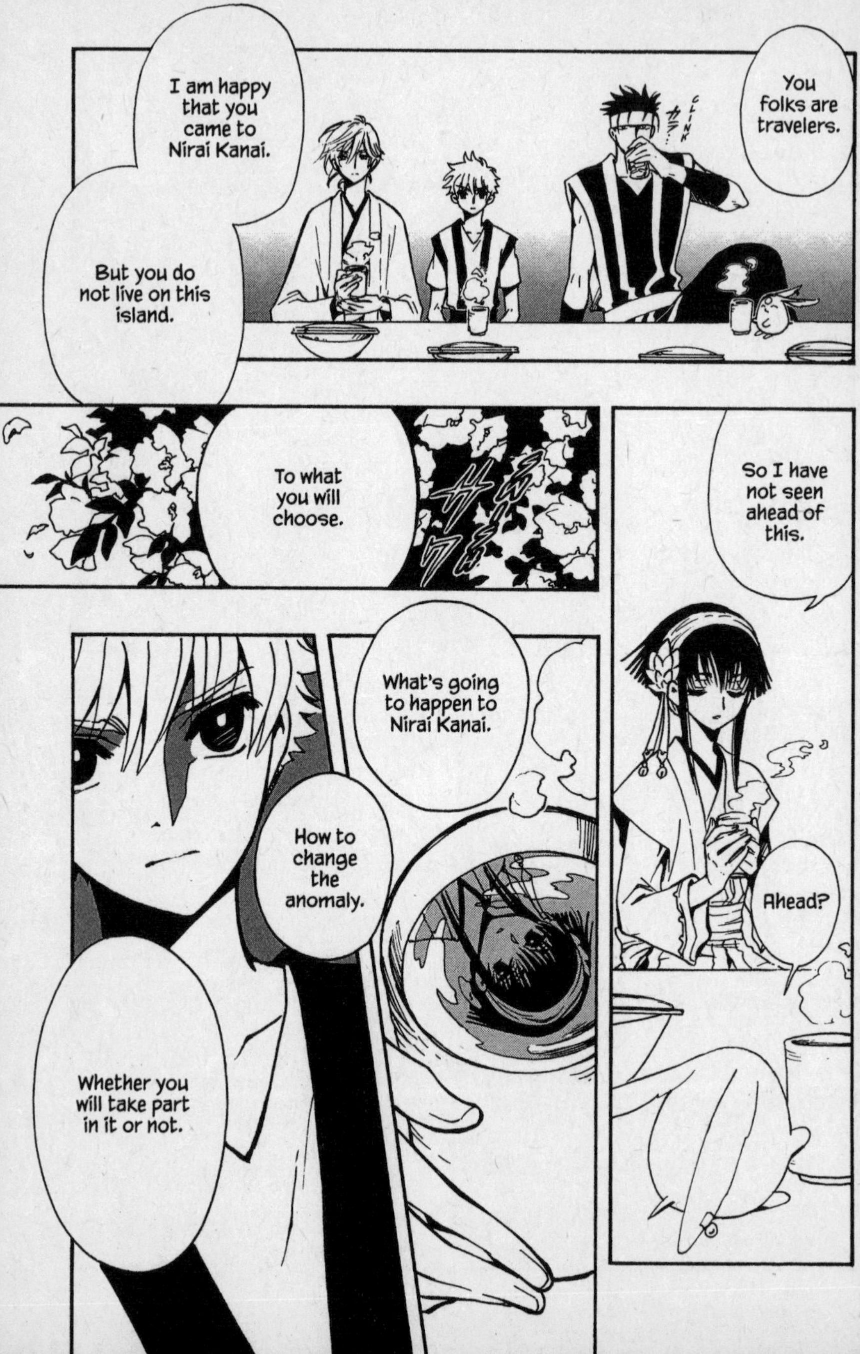

You folks are travelers.
CLINK
I am happy that you came to Nirai Kanai.
But you do not live on this island.
So I have not seen ahead of this.
Ahead?
To what you will choose.
What's going to happen to Nirai Kanai.
How to change the anomaly.
Whether you will take part in it or not.

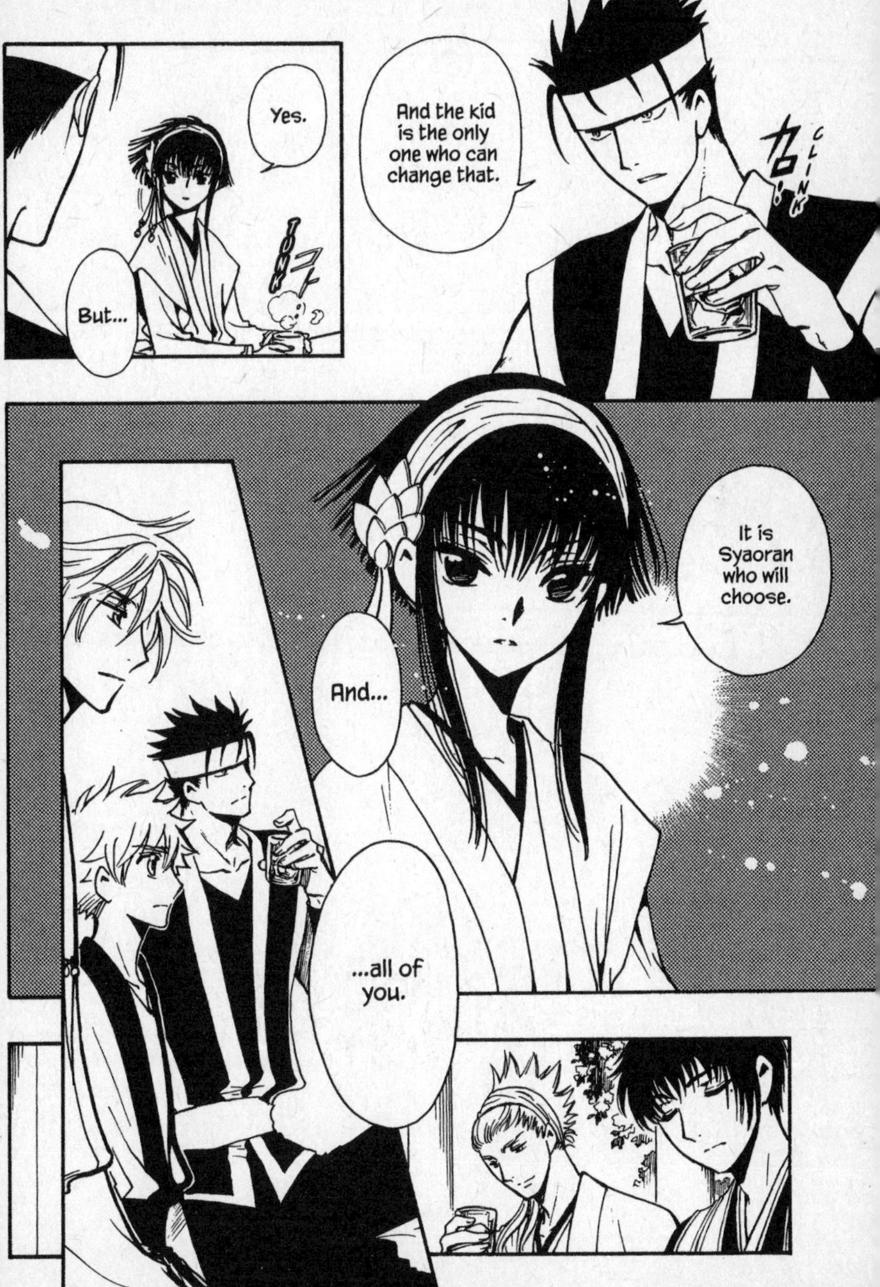
And the kid is the only one who can change that.
CLINK
Yes.
TONK
But...
It is Syaoran who will choose.
And...
...all of you.

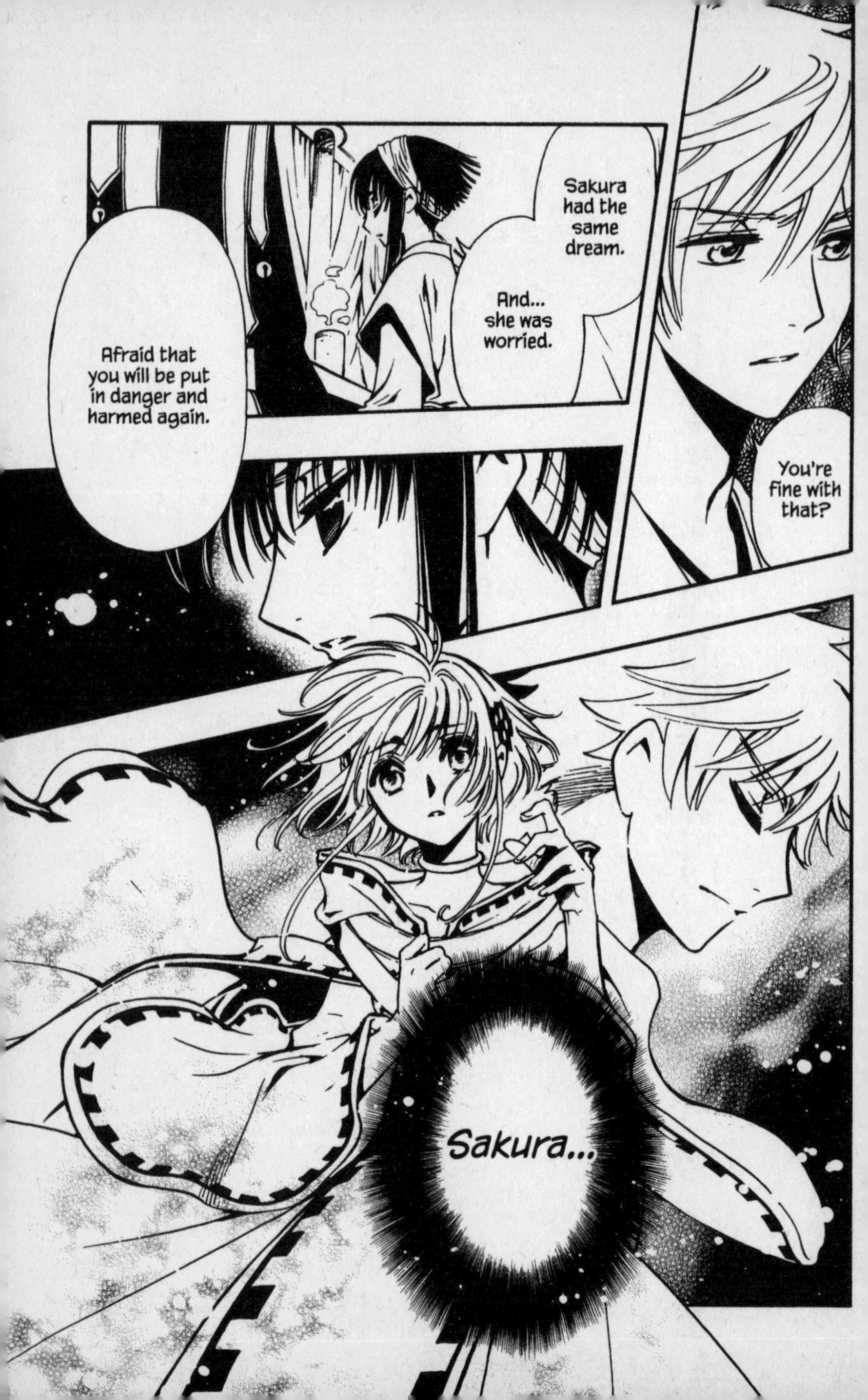
Sakura had the same dream.
And... she was worried.
Afraid that you will be put in danger and harmed again.
You're fine with that?
Sakura...

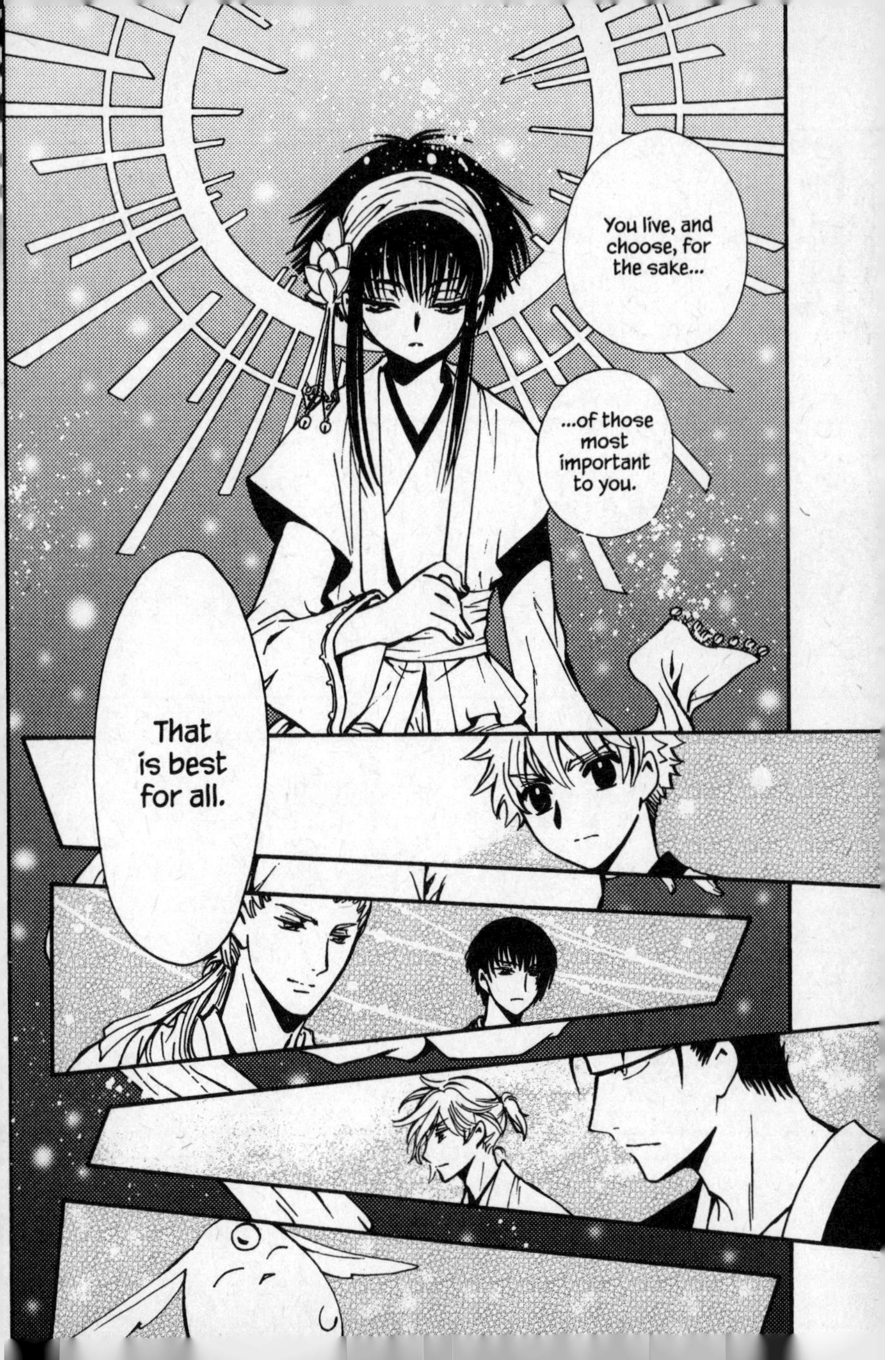
You live, and choose, for the sake...
...of those most important to you.
That is best for all.

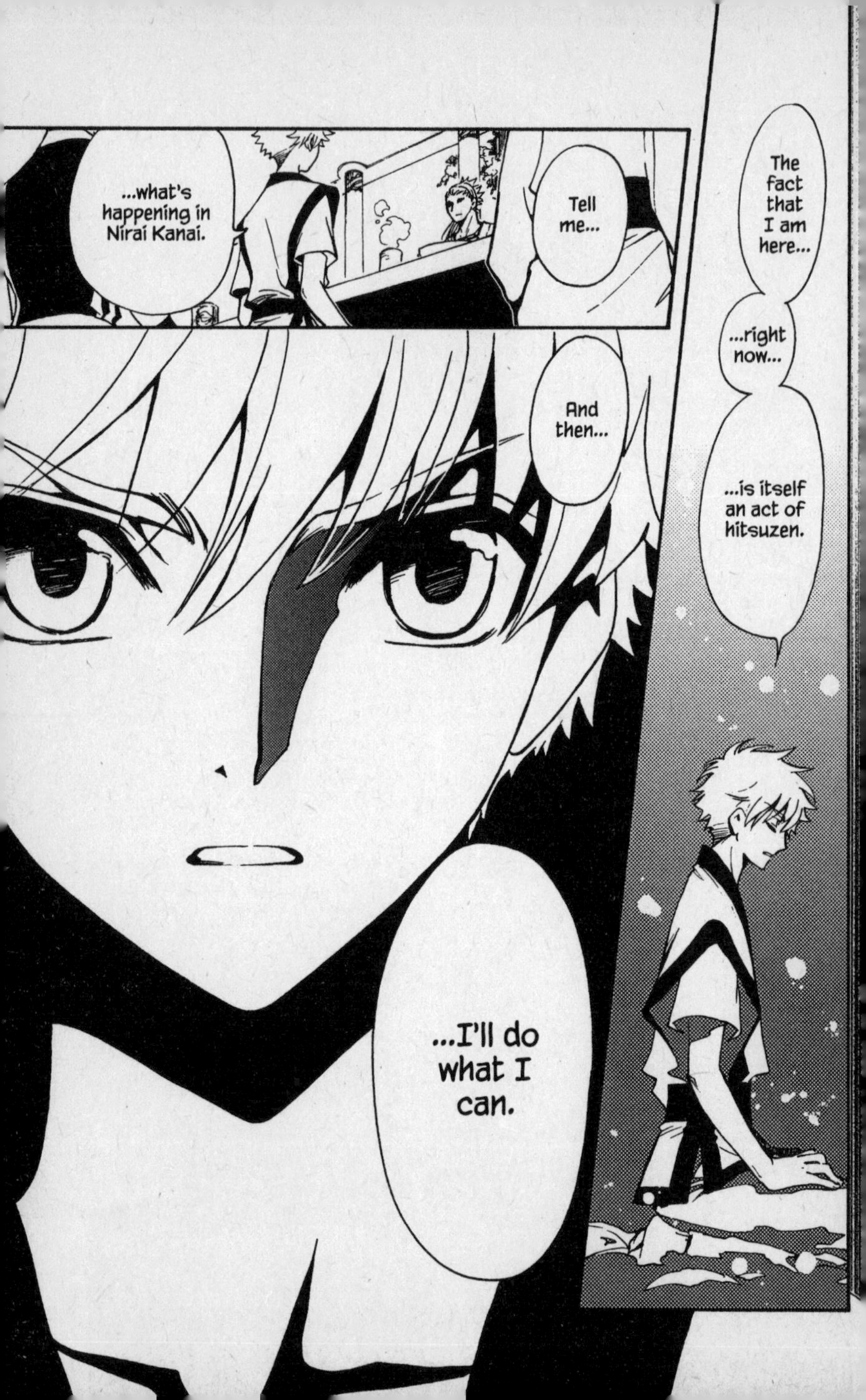
The fact that I am here...
...right now...
...is itself an act of hitsuzen.
Tell me...
...what's happening in Nirai Kanai.
And then...
...I'll do what I can.

TSUBASA

WoRLD CHRoNiCLE: NIRAIKANAI

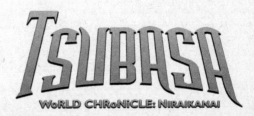

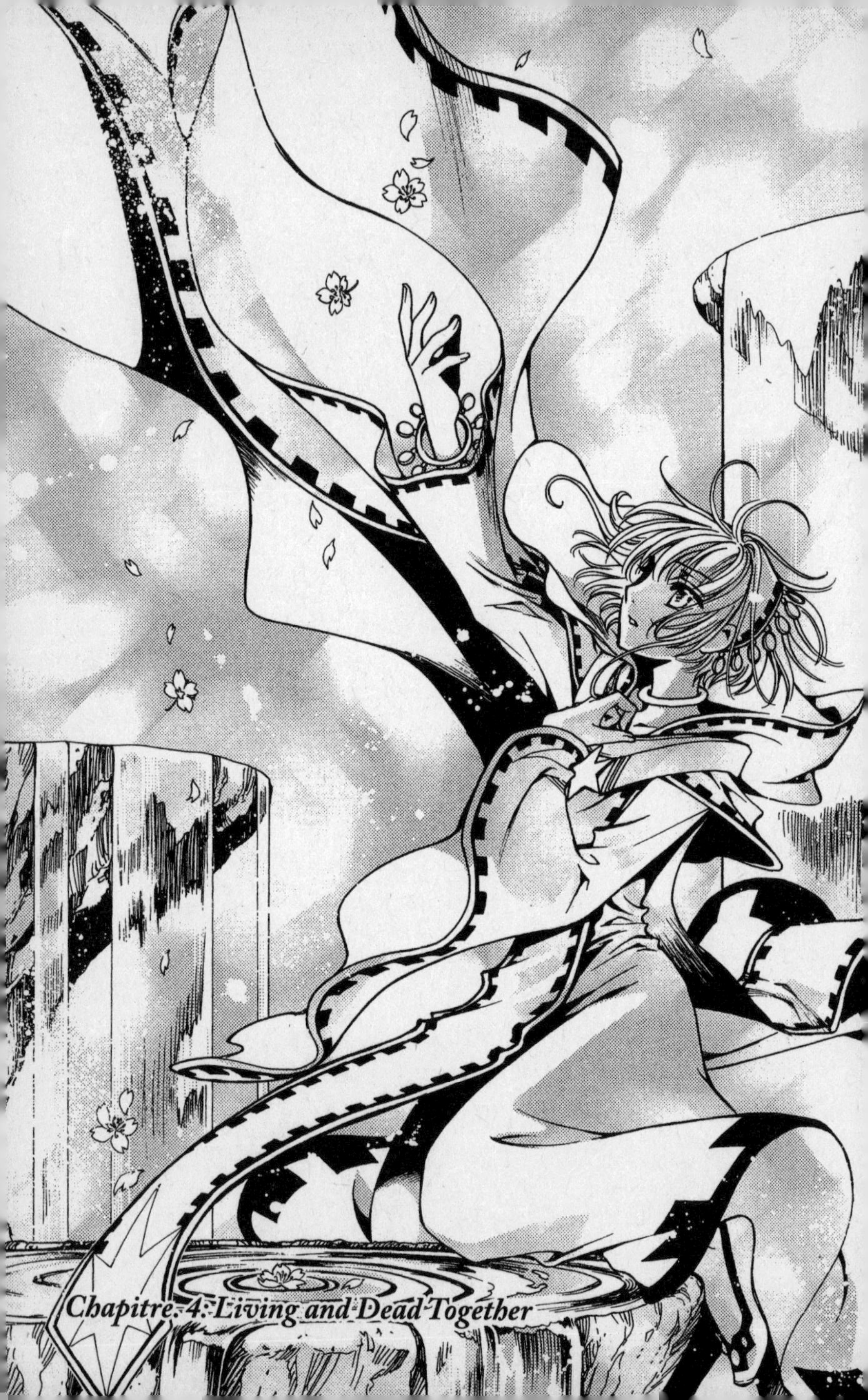
Chapitre. 4: Living and Dead Together

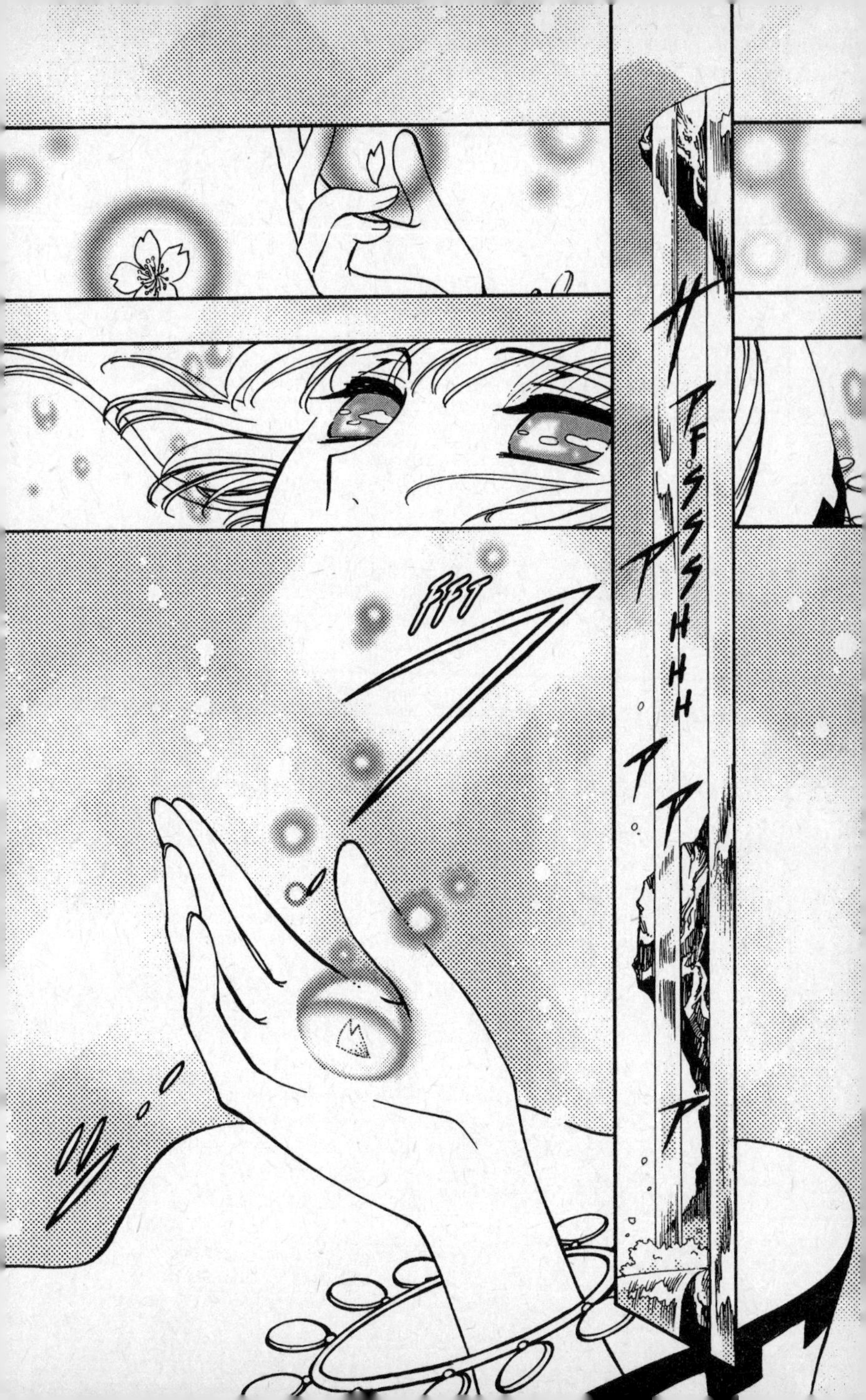
PFSSSHHH
FFT

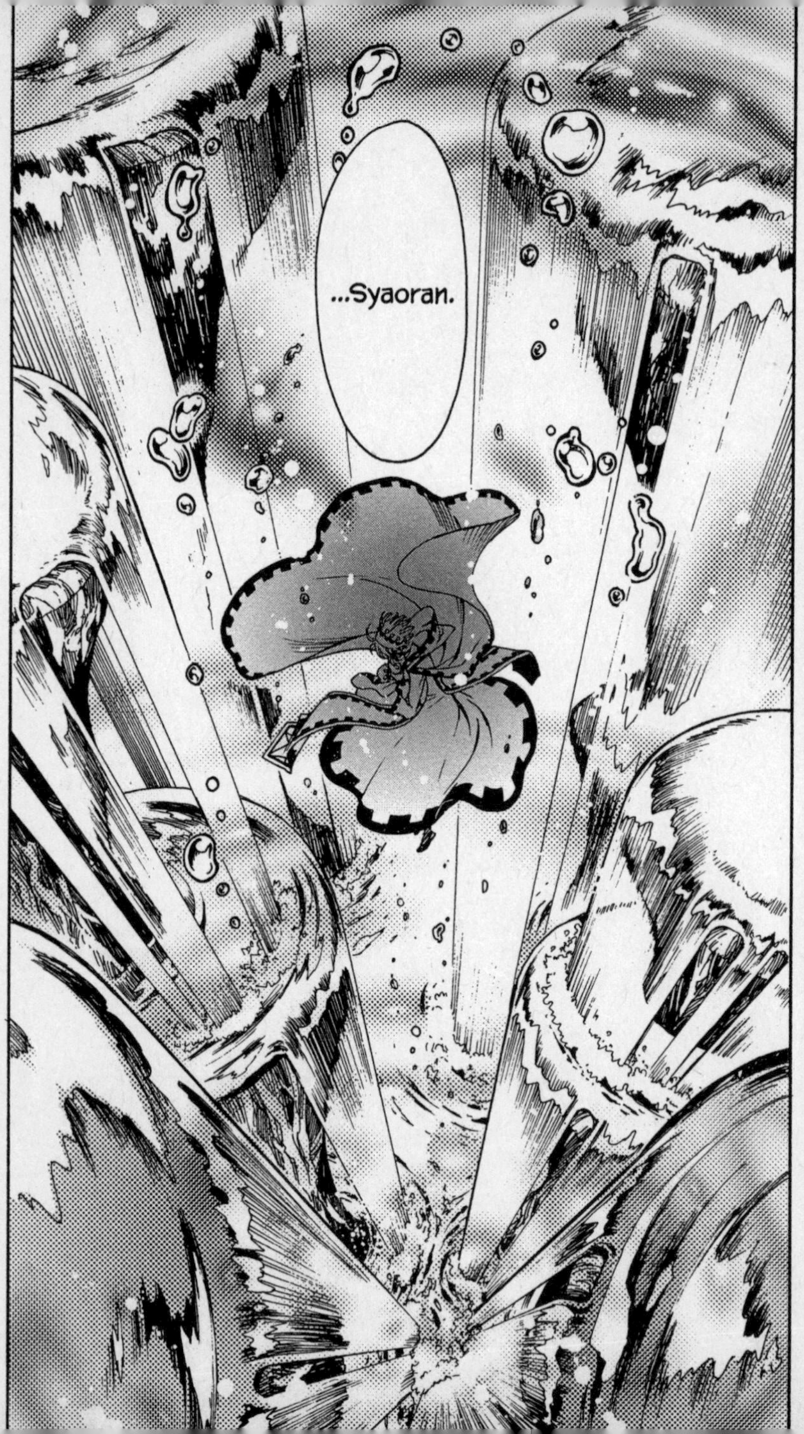
...Syaoran.

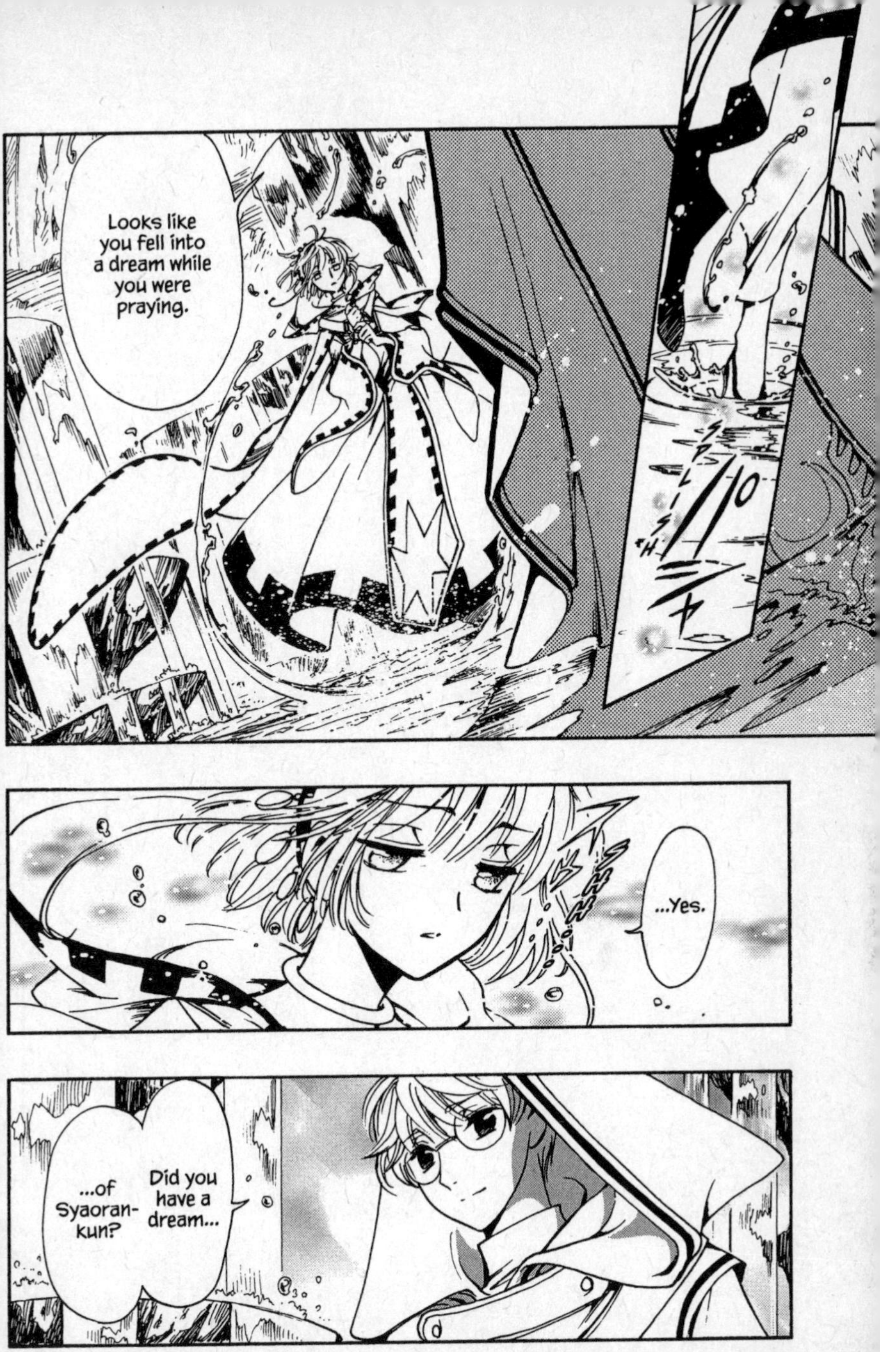
Looks like you fell into a dream while you were praying.
SPLISH
...Yes.
Did you have a dream...
...of Syaoran-kun?

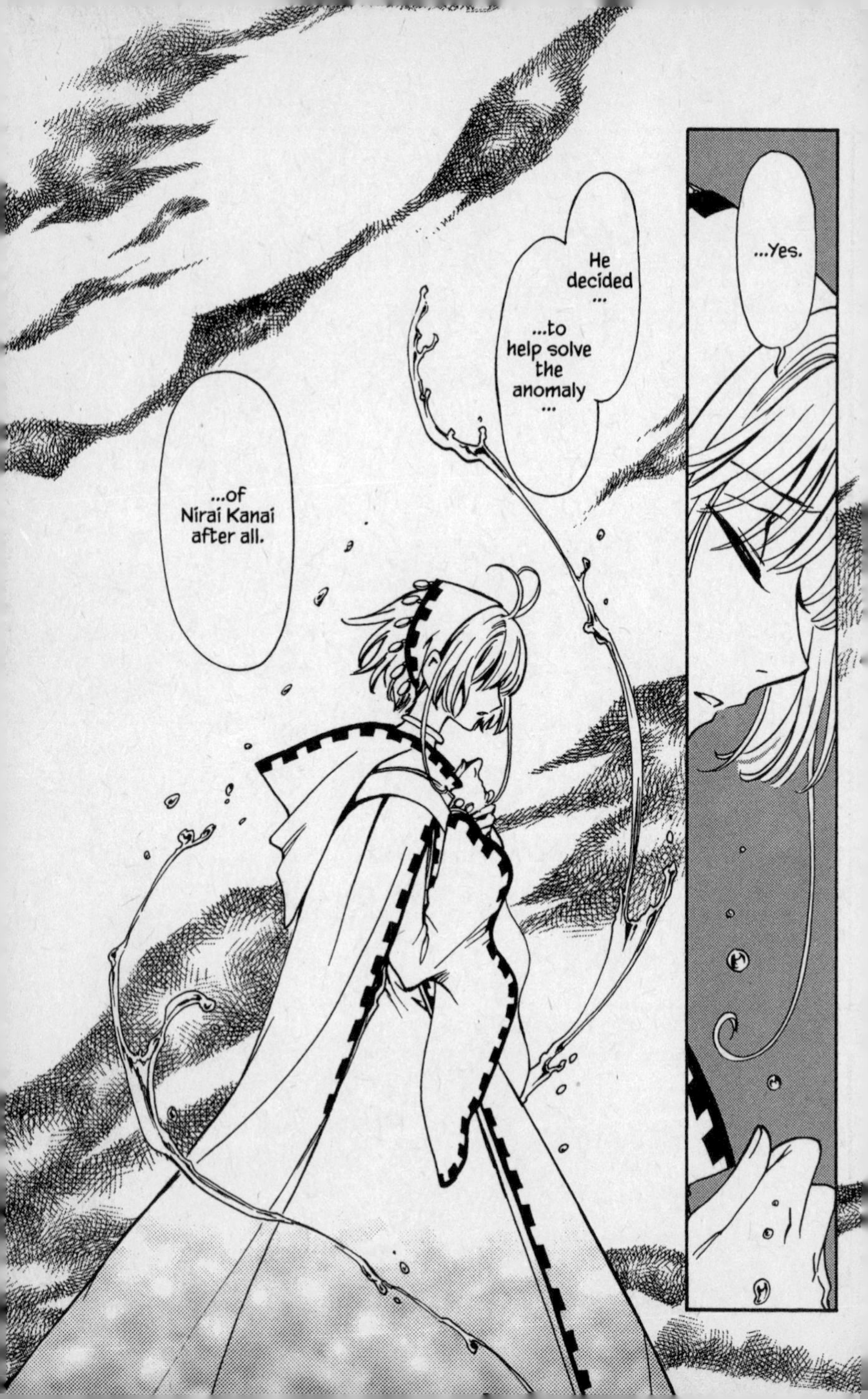
...Yes.
He decided ...
...to help solve the anomaly ...
...of Nirai Kanai after all.

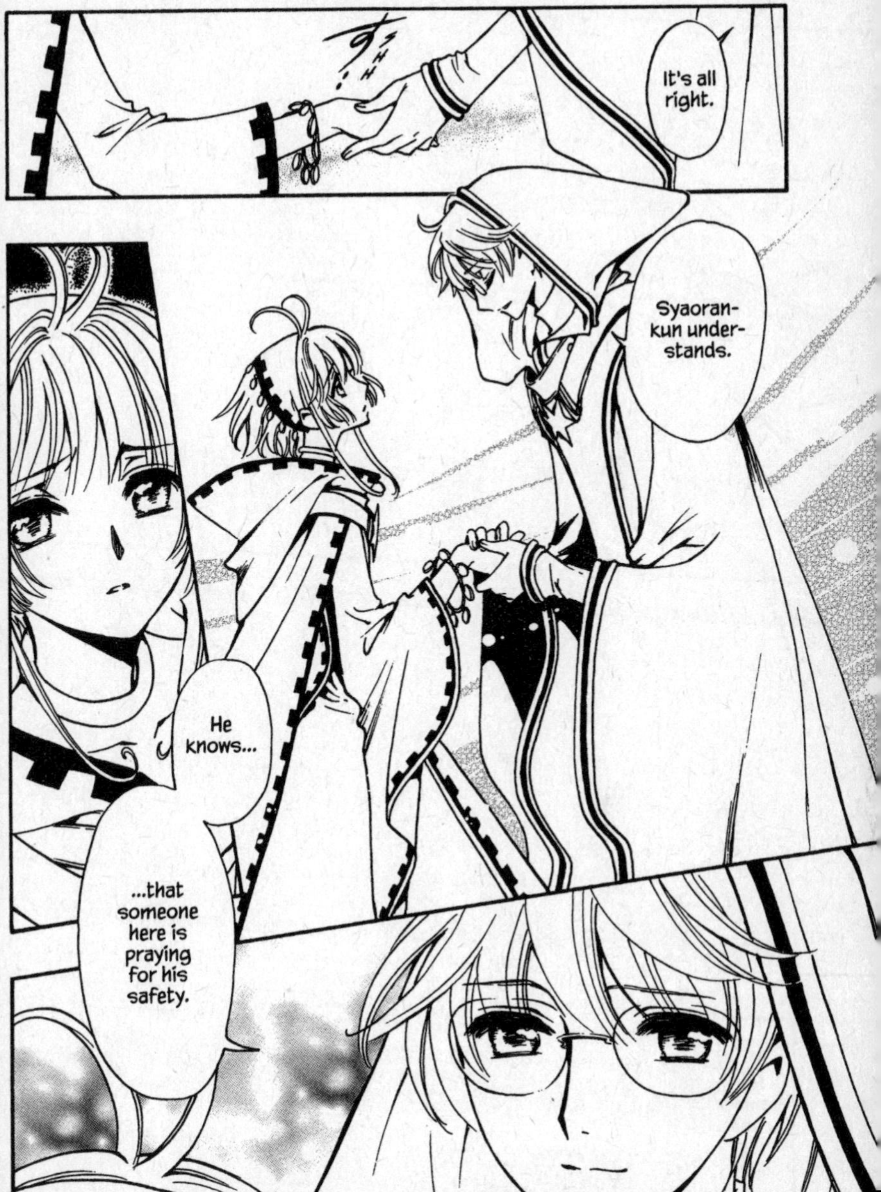
It's all right.
Syaoran-kun under-stands.
He knows...
...that someone here is praying for his safety.

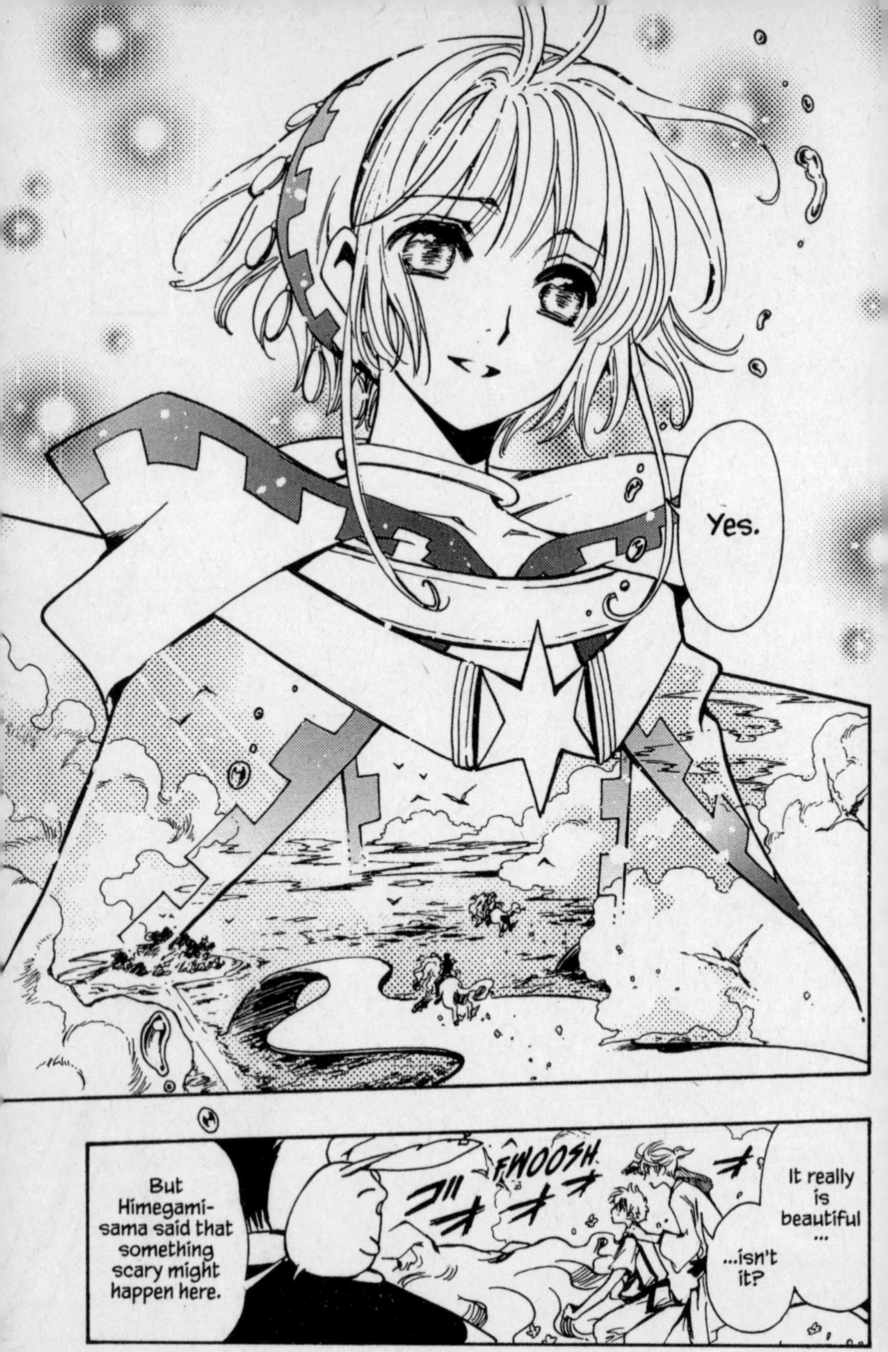
Yes.
It really is beautiful ...
...isn't it?
FWOOSH
But Himegami-sama said that something scary might happen here.

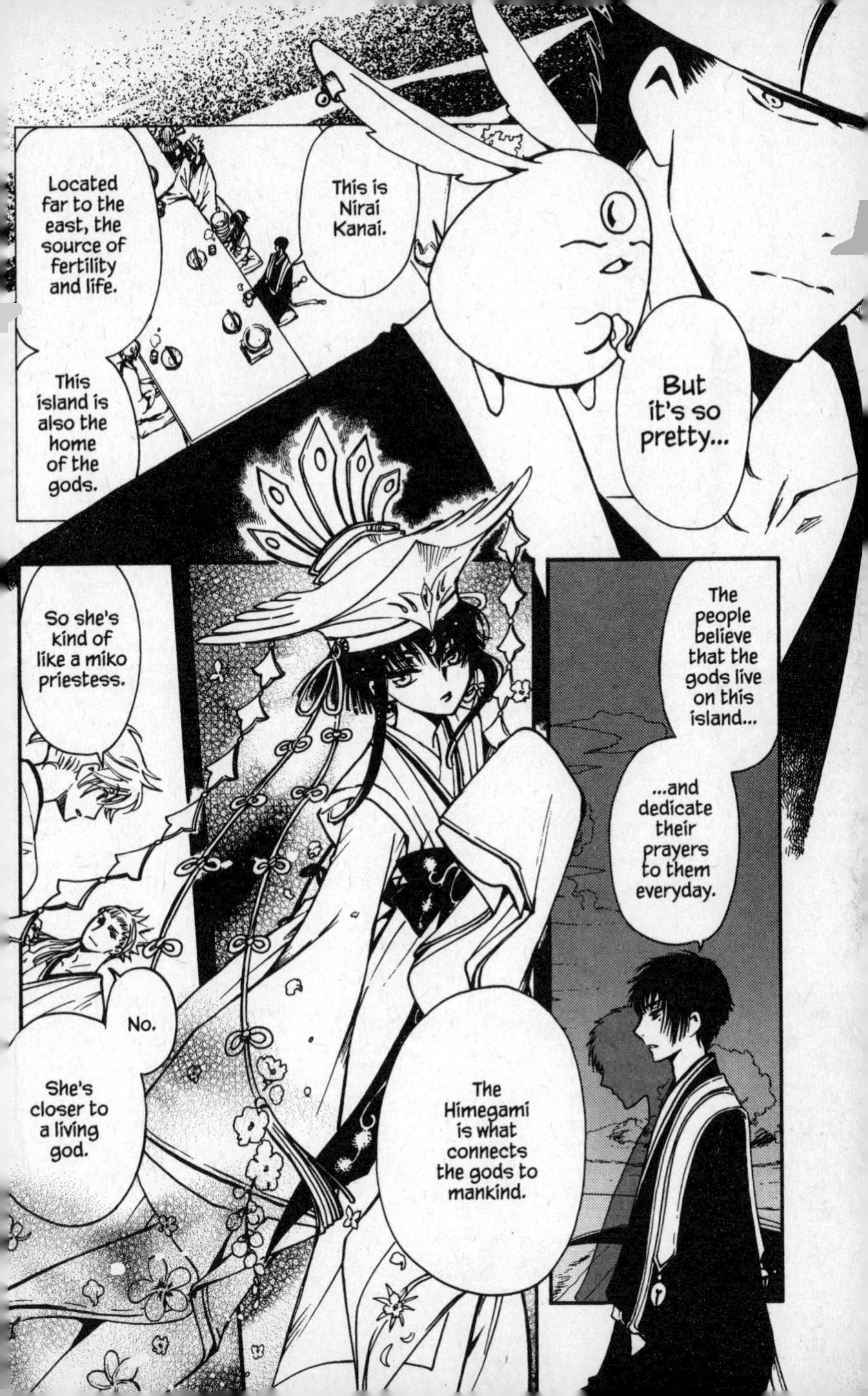
This is Nirai Kanai.
But it's so pretty...
Located far to the east, the source of fertility and life.
This island is also the home of the gods.
The people believe that the gods live on this island...
...and dedicate their prayers to them everyday.
The Himegami is what connects the gods to mankind.
So she's kind of like a miko priestess.
No.
She's closer to a living god.

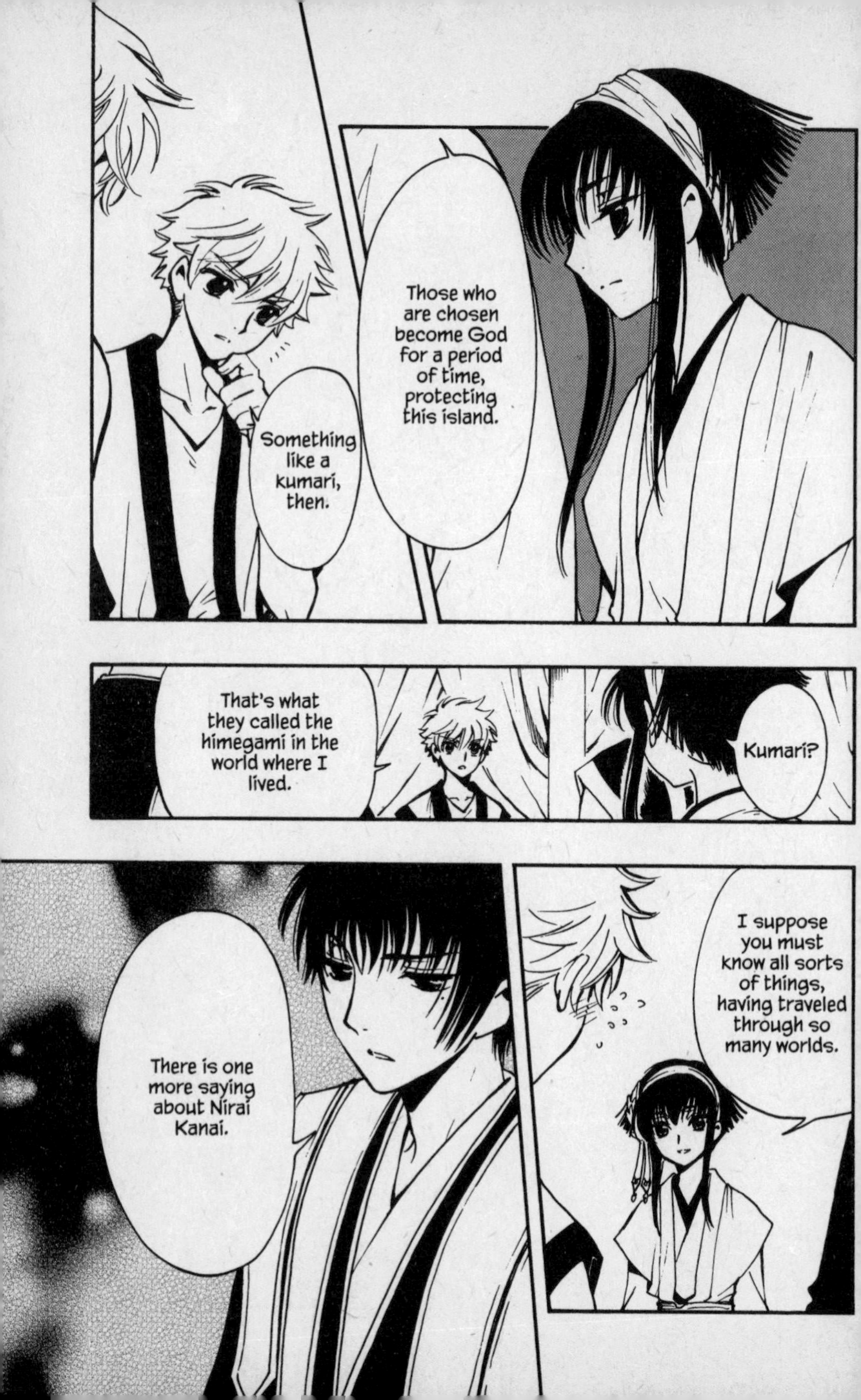

Those who are chosen become God for a period of time, protecting this island.
Something like a kumari, then.
Kumari?
That's what they called the himegami in the world where I lived.
I suppose you must know all sorts of things, having traveled through so many worlds.
There is one more saying about Nirai Kanai.

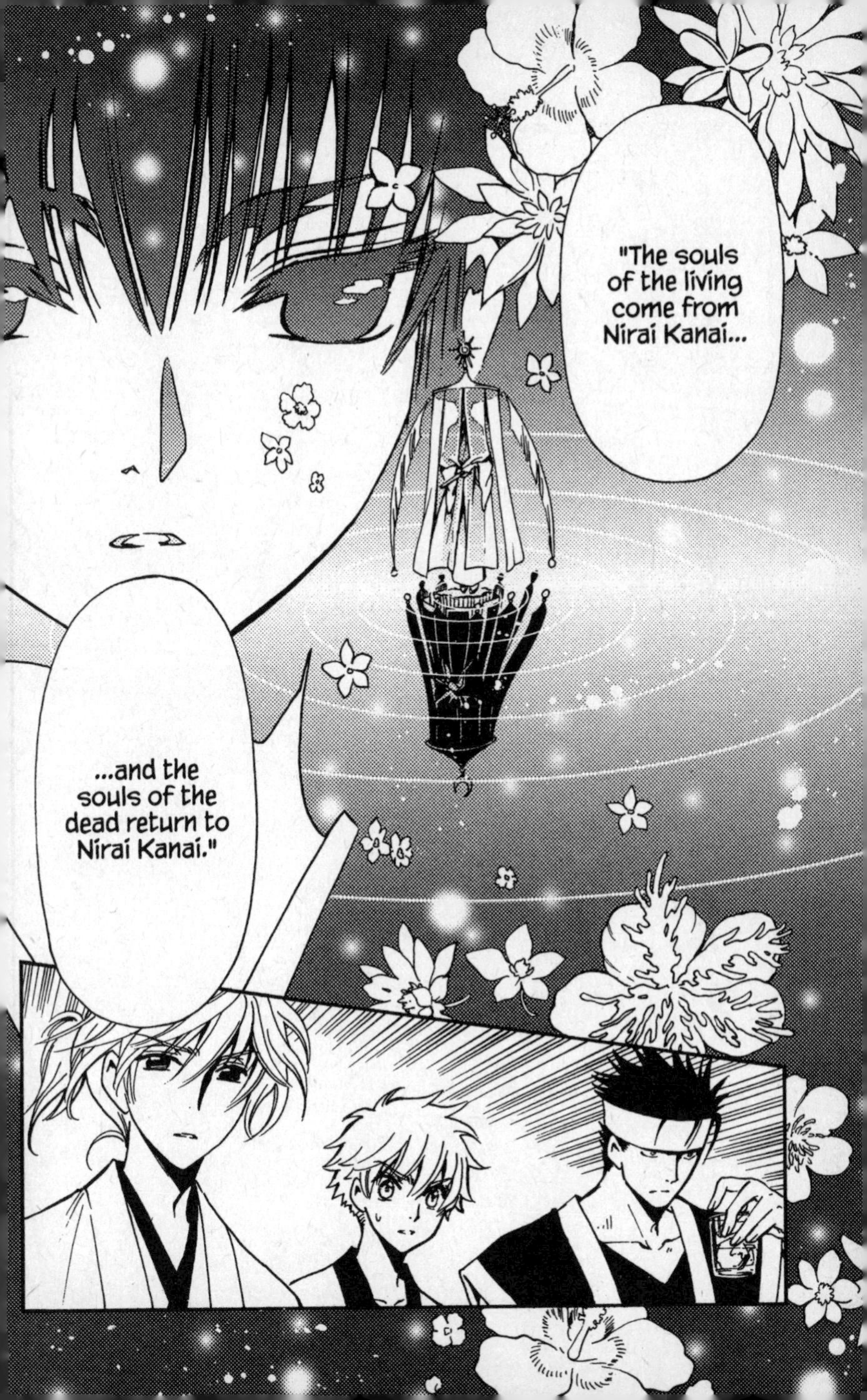
"The souls of the living come from Nirai Kanai...
...and the souls of the dead return to Nirai Kanai."

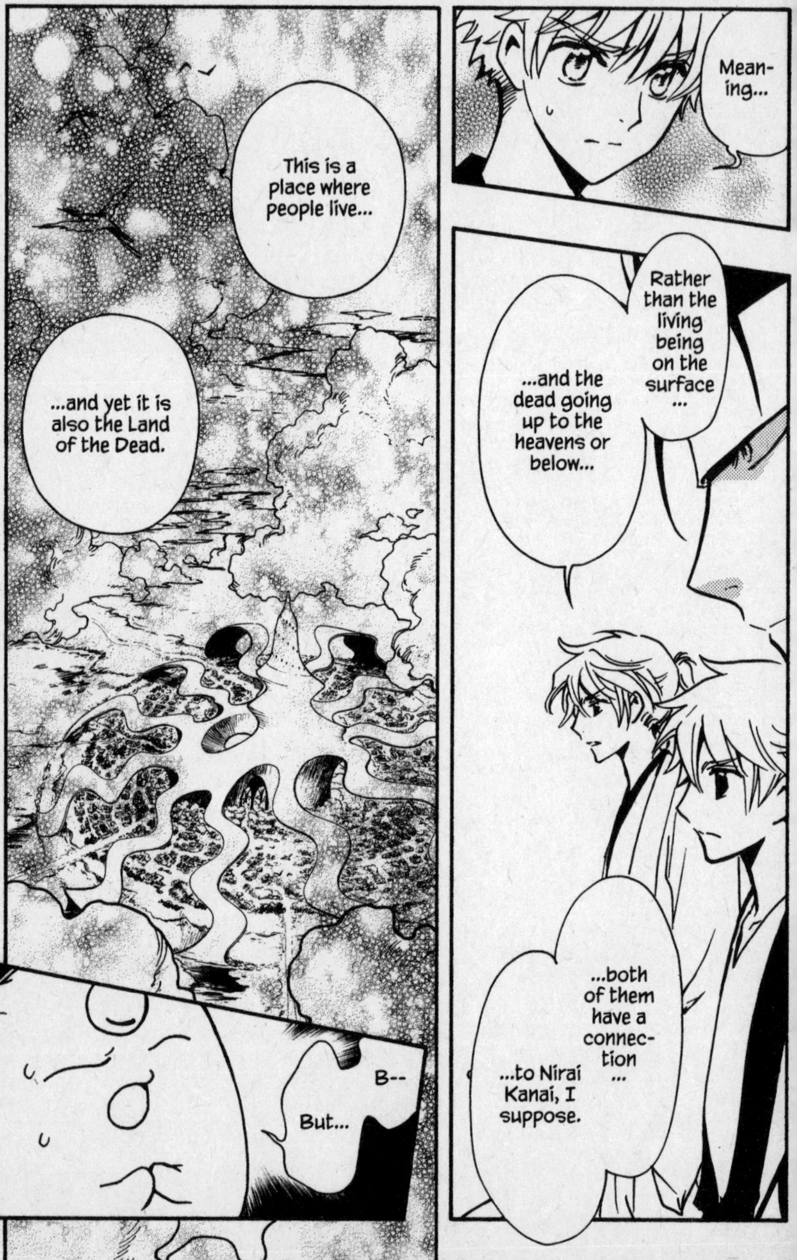
Meaning...
Rather than the living being on the surface...
...and the dead going up to the heavens or below...
...both of them have a connection...
...to Nirai Kanai, I suppose.
This is a place where people live...
...and yet it is also the Land of the Dead.
B--
But...

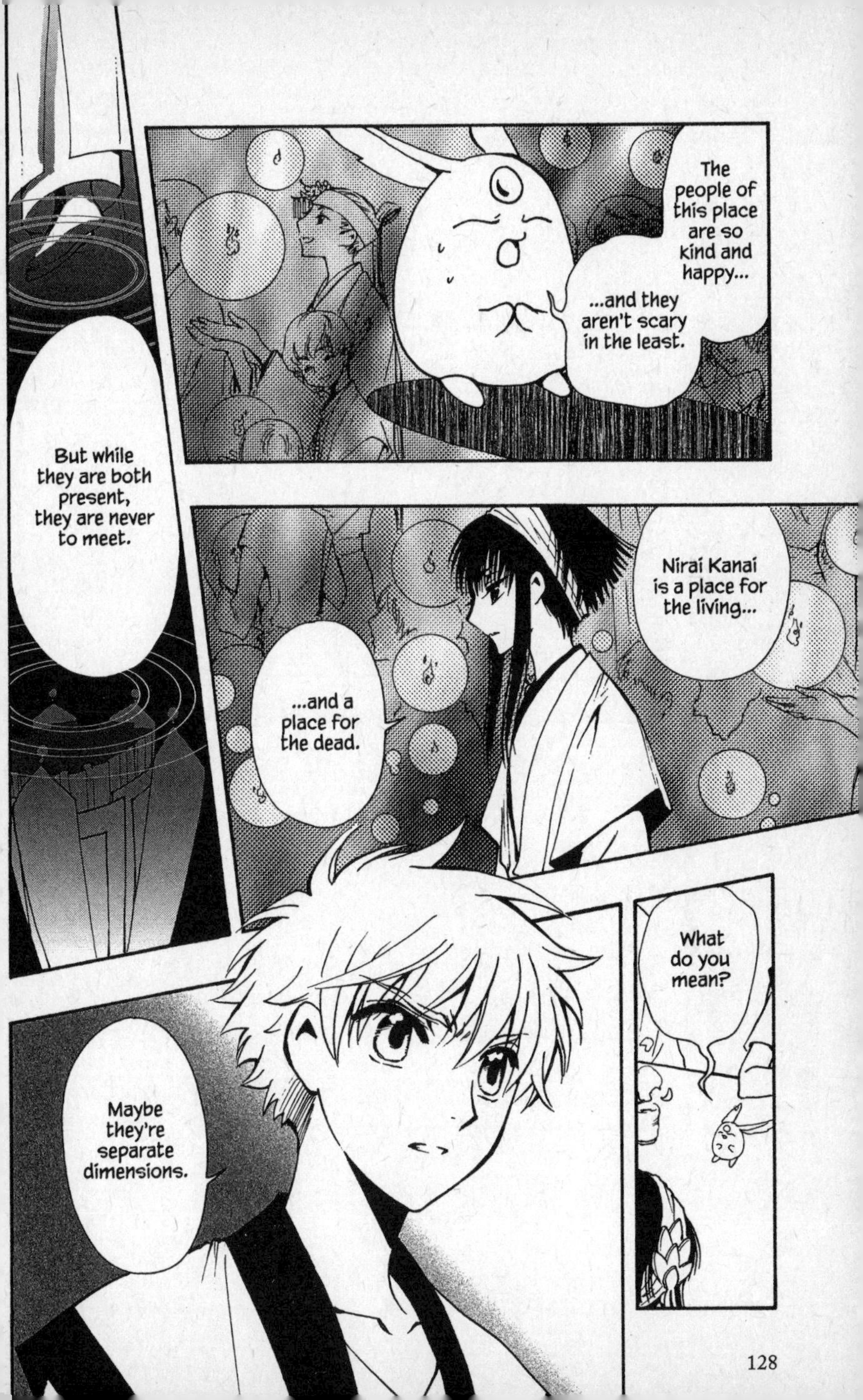
The people of this place are so kind and happy...
...and they aren't scary in the least.
Nirai Kanai is a place for the living...
...and a place for the dead.
But while they are both present, they are never to meet.
What do you mean?
Maybe they're separate dimensions.

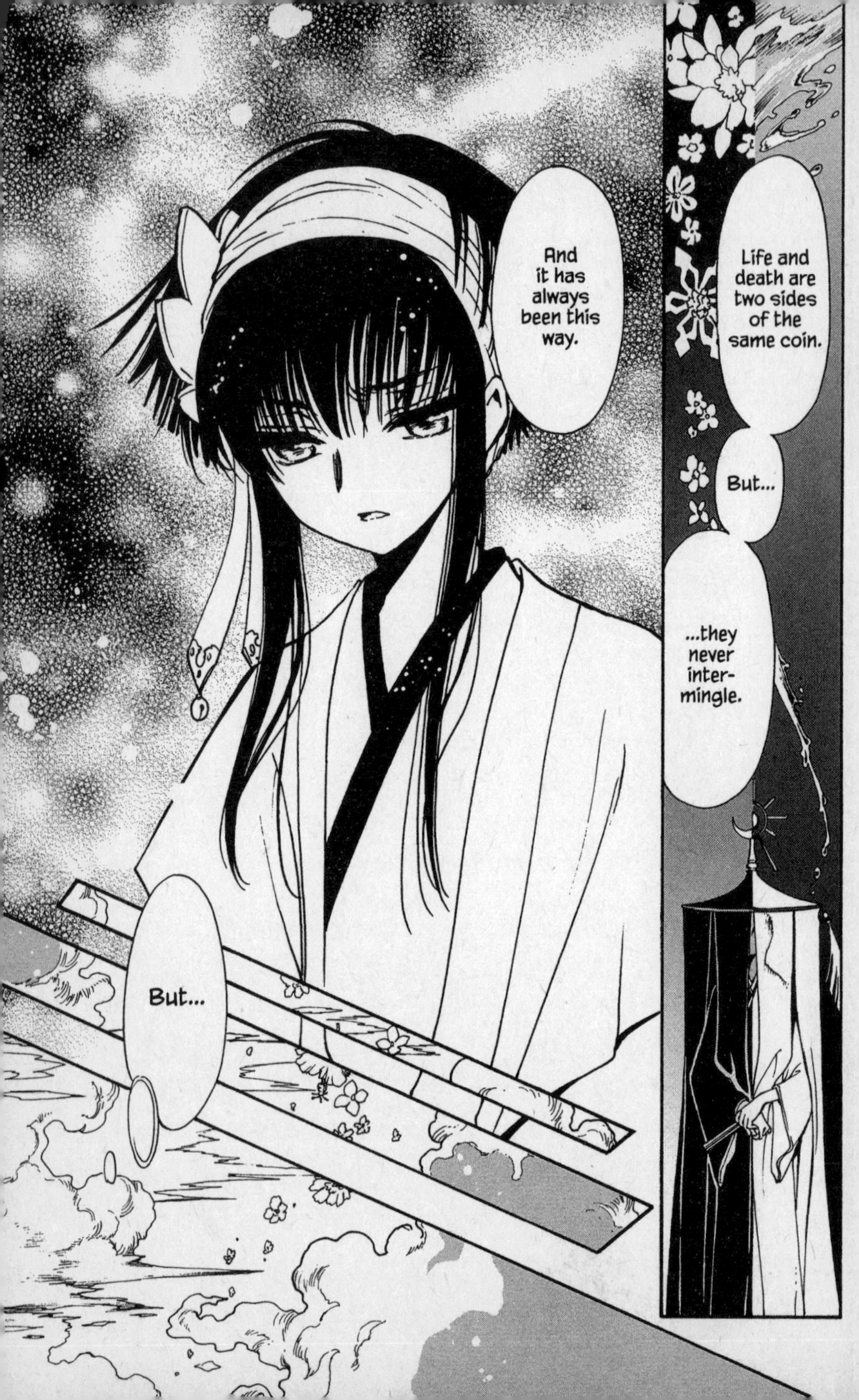
Life and death are two sides of the same coin.
But...
...they never intermingle.
And it has always been this way.
But...

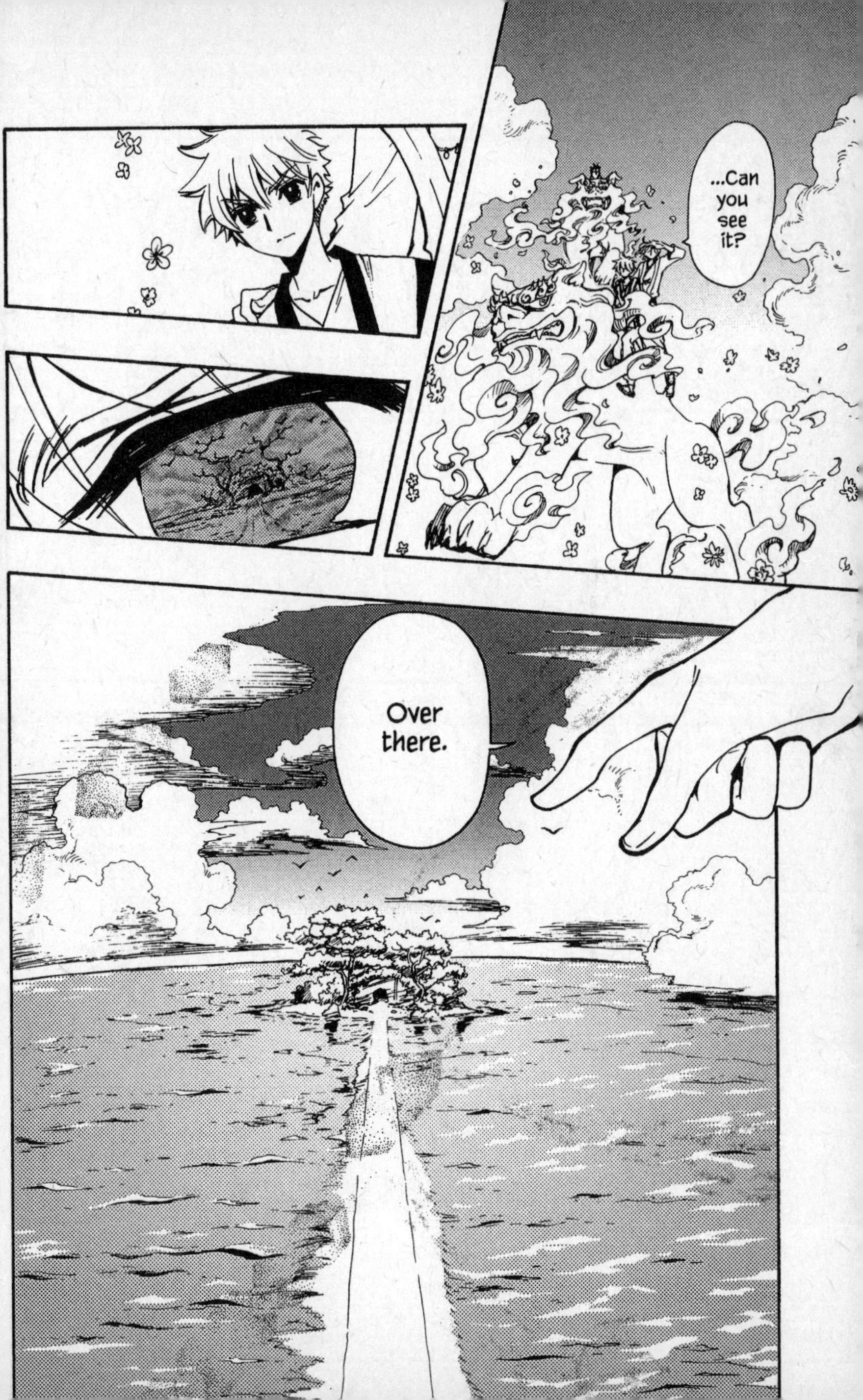
...Can you see it?
Over there.

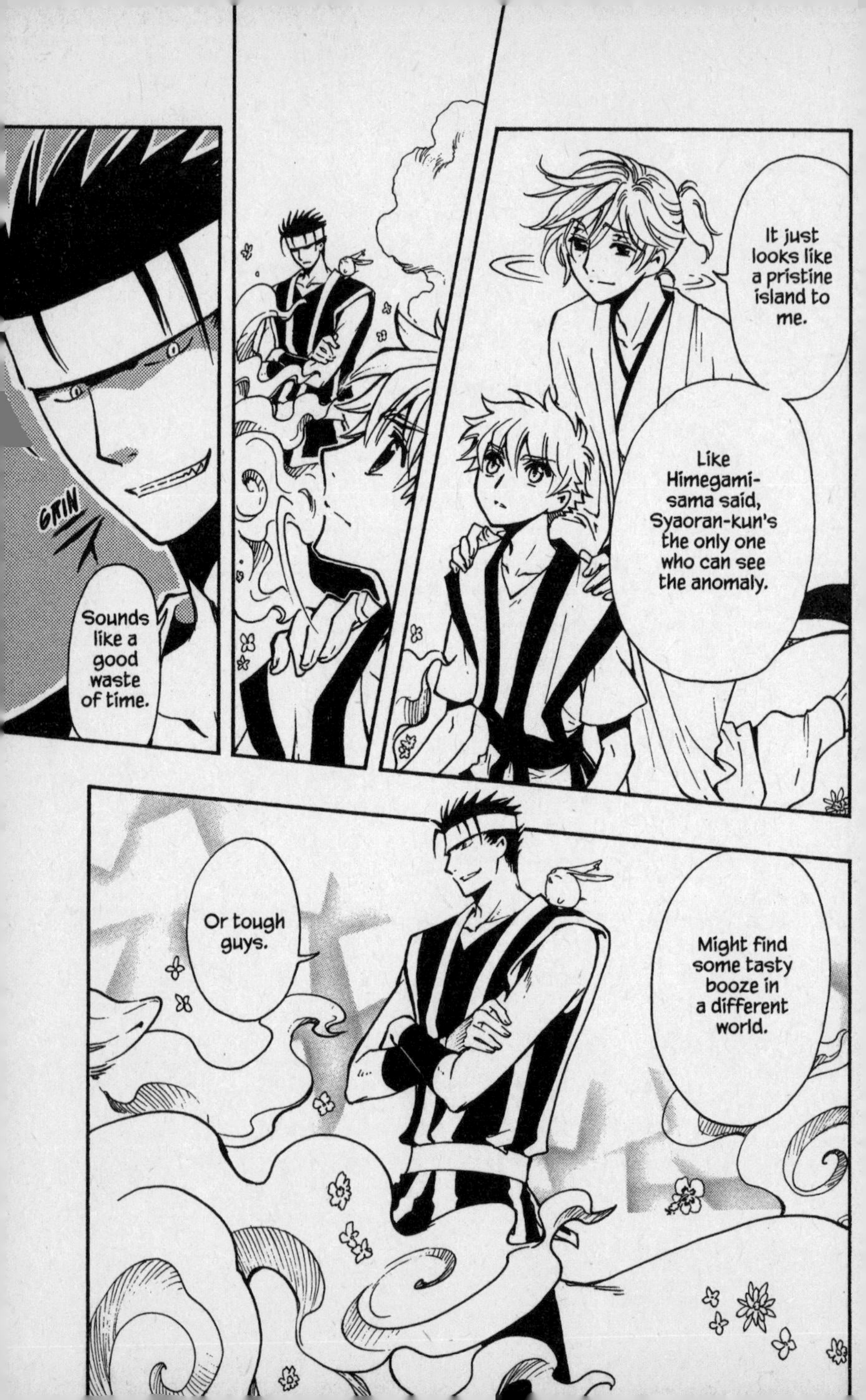
It just looks like a pristine island to me.
Like Himegami-sama said, Syaoran-kun's the only one who can see the anomaly.
GRIN
Sounds like a good waste of time.
Might find some tasty booze in a different world.
Or tough guys.

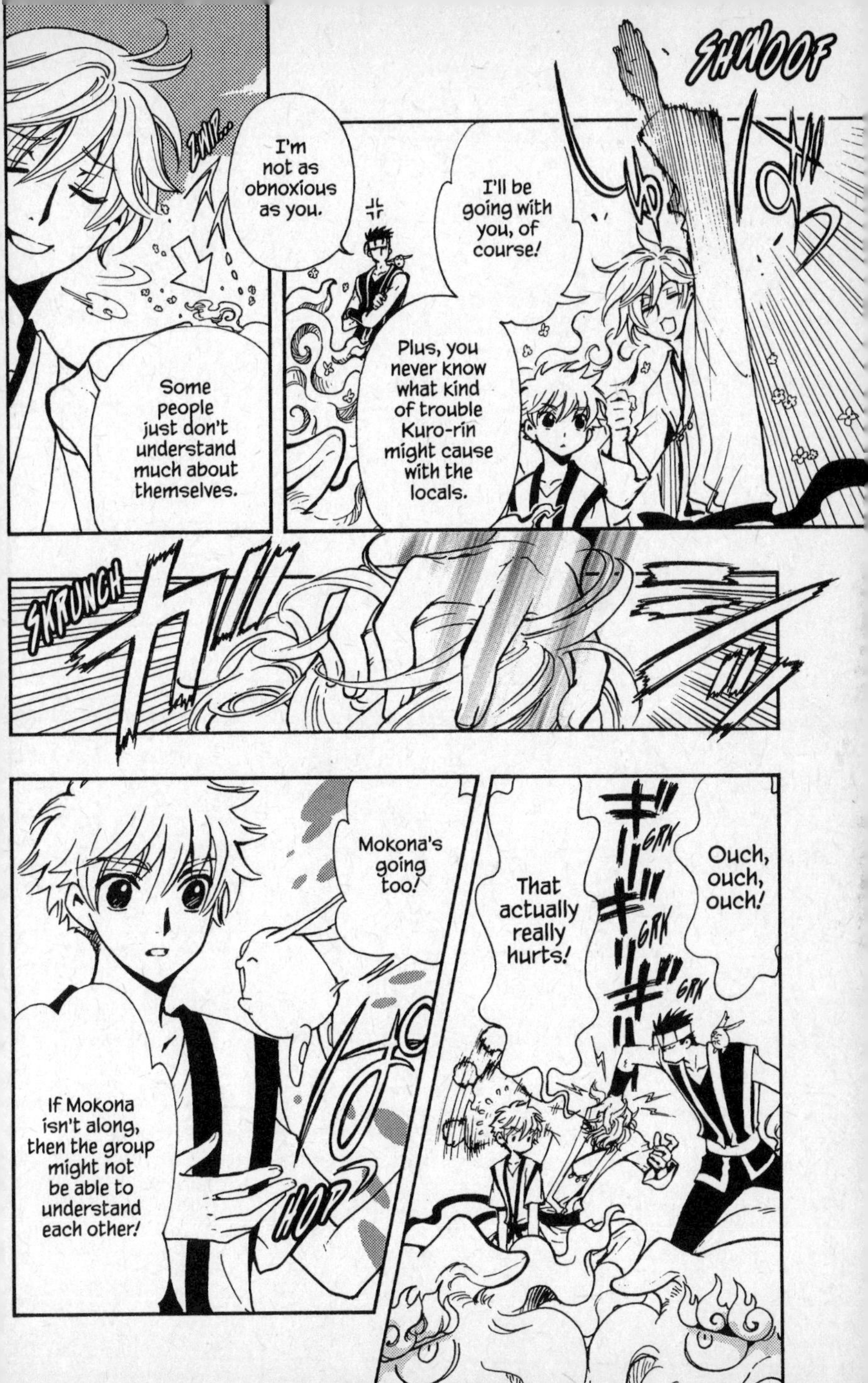
SHWOOF
I'll be going with you, of course!
Plus, you never know what kind of trouble Kuro-rin might cause with the locals.
I'm not as obnoxious as you.
ZWIP...
Some people just don't understand much about themselves.
SKRUNCH
Ouch, ouch, ouch!
That actually really hurts!
GRN
GRN
GRN
Mokona's going too!
HOP
If Mokona isn't along, then the group might not be able to understand each other!

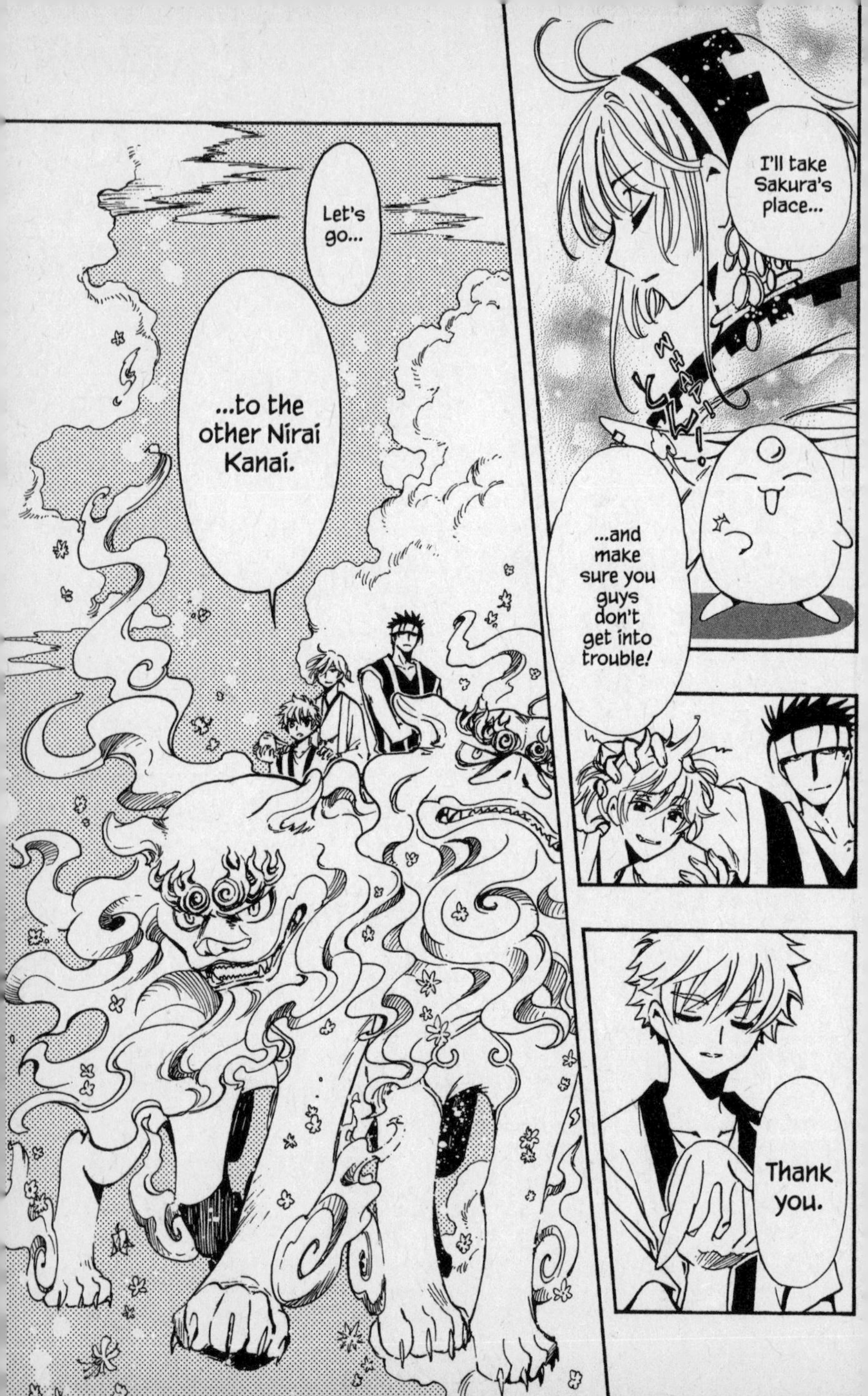
I'll take Sakura's place...
WHAAA!
...and make sure you guys don't get into trouble!
Thank you.
Let's go...
...to the other Nirai Kanai.

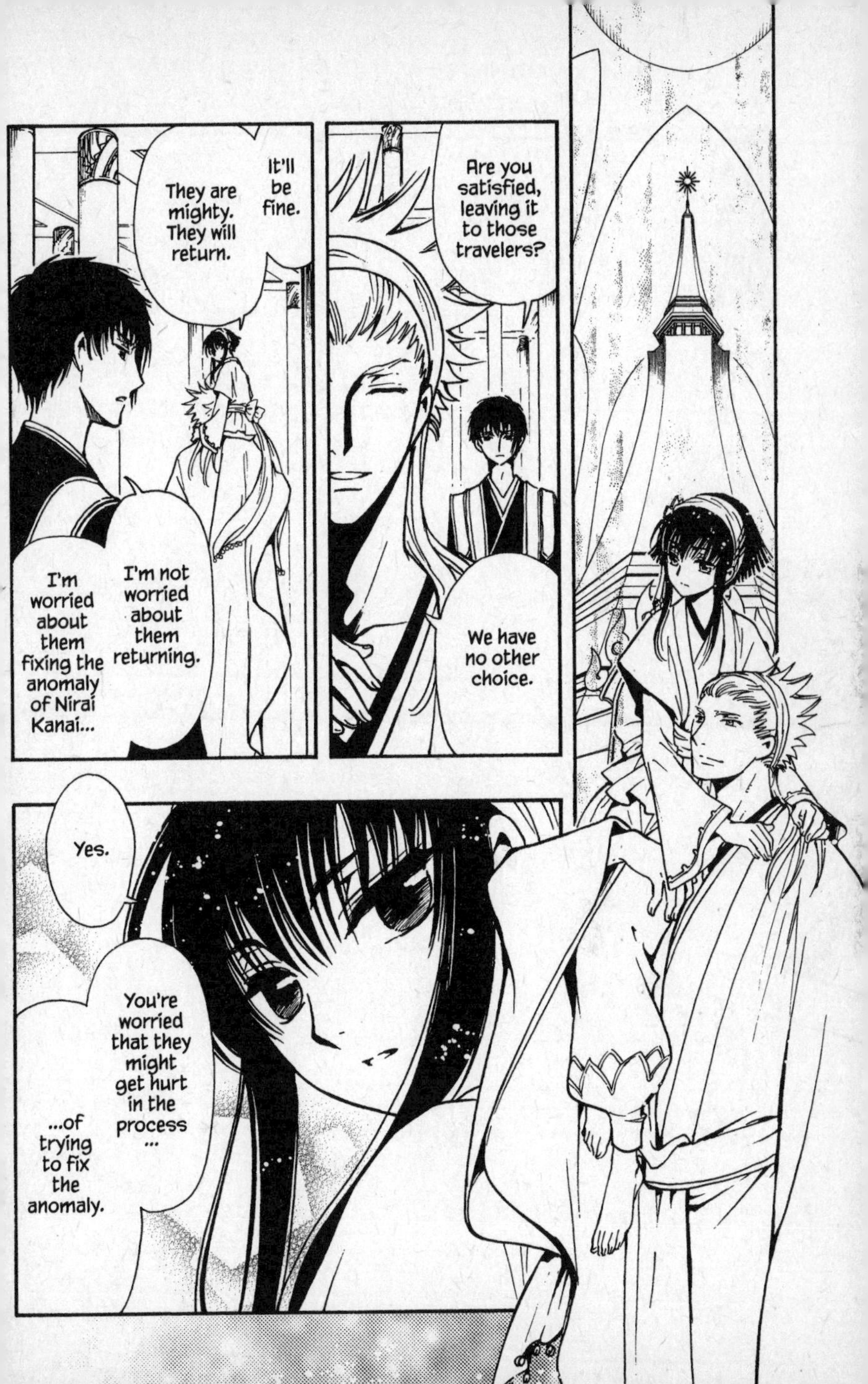
Are you satisfied, leaving it to those travelers?
We have no other choice.
It'll be fine.
They are mighty. They will return.
I'm not worried about them returning.
I'm worried about them fixing the anomaly of Nirai Kanai...
Yes.
You're worried that they might get hurt in the process...
...of trying to fix the anomaly.

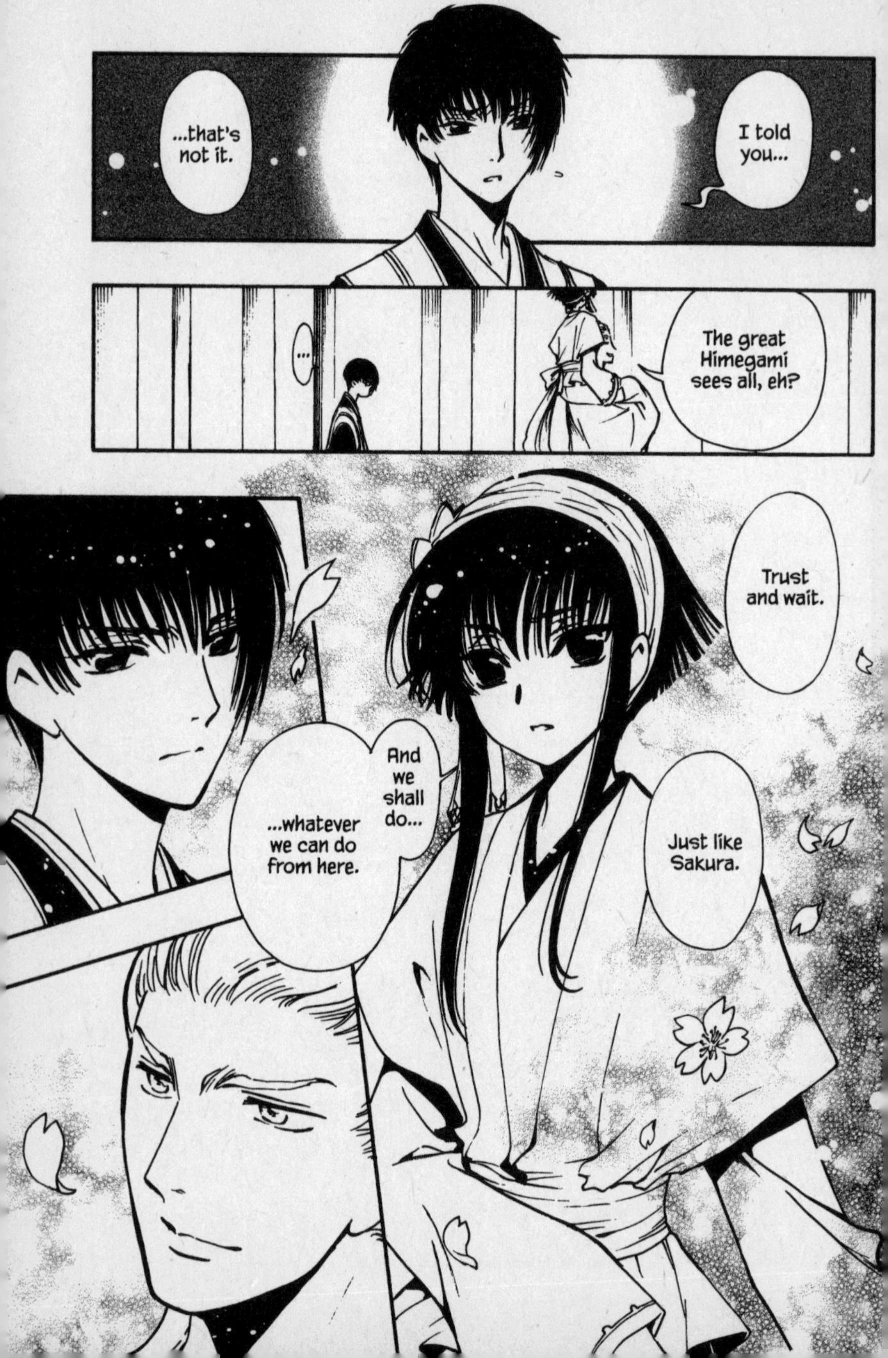
I told you...
...that's not it.
The great Himegami sees all, eh?
...
Trust and wait.
Just like Sakura.
And we shall do...
...whatever we can do from here.

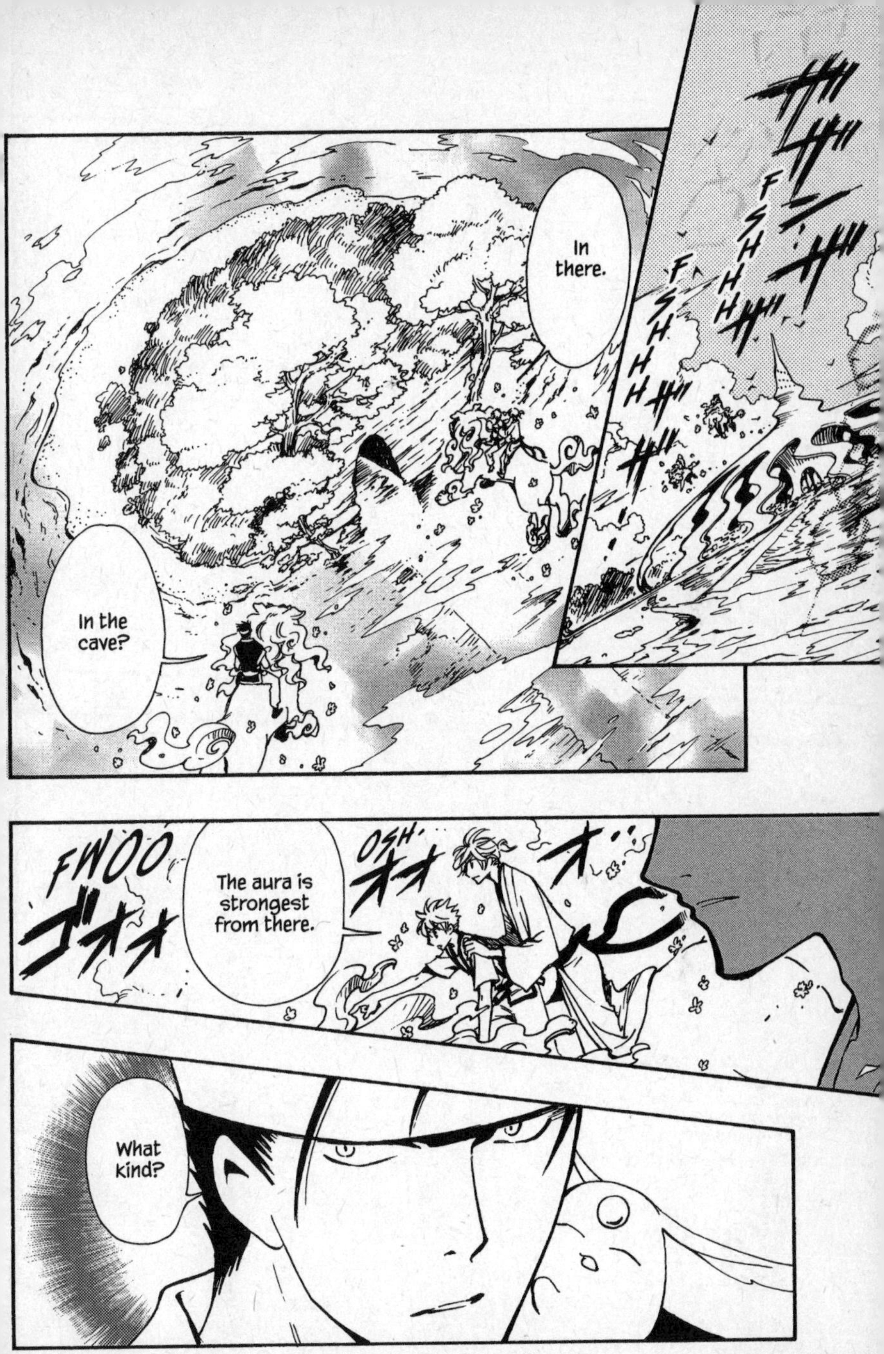
FSHHHH
FSHHHHH
In there.
In the cave?
OSH
The aura is strongest from there.
FWOO
What kind?

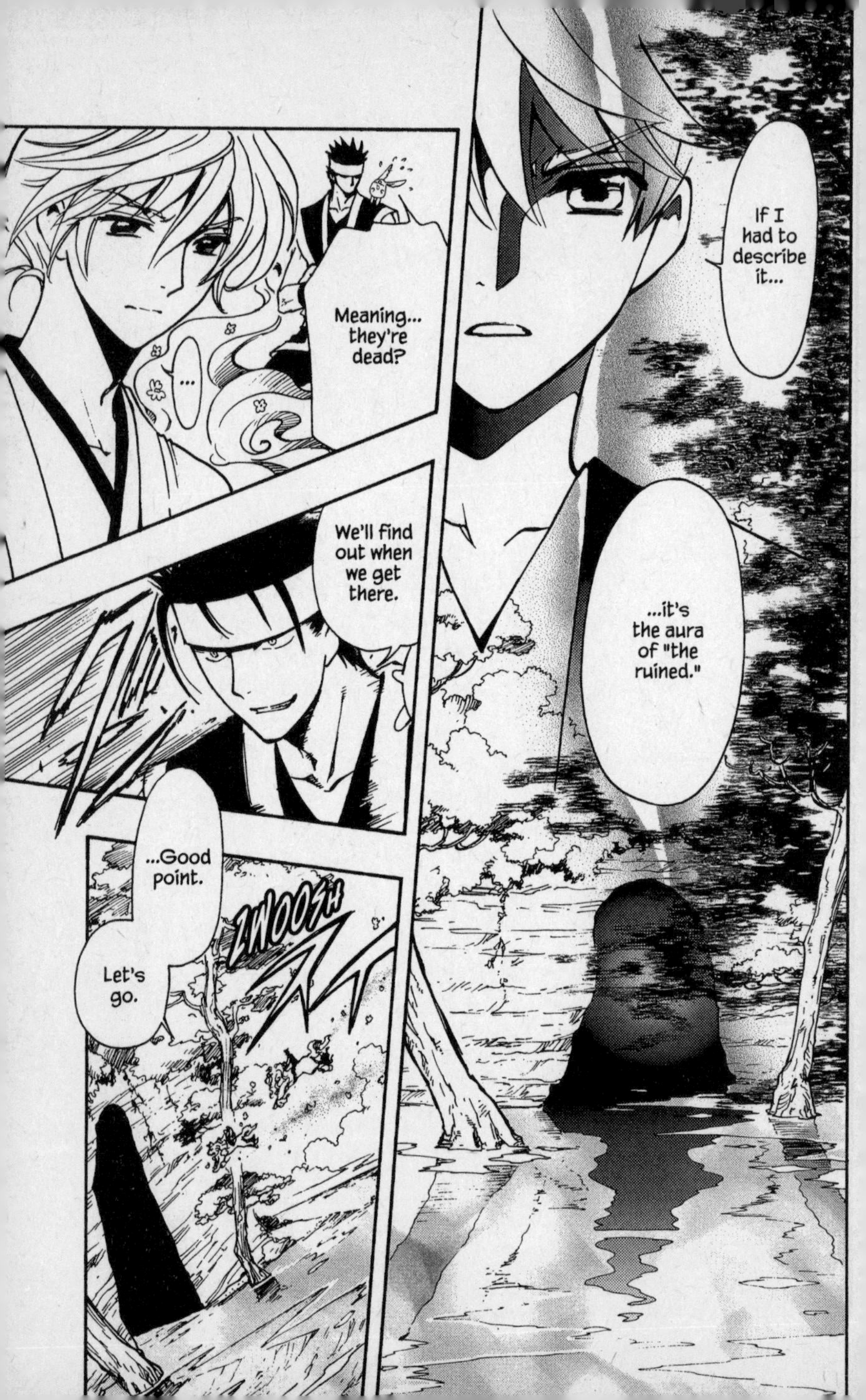
If I had to describe it...
...it's the aura of "the ruined."
Meaning... they're dead?
...
We'll find out when we get there.
...Good point.
Let's go.
ZWOOSH

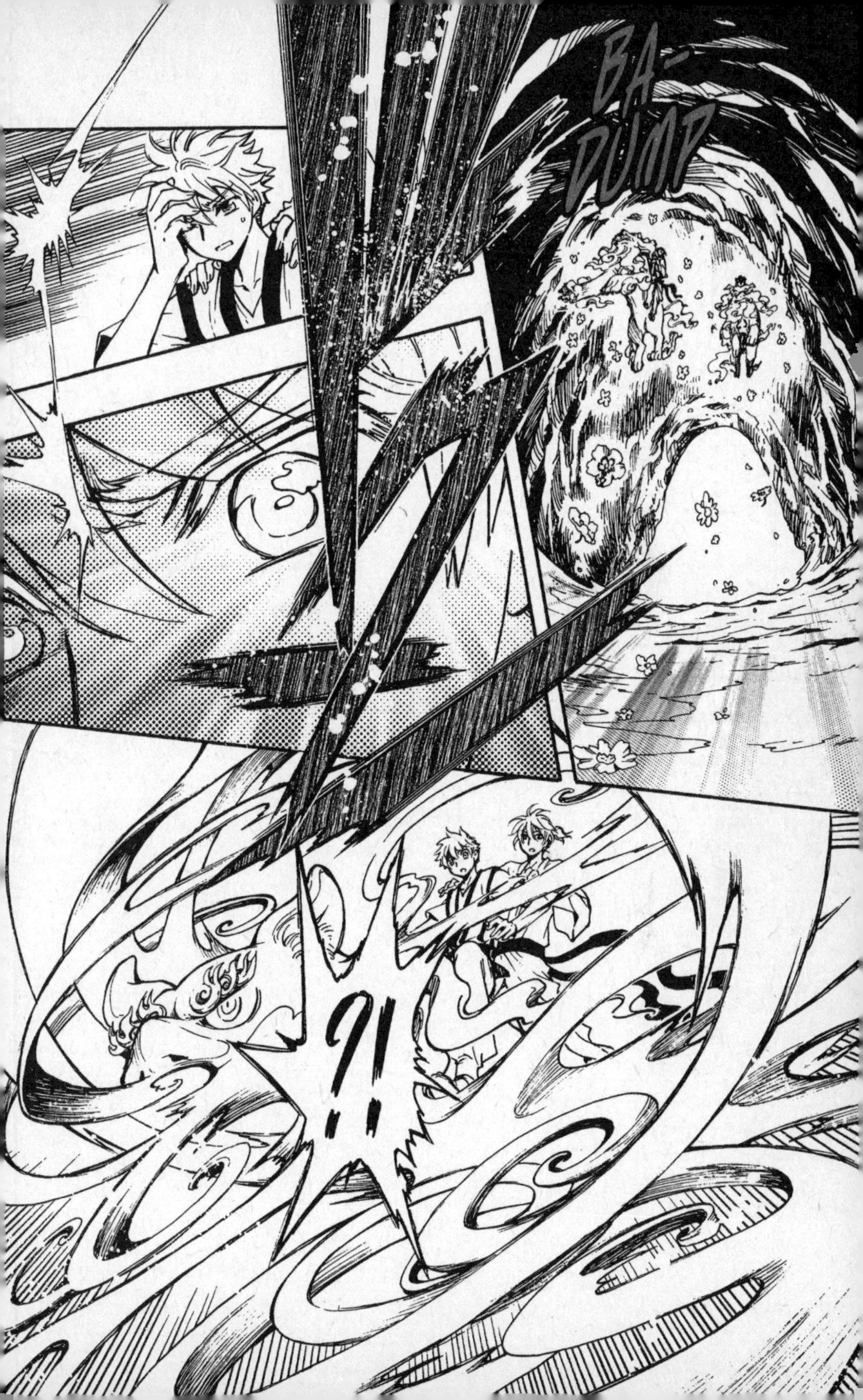
BA-DUMP
?!

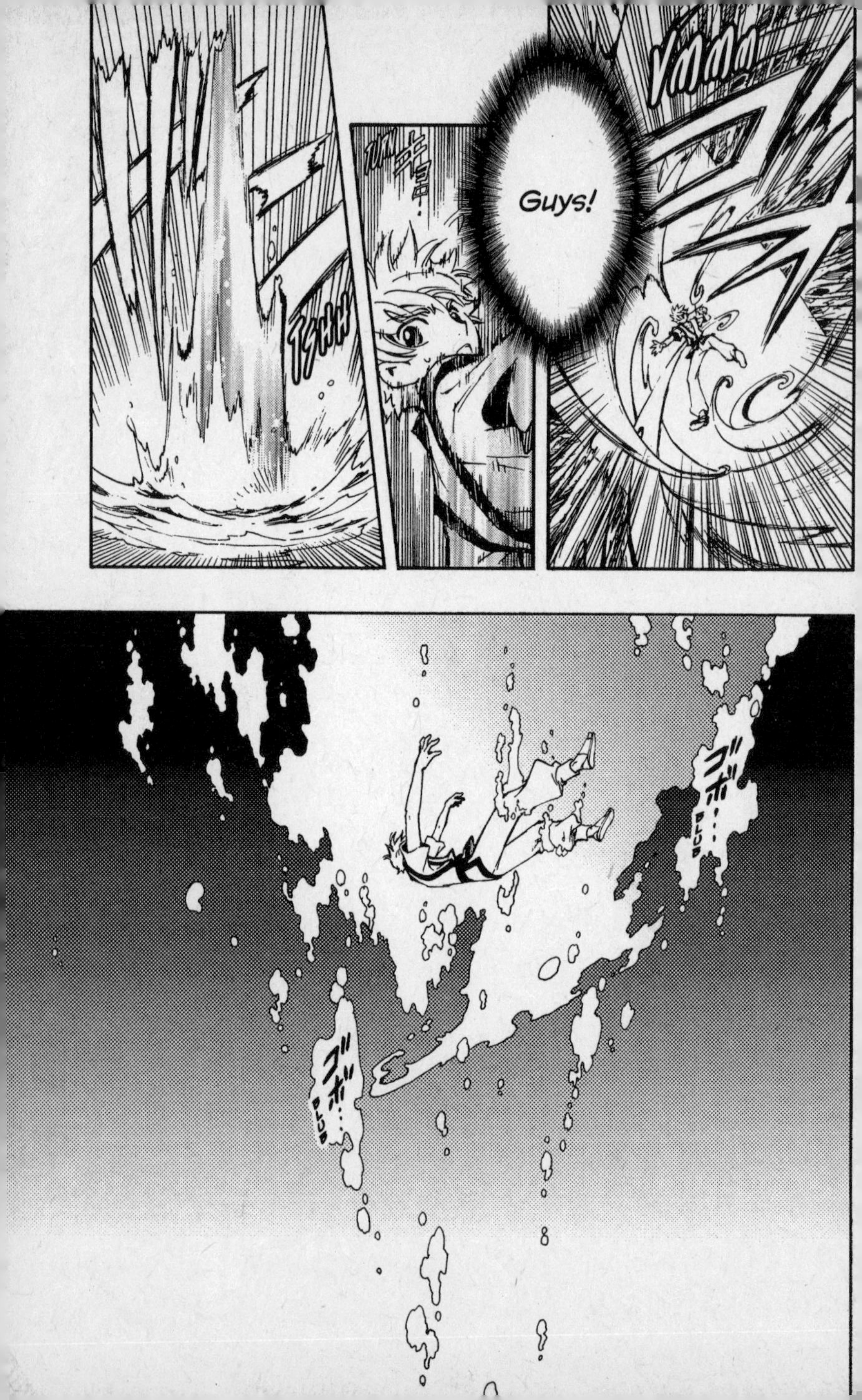

VMMM
Guys!
TSHH
ゴボ…
BLUB
ゴボ…
BLUB

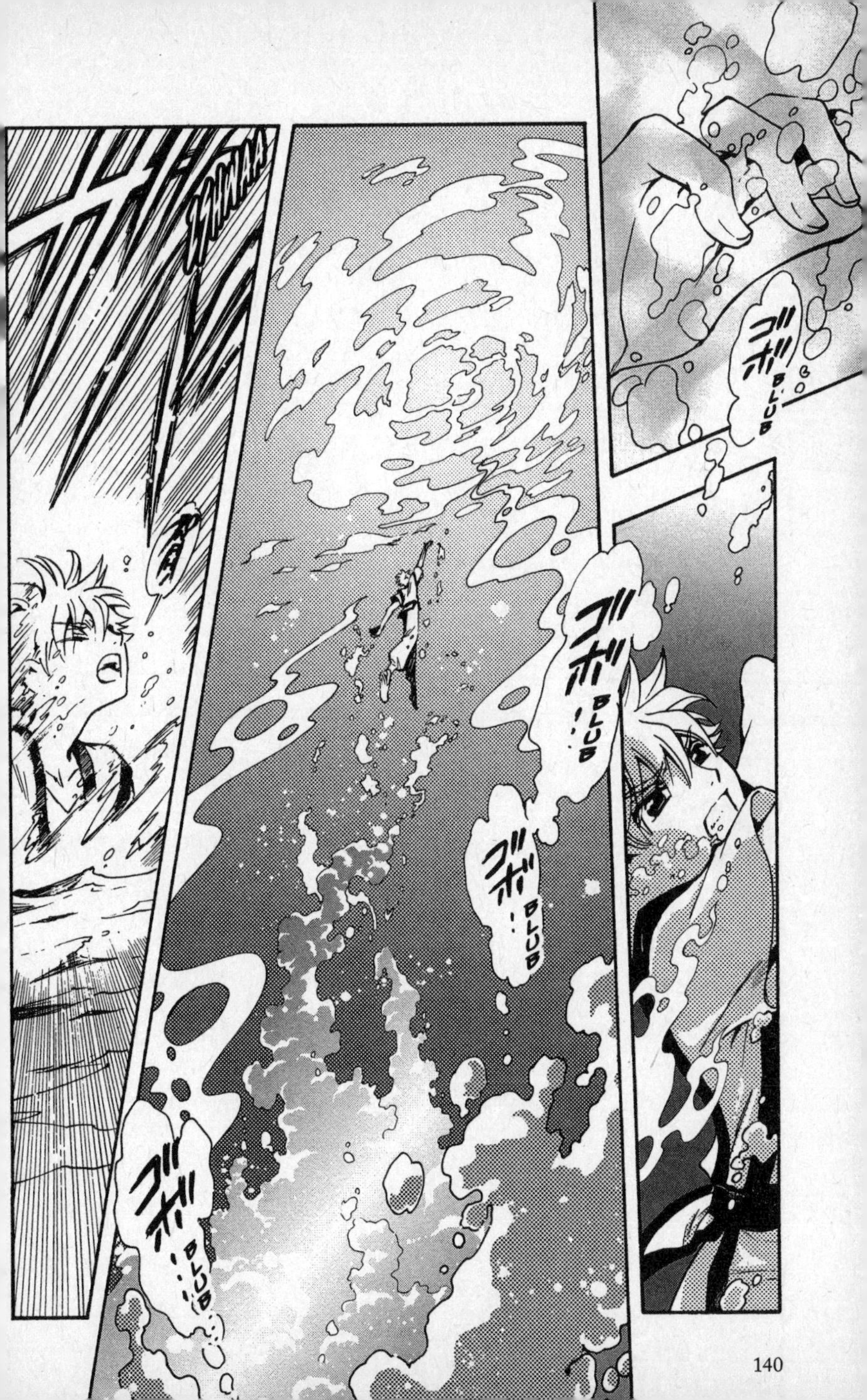
ゴボ BLUB
ゴボ BLUB
ゴボ BLUB
ゴボ BLUB
SHWAA

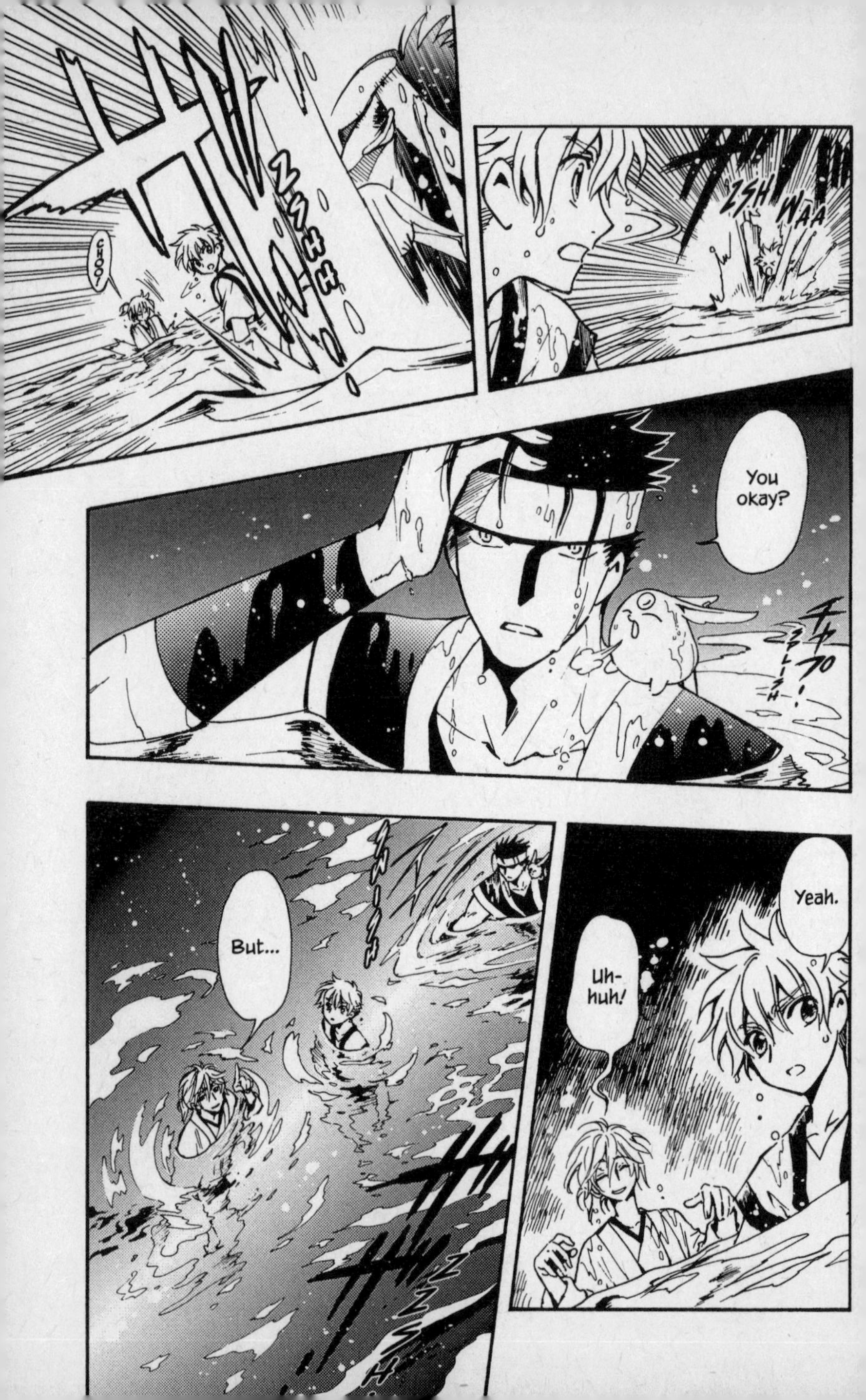
ZSHWAA
CHOO!
ZSHHH
You okay?
SPLASH!
Yeah.
Uh-huh!
But...
ZZZSH

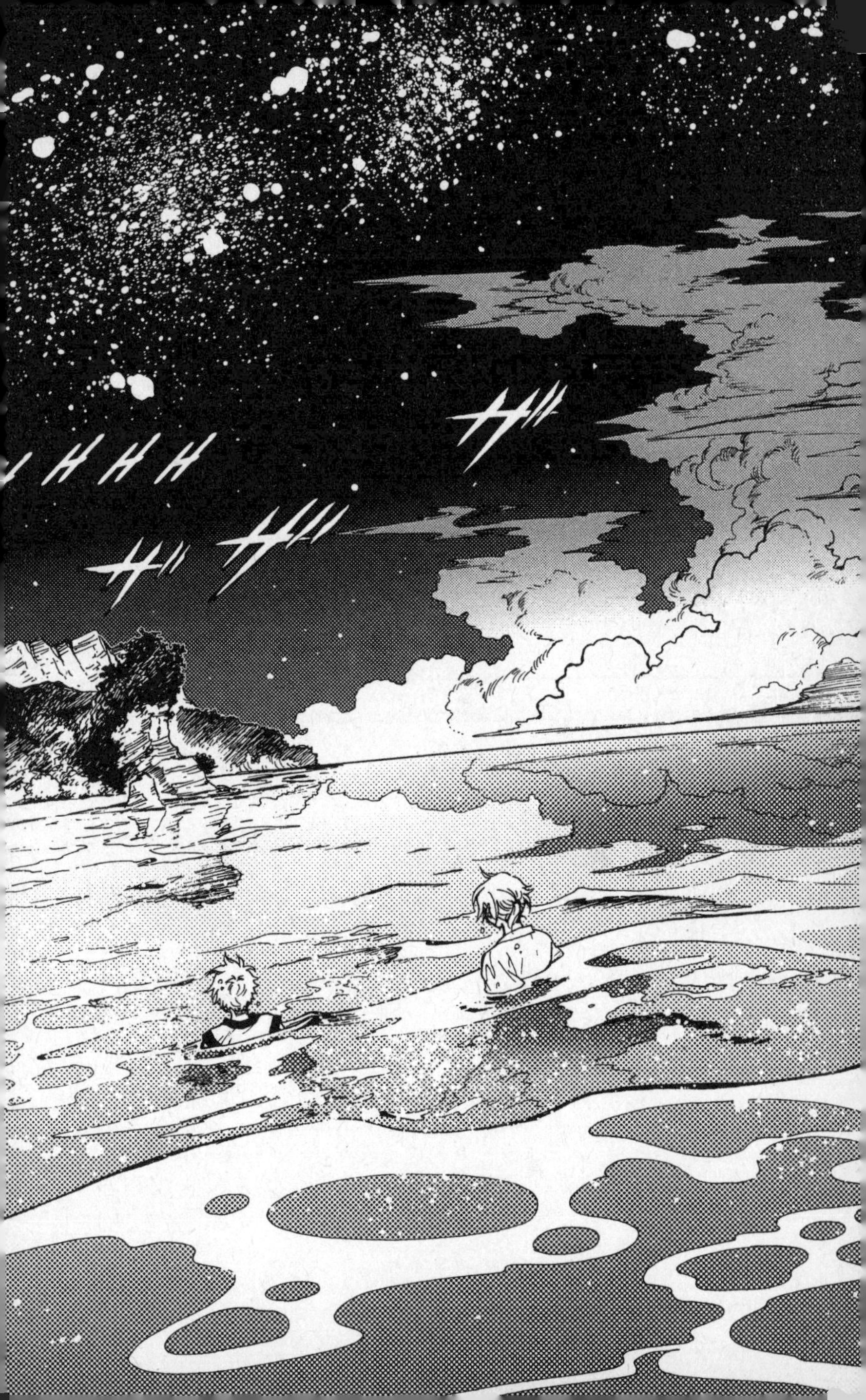

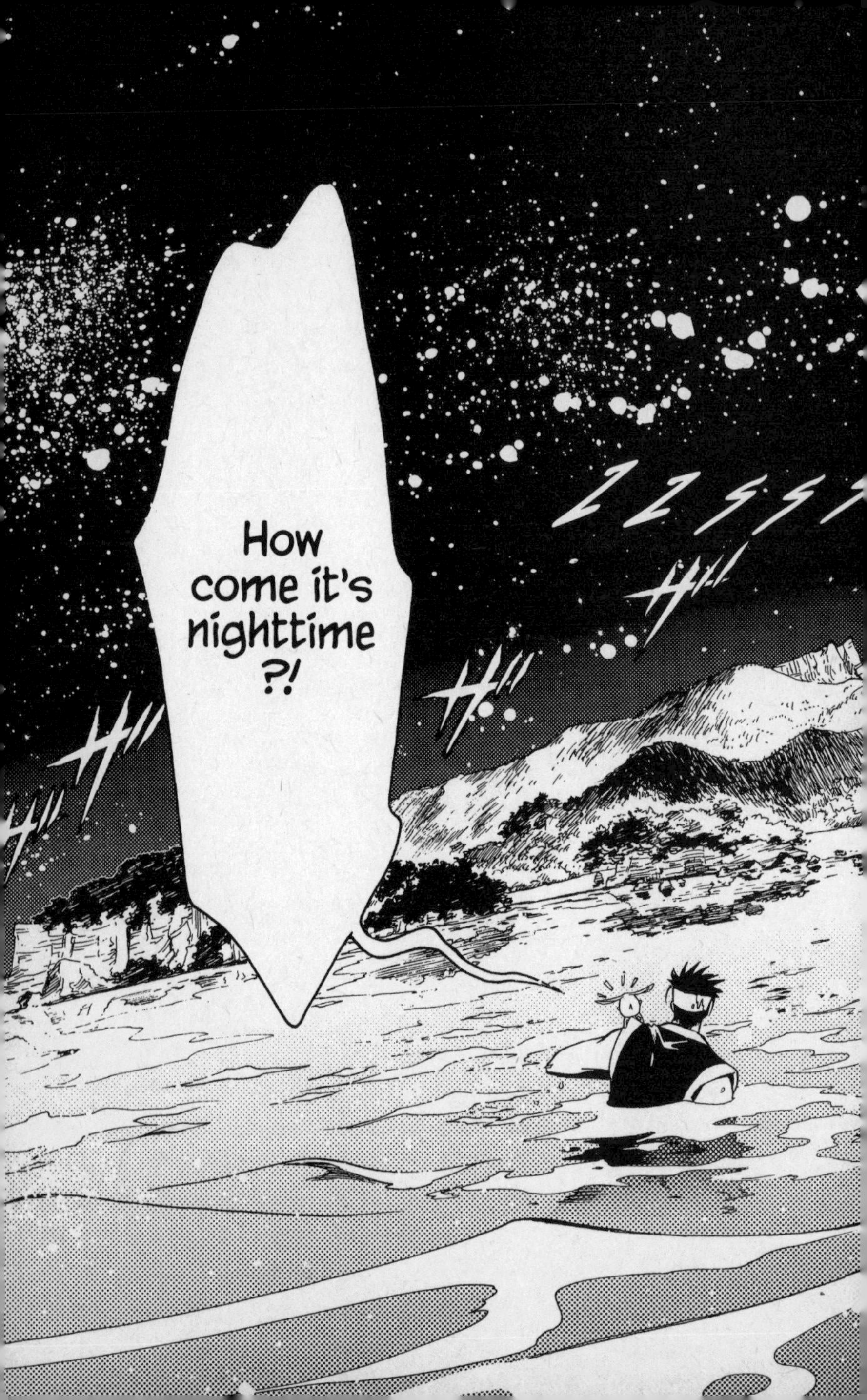
How come it's nighttime ?!

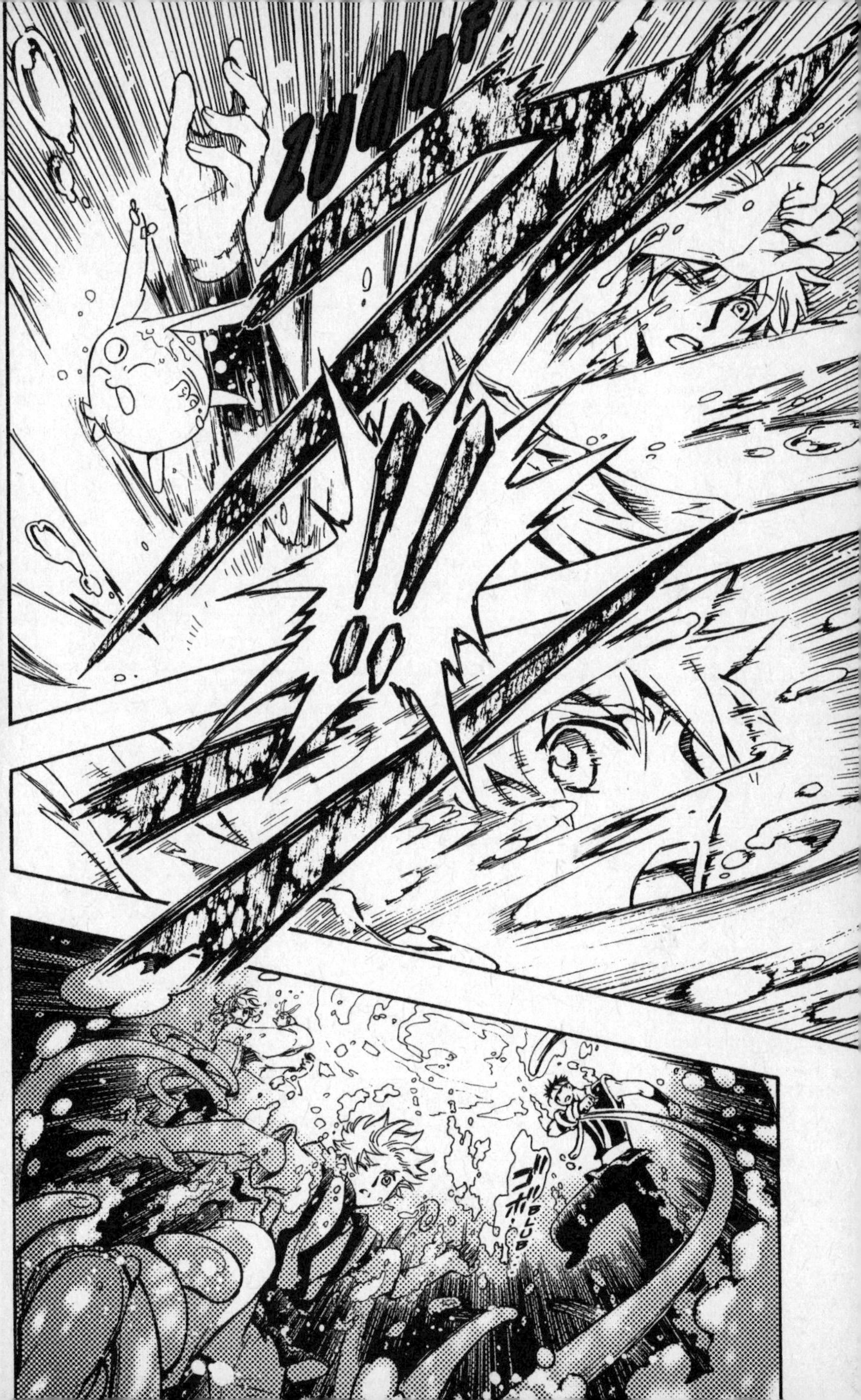
ZUAAAF
ゴボ…
BLUB

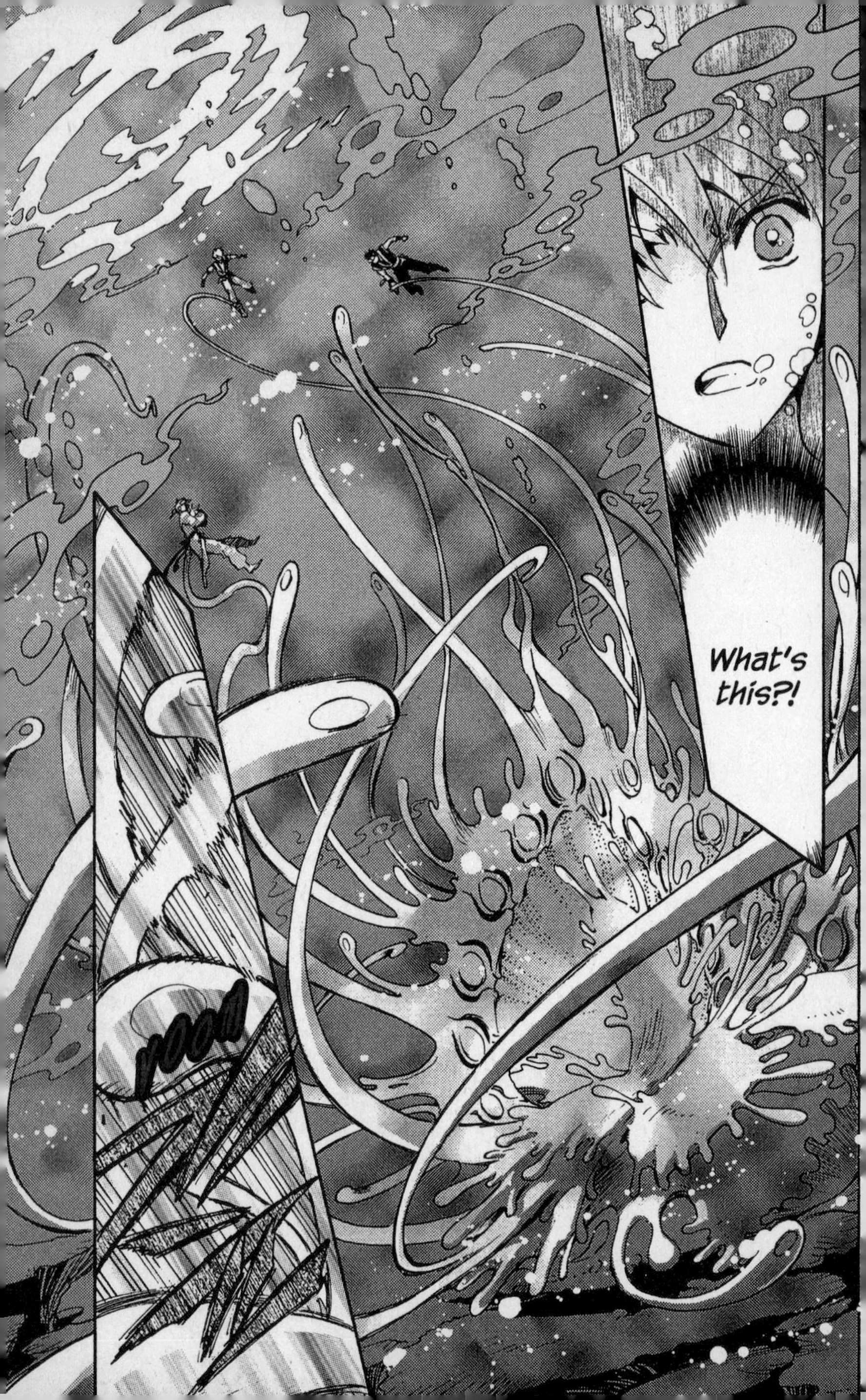
What's this?!
voom

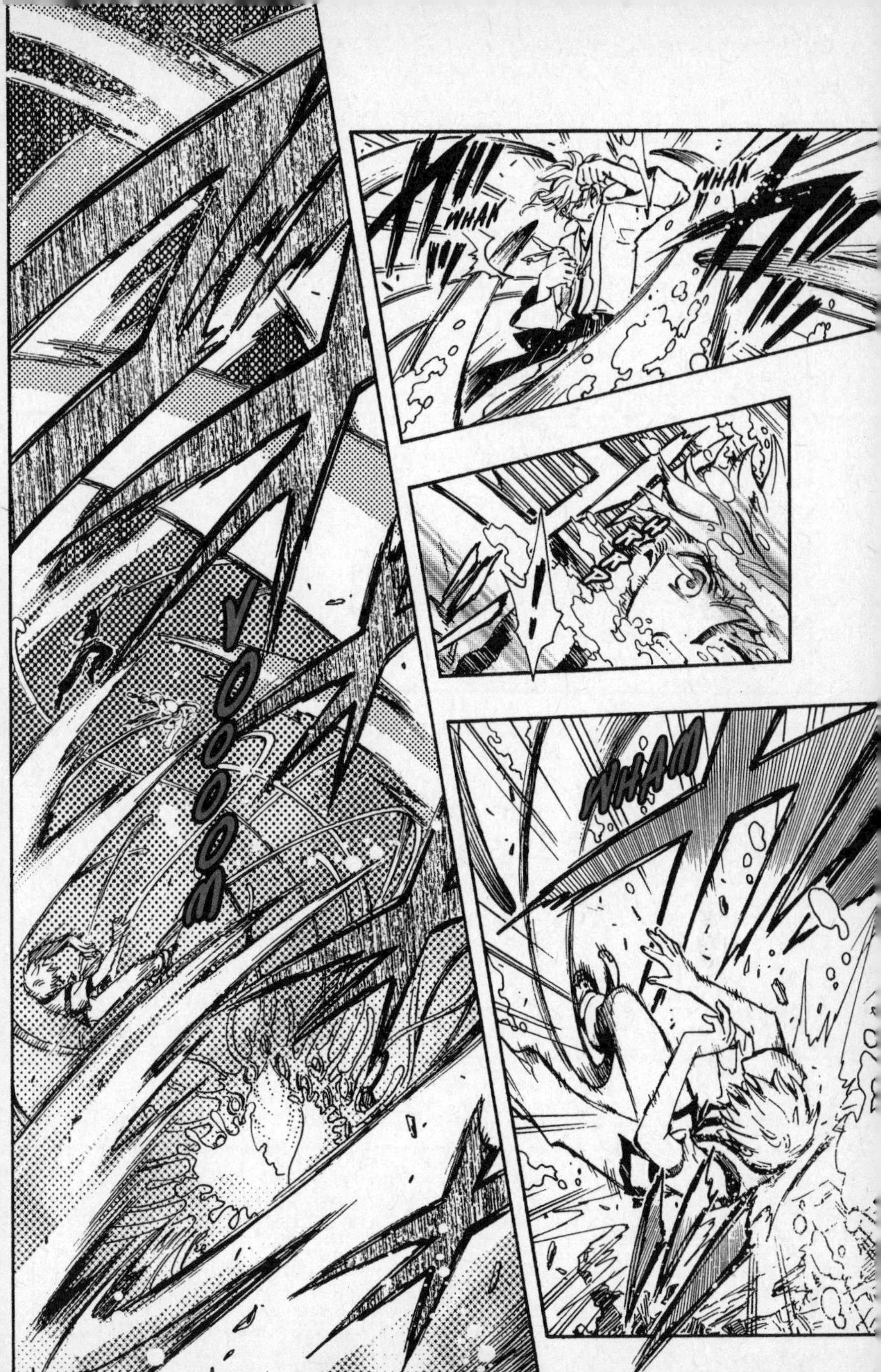
WHAK
WHAK
HRRP
WHAM
VOOOOOOM

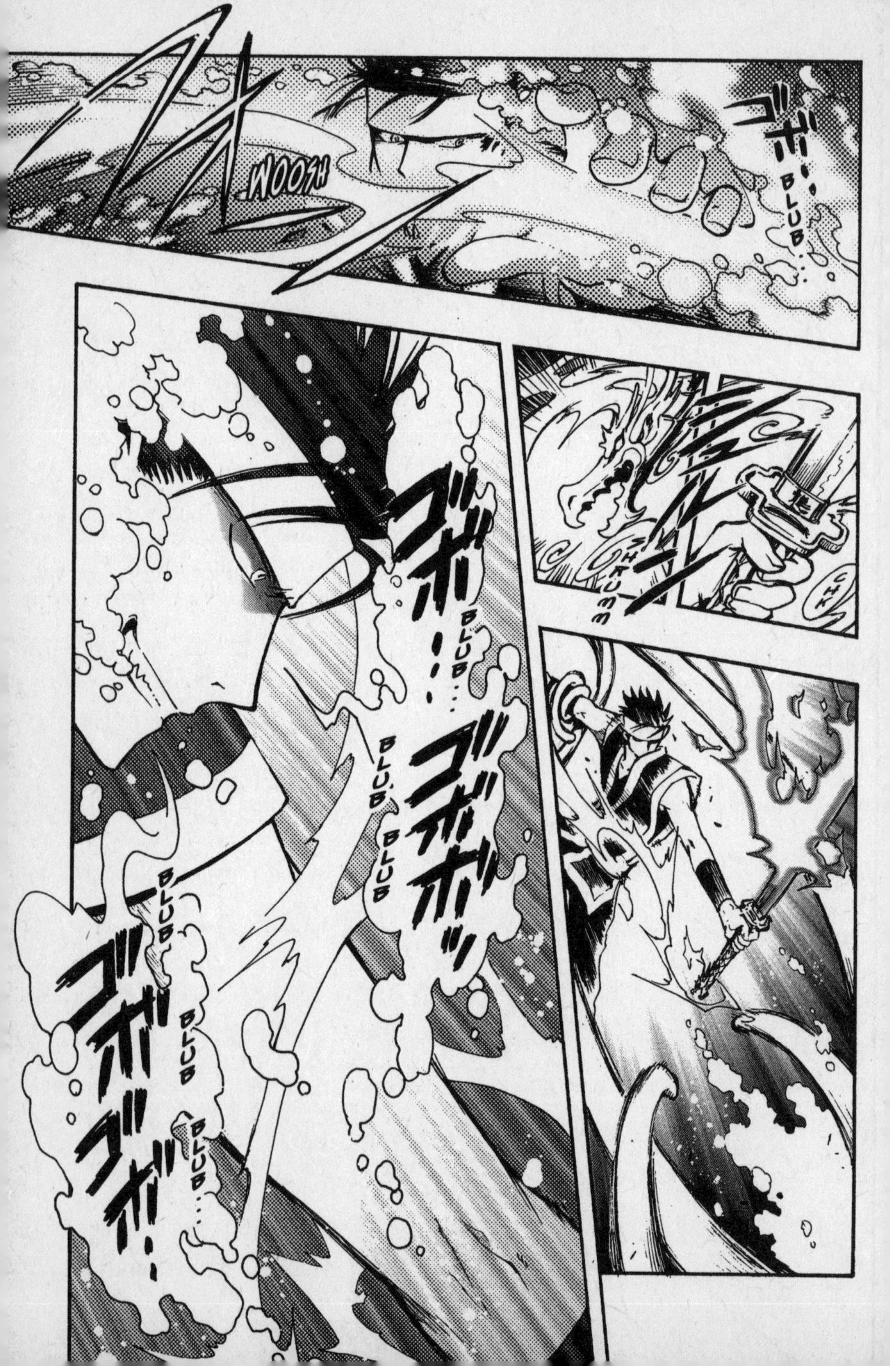

ゴボ…
BLUB…
WOOSH
SHRUMM
CHK
ゴボ!!
BLUB…
ゴボボッ
BLUB BLUB
BLUB
ゴボゴボ…
BLUB
BLUB…

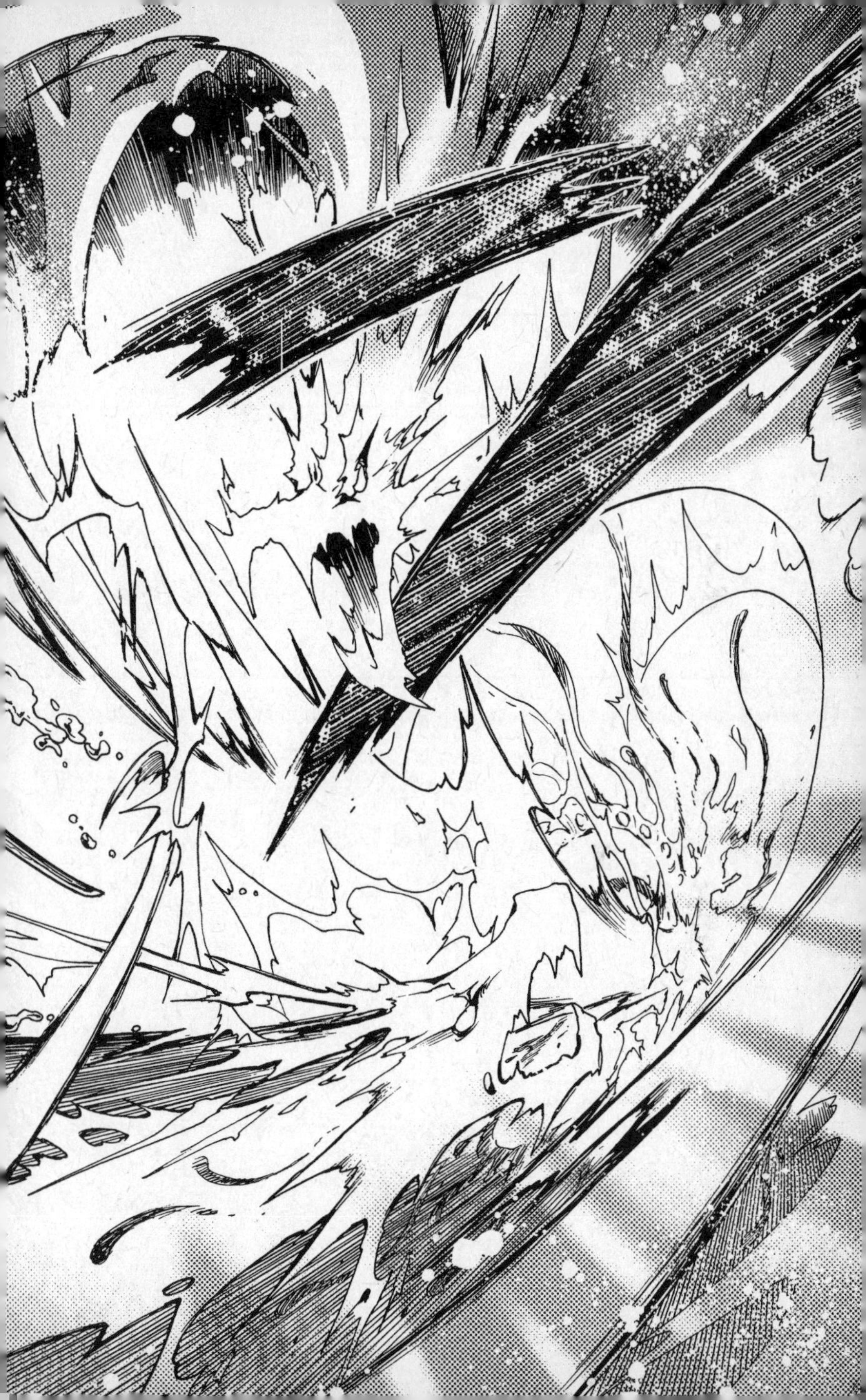

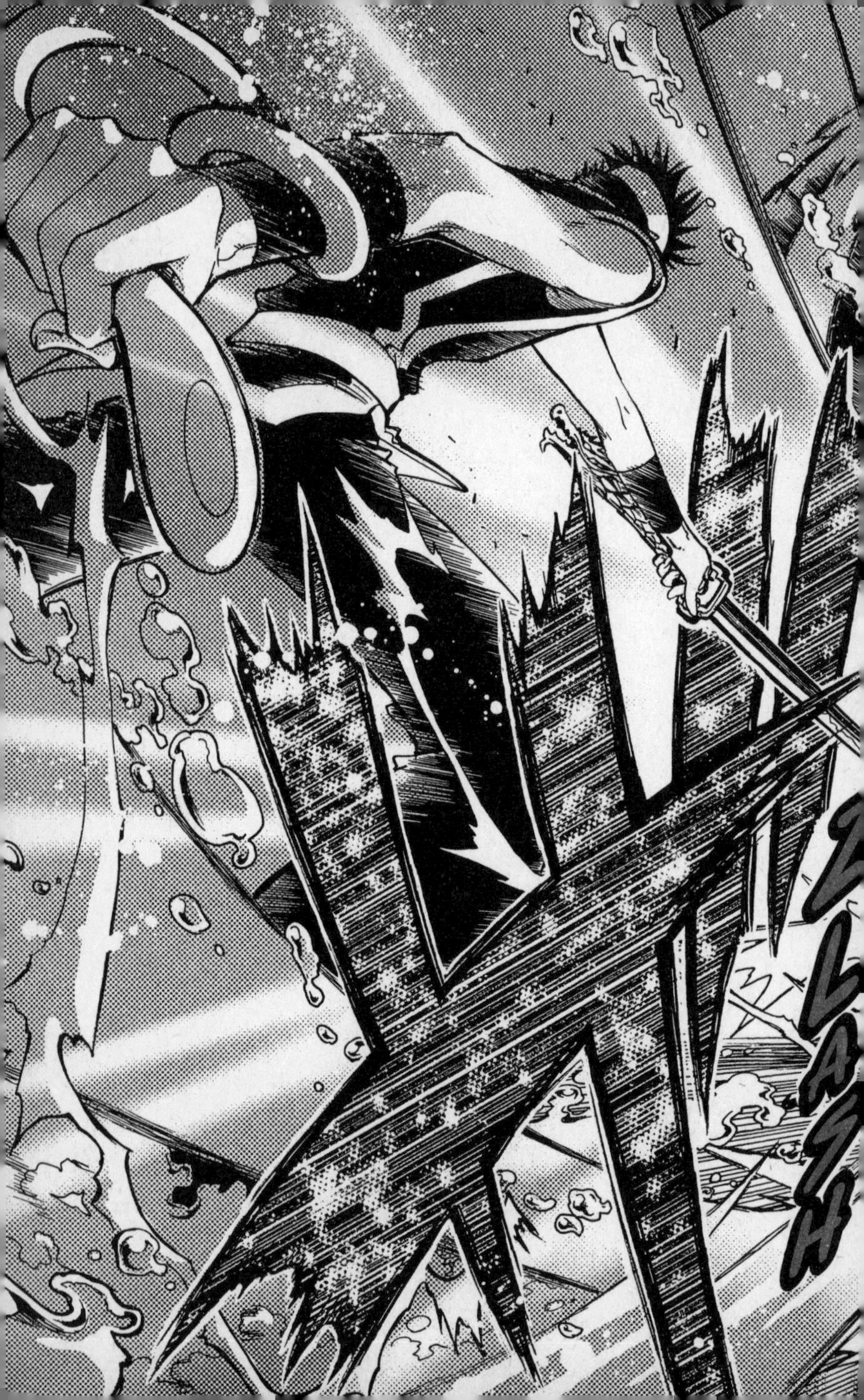
ZLLASH

TSUBASA

WoRLD CHRoNiCLE: NIRAIKANAI

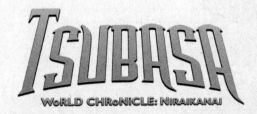

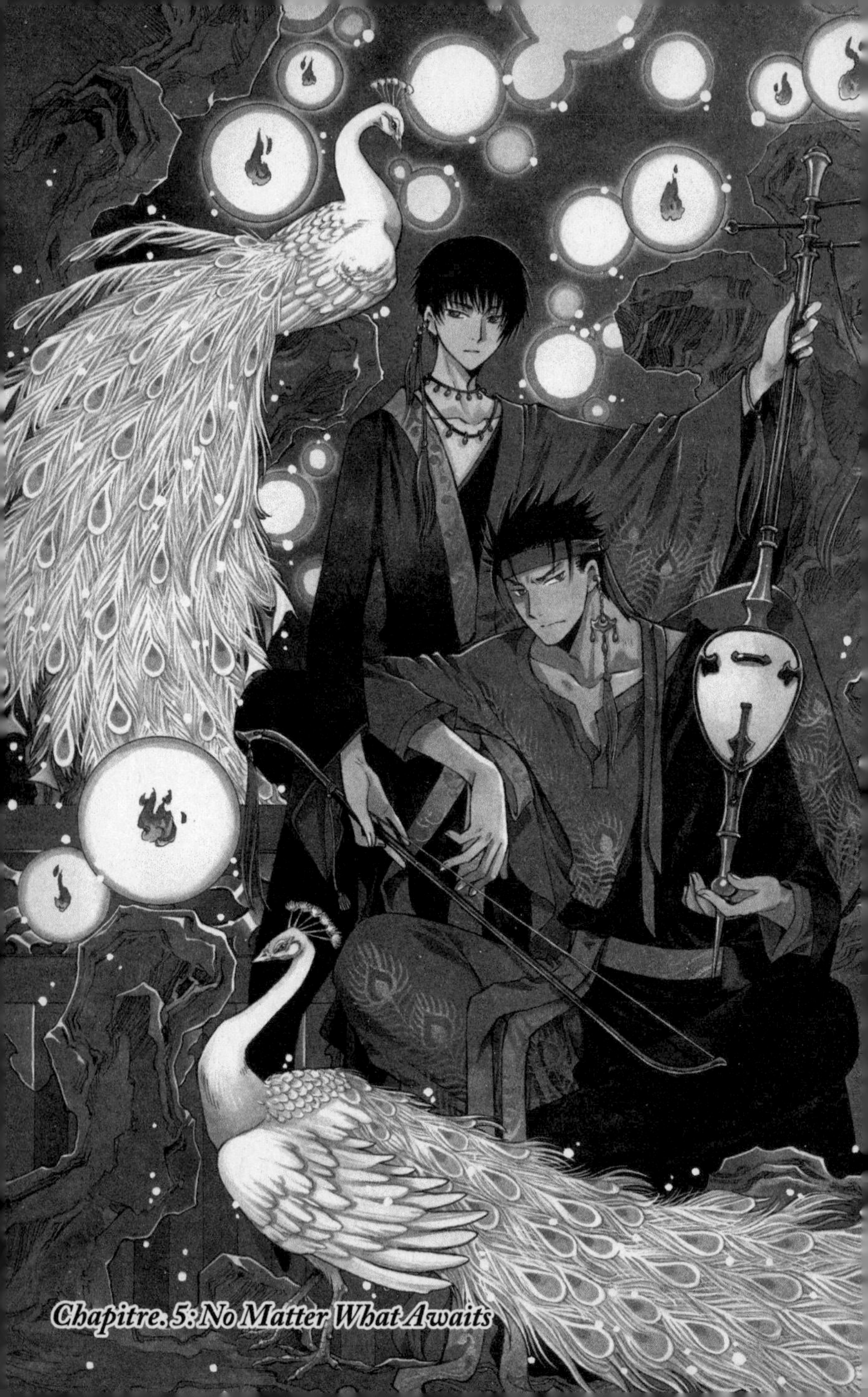
Chapitre. 5: No Matter What Awaits

TSUBASA

WoRLD CHRoNiCLE: NIRAIKANAI

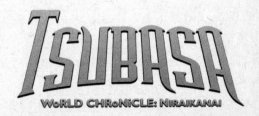

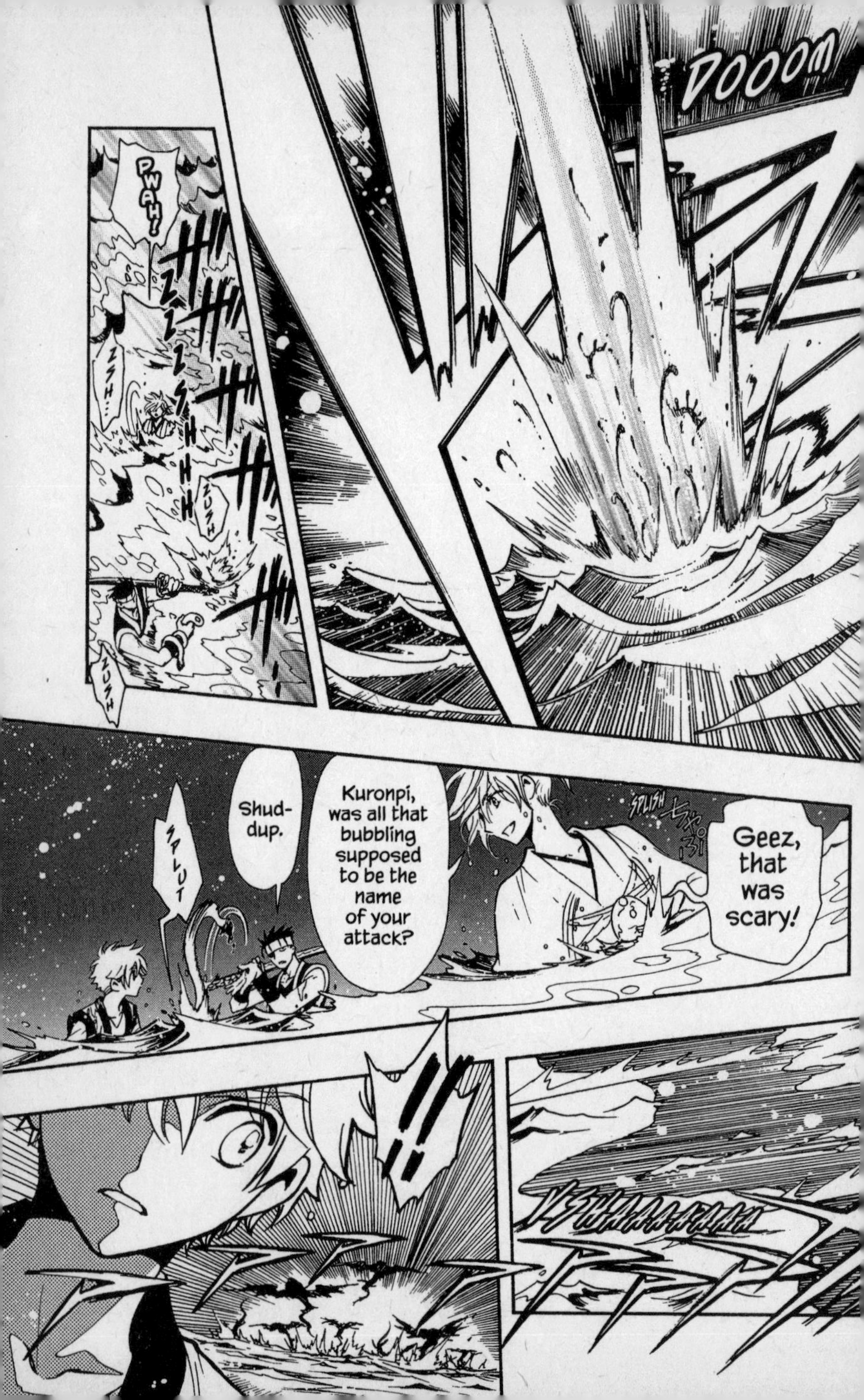
DOOOM
PWAH!
ZZZZSHHHH
ZSH...
ZUSH
ZUSH
Geez, that was scary!
SPLISH
Kuronpi, was all that bubbling supposed to be the name of your attack?
Shud-dup.
SPLUT

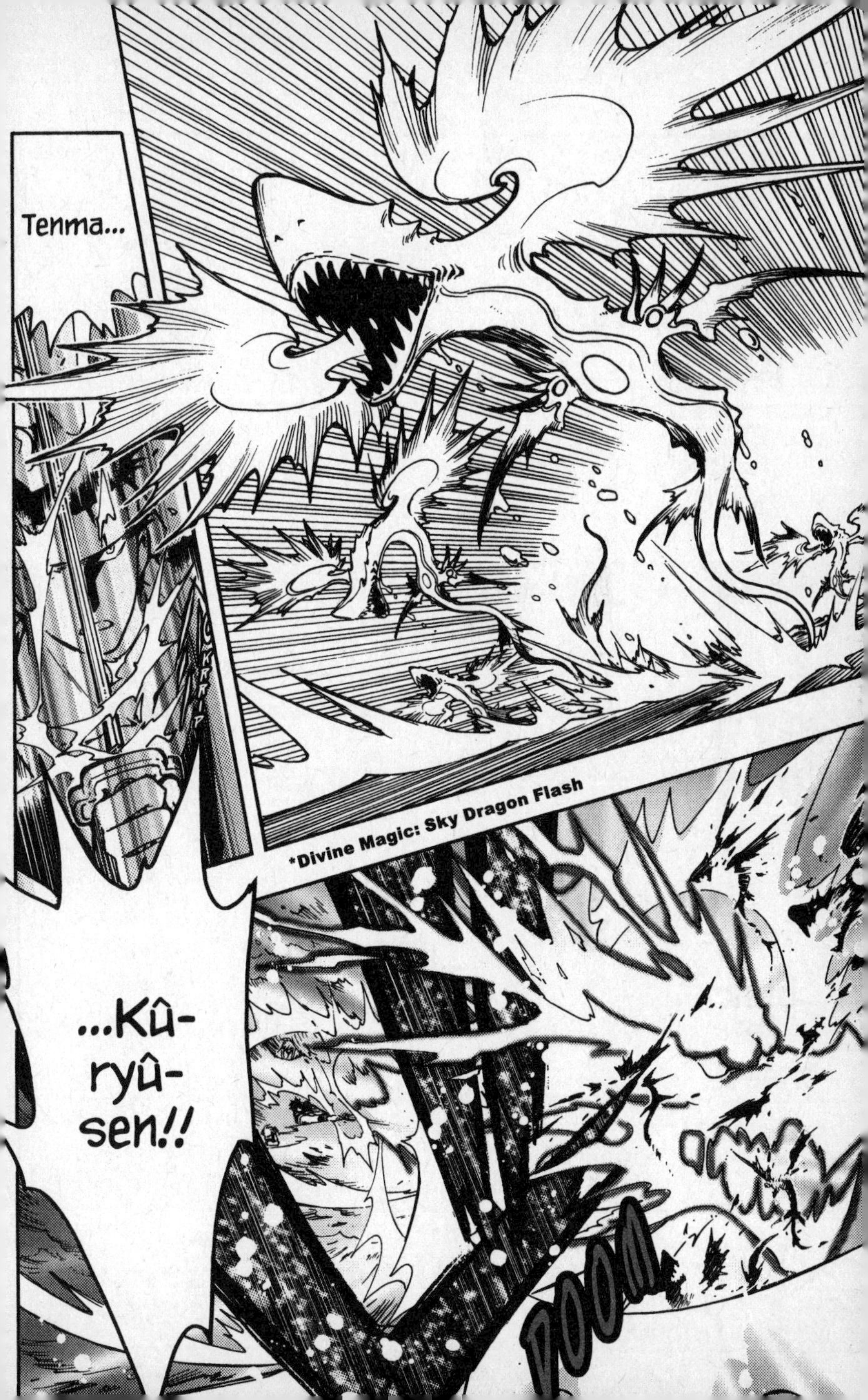
*Divine Magic: Sky Dragon Flash
Tenma...
KRRIP
...Kû-ryû-sen!!
DOOM

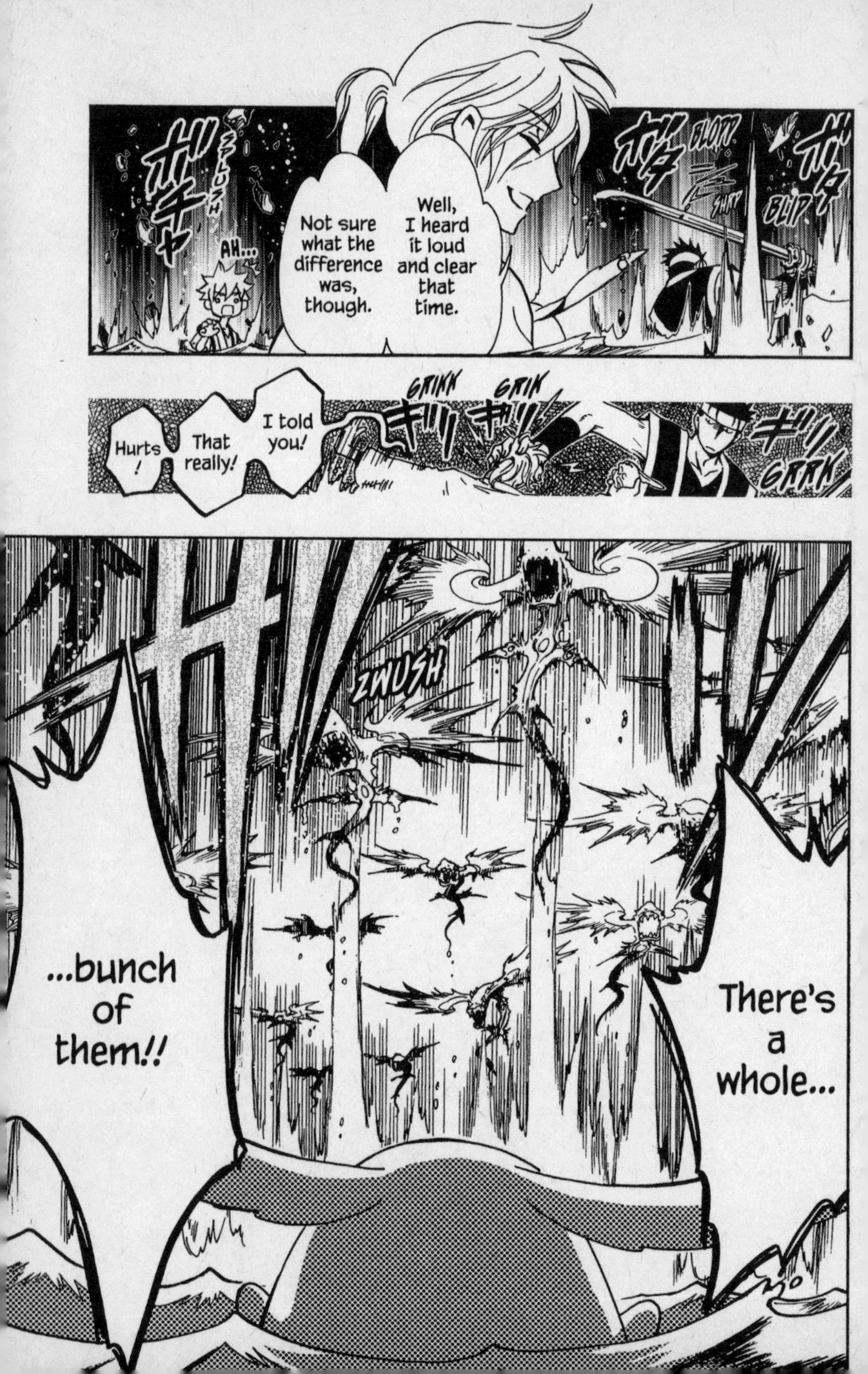
BLIP
BLOTT
SHRP
Well, I heard it loud and clear that time.
Not sure what the difference was, though.
AH...
SPLUSH
GRRK
GRIK
GRIKK
I told you!
That really!
Hurts!
There's a whole...
ZWUSH
...bunch of them!!

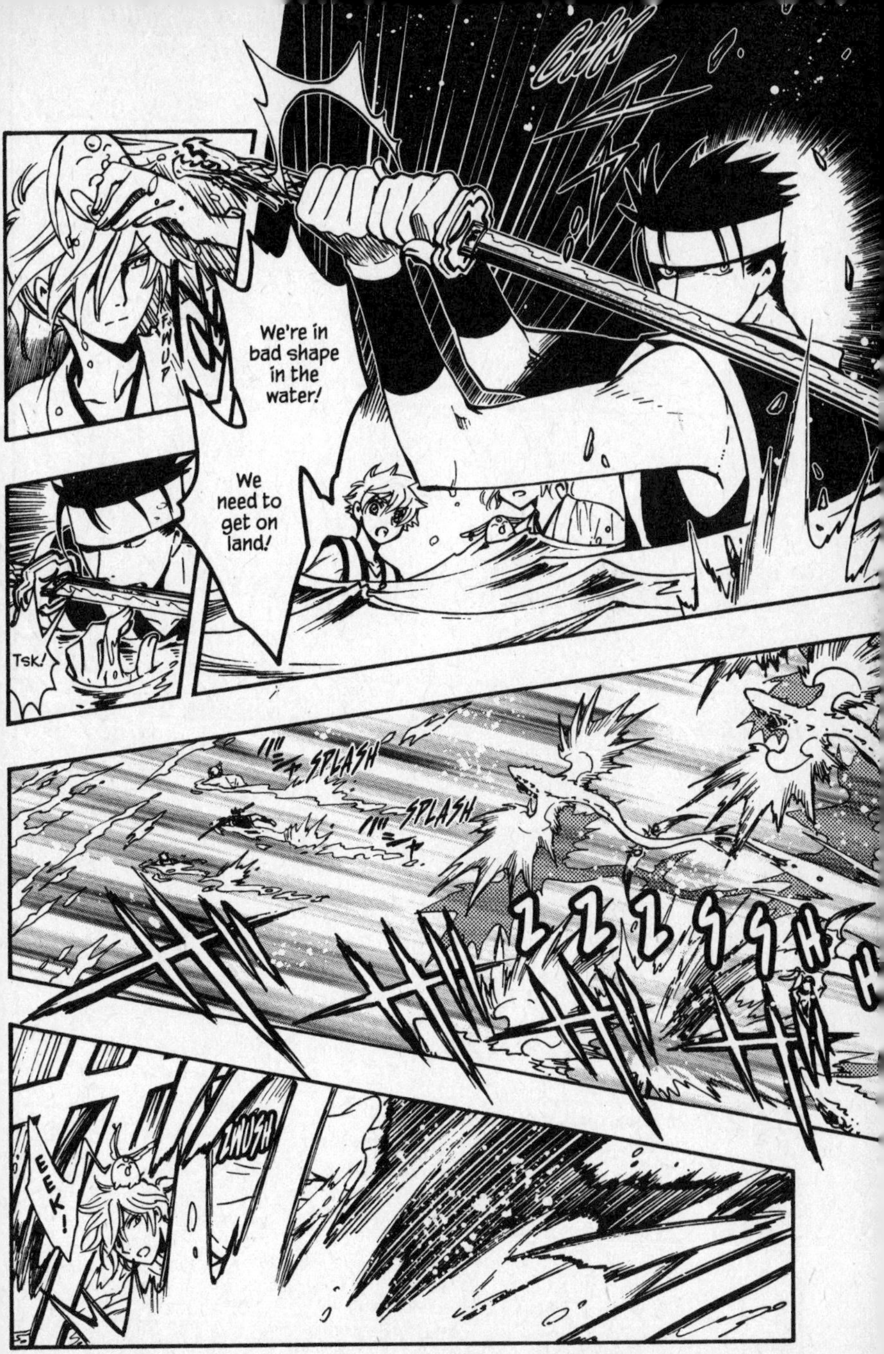
We're in bad shape in the water!
We need to get on land!
FWUP
TSK!
SPLASH
SPLASH
ZZZSSSHH
ZWOSH
EEEK!

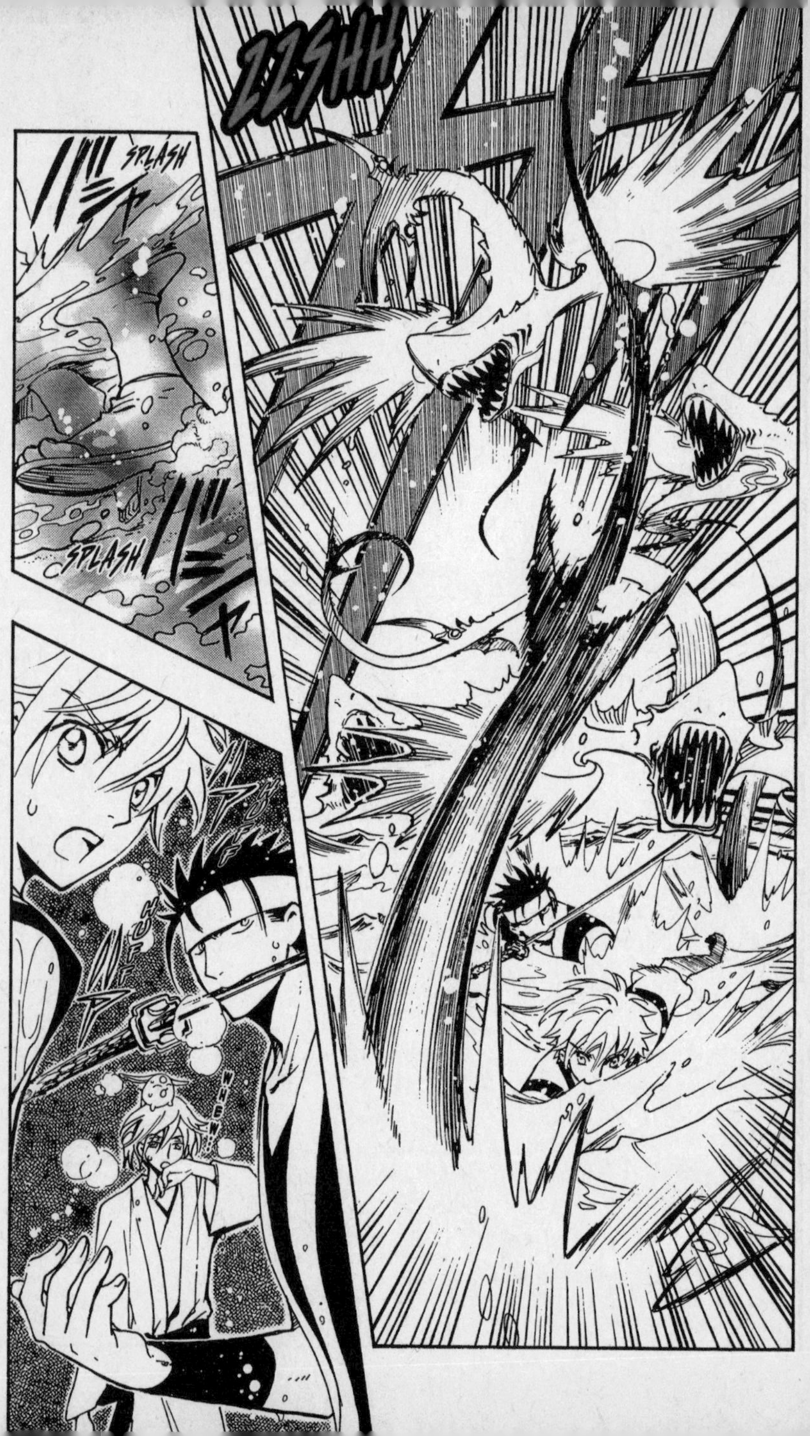
ZZSHH
SPLASH
SPLASH
HUFF
HUFF
WHEW...

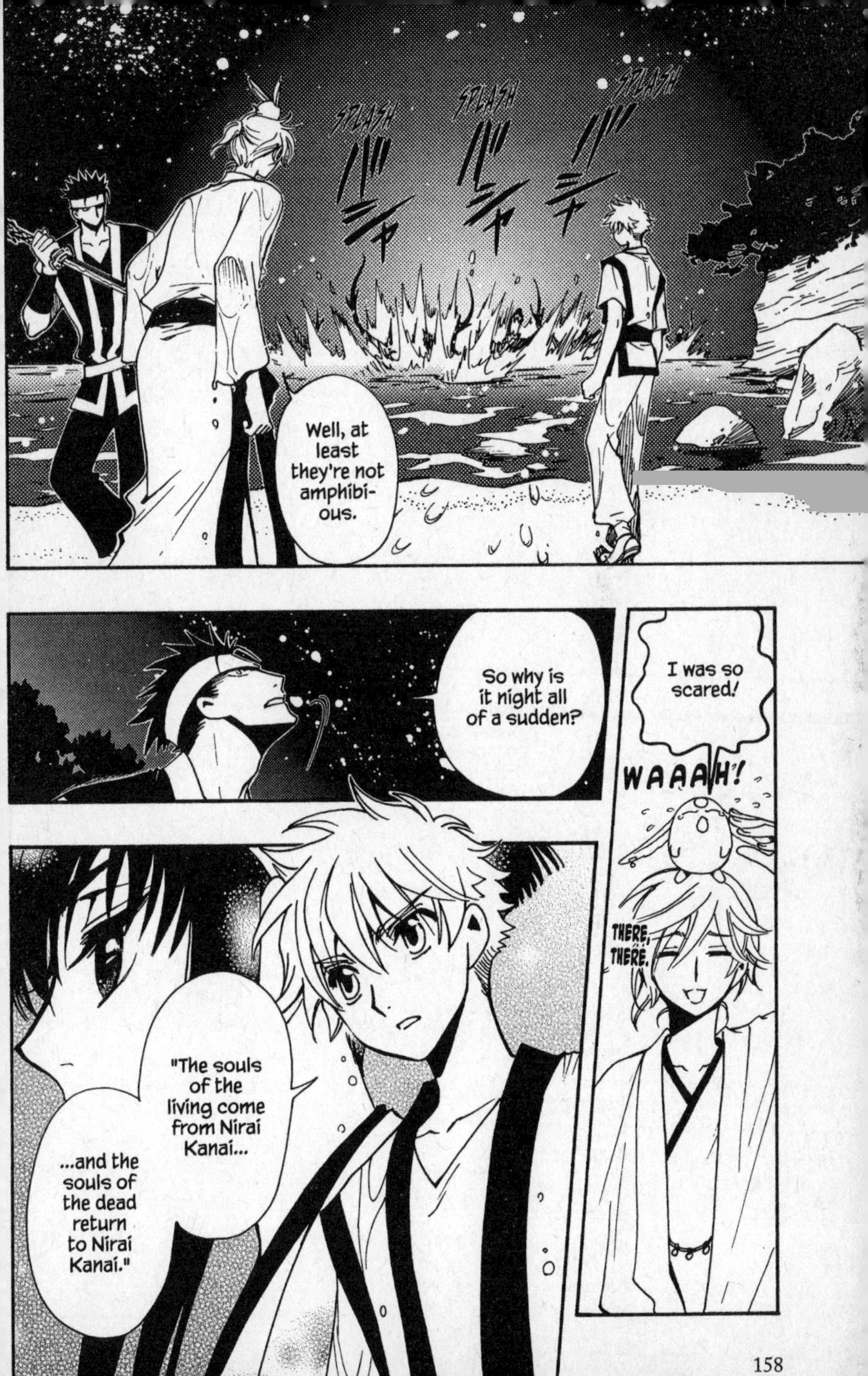
SPLASH
SPLASH
SPLASH
Well, at least they're not amphibi-ous.
I was so scared!
WAAAH!
THERE, THERE.
So why is it night all of a sudden?
"The souls of the living come from Nirai Kanai...
...and the souls of the dead return to Nirai Kanai."

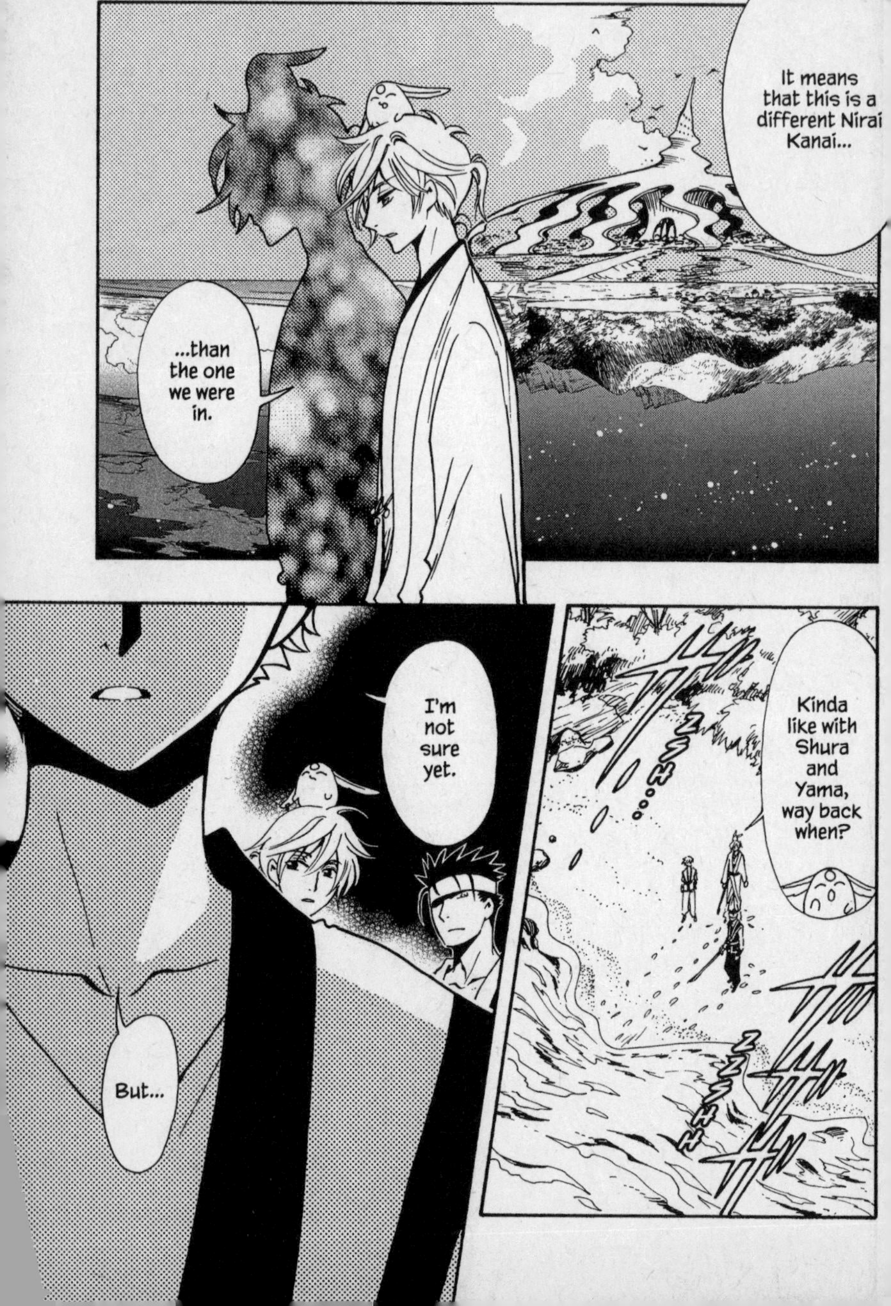
It means that this is a different Nirai Kanai...
...than the one we were in.
Kinda like with Shura and Yama, way back when?
I'm not sure yet.
But...

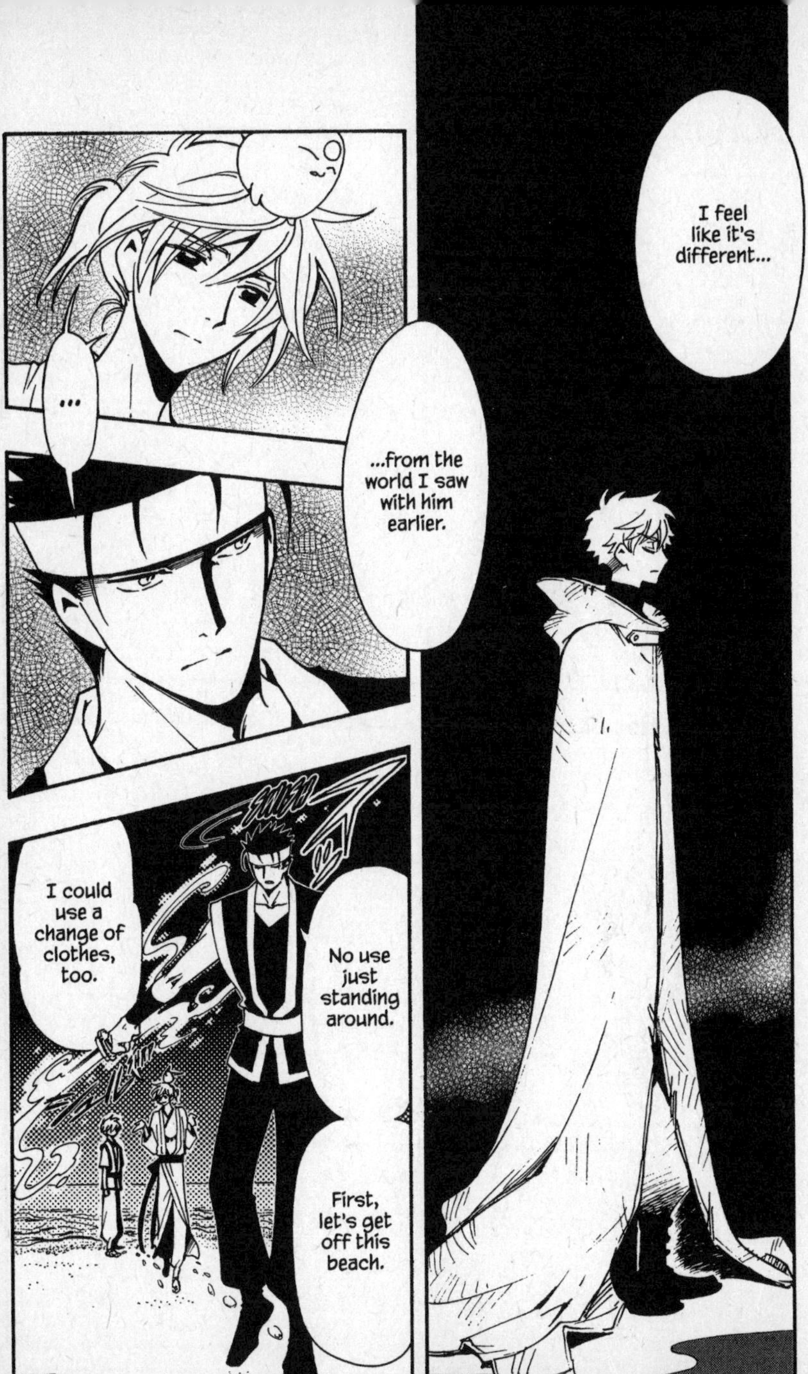
I feel like it's different...
...from the world I saw with him earlier.
...
No use just standing around.
First, let's get off this beach.
I could use a change of clothes, too.

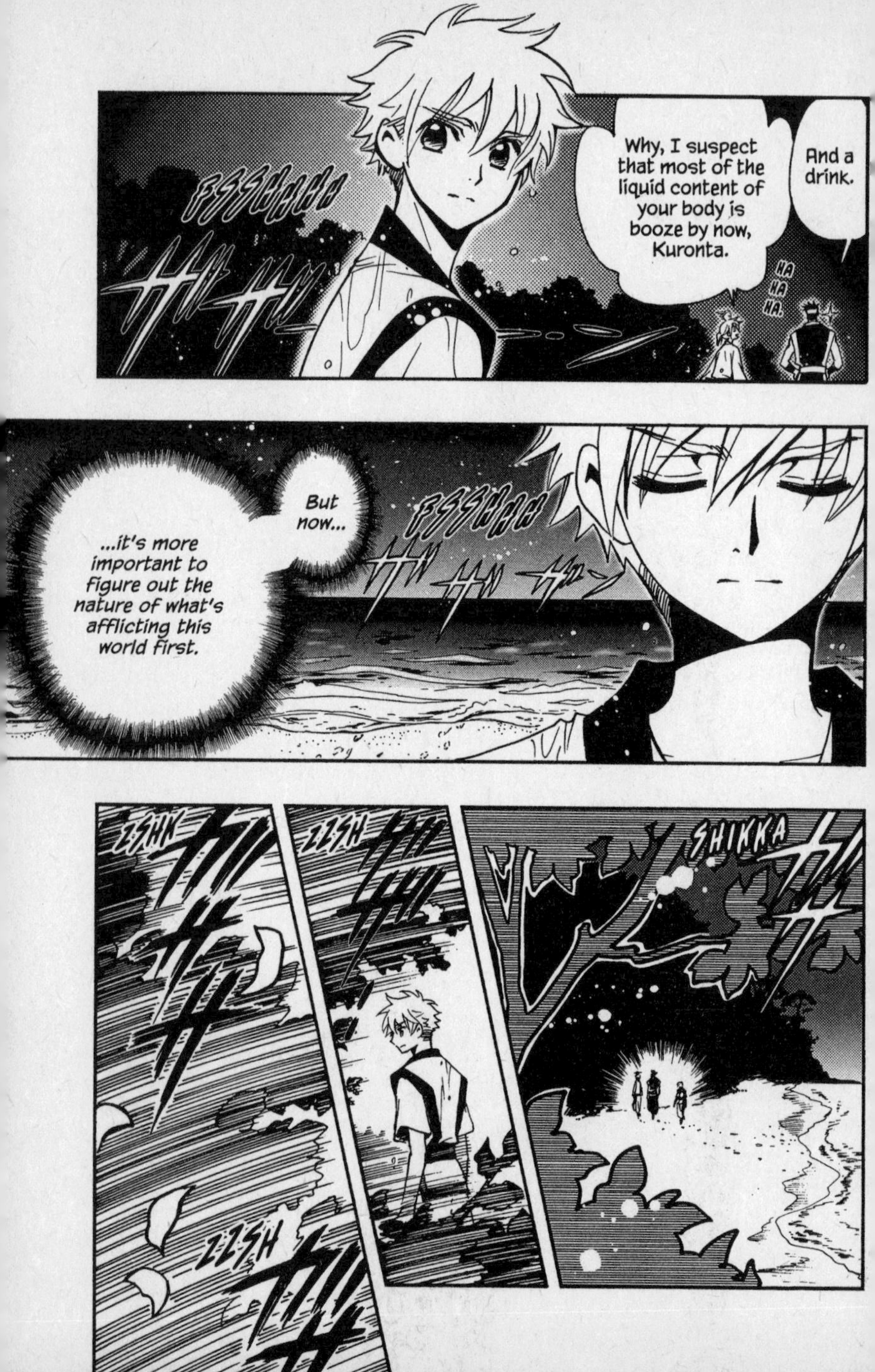
And a drink.
Why, I suspect that most of the liquid content of your body is booze by now, Kuronta.
HA HA HA.
But now...
...it's more important to figure out the nature of what's afflicting this world first.
SHIKKA
ZZSH
ZSHK
ZZSH

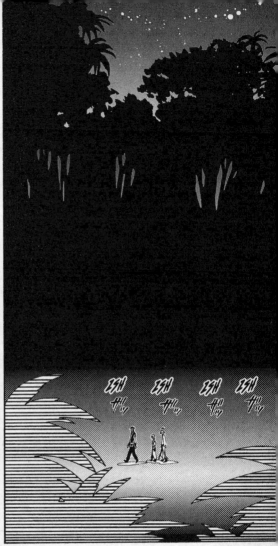

It's so dark.

IT'S SPOOKY!

I can barely see.

INDEED.

WHAT?

You're kidding-- it's a piece of cake.

There's a fork in the road ahead.

Kuro-rin's incredible night vision strikes again!

NIN-NIN!

You're practically a ninja!

SQUIIIISH

& I GIVE!

I GIVE!

OUCH!

I am a ninja.

162

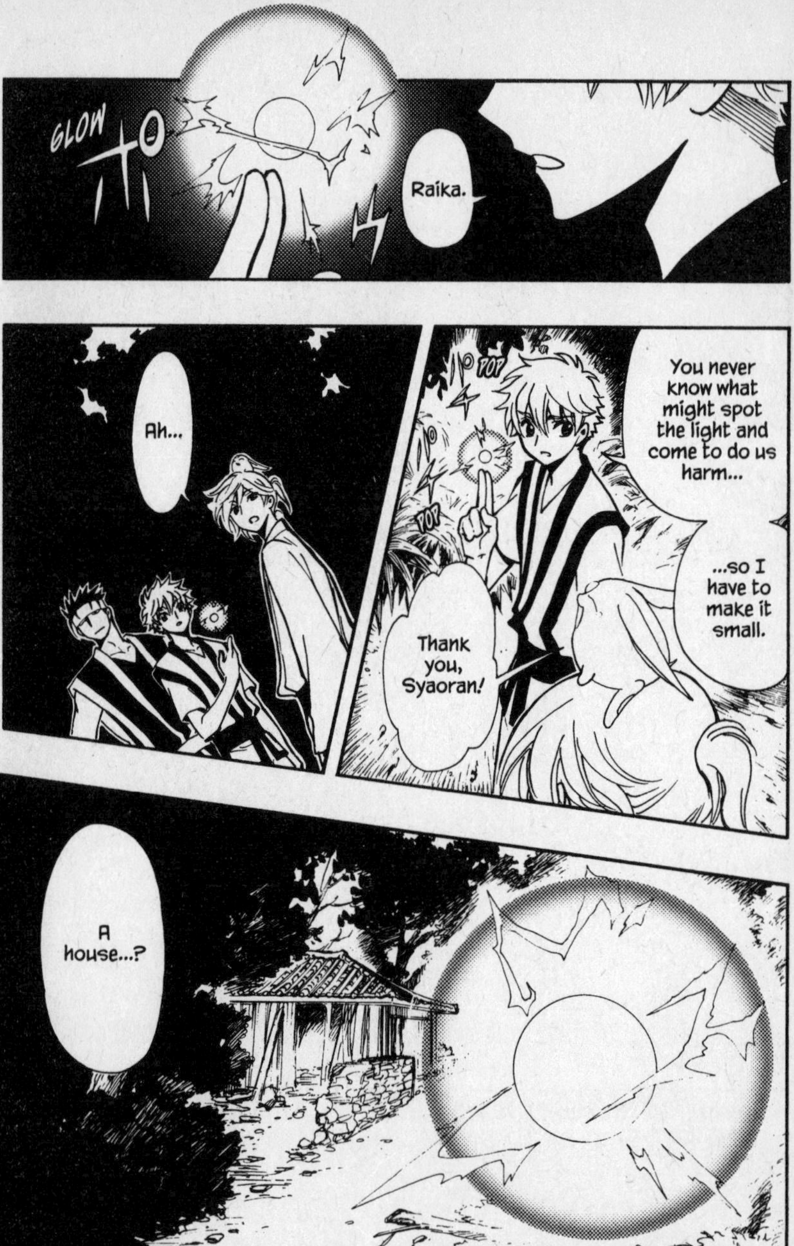
Raika.
GLOW
You never know what might spot the light and come to do us harm...
POP
...so I have to make it small.
POP
Thank you, Syaoran!
Ah...
A house...?

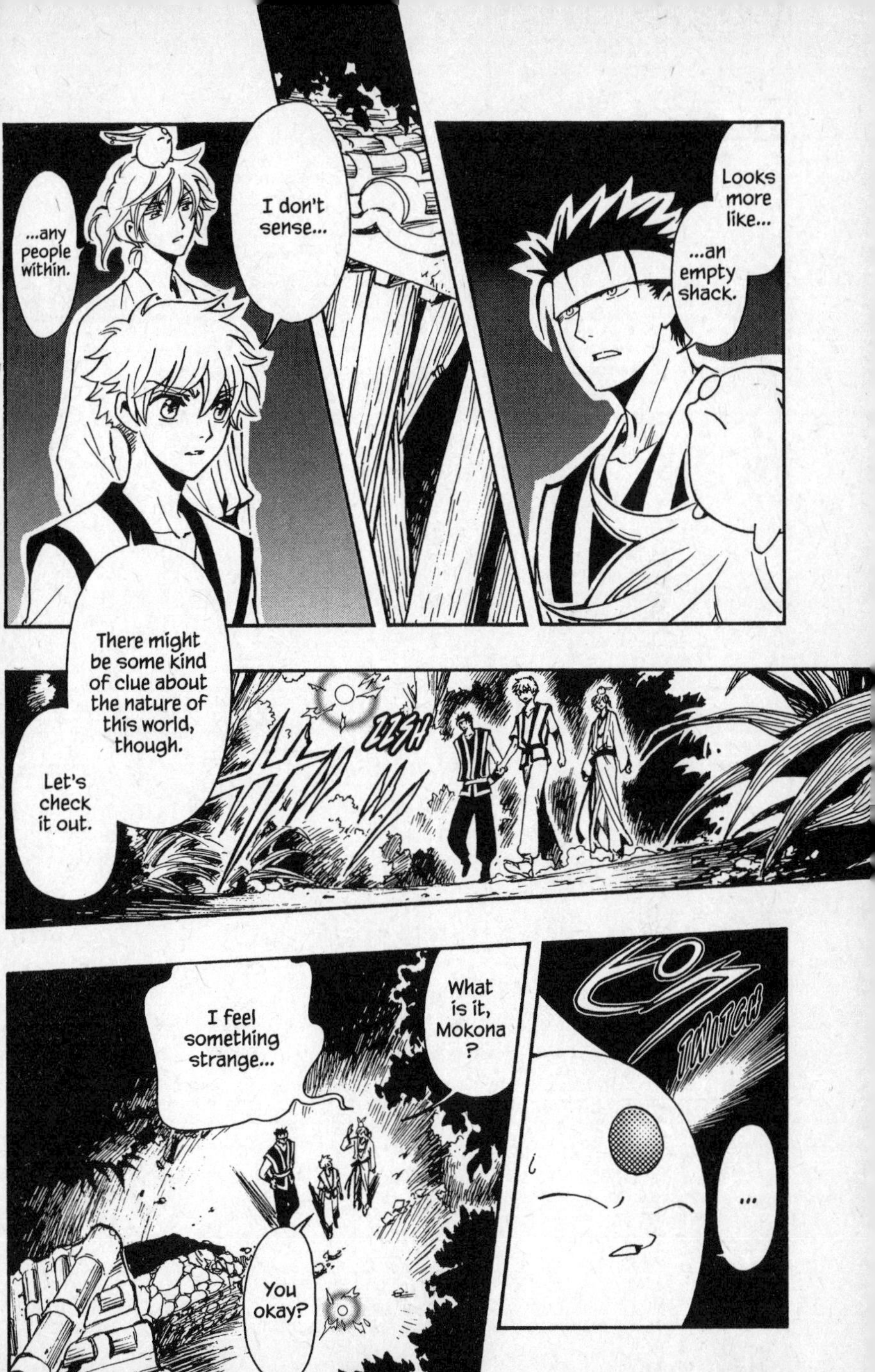
Looks more like...
...an empty shack.
I don't sense...
...any people within.
There might be some kind of clue about the nature of this world, though.
Let's check it out.
ZZSH
TWITCH
...
What is it, Mokona?
I feel something strange...
You okay?

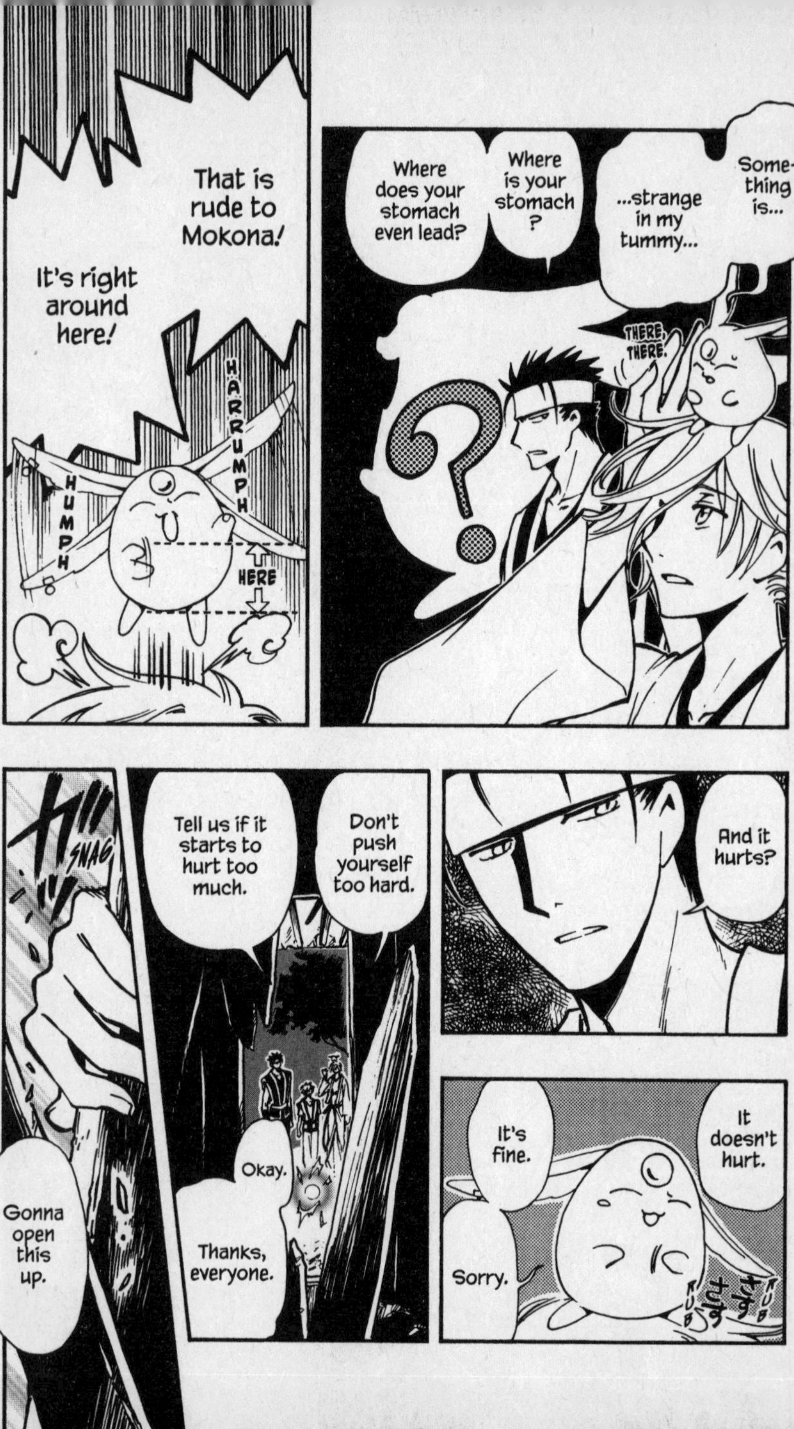
Some-thing is...
...strange in my tummy...
THERE, THERE.
Where is your stomach?
Where does your stomach even lead?
That is rude to Mokona!
It's right around here!
HARRUMPH
HUMPH
HERE
And it hurts?
It doesn't hurt.
It's fine.
Sorry.
RUB RUB
Don't push yourself too hard.
Tell us if it starts to hurt too much.
Okay.
Thanks, everyone.
SNAG
Gonna open this up.

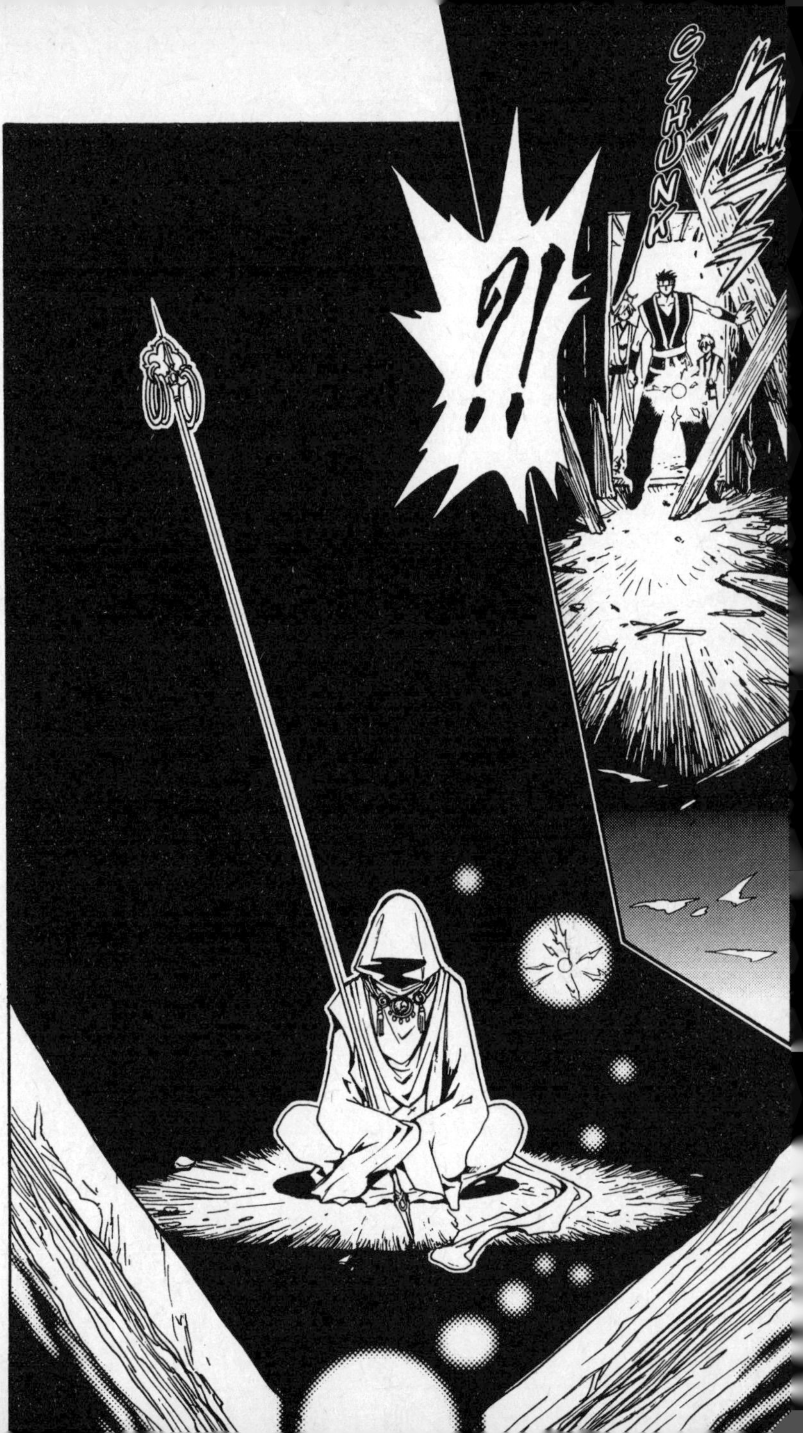

SHUNK
?!

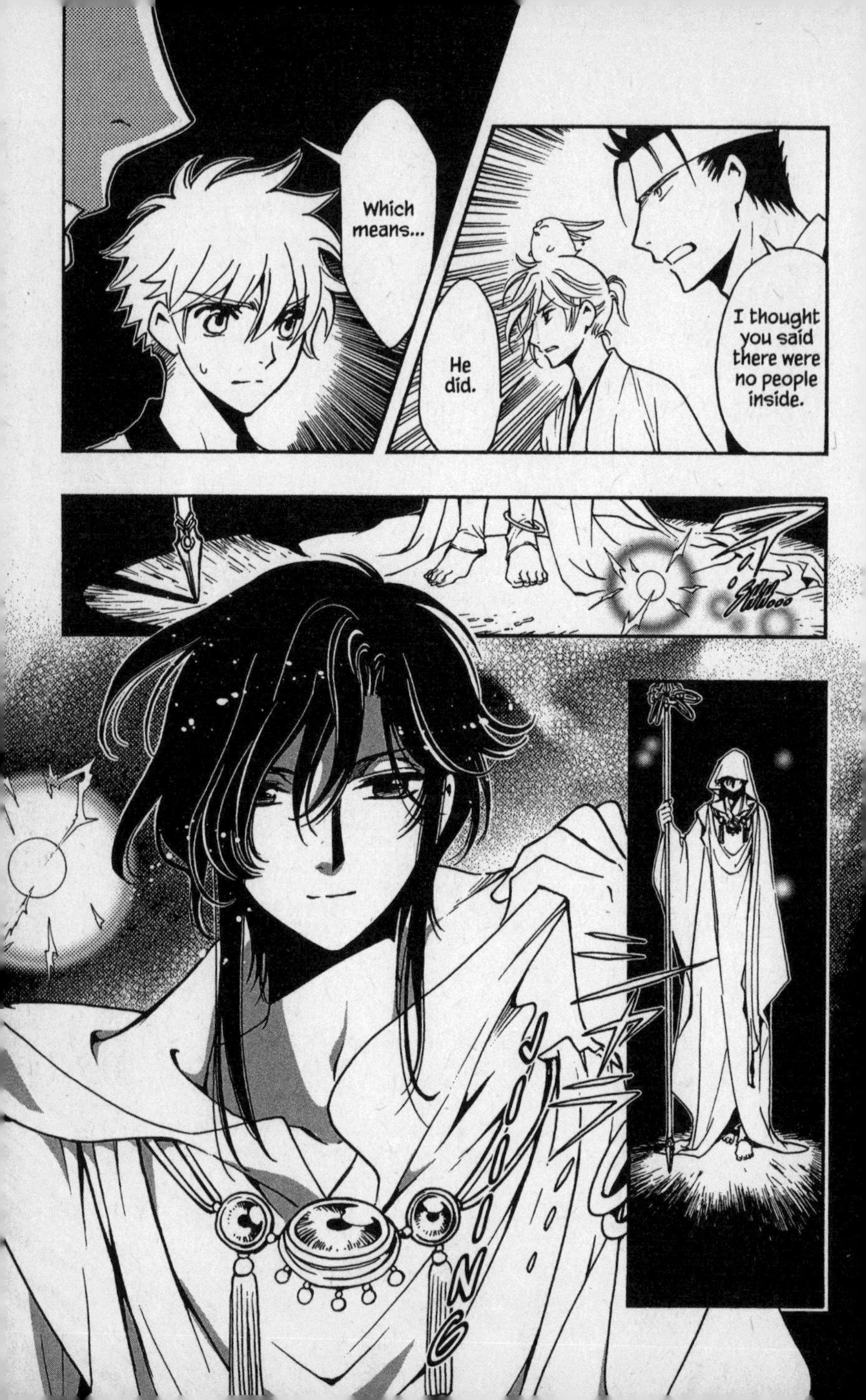
I thought you said there were no people inside.
He did.
Which means...

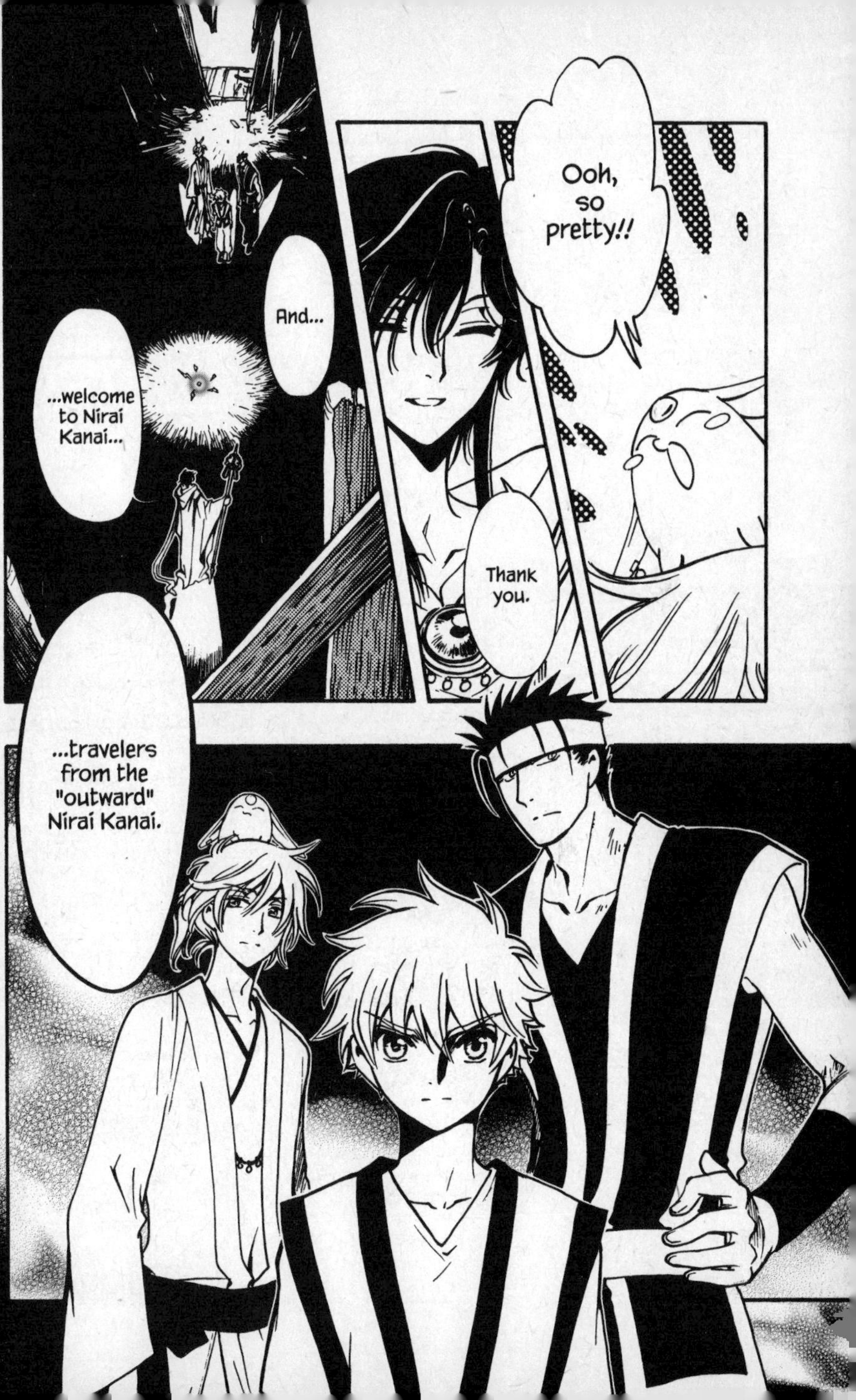
Ooh, so pretty!!
Thank you.
And...
...welcome to Nirai Kanai...
...travelers from the "outward" Nirai Kanai.

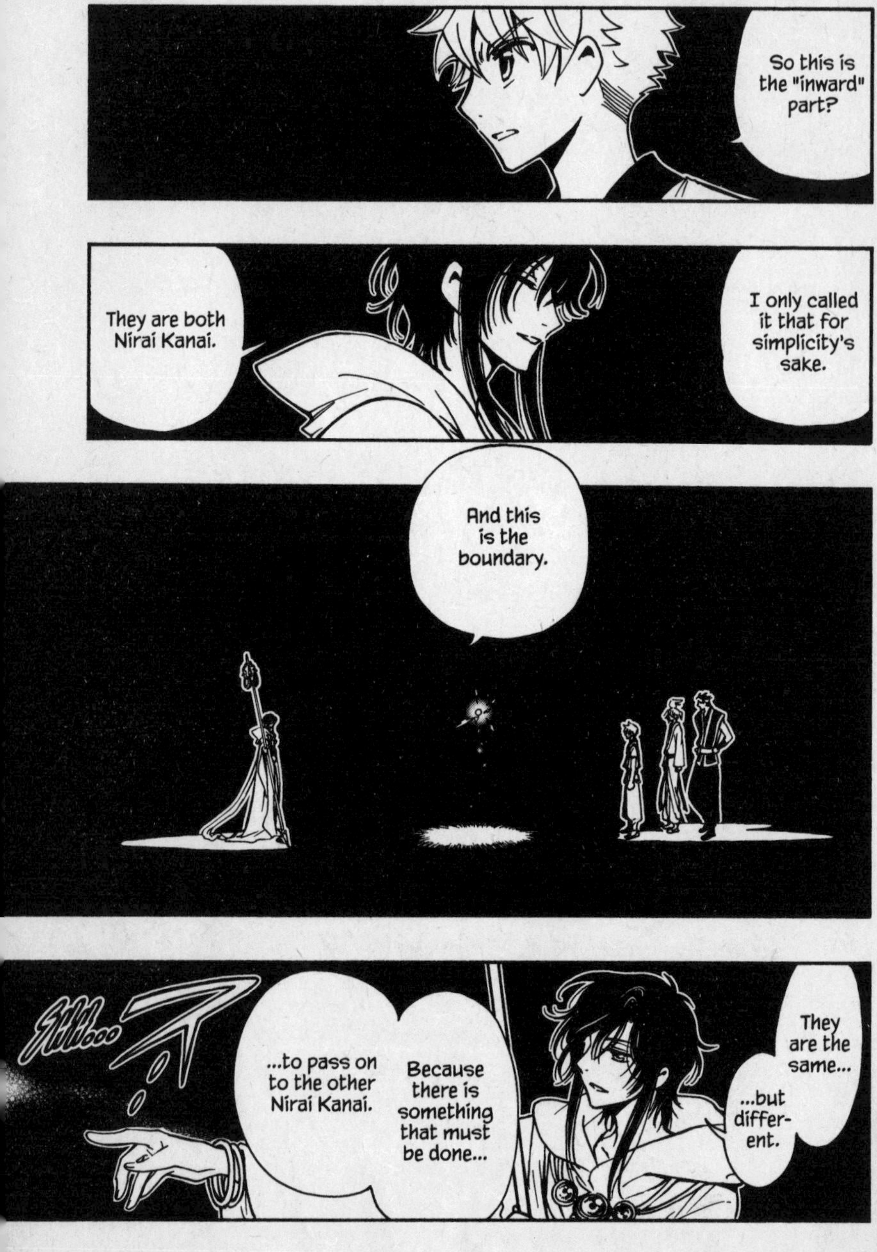
So this is the "inward" part?
I only called it that for simplicity's sake.
They are both Nirai Kanai.
And this is the boundary.
They are the same...
...but different.
Because there is something that must be done...
...to pass on to the other Nirai Kanai.

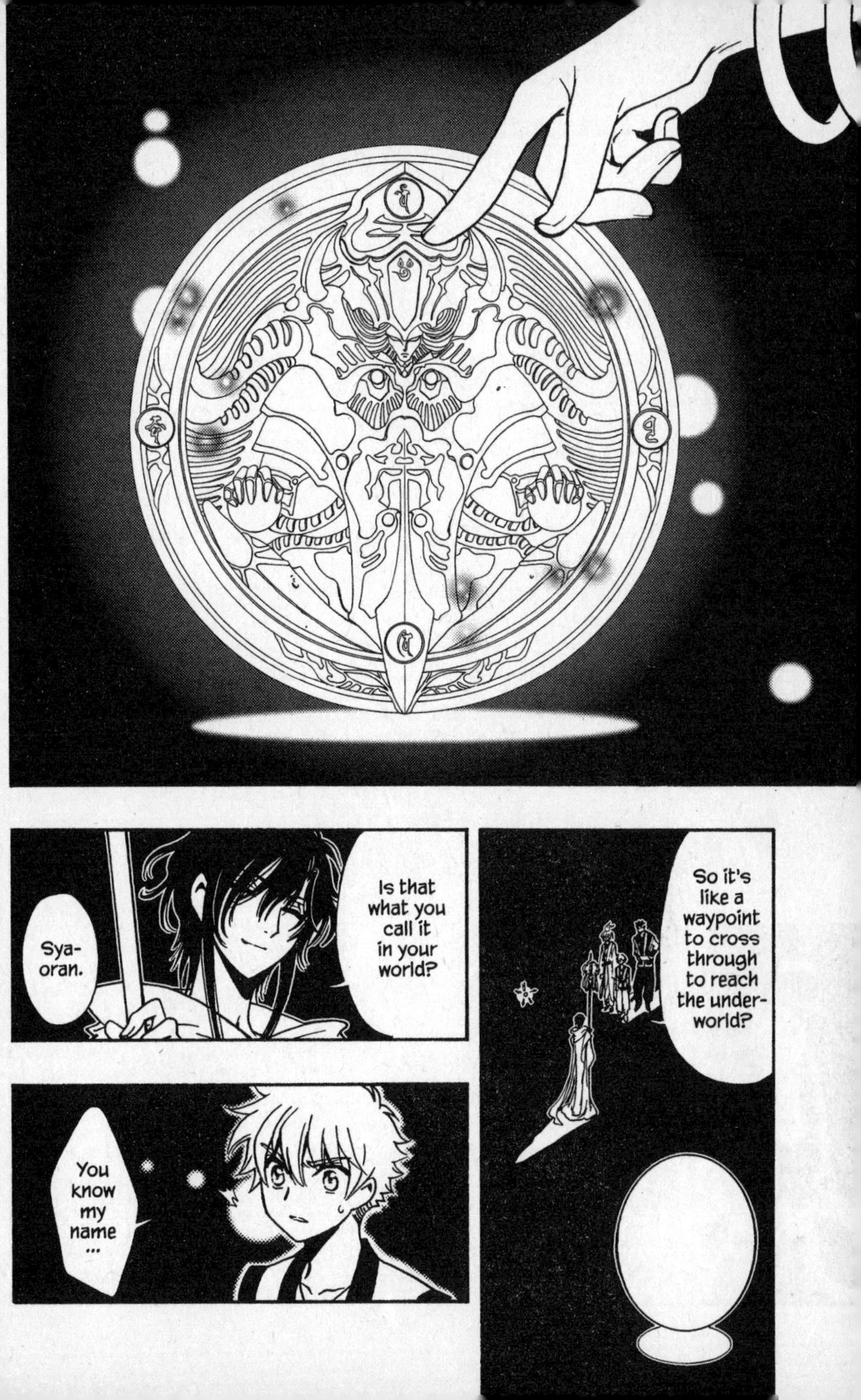
So it's like a waypoint to cross through to reach the under-world?
Is that what you call it in your world?
Sya-oran.
You know my name ...

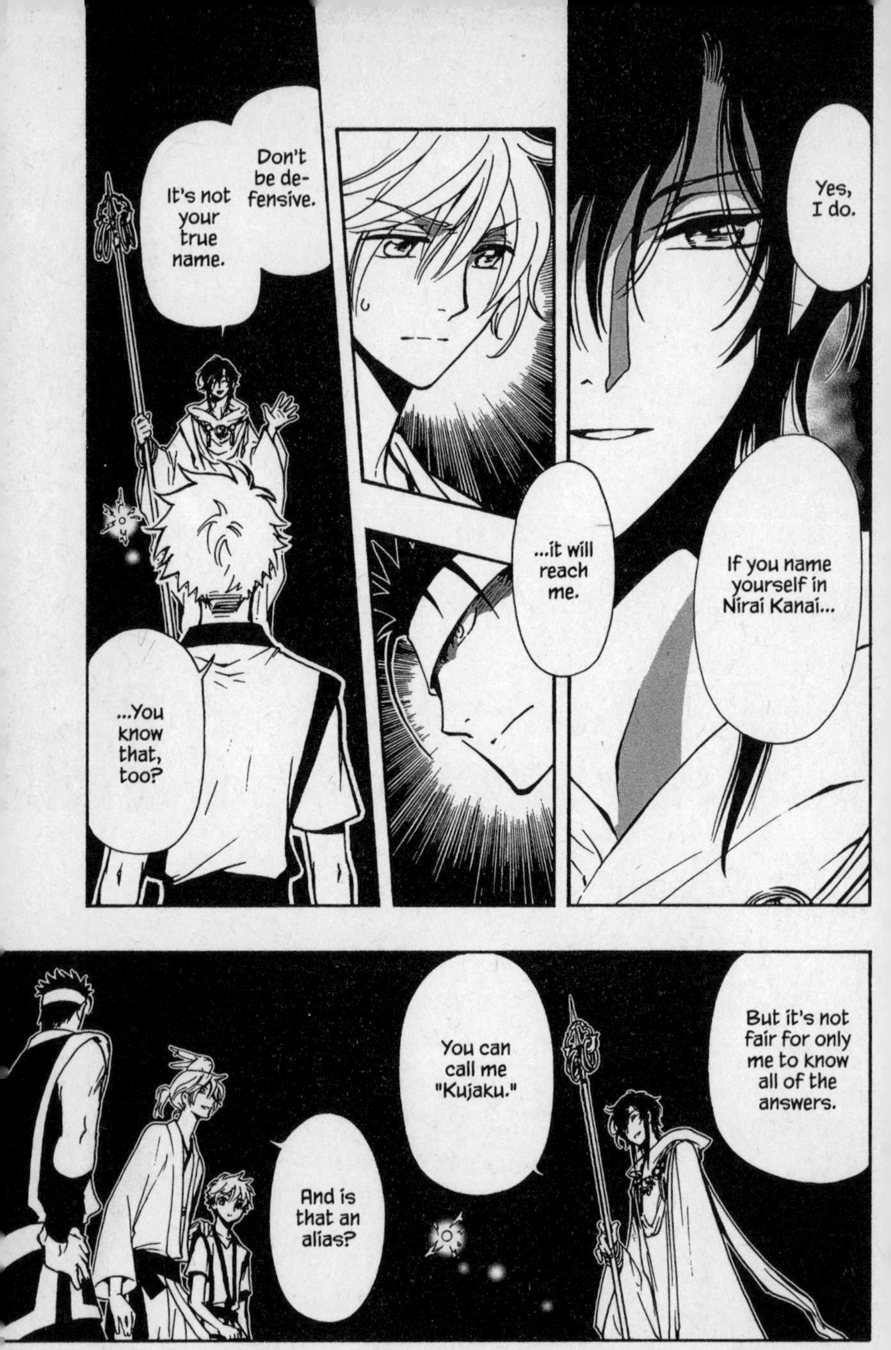
Yes, I do.
If you name yourself in Nirai Kanai...
...it will reach me.
Don't be defensive.
It's not your true name.
...You know that, too?
But it's not fair for only me to know all of the answers.
You can call me "Kujaku."
And is that an alias?

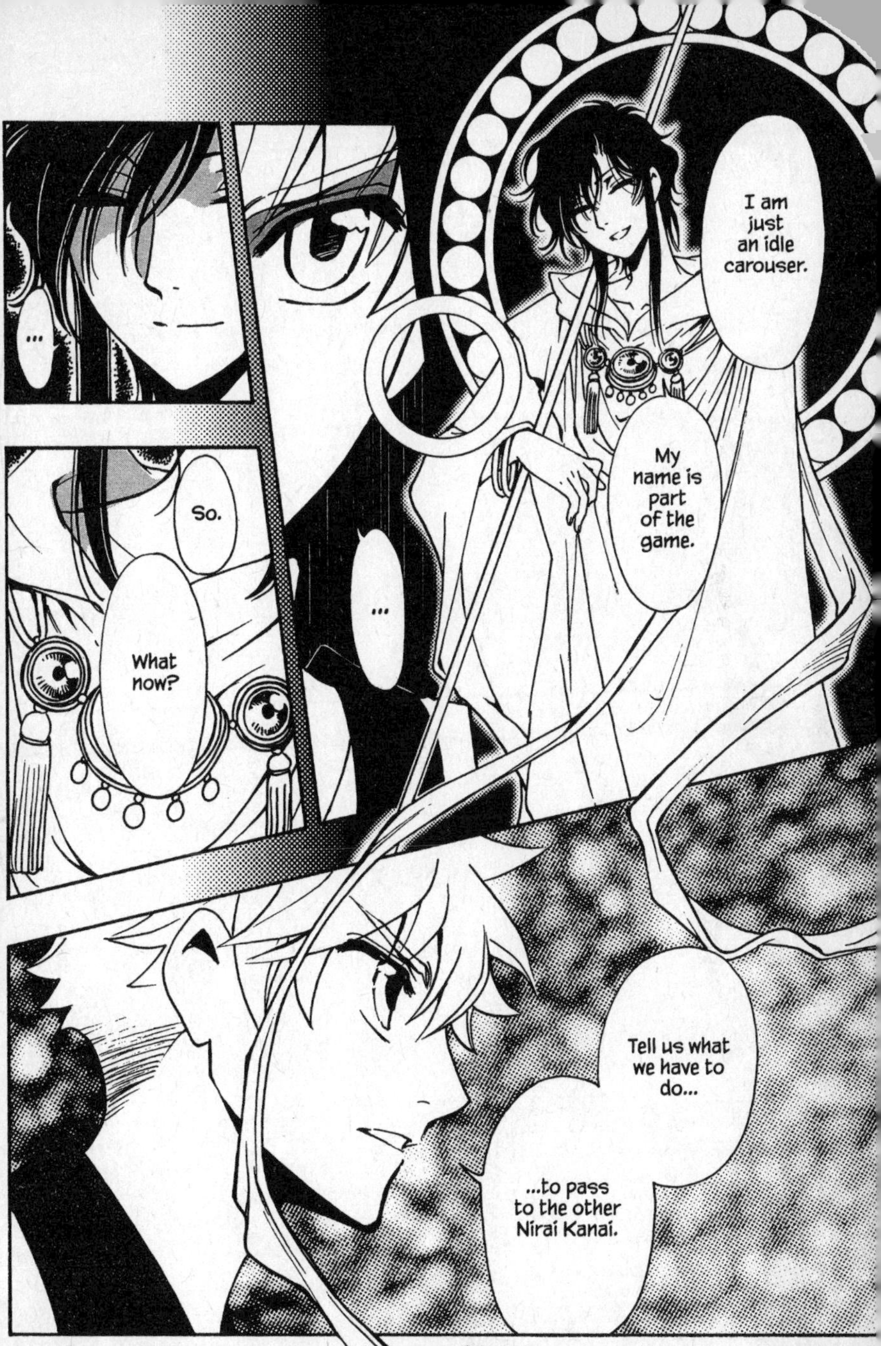
I am just an idle carouser.
My name is part of the game.
...
...
So.
What now?
Tell us what we have to do...
...to pass to the other Nirai Kanai.

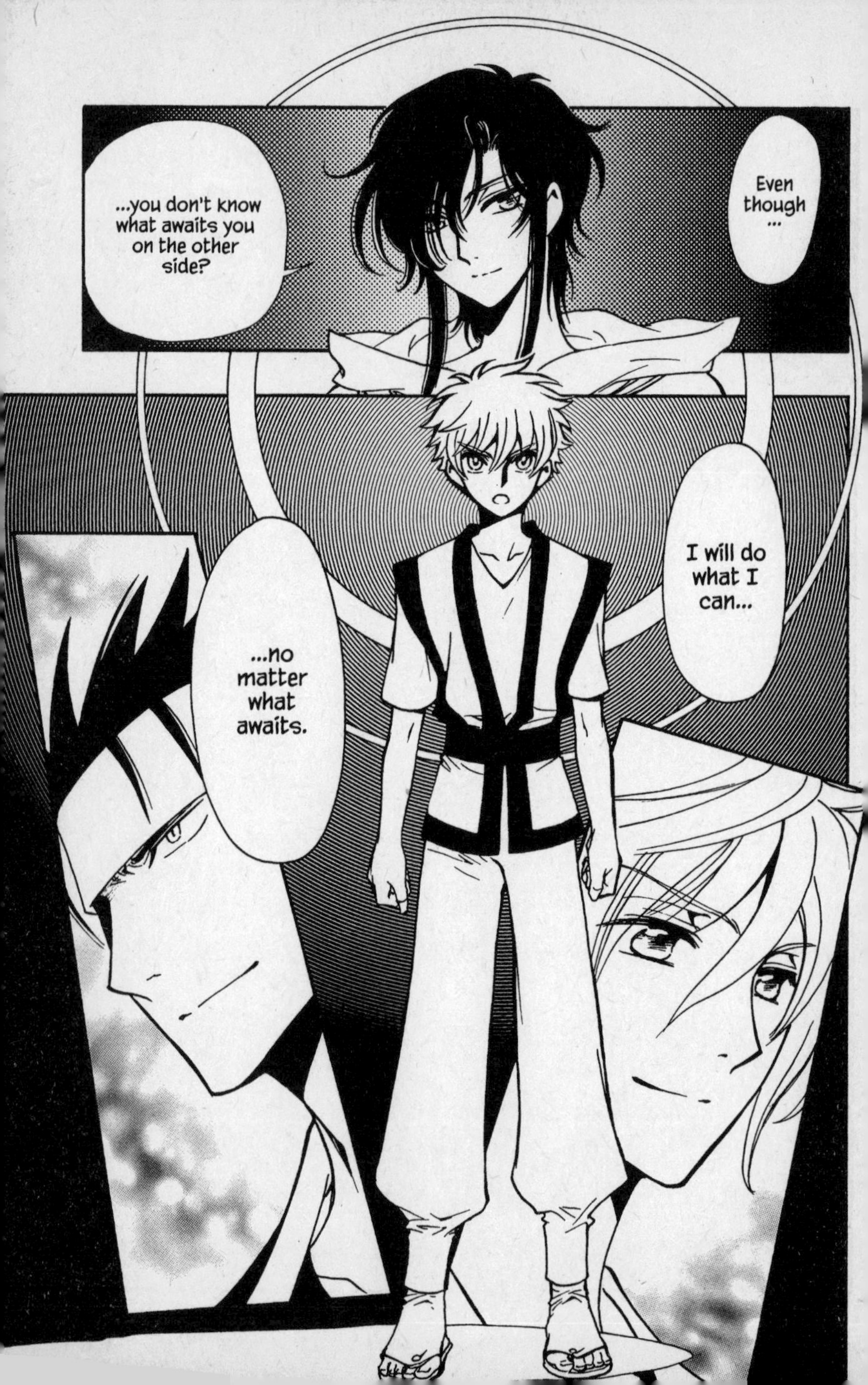
Even though ...
...you don't know what awaits you on the other side?
I will do what I can...
...no matter what awaits.

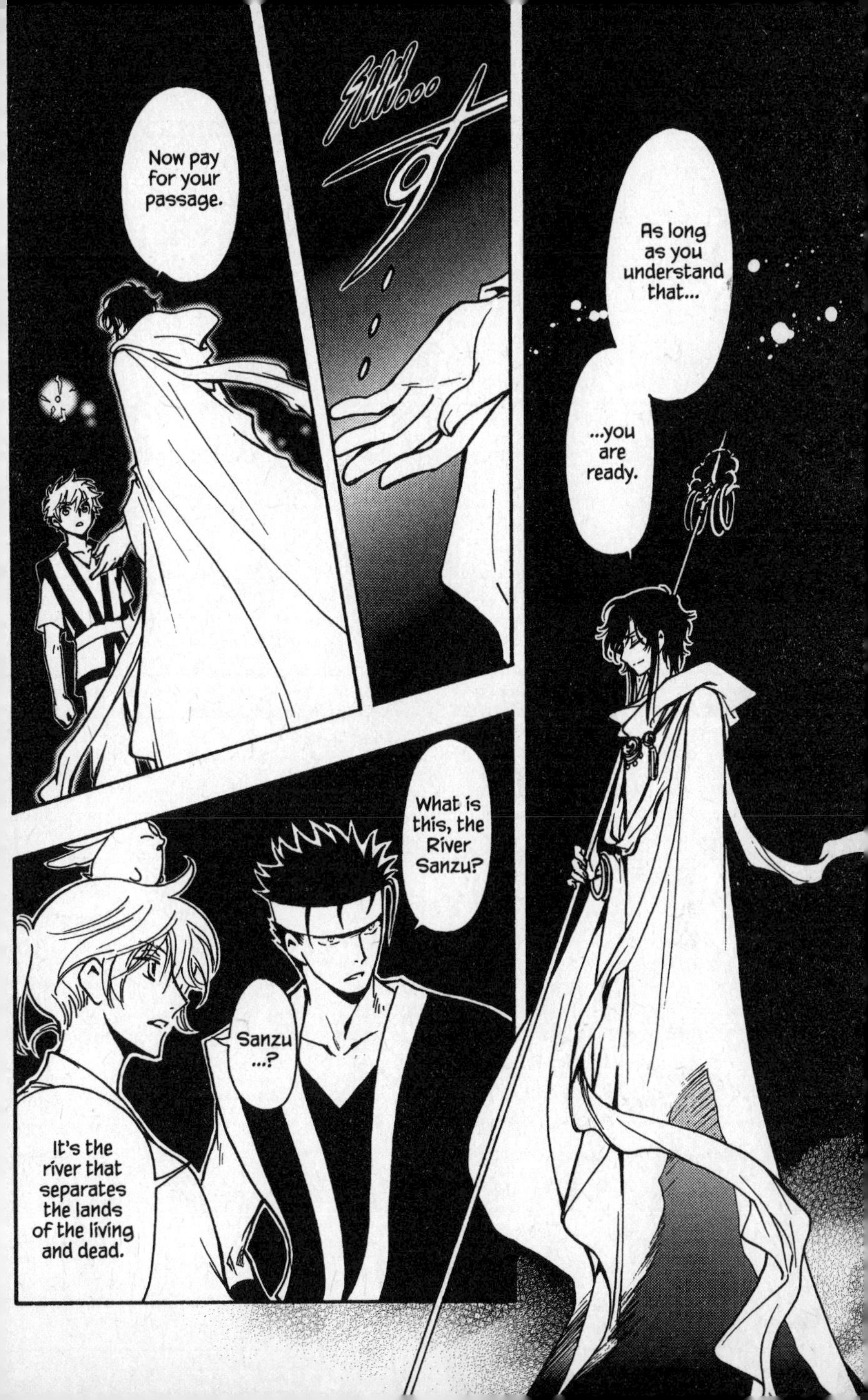
As long as you understand that...
...you are ready.
SHHH...
Now pay for your passage.
What is this, the River Sanzu?
Sanzu ...?
It's the river that separates the lands of the living and dead.

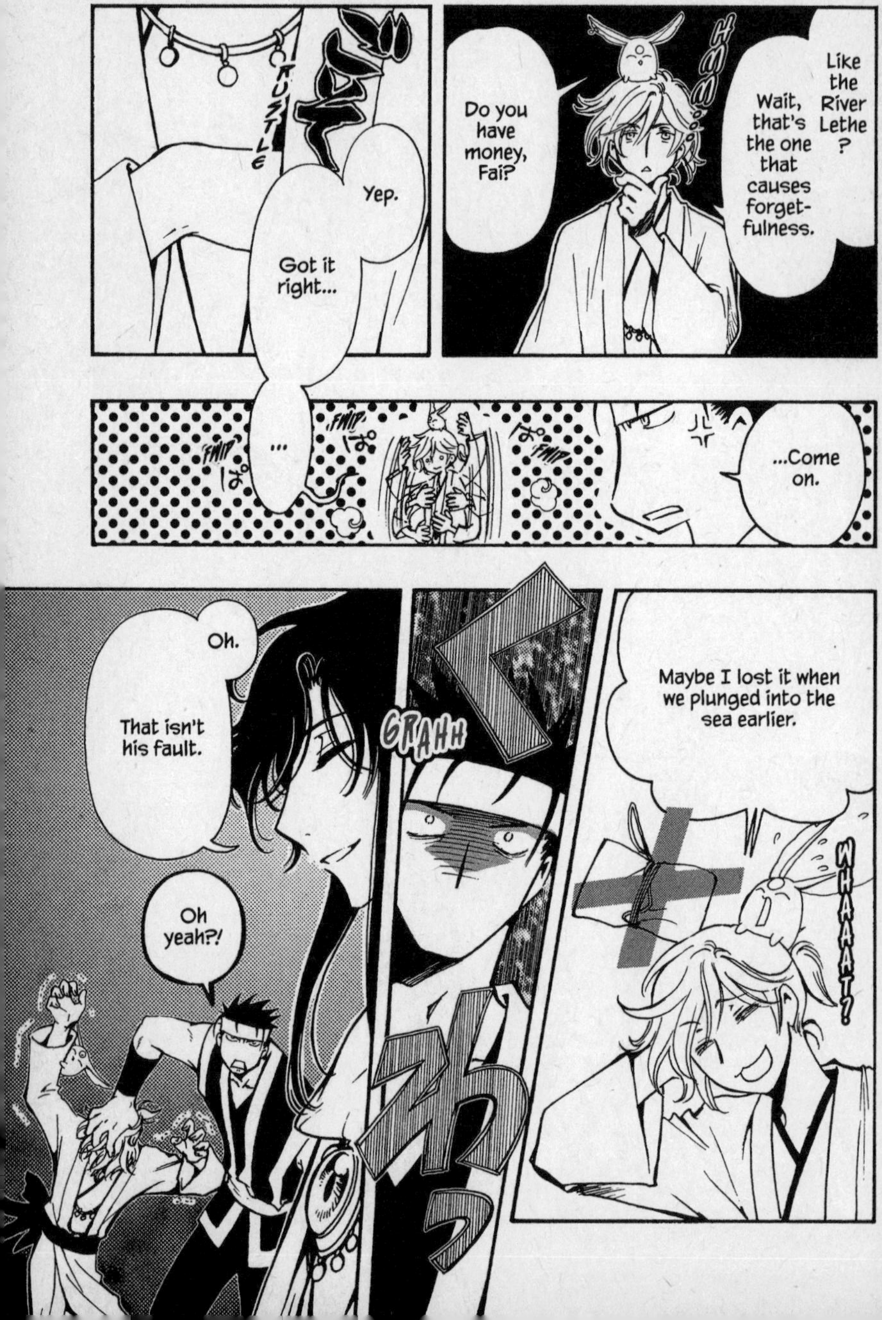
Like the River Lethe?
Wait, that's the one that causes forget-fulness.
HMMM...
Do you have money, Fai?
RUSTLE
Yep.
Got it right...
...Come on.
FWIP
ぱ
FWIP
ぱ
...
FWIP
ぱ
Maybe I lost it when we plunged into the sea earlier.
WHAAAAT?
GRAHH
Oh.
That isn't his fault.
Oh yeah?!

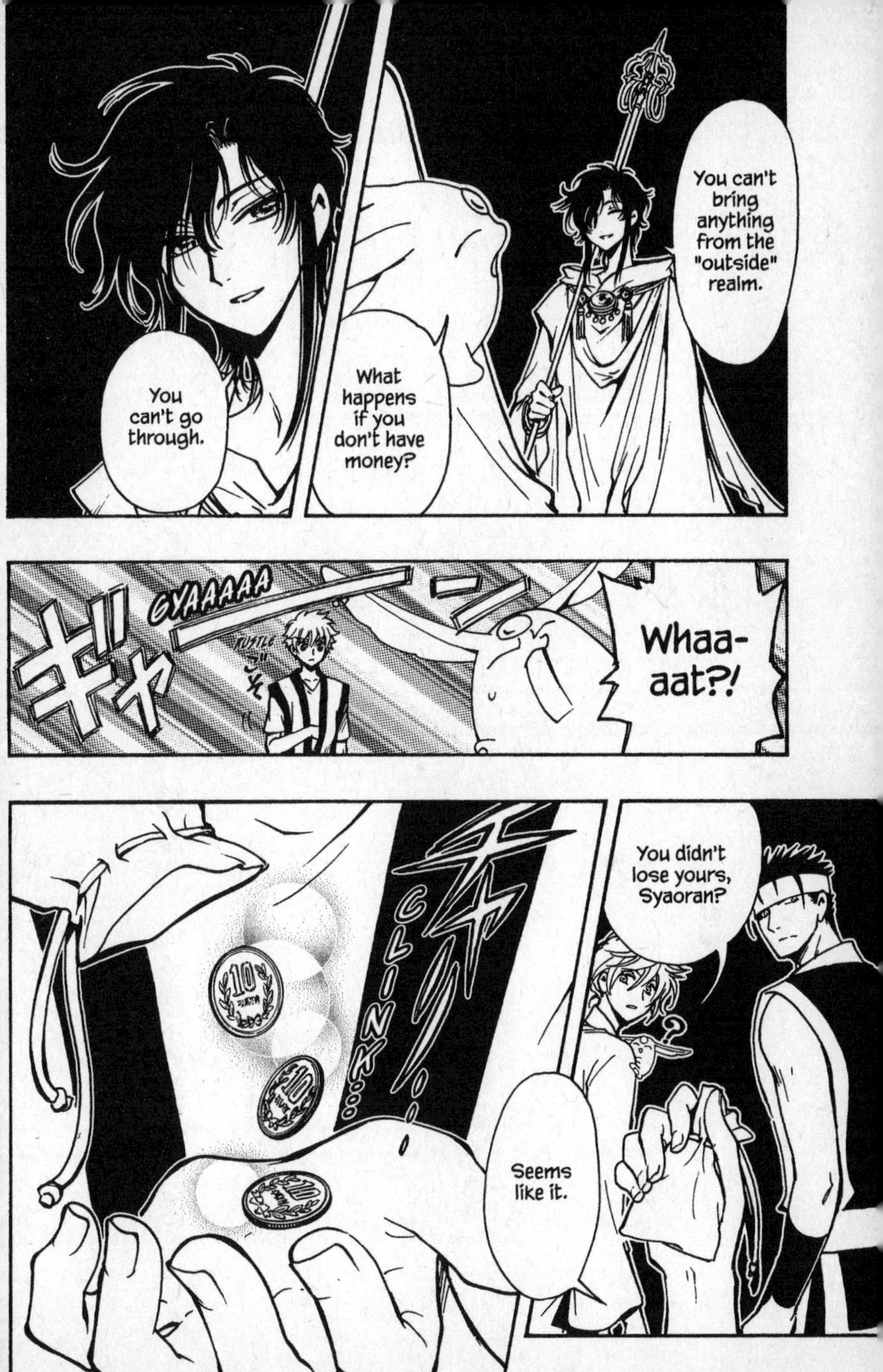
You can't bring anything from the "outside" realm.
What happens if you don't have money?
You can't go through.
Whaaa-aat?!
GYAAAAA
ギャ
RUSTLE
You didn't lose yours, Syaoran?
Seems like it.
CLINK...

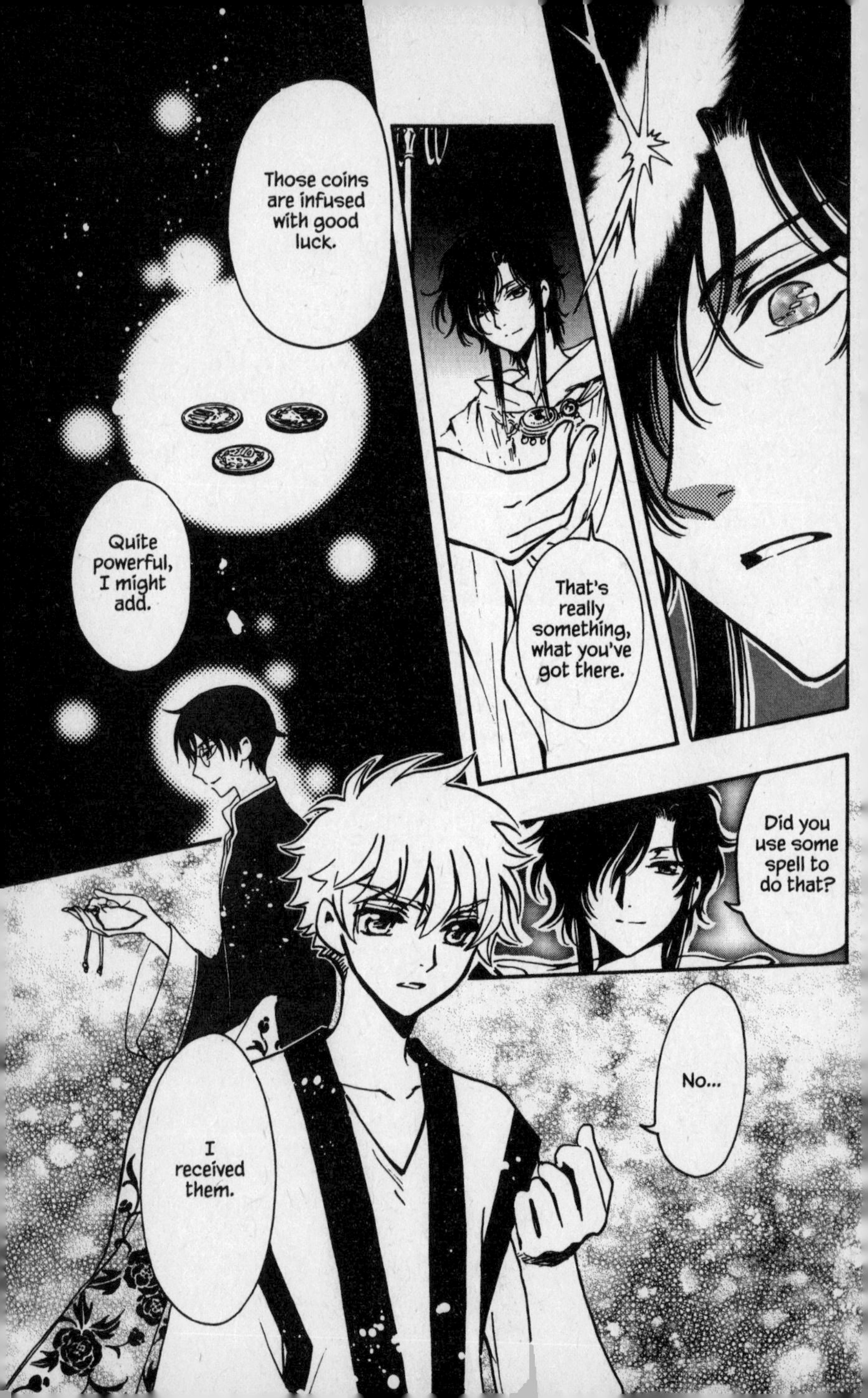
That's really something, what you've got there.
Those coins are infused with good luck.
Quite powerful, I might add.
Did you use some spell to do that?
No...
I received them.

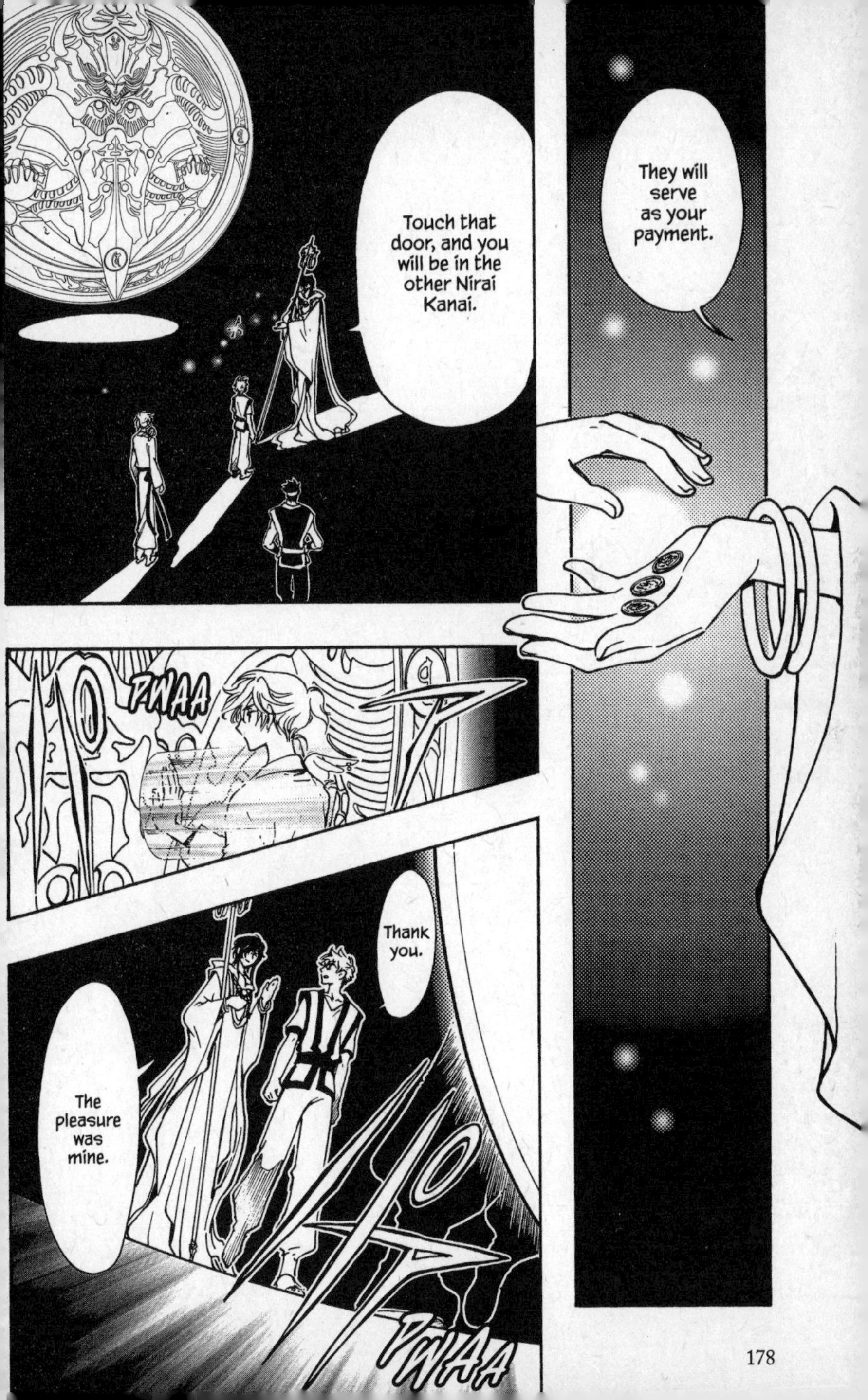
They will serve as your payment.
Touch that door, and you will be in the other Nirai Kanai.
PWAA
Thank you.
The pleasure was mine.
PWAA

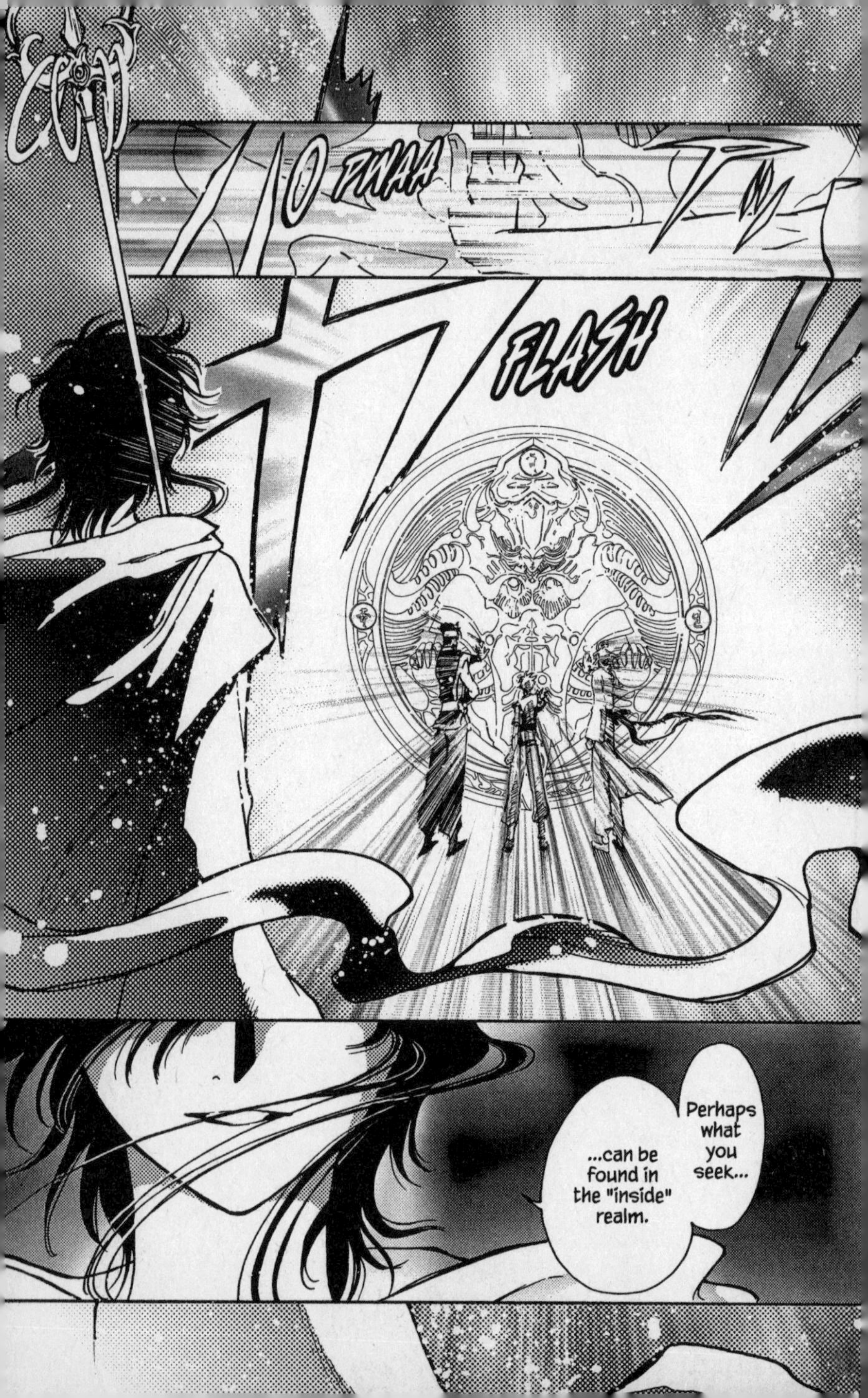
PWAAA
FLASH
Perhaps what you seek...
...can be found in the "inside" realm.

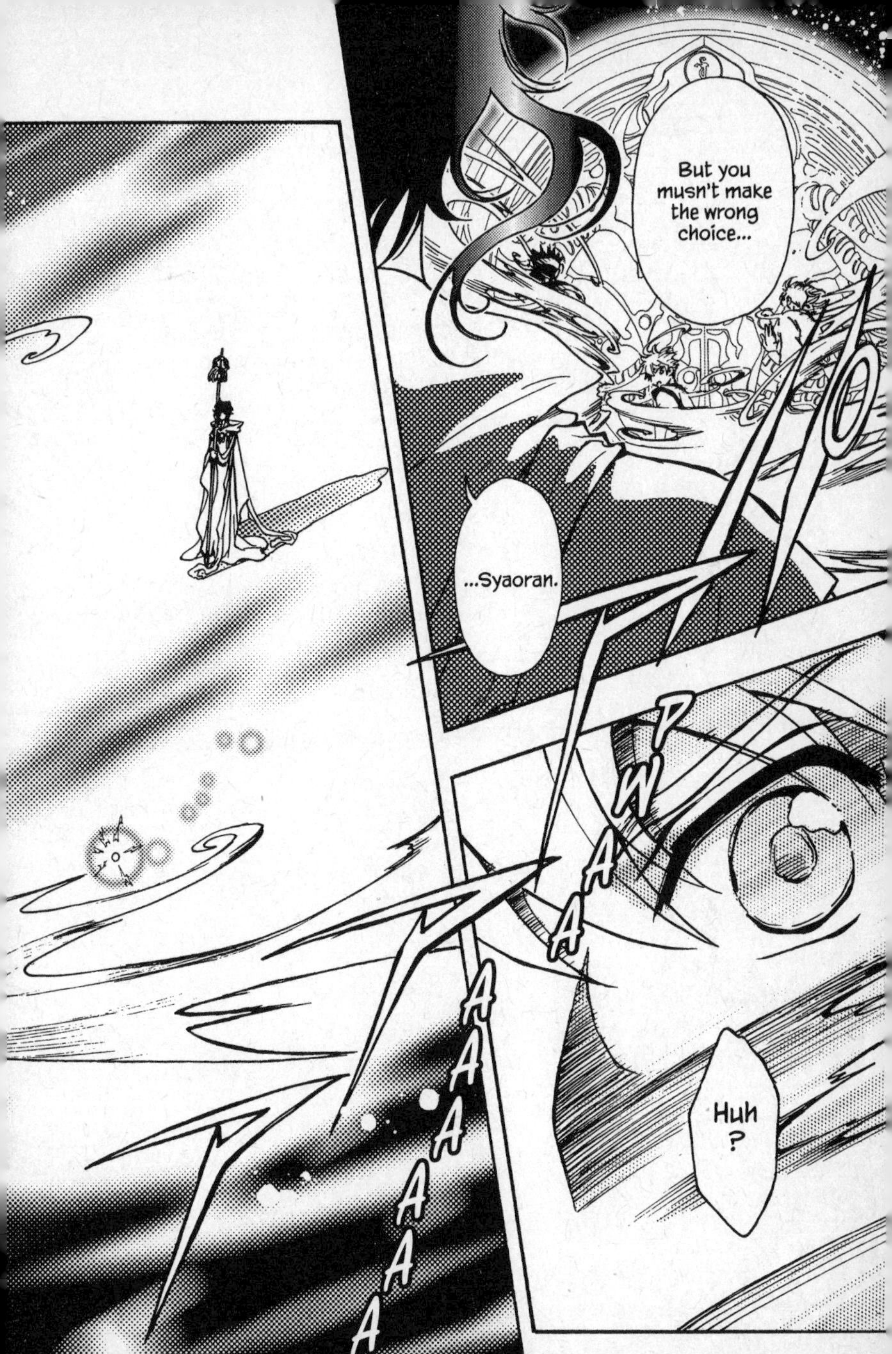

But you musn't make the wrong choice...
...Syaoran.
Huh?
PWAAAAAAAAAA

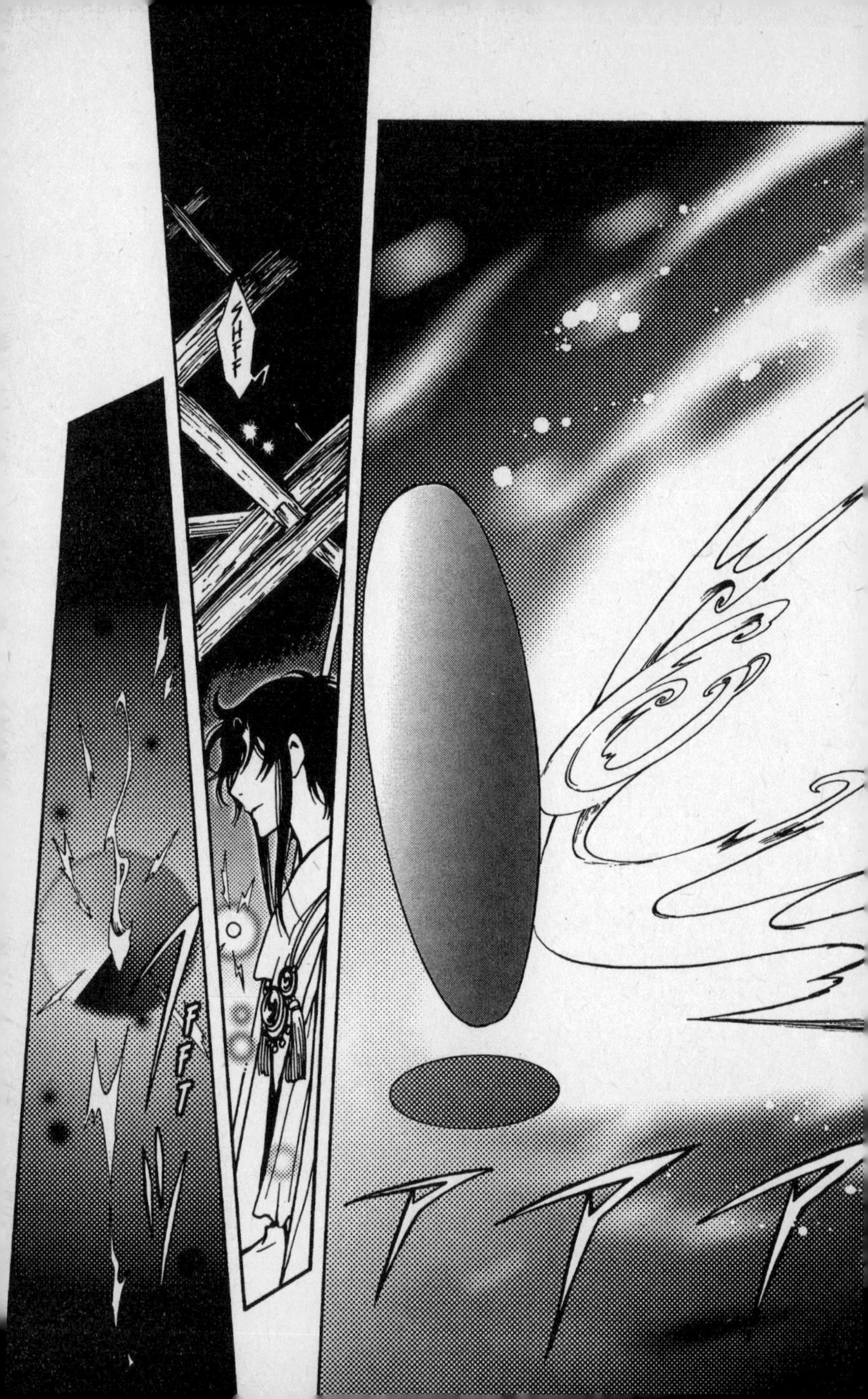
SHFF
FFFT

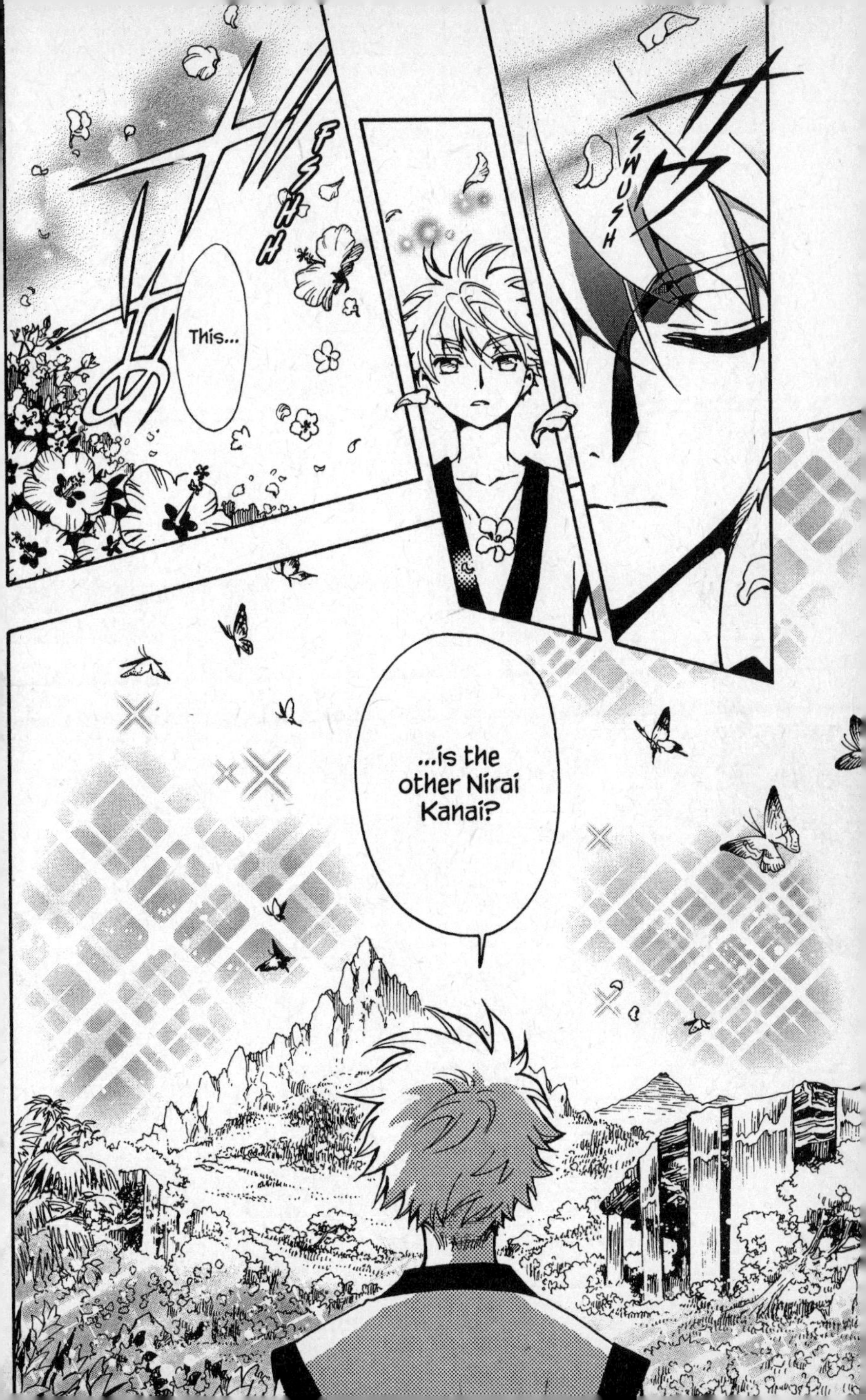
SWUSH
FSHH
This...
...is the other Nirai Kanai?

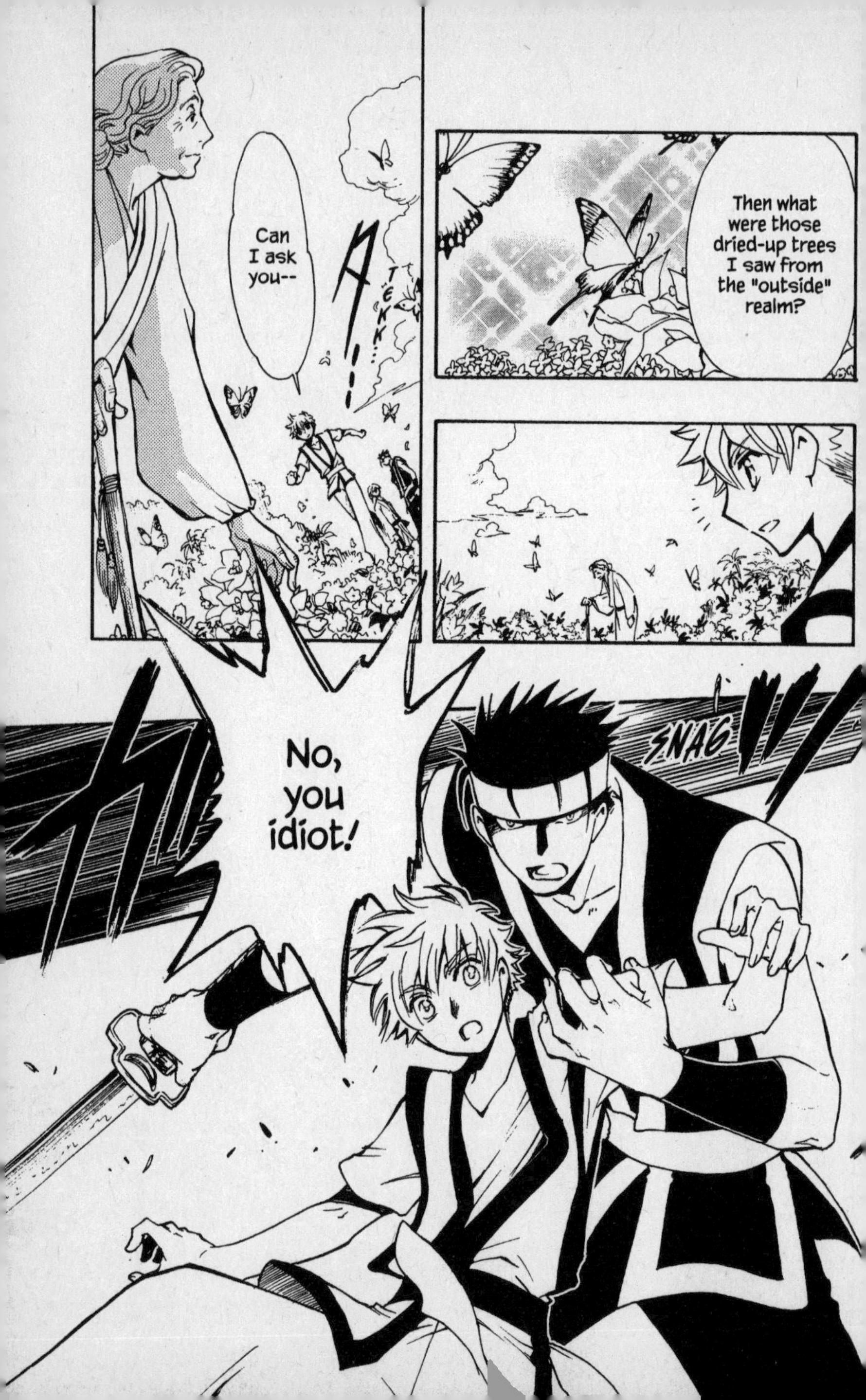
Then what were those dried-up trees I saw from the "outside" realm?
Can I ask you--
TEKK...
No, you idiot!
SNAG

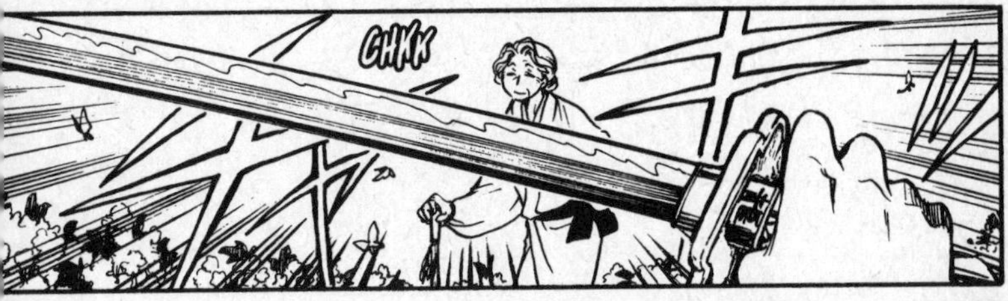
CHKK

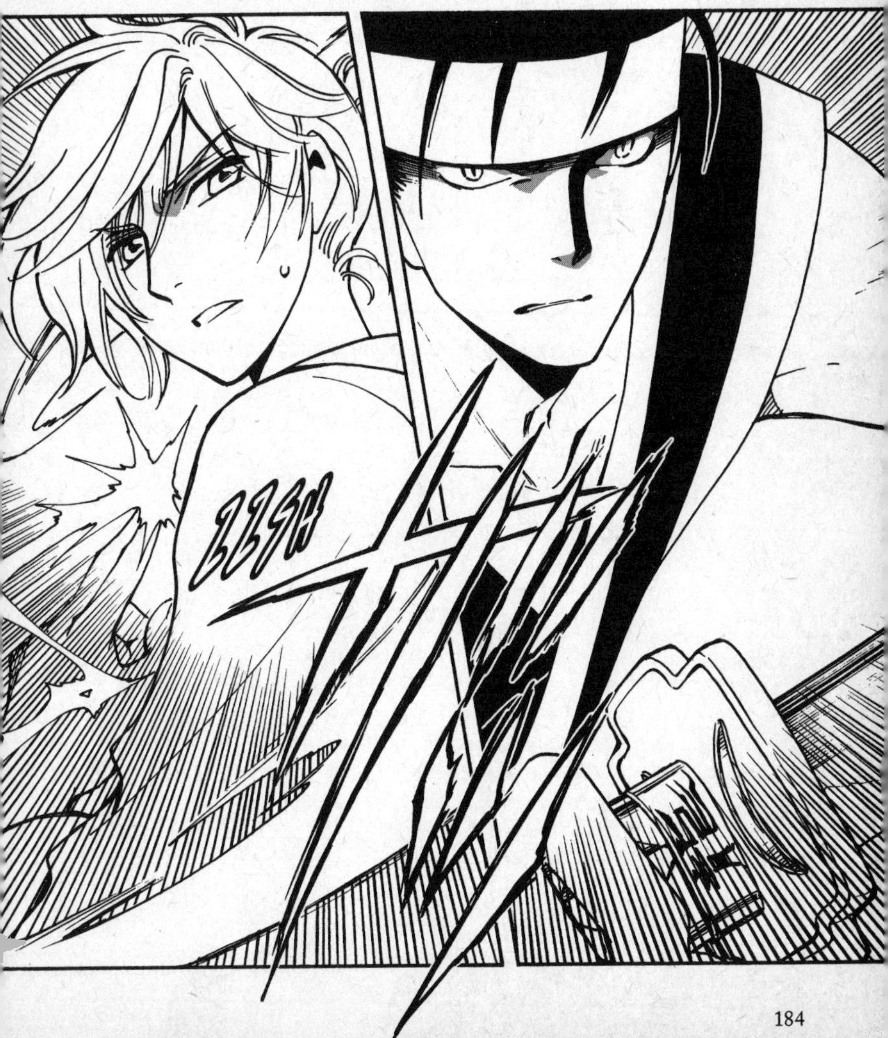
ZZSCH

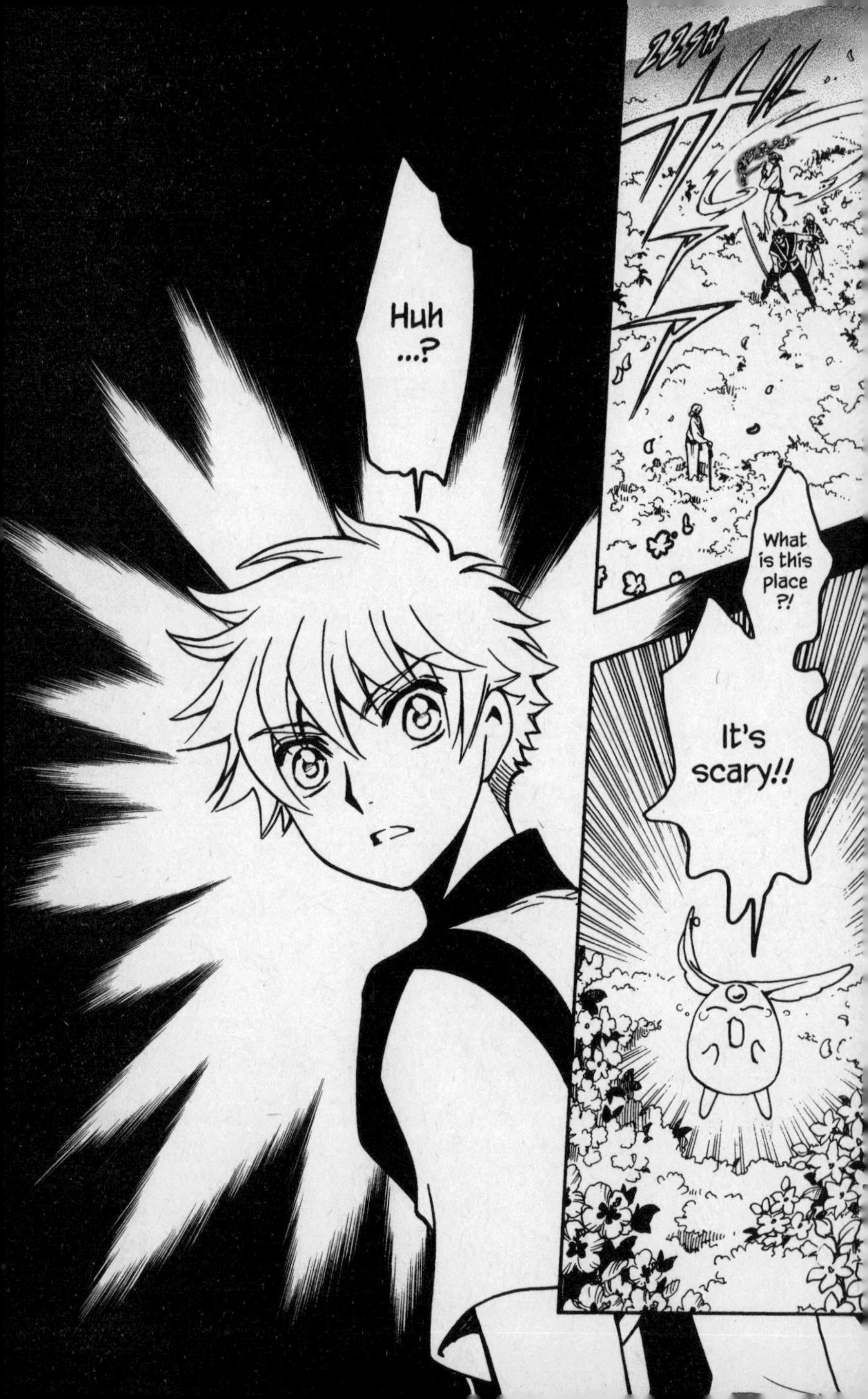
What is this place?!
It's scary!!
Huh...?

Originally published in *Shonen Magazine Special*,
No. 9 - No. 12, 2014; No. 1, 2015

To Be Continued

TRANSLATION NOTES

Japanese is a tricky language for most Westerners, and translation is often more art than science. For your edification and reading pleasure, here are notes on some of the places where we could have gone in a different direction in our translation of the work, or where a Japanese cultural reference is used.

Nirai Kanai, page 26

A construct of Ryukyuan religion (Ryukyu being the series of islands that stretch from the southwest of Japan to Taiwan, the most notable of which is Okinawa). Nirai Kanai is the realm of the gods and thus the source of both good and bad fortune. The practice of festivals is meant to summon the gods from Nirai Kanai to either bring good fortune, or to have them take bad fortune back with them. It should be noted that while there are many elements of the "real" Nirai Kanai present in this manga--such as the sunny, subtropical climate of Okinawa--this depiction of Nirai Kanai, like other mythologically-based locations in the original Tsubasa series, is CLAMP's own take with its own unique details.

Soba, page 35

One of the classic Japanese noodles, soba is made of buckwheat and can range from lighter to a dark, almost purple color. It has more of a texture than wheat noodles such as Chinese noodles (ramen) or udon. Soba is enjoyed both in hot broth, or chilled in the summer. "Suba" is the term for soba in Okinawan dialect.

Kakuni, page 35
Kakuni is a dish stemming from the southern end of Japan that most likely is a combination of Japanese and Chinese technique. It is made of thick slices of pork (the name means "simmered square") that are simmered in sauce at low heat for a long time, which makes the meat extremely tender.

Crossover characters, page 40
The trio of Himegami, Sakon and Ukon are crossover characters from CLAMP's recent series Gate 7, modeled very loosely around famous historical figures of Japan. The character of Himegami (meaning "princess god") is played by Hana from Gate 7, who shares her love of noodles. Meanwhile, her two attendants Sakon and Ukon are based on, respectively, the characters of Sakura and Tachibana, who fill similar roles to their characters in Gate 7. As this series started publication in 2011, several years after the conclusion of the original Tsubasa series, no doubt CLAMP was eager to throw them into the continuation of their epic crossover work!

Nukazuke, page 69
The Japanese art of pickling with rice bran, known as nuka. These pickles can be made of a variety of vegetables (in this case, it's clearly cucumbers) and the result is, depending on the particular batch of nuka culture used to ferment the pickles, anywhere from tangy to ultra sour and pungent.

Kijimu, page 71
A corruption of the word kijimuna, which is a kind of folklore creature in Okinawa. Kijimuna are tree spirits, and

typically depicted as children with wild red hair and trickster personalities. The great manga artist Shigeru Mizuki, who depicted all kinds of yôkai and other traditional goblins and spirits in his works, drew the kijimuna in a small, rounded form that looks fairly similar to Mokona's shape.

Yomi, page 108
In traditional Japanese mythology, Yomi or Yomi-no-kuni is the name for the land of the dead, commonly held to be underground much like the Christian Hell, or Hades.

Hitsuzen, page 115
A central concept of the xxxHOLiC series, defined by Yûko as "a naturally foreordained event, a result which can only be obtained by a single causality, and other causalities would necessarily create different results."

Miko, page 124
A priestess in the Shinto tradition. In a contemporary sense, a miko performs certain traditional rites and cleansing rituals, but in the past, the concept of a miko evolved from ancient female shamans who performed exorcisms.

Kumari, page 125
In the real world, a kumari is a "living goddess" in Nepalese tradition, a virgin girl who represents an incarnation of the Hindu goddess, the source of all energy in the universe. The kumari are chosen by a strict set of criteria and are "retired" when they reach puberty.

Kujaku, page 167
A character from CLAMP's debut series, RG Veda, Kujaku is a mysterious wanderer who crosses the path of the main cast on several occasions. While his motivations are initially mysterious, he is eventually revealed to have a central role in the story. His name on its own means "peacock," but can also be short for Kujaku-Myô-ô, the Japanese name for Mahamayuri, one of the Buddhist Wisdom Kings that is typically represented in the form of a peacock.

Sanzu, page 174
The river in Japanese Buddhist belief that must be crossed to reach the afterlife. It is very similar in concept to the River Styx in Greek mythology, down to the toll required to pass.

Tsubasa WoRLD CHRoNiCLE: Niraikanai volume 1 is a work of fiction. Names, characters, places, and incidents are the products of the author's imagination or are used fictitiously. Any resemblance to actual events, locales, or persons, living or dead, is entirely coincidental.

A Kodansha Comics Trade Paperback Original.

Tsubasa WoRLD CHRoNiCLE: Niraikanai volume 1 copyright © 2015
CLAMP • ShigatsuTsuitachi CO., LTD./Kodansha
English translation copyright © 2015 CLAMP • ShigatsuTsuitachi CO., LTD./Kodansha

Published in the United States by Kodansha Comics, an imprint of
Kodansha USA Publishing, LLC, New York.

Publication rights for this English edition arranged through
Kodansha Ltd., Tokyo.

First published in Japan in 2015 by Kodansha Ltd., Tokyo, as
Tsubasa WoRLD CHRoNiCLE: Niraikanaihen volume 1.

ISBN 978-1-63236-124-0

Printed in the United States of America.

www.kodanshacomics.com

9 8 7 6 5 4 3 2 1

Translator: Stephen Paul
Lettering: James Dashiell
Kodansha Comics edition cover design: Phil Balsman